Lawfare is a timely and important work that provokes and confronts the growing debate on constitutionalism and the material transformation of our society. The one end argues that the Constitution and the meaning the courts have given it have failed to reverse our inherited framework of privilege, racism, socio-economic exclusion and inequality. This because the constitutional project is animated by Eurocentric notions of law that preserve that foreign paradigm and continue to privilege and protect unequal colonial power relations in society. The other view is that the promise of our Constitution is a legitimate outcome of our own struggles and historical demands for a just society. It is rooted in our collective African location and ubuntu, and properly applied, the Constitution is emphatically transformative and capable of dismantling a horrific past and birthing a new and just society.

Let the debate rage on. This work will prove a valuable addition to the controversy and the notion of lawfare.
- DIKGANG MOSENEKE, former Deputy Chief Justice

GW00391234

LAWFARE

Judging Politics in South Africa

MICHELLE LE ROUX
AND DENNIS DAVIS

Jonathan Ball Publishers
Johannesburg & Cape Town

Originally published in South Africa in 2019 by
JONATHAN BALL PUBLISHERS
A division of Media24 (Pty) Ltd
PO Box 33977
Jeppestown
2043

ISBN 978-1-86842-960-8
ebook ISBN 978-1-86842-961-5

Every effort has been made to trace the copyright holders and to obtain their permission for the use of
copyright material. The publishers apologise for any errors or omissions and would be grateful to be
notified of any corrections that should be incorporated in future editions of this book.

Twitter: www.twitter.com/JonathanBallPub
Facebook: www.facebook.com/JonathanBallPublishers
Blog: http://jonathanball.bookslive.co.za/

Cover by Michiel Botha
Front cover image: Palace of Justice, Pretoria, South Africa © Shutterstock
Design and typesetting by Catherine Coetzer
Editing by Mark Ronan
Printed and bound by CTP Printers, Cape Town
Set in ITC Garamond Light

CONTENTS

Acronyms and abbreviations   vii

Foreword   ix

Preface   xiii

1 The ascendancy of lawfare   1

2 Why these cases?   22

3 Who can rid me of this troublesome court?
   The Executive v The Judiciary   43

4 The Rivonia trial: Competing visions for South Africa   66

5 The challenge to the pass laws: The beginning
   of the end   96

6 Exposing detention without trial   120

7 A bridge over our troubled waters?   147

8 A break with the past, a view of the future   173

9 Activism, denialism, socio-economic rights
   (and beetroot)   196

10 A special relationship   216

11 Gay marriage: From possibility to reality   239

12 The great escape   248

13 'State capture' (*noun*)   267

14 Conclusion: Precedent and possibility   297

Notes   309

Acknowledgements   337

Index   339

ACRONYMS AND ABBREVIATIONS

ANC	African National Congress
ARV	antiretroviral
AWB	Afrikaner Weerstandsbeweging
AZAPO	Azanian Peoples Organisation
CALS	Centre for Applied Legal Studies
CASAC	Council for the Advancement of the South African Constitution
CODESA	Convention for a Democratic South Africa
COSATU	Congress of South African Trade Unions
DA	Democratic Alliance
EFF	Economic Freedom Fighters
ESTA	Extension of Security of Tenure Act
ICC	International Criminal Court
IFP	Inkatha Freedom Party
KC	King's Counsel
LRC	Legal Resources Centre
MEC	Member of the Executive Council
MK	Umkhonto we Sizwe
MTCTP	mother-to-child transmission prevention of HIV
NDPP	National Director of Public Prosecutions
NERSA	National Energy Regulator of South Africa
NGO	non-governmental organisation
NPA	National Prosecuting Authority of South Africa
NUSAS	National Union of South African Students
PAC	Pan Africanist Congress
QC	Queen's Counsel
SABC	South African Broadcasting Corporation
SAPS	South African Police Service
SARFU	South African Rugby Football Union
SARS	South African Revenue Service
SC	Senior Counsel
TAC	Treatment Action Campaign
TEC	Transitional Executive Council
TRC	Truth and Reconciliation Commission
UCT	University of Cape Town

FOREWORD
BY PRAVIN GORDHAN

Through the dark and devastating periods of colonialism and apartheid, the lodestar for democrats, activists and the majority of the oppressed was an aspiration to freedom: to create a democratic state, with racial and gender equality; to enjoy freedom from want, fear, oppression and exploitation; and to live a dignified life.

The law was a pivotal instrument during that period.

Today, the law constitutes the foundation of our young democracy, providing an all-embracing framework where our collective rights and obligations are preserved in the Constitution, which also limits the abuse of executive power and public funds.

The Constitution commits us to uplift the poor – to eliminate inequalities, to promote economic development for the benefit of all, and to create a society in which social justice and economic emancipation occur within a far-reaching transformation of our society.

> Government's objective is not merely to transfer ownership of assets or opportunities to contract with the state: it is to change the structure of the economy. Broad-based transformation should promote growth, mobilise investment, create jobs and empower citizens. It must create new resources to support social change, including assets and livelihoods for the majority, and strengthen South Africa's constitutional foundations.[1]

So participation in government is not just a technical or technocratic role. It is, and has been for me, one aimed at achieving the vision and goals of leaders such as Nelson Mandela, Walter Sisulu, Lillian Ngoyi and Bram Fischer to advance a profound, fundamental transformation.

But, in today's geopolitics – with mounting alienation between elites and citizens, insecurity for workers, the rise of right-wing populism and identity politics – the law, the Constitution and the courts also have a role beyond holding the executive to account.

Now the courts – through the process of lawfare, as the authors of this book, Michelle le Roux and Dennis Davis, observe – together with other institutions, need to defend democratic values against the worst in populist politics, identity essentialism and repressive economic policies.

The law and lawfare should become instruments of a progressive transformation of society, the economy, politics and culture, in the context of the Bill of Rights, and thus in defence of individual rights and economic rights. The law should seek to challenge patterns of concentration in the economy, confront hate speech and tribalism, and promote the process of nation-building.

But transformation and transitions can also unleash the forces of greed, corruption and new means of exploitation. What we have experienced are the consequences of the worst human instincts – self-enrichment, neglect of the higher mission, placing one's self-interest before the community's interests.

All this begs the question: what went wrong in the functioning of government?

In a context of poor governance, questionable executive conduct and the forces of state capture and corruption for nearly a decade, we need to examine what the role of a new phase in lawfare should be to restore the democratic state as a servant of citizens, and to ensure that social and economic development advances social justice.

The law and civil-society activism have been key features of our political discourse over recent years. And they should continue to inculcate a culture of accountability in the private and public sectors.

We have been through a torrid time over the past nine years. The authors of *Lawfare* examine why our acclaimed Constitution could not be a sufficient safeguard against the mendacity of state capture and why institutions that were built with resilience can be destroyed without too much resistance, notwithstanding the vigilance of a few civil-society organisations.

In 2014 Judge Edwin Cameron told the Johannesburg Bar: 'The Constitution itself cannot save South Africa from crime, corruption, misgovernance, governmental inefficiency and police brutality. What can save us is the Constitution in combination with a proud, deeply sceptical population, together with principled lawyering.'[2]

State capture damaged the institutional fabric of our state; a culture of malfeasance was legitimised and tolerated with increasing impunity and a lack of accountability.

Democracy, we have learnt the hard way, is not a smooth, frictionless ride. A number of seminal cases, challenging the authority and conduct of the executive, have been instructive in expounding the resolve of our constitutional democracy.

Thus, the courts have held political office-bearers to a high standard of honesty – even those who lie under oath (see *Minister of Home Affairs and Another v Fireblade Aviation Proprietary Limited and Others*); they have confirmed the independence of Chapter 9 Institutions (*McBride v Minister of Police and Another*), and have prescribed the qualities for a 'fit and proper person' to hold public office (in the *Simelane* and *Ntlemeza* judgments).

As Le Roux and Davis argue in Lawfare: 'The courts stood alone as a credible institution – hence the intensification of lawfare during this past decade.'

In contrast, we have now arrived at a moment where we are recalibrating our perspectives on ethical leadership, where we are restoring good governance, introducing greater boldness of vision, and showing a new urgency in our actions towards transforming our economy and our society towards greater inclusivity. This must occur in both the public and private sectors.

We know from research by the MIT Sloan School that 'countries rise when they put in place the right pro-growth political institutions and they fail – often spectacularly – when those institutions ossify or fail to adapt. Powerful people always and everywhere seek to grab complete control over government, undermining broader social progress for their own greed. Keep those people in check with effective democracy or watch your nation fail.'[3]

In this respect, *Lawfare* draws from an extensive and diverse body of domestic law that concerns, primarily, the contestation between political power, the public interest, social justice and, ultimately, the rule of law to strengthen democracy.

I know that Le Roux and Davis, as exemplary lawyers, attempted this detailed analysis of case law to help ensure we do not again arrive at a point where nefarious intent and irrationality determine how this country is governed.

What divides us is not colour or race, or even ideology. It is ethics.

We should heed the words of Nelson Mandela: 'Never, never and never again shall it be that this beautiful land will again experience the oppression of one by another and suffer the indignity of being the skunk of the world. Let freedom reign.[4]

Gordhan is South Africa's Minister of Public Enterprises, a former Minister of Finance and a former Commissioner of the South African Revenue Service.

PREFACE

This book is about this use and abuse of law. It analyses the stories of
key cases litigated during apartheid and over the past 20 years to show
the potential – and the limitations – of law. Throughout South African
history, the law has both constructed and transformed society. Law
created and entrenched the racist, corrupt framework of apartheid. Now,
the law is being used to dismantle that state and build a constitutional
democracy for all who live in this country.

The law, in our recent constitutional era, brought the promise of
transforming the society and economy organised under apartheid. This
process was almost immediately threatened by the arms-deal corruption
allegations and, more recently, the systematic hollowing out of our
constitutional institutions. In the landmark legal cases described in this
book, one side had a firm and fervent belief in the rule of law and in
the rights to be enjoyed under it, while the other felt that the very same
legal concepts frustrated its particular political or social objectives.

Fortunately, the rule of law largely survived these institutional assaults
in the past decade of the state-capture era. In particular, powers of the
judiciary were not captured, and the law even held our leaders accountable in some important cases brought by civil society and opposition
parties, manifesting a phenomenon we explore here: lawfare.

However, the wholesale degradation of the police and prosecution
authorities, in particular, has fundamentally compromised governance
and placed at risk the ongoing reliability, predictability and certainty

demanded by the rule of law. It remains to be seen whether our criminal-justice system can be 'recaptured', and whether the perpetrators and predators will be compelled to wear orange prison uniforms for their crimes – whether they be apartheid-era killers or corrupt officials.

South Africa's tradition of progressive lawyering, even during the darkest days of apartheid, coupled with our ambitious Constitution, gave us hope in 1994 that law could be a core tool for the construction of a meaningful democracy. It must be recognised that, regardless of the theoretical and conceptual possibility of law, too little has actually changed in South Africa for most of the country's citizens. Where we live, what we live in, and whether we get a good education, a decent job and healthcare when we are sick, all still depend too much on our race. Corruption and the looting of our state resources only deepen inequality and accelerate the immiseration of far too many. No one can feed law to their hungry children.

At the same time, populism, often linked to identity politics, is on the rise in South Africa. This endangers our constitutional project and is a deadly threat to the building of a non-racial, non-sexist country, as promised in the Constitution. As long as the way we look or the colour of our skin continues to be the main determinant of our path in South Africa, politicians will be tempted to tell us that those who look like them will be first to eat.

Our Constitution describes a united and diverse society. Ubuntu is central to this vision. But it is a vision that is under threat. For some South Africans, perhaps an increasing number, the Constitution is seen as a sell-out of the majority, a compromise, an obstacle. Or just irrelevant to the lived experience of most.

Globally, this turn away from constitutionalism towards populism and strong-man politics is giving rise to forms of authoritarian constitutionalism. This sees the tropes and rhetoric of democracy used to justify undemocratic executive action on the basis that the President has been elected by the people and should not be constrained by rights claims enforced by un-elected judges. At the same time, suspicion and distrust of the Other are used to justify a hardening of policing and law-enforcement, censorship, crackdowns on movement and increased intolerance. So, while a notional constitutional state remains in play, it has actually been gutted in a number of countries (see Turkey, Hungary and Zimbabwe, for example).

This book shows that those of us who believe in equality, dignity and freedom for all – values that should flourish in the constitutional framework – continue to have a lot of work to do: restoring our institutions to ensure capable leadership; retaining the vibrancy of civil society and active citizenship; dismantling the racist inequality of apartheid; and holding government accountable for its exercise of public powers and spending of public money. Critically, in our immediate context, we need to reach across our differences, abandon our privileges and respect every single person who lives in South Africa – as the Constitution demands.

Nothing is inevitable in this project – neither success nor failure. The Constitution is a powerful tool for the building of accountable and meaningfully participative democracy, but it is only a book of words if there is not a supportive politics and vigilant citizenry striving to realise its vision. A reaffirmation of our constitutional values is needed.

The cases described in this book show the possibilities and the precedents for progressive, transformative law, and the dangers and risks posed by its opposite.

Note on the text

Chapters 3 to 10 were originally published in a book we wrote in 2008 titled *Precedent and Possibility: The (Ab)use of Law in South Africa*. Each has been carefully reconsidered in the light of legal and political developments that have taken place over the decade since they were initially written. These chapters have been revised and updated to draw out the implications for the overall argument advanced in this book, namely the role and significance of lawfare in the third decade of South African constitutional democracy. We hope that the stories they tell remain of interest and relevance to a wider audience here.

Michelle le Roux
Dennis Davis
March 2019

1

THE ASCENDANCY OF LAWFARE

'The Nkandla moment presented that opportunity to interact with our people and to tell them about the legal, constitutional and normative underpinning of public power and why we are duty bound to deploy it honestly [and] effectively in order to produce good outcomes and to produce a just society.'[1]
– FORMER DEPUTY CHIEF JUSTICE DIKGANG MOSENEKE,
   28 January 2017

'This judgment signifies unfettered encroachment of the judiciary into the realm of the executive – pandering to the whims of the opposition who want to co-govern with the popularly elected government through the courts.'[2]
– ANC NATIONAL SPOKESPERSON ZIZI KODWA reacting to an order that
   President Zuma must disclose his reasons for his 2017 cabinet reshuffle

'Politics itself is migrating to the courts … Conflicts once joined in parliaments, by means of street protests, mass demonstrations, and media campaigns, through labour strikes, boycotts, blockades, and other instruments of assertion, tend more and more … to find their way to the judiciary. Class struggles seem to have metamorphosed into class actions.'[3]
– JEAN AND JOHN L COMAROFF

'You ain't seen nothing yet'
– BACHMAN TURNER OVERDRIVE, 1974

The birth of democracy in 1994 held out the promise of the construction of a new nation, in which the equality, dignity, freedom and humanity that could unite all South Africans would replace the systemic racism, sexism, discrimination, exclusion and homophobia that had fractured the country throughout its history. That possibility is contained in the Constitution, the foundational text for South Africa's new society. The Constitution is both allocative and normative, meaning that it assigns roles and imposes obligations upon various institutions, organs of state and spheres of government, while it also prescribes the creation of a new society described in compelling terms in its pages.

Key to the constitutional democratic state established by the Constitution is the concept of separation of powers. As the label suggests, this is the creation of three distinct arms of government, each with its own interrelated powers – the executive, legislature and judiciary. Each is assigned a specialised role to build the society promised in the Constitution. The executive formulates policy and implements legislation passed by Parliament, which is the sole lawmaker in the republic. The conduct and performance of the executive and the legislature are, in turn, subject to judicial scrutiny.

Underpinning this interlocking scheme is the principle of legality, or the notion that all public power is sourced in the Constitution, expressed in national legislation and exercised in a way that needs to be rational, fair and reasonable. In other words, government has no authority or power other than that sourced in the Constitution – hence it is referred to as 'the supreme law'. With the Constitution, there is no royal prerogative power or any other residual power for those who govern our country.

And all public power is held accountable – to the courts, to Parliament and to the key institutions created by Chapter 9 of the Constitution to support constitutional democracy. These are the Public Protector, the South African Human Rights Commission, the Commission for the Promotion and Protection of the Rights of Cultural, Religious and Linguistic Communities, the Commission for Gender Equality, the Auditor-General and the Electoral Commission.

As an aside, readers are forgiven if they have only heard of about three and a half of these institutions and then only of those whose leaders were distinguished by either spectacular incompetence or striking excellence at fulfilling their mandates. The 'Chapter 9s' are supposed to be partners in advancing the Constitution's transformative project, as well as scrutinisers of government power and performance. They are important because they further support our faith in law and the Constitution, our fidelity to the constitutional scheme of governance, and our commitment to the transformative outcomes prefigured in the Constitution. A society of dignified, free and equal South Africans, as described in the Constitution, is both the goal and the measure of our progress towards it. Unfortunately, we have still far to go in having the Chapter 9s fulfil our expectations of them as we do in ensuring that the constitutional promise is the lived reality of all South Africans, rather than racialised inequality and poverty.

The political, social and economic promises contained in the Constitution were framed as legal claims. These claims are expressly made in the Bill of Rights (Chapter 2 of the Constitution). Hence it should have been foreseen that struggles for both the political and economic rights set out in the Constitution would be increasingly fought in the courts once politics had failed to deliver immediate redress, transformation and justice to the victims of apartheid.

When we wrote *Precedent & Possibility: The (Ab)use of Law in South Africa*, we were concerned at the time of writing in 2008 that, if politics failed (or even if government was simply ineffective), the courts alone would not be able to power this journey away from apartheid and towards constitutional nirvana. For this reason, we warned that a turn to lawfare carried its own risks for the constitutional enterprise, which, at the time, was scarcely a decade and a half old. The concern was that political struggle by active citizens, civil-society groups, political parties and organised labour should not be converted into litigation alone. Displacing our constitutional political project (of 'nation-building' or 'transformation' for 'the rainbow nation') into legal processes fails for two reasons. First, litigation is slow, often incremental and relatively narrow in what it can change. Politics should be more responsive and comprehensive in reflecting the will of the people. Secondly, pending litigation seems to halt other processes or institutions from delivering on their obligations to realise the constitutional vision of our society, facilitated by a competent and capacitated state. Cabinet ministers and other public servants seem to feel that they are 'off the hook' while litigation about something for which they are responsible proceeds. The country waits for judgments at each level of the court system, rather than seeing its government deliver services and meaningful change. All of the arms of government and institutions of state in all spheres of government must do their bit. The constitutional project works only if all of its parts are functional and engaged and deliver on their mandates.

We had underestimated the extent of this rush towards litigation. The degradation of state institutions began relatively slowly. But by the end of a decade, a parallel state with compromised heads of security and law-enforcement agencies, including the critical revenue service, was revealed (see the revelations at the commissions of inquiry into state capture and the South African Revenue Service [SARS], for example). Parliament became as politically sheepish as the head of the National Prosecuting Authority (NPA). The courts stood alone as a credible institution – hence the intensification of lawfare during this past decade.

The exponential increase in lawfare

We have described the use of the courts in this fashion as constituting a form of lawfare, a term we borrowed from John and Jean Comaroff, who observed that, as society increasingly uses law as a means of control, the targets of the state invoke the cry of human rights to persuade courts that law has an intrinsic quality of accountability, certainty and the recognition of the basic freedom of the individual citizen. In this way, citizens fight attempts to control them through the law by using the law. Thus politics in many societies is played out more in the courts than it is in the streets, more by the use of law and its disguised violence than by unfettered brutal force, absent of any legal constraint.[4]

Political claims became legal complaints as, increasingly, the courts became the primary dispute-resolution mechanism replacing Parliament, political struggles, community activism and engagement, and media campaigns.

This is not a phenomenon exclusive to South Africa, which prompts the question, why do governments then employ law as a means of political and social control if it can work against social control? The

Comaroffs provide a plausible answer in their concept of 'lawfare': 'As a species of political displacement, [lawfare] becomes most readily visible when those who act in the name of the state conjure with legalities to act against some or all of its citizens.'[5] For example, former President Zuma's government used law to advance an ideological battle by introducing controversial legislation and regulation, such as the Mining Charter proposed by Minister Mosebenzi Zwane or when it repeatedly floated the idea of a media tribunal to deal with unflattering coverage and effective investigative journalism.

Within a few years after democracy had dawned in South Africa, the political energy that had powered the sustained struggle against the apartheid regime began to be replaced by vigorous contests in court in the Zuma era, and the phenomenon continues. The stampede to the courts to invalidate elective conferences held by the provincial structures of the African National Congress (ANC) is a case in point. The courts have become a battleground for contesting political forces, not only between the state and its opponents, as was the case during apartheid, but even between contending forces within the governing party.

Lawfare should be understood as having a duality to it; it can be a good or a bad thing. It is a good thing for adjudication to be political, in the sense that it advances the constitutional project and is undertaken by litigants and judges as an instrument to ensure that the constitutional vision is realised. However, it is a bad thing when courts become the site of pure political contestation because politicians seek to usurp judicial powers to achieve their objectives. In both contexts, it draws the judiciary far further into the political arena than has traditionally been the case. It holds the promise of promoting more reasoned deliberation about key political and distributional claims, but it can also turn the courts into a juristocracy, thereby reducing the importance of politics and the vibrancy of civil society. It is here that the two parts of lawfare meet each other. Lawfare in its negative sense is most clearly seen when politicians employ the courts in political trials to marginalise or remove their political opponents. When civil society is vibrant, the use of law in this fashion contests the attempt to criminalise political opposition and, in turn, may employ the courts as a means to curb the (ab)use of law. And the stronger the voices of civil society, the more likely it is that a court will feel less constrained by political pressure

5

and freer to exercise accountability over these forms of abuse.

Let us then begin with what could and should have been seen, at least from the moment that the criminal law was employed against Zuma before he became President. To be clear, ours is not an argument that Zuma should not be held accountable in a criminal court in respect of the 16 charges brought against him of corruption, money laundering and racketeering for 783 payments he received from his one-time financial advisor, Schabir Shaik. However, once he was charged, law and politics fused as competing factions in the ANC battled for political ascendancy. After the conviction of his co-accused, Shaik, in 2005, Zuma was dismissed as deputy president by President Thabo Mbeki. Expertly casting himself as the victim of a campaign of political interference aimed at preventing his rise to Number 1 citizen, Zuma turned to the courts. In 2007 he was charged on various counts of money laundering and corruption. On 12 September 2008, Judge Chris Nicholson held on procedural grounds that these charges were unlawful. This judgment proved to hold huge political implications. Not only did the judge set aside the prosecution of Zuma, but he also offered a number of scathing observations about the motivation for the prosecution, in particular about the political influence brought to bear by Mbeki and certain of his acolytes.

The result of the appeal against this judgment was an intemperate excoriation of Judge Nicholson by Judge Louis Harms, on behalf of a unanimous Supreme Court of Appeal. Correctly described by journalist Adriaan Basson as overwrought, Judge Harms accused Judge Nicholson of failing to apply basic rules of procedure and evidence in his critique of the prosecution. Although the harsh language of the rebuke was unjustified in our view, it is also clear that Judge Nicholson had over-reached himself by delving into political questions that were not before him for determination, and his judgment's findings about the ANC's succession politics, which had surrounded the prosecutorial decision to pursue Zuma, far exceeded the narrow procedural case that he was called on to decide.

It is worth noting, though, that Nicholson's musing on the need for a commission of inquiry to provide closure to the saga seems strangely prescient today, when commissions of inquiry are demanded and formed on a daily basis – as if they could substitute for effective law enforcement, diligent investigation, vigorous prosecution or a capable state intent on service delivery.

What was less known were the tactics alleged to have been adopted by the competing factions in the battle for political control in the ANC, and hence the country. Recently it has been suggested by historian and journalist RW Johnson that when the state prosecuted Shaik, in effect for having a corrupt relationship with Zuma, Mbeki sent an emissary to the then Judge President of the KwaZulu-Natal High Court to ensure the appointment of the presiding judge for the Shaik trial. Johnson also claims that Zuma warned Shaik not to appoint a technical criminal advocate (Shaik's choice had been the eminent silk Francois van Zyl, who successfully defended Shrien Dewani, who had been charged with the high-profile murder of his wife while visiting Cape Town) but to deploy political/legal tactics, as he subsequently did with his so-called Stalingrad litigation strategy.[6] This is the strategy of delay, made possible by undertaking appeals with little prospect of success and the pursuit of preliminary or interlocutory points to postpone consideration of the merits, all coupled with an extra-curial resort to the much misunderstood but frequently invoked *sub judice* rule to avoid accountability or the need to justify this grotesque waste of public funds spent on litigation.

The anticipated application to stay (or halt) Zuma's prosecution altogether (rerunning the political interference point and adding to it the self-created delay in bringing the prosecution to trial) is the final available ploy. Even today it appears that further appeals against any decision on the application will ensure that Zuma avoids the trial court for years to come. The retort that 'if the law and rules of procedure permit it, it's OK' is no answer to this strategy. The legal system should not be abused with frivolous, baseless, vexatious or tendentious cases. Sound legal judgement and advice, given by lawyers guided by their obligations to ensure the proper and efficient use of the legal system, would not result in some of the litigation strategies pursued in our courts. Abuse of process and litigation undertaken not to resolve real disputes or to vindicate rights, but to avoid or delay politically unpalatable outcomes, should be discouraged.

In 2008, we woefully underestimated the extent of state capture and the intensity of lawfare that would unfold. The subsequent assault on key institutions created by the Constitution – disempowering and decapacitating them – was also inadequately predicted. Since then, a programme of what is now referred to as state capture was rolled out. Institutions of state have two purposes – service delivery, and preserving and strengthening our constitutional democracy. What we have seen in too many government departments, agencies and institutions is that the service deliverers have become corrupted for their own enrichment through cronyism, nepotism, and tender and procurement fraud, while accountability has been incapacitated by the appointment of leaders of key institutions who seemingly do not have the will to fulfil their mandates.

First to fall were the Scorpions, set up in 2001 as a multidisciplinary, independent institution to deal with the increasing scourge of corruption, combining investigative and prosecutorial competence. By 2009, the unit had been disbanded and replaced with the Hawks, whose legal design placed it within the clutching grasp of the then Minister of Safety and Security. The decision to be rid of the Scorpions was taken by the ANC at its 2007 Polokwane electoral conference, where Zuma emerged victorious against Mbeki and ascended to the ANC throne. The Scorpions, which had played an important role in the Shaik corruption trial and the subsequent investigation of Zuma, were doomed once the political dominance of the Zuma faction was cemented. The name change between these two law-enforcement predators barely captured the devastating effect of the changes made on the unit's ability to crush corruption. The new unit was no swift and efficient crime killer.

Thanks to the tireless efforts of Johannesburg businessman Hugh Glenister, the birth of the Hawks was at least a troubled affair. Glenister launched an intensive campaign of lawfare, seeking to win from the courts what the losing ANC factions and opposition parties could not deliver. Three cases dealing with the constitutionality of the Hawks made their way to the Constitutional Court, the most significant of which was *Glenister 2*. Here, Glenister and the Helen Suzman Foundation, as amicus,[7] argued that the legislation that established the Hawks did not give the unit the necessary structural and operational independence to be an effective corruption-fighting mechanism. And, for that reason, the impugned legislation was inconsistent with international obligations of the republic to have independent corruption busters and, hence, it was also incompatible with the Constitution, which requires compliance with treaties that South Africa has ratified and adopted.

In their majority judgment, former Deputy Chief Justice Dikgang

Moseneke and Justice Edwin Cameron found for the applicants. Their bold judgment sourced an obligation to establish a viable, and thus independent, anti-corruption unit in a reading of South Africa's international obligations coupled with the Constitution. The announcement by President Ramaphosa in his February 2019 State of the Nation address that the 'Scorpions 2.0' would be re-established under the direction of the new National Director of Public Prosecutions (NDPP), Shamila Batohi, is a promising ending to this saga.

This kind of judicial oversight aimed at ensuring institutional competence and independence was not an exception. In 2012, the official opposition failed in Parliament to prevent the appointment of Menzi Simelane by Zuma to the all-important position as NDPP (at least his appointment was certainly important to the President). In keeping with the move to lawfare, an application was launched to set aside this appointment. Again the stakes were high: the early stench of public corruption had begun wafting through the state and it seemed as if the executive wanted to ensure not just an unreliable anti-corruption unit, but also to prevent an excessively (or even vaguely) independent NDPP.

The case again required judicial scrutiny of an executive decision – this time whether Simelane met the requirements of integrity and conscientiousness to be the fit and proper person required by the relevant legislation. The government argued that the President had a wide discretion in the appointment of the NDPP. It was for the President to make the decision – which involved a value judgment – and the requirement that the person appointed 'must be a fit and proper person with due regard to his experience, conscientiousness and integrity' could not be said to be an objective one. However, just because the President has the power to make this appointment does not mean that his decision cannot be objectively scrutinised by a court.

A careful evaluation of the evidence relating to Simelane's performance in his previous position as director general in the Department of Justice showed compellingly that he did not meet the tests of conscientiousness and integrity to rationally be considered a fit and proper person for appointment to such high office generally, let alone one that requires the strength of character and integrity of the NDPP. The highest court agreed, and Simelane was removed.

But Simelane should not feel as if he was the only 'victim' of courts diligently ensuring that compromised leaders picked for critical law-enforcement positions were removed from office. In a similar vein, decisions in the High Court went against the NPA's senior prosecutors, Nomgcobo Jiba and Lawrence Mrwebi; the Hawks head, Berning Ntlemeza, and crime-intelligence boss Richard Mdluli were also declared to be unfit and improper to hold these offices. In keeping with the general intensity of the lawfare waged, Jiba and Mrwebi appealed the decision to strike them from the roll of advocates. Five judges of the Supreme Court of Appeal heard the appeal and, by three to two, ruled that neither Jiba nor Mrwebi should be struck off. The General Council of the Bar appealed this decision to the Constitutional Court. The decision to appeal was not unanimous, and caused Advocates for Transformation to accuse the General Council of the Bar of racism,[8] yet another example of the contested nature of lawfare.

Another compelling exercise in lawfare was seen in the saga that sought to reinstate Mxolisi Nxasana as NDPP, one in which allegations were made that the former President had lied under oath when he said that Nxasana had requested to leave office. In that case – and the resolution of the dispute of fact arising from the two seemingly mutually destructive versions put up by the ex-President and Nxasana – the Pretoria High Court held that Shaun Abrahams had been improperly appointed as the head of the NPA but that Nxasana, his predecessor, should not be reinstated. It ordered that the then deputy president, Cyril Ramaphosa, should appoint a new head of the NPA. By the time the case reached the Constitutional Court, Ramaphosa was President.

The Constitutional Court removed the head of the NPA and gave President Ramaphosa 90 days to appoint a new head prosecutor. A minority decision found that this was an outcome that required the majority of the court to engage in unfounded speculation about whether there would be further instability in the NPA if Nxasana were reinstated, which is an eventuality that those judges chose to avoid. The majority judgment appears to have fallen into the same trap of which it criticised the former President: removing lawfully appointed public servants in ways that smacked of political expedience.

And, a decade ago we were not yet aware that disputes over improvements made to former President Zuma's homestead, Nkandla, would build into a tsunami of taxpayers' money spent wastefully on the legal system. When the then Public Protector, Thuli Madonsela, found that some of the improvements to Nkandla had been made not to ensure the security of the President but for his private benefit, and for which he was obliged to reimburse the fiscus, the attack on her office was unbridled. Both the then ANC secretary general, Gwede Mantashe, and his deputy, Jessie Duarte, accused the Public Protector of behaving as if she was above Parliament. In the words of Duarte, she was 'very populist in her orientation' and did 'not present a full picture to the public'.[9]

For almost two years, the nation was told that the executive could commission its own report on the Nkandla improvements and that it was not, in any way, bound by the Public Protector's completed report. But, finally, in early 2016, the Economic Freedom Fighters (EFF) applied to the Constitutional Court for an order declaring the President in breach of his constitutional obligations because he had refused to comply with the Public Protector's report and had not 'paid back the money'.

The outcome of the EFF application before the Constitutional Court was inevitable after Advocate Jeremy Gauntlett, on behalf of the President, conceded that the remedial action in the Public Protector's report was binding. Hence the Constitutional Court was hardly confronted with a hard case. However, it was in the wording chosen by the Chief Justice that the core importance of the judgment was to be found:

> One of the crucial elements of our constitutional vision is to make a decisive break from the unchecked abuse of State power and resources that was virtually institutionalised during the apartheid era. To achieve this goal, we adopted accountability, the rule of law and the supremacy of the Constitution as values of our constitutional democracy. For this reason, public office-bearers ignore their constitutional obligations at their peril. This is so because constitutionalism, accountability and the rule of law constitute the sharp and mighty sword that stands ready to chop the ugly head of impunity off its stiffened neck.[10]

The Nkandla judgment held major political ramifications, to the extent that even the President felt constrained to inform the nation of his (non-) response by convening a late-night press conference to share his sorry/

not sorry non-apology/non-resignation statement with the nation. The Nkandla decision was a rallying cry for further legal action by opposition parties and civil-society groups. Its findings were used to challenge Speaker of Parliament Baleka Mbete and Zuma during parliamentary sittings. Following its decision, the Constitutional Court was required to deal with the proper parliamentary mechanism for impeaching a President as a consequence of its earlier finding that he had failed to uphold his oath of office and fulfil his constitutional obligations. The majority of the court found that Parliament had to hold a preliminary inquiry to determine whether a ground for impeachment existed and, in turn, this obliged the National Assembly to make rules specifically tailored to conducting an impeachment process. The Chief Justice penned an irate dissent, accusing his colleagues in the majority of 'a textbook case of judicial overreach' by intruding impermissibly into the terrain of Parliament.

Many of the cases where the courts have required executive compliance with the Constitution have been swiftly followed by sustained attacks against the judiciary from outsiders, questioning its role. This has placed the courts in the line of political fire. In reaction to this lawfare, and faced with a series of adverse findings against government, the ANC has rolled out its attack machine on several occasions.

The governing party was particularly incensed by the manner in which the courts dealt with the government's handling of the case of Sudanese President Omar al-Bashir. In June 2015, al-Bashir, arrived in South Africa for the African Union assembly. Two warrants had been issued by the International Criminal Court (ICC) for his arrest on charges of crimes against humanity and war crimes. On 27 November 2000, South Africa had ratified the Rome Statute, which conferred jurisdiction on the ICC to try cases such as those involving al-Bashir.

One might therefore have reasonably expected that, when the ICC asked for assistance in the arrest of al-Bashir, the South African authorities would have complied with their obligations under both the Rome Statute and the domestic legislation passed to ensure implementation of its obligations. But they did no such thing. And when the Southern African Litigation Centre applied to the Pretoria High Court for an interdict preventing al-Bashir from leaving the country, the court was assured by government lawyers that he was still present in the country.

Sadly, that was not true.

The government reaction was strident, particularly after the outcome in the Pretoria High Court. An interim order was granted by the court preventing al-Bashir from leaving South Africa pending a hearing on the application. The South African government then allowed the Sudanese leader to leave, the court order notwithstanding. The court took a very dim view of this violation of a court order, saying, 'If the State, an organ of State, or a State official does not abide by Court orders the democratic edifice will crumble stone by stone until it collapses and chaos ensues.'[11]

Mantashe did not take lightly to this criticism: 'There is a drive in sectors of the judiciary to create chaos for governance ... we know if it doesn't happen in the Western Cape High Court it will happen in the North Gauteng. These are two benches where you always see the narrative is totally negative ...'[12]

On 1 July 2015, the ANC warmed to the theme of describing judgments as judicial overreach – as if they breached the doctrine of separation of powers. The organisation also expressed concern at statements of the former Deputy Chief Justice, speaking at Georgetown University in Washington, when he said that in South Africa the judiciary should take a more direct political stance than even in the US.

Justice Moseneke had earlier raised concern at the 'uncanny concentration of power' in the President in regard to appointments provided for in the Constitution. Among other things, he referred to the President's responsibility (after consultation with the Judicial Service Commission and the leaders of parties in the National Assembly) to appoint the Chief Justice and Deputy Chief Justice. Justice Moseneke had questioned whether the design of this part of the Constitution was not at war with the dominant idea of preventing a concentration of power in the hands of the President. In response, the ANC asked, 'Is he proposing changing the Constitution in the name of defending the Constitution?'[13]

This all proved to be a bridge too far for Chief Justice Mogoeng Mogoeng, who reacted vigorously to these attacks and convened a meeting of the President and senior ministers with representative heads of courts. This unprecedented encounter with the arms of government appeared to end in a conciliatory way. However, it would be naive to assume that we have heard the last of this tension as courts continue to decide who leads party structures and organs of state.

As described in more detail later in this book, the courts have been called upon to deal with egregious conduct on the part of the executive on various occasions. But we should add a word of caution: on occasion an adverse judgment, whether it be in the Nkandla case or the litigation to remove Berning Ntlemeza as head of the Hawks, has been accepted by government without demur. It may well be, therefore, that attacks on the judiciary are partly dependent upon the balance of political forces within and between political parties at the time a case is decided. When the Constitutional Court delivered its unanimous Nkandla judgment, for example, there was not a peep of criticism of the court. The ANC tactic shifted to an argument that the judgment had not found that the President had deliberately breached the Constitution sufficiently to justify any constitutional basis for impeachment. When the judgment came down, Zuma was facing a series of crises all linked to his alleged connection to the Gupta family and their business dealings in South Africa. It would have been foolhardy to attack the Constitutional Court for delivering a judgment based, to a large extent, on a concession made by the President's own lead counsel, when the political forces within the governing party were already engaged in a ferocious war of position.

The Eurocentric/neoliberal attack

In addition to the consequences of the deepening phenomenon of lawfare, another set of challenges to the constitutional project has emerged, namely the fact the Constitution itself has become an object of criticism by those who see it as an obstacle to transformation. This thinking that the Constitution prevents social and economic change, particularly as it is a Eurocentric document, is unsurprising, given the slow pace of economic transformation (radical or otherwise) the country has seen over the past two decades. Some of the content of this line of attack has been around from the inception of the Constitution, but the volume and intensity of this form of discourse has increased since 2008.

In responding to this criticism, it is wise to recall the text of the Republic of South Africa Constitution Act of 1996, which boldly proclaims that the country aspires to be a non-racial, non-sexist society based on the core principles of freedom, dignity and equality. The ambitiousness of the constitutional enterprise was captured in a truly remarkable speech delivered by the then deputy president, Thabo Mbeki, who addressed

Parliament as it met to adopt the Constitution:

> The Constitution, whose adoption we celebrate, constitutes an unequivocal statement that we refuse to accept that our African-ness shall be defined by our race, our colour, our gender or our historical origins.

> It is a firm assertion made by ourselves that South Africa belongs to all who live in it, Black and White.

> It gives concrete expression to the sentiment we share as Africans, and will defend to the death, that the people shall govern.

> It recognises the fact that the dignity of the individual is both an objective which society must pursue, and is a goal which cannot be separated from the material well-being of that individual.

Mbeki went on to claim that the Constitution

> creates a law-governed society which shall be inimical to arbitrary rule.

> It enables the resolution of conflicts by peaceful means rather than resort to force.

> It rejoices in the diversity of our people and creates the space for all of us voluntarily to define ourselves as one people.

> As an African, this is an achievement of which I am proud, proud without reservation and proud without any feeling of conceit.[14]

In a moment of magnificent expression, Mbeki had captured the animating idea behind the enterprise: a people defined by our diversity, cognisant of our racist past and of how far we must still travel in order to all become Africans, and thus a people with a shared common identity. To achieve this, we were to destroy the myth of racialised cultural and economic superiority that prevented us from claiming a fresh identity as South Africans. As Cameroonian philosopher Achille Mbembe has argued,[15] democracy was dependent on this construction. If we could not break the myth and replace it with a new form of citizenship, the very enterprise set out in the Constitution was fatally doomed.

Now, however, there is a growing chorus claiming that the Constitution was employed by recalcitrant whites to subvert majority rule. This mode of attack, located at the margins of politics back in 2008, is now assuming increasing importance in the national discourse. It sees the Constitution as a compromise aimed at preserving so-called white monopoly capital, and casts Mandela and his team of negotiators as sell-outs of their people, especially on the question of land redistribution and apartheid restitution. The argument is that the constitutional promise preserves the ill-gotten gains obtained during apartheid. The slow, almost non-existent, pace of meaningful land reform in particular has proved to be fertile ground for casting the Constitution as the obstacle or, worse, the mechanism to retain apartheid-era economic and ownership structures of land and other productive assets.

What is most apparent in the ongoing debate regarding land reform is that the Constitution is now labelled as part of the problem. We say that it is rather the seeming absence of a coherent land policy implemented with determination and expedition that is the source of the present crisis in land restitution. Assume away the property clause, Section 25 of the Constitution, and we would be in the same factual position. The land-reform problem is political, not constitutional. The same observation is applicable to the stark patterns of inequality, the grinding poverty encountered by millions and the structural racism that continues to blight this land – unaddressed by government. These are not the products of the Constitution.

Even ignoring the deployment of the hollow Bell Pottinger catch-phrase 'white monopoly capital', spouted as a response to the nation's vocal rejection of state capture in South Africa, the government's failure to address the disgraceful material conditions of poverty and landless-ness in this most unequal of societies is evidence of the failure of the ANC government to fully realise the transformation promised in the Constitution.

An academic version of the line of argument that the Constitution is the problem has been developed by University of Pretoria academic Joel Modiri. In a series of articles, Modiri argues that, while the advent of a new constitutional order did alter the moral and political foundation of the country, there can be no guarantee that the Constitution will not reproduce a formalist and conservative legal culture. It is also based upon the assumption that Western liberal constitutionalism is superior to African alternatives. Thus, the South African Constitution represents a Western (and hence colonial) order of legal knowledge that 'suppresses and marginalises indigenous African ways of knowing and doing law'.[16] In similar fashion, Tshepo Madlingozi claims that the call for a supreme Constitution and a Bill of Rights came overwhelmingly from whites 'with a view to keeping the main edifice of the anti-black bifurcated policy intact'.[17]

These critical voices call seriously into question the possibilities of which many spoke when the Constitution passed into law; hence they require a careful response. In fact these criticisms necessitate two related replies: to the attack on the failure to transform the economic structure inherited from apartheid and to the contention that, far from being the poster child of progressive constitutionalism, the South African text is wholly inappropriate for an African country.

There can be little doubt that this line of attack on the Constitution has highlighted the mistakes made through the almost unqualified praise, indeed the triumphalism, that has accompanied constitutional writings over the past two decades. Read, for example, the standard textbooks on constitutional law, the comprehensive and careful assessment of the so-called Chaskalson court by Theunis Roux,[18] the breathless enthusiasm for the mystical Constitution in the work of the court by retired Justice Albie Sachs and you will find not a scintilla of the kind of criticism that Modiri, Madlingozi and the hosts of social-media users have articulated consistently over the past year or so.

Is the Constitution a Eurocentric imposition or a uniquely South African achievement? Will it inevitably retard the structural changes needed to achieve a substantive model of democracy, as claimed by its antagonists and energetically denied by its proponents? These are questions that now bedevil the political and legal debate. In summary, we now need to revisit the role of the judiciary in a constitutional democracy grounded in South African society. But we cannot do this without an answer to a prior question: can our Constitution promote substantive structural change to achieve its proclaimed vision, a non-racial, non-sexist democracy based on freedom, dignity and equality for all?

Just as economic sanctions hastened the end of apartheid, can and will downgrades to junk status, coupled with years of stagnant growth and debilitating youth unemployment, herald an irresistible opposition to constitutional democracy? Is it then correct to blame the Constitution for our recession? Our unemployment? Our deindustrialisation? Our failing schools? Our inadequate healthcare system? We say not.

So, is the Constitution a tool of self-preservation for the beneficiaries of apartheid? We have emphasised Thabo Mbeki's 'I am an African' speech that he made in his address to Parliament when the Constitution was passed into law. This was to emphasise our argument that the Constitution was based on an essential truth – to be a democratic country we needed to embrace the idea of 'us as Africans' transcending our past understandings of race and gender. To say we are (South) Africans poses the urgent existential challenge to construct a fresh national identity, respectful of the dignity of difference but committed to the sharing of our common goods, to offer our skills, work ethic, resources, opportunities and commitment to the benefit of all South Africans, and to redress the racist discrimination of our colonial and apartheid past.

That redress of the past and adequate protection for those on the margins have not taken place is undeniable. We would argue that the blame for this political, or indeed legal, failure cannot be placed on the Constitution. On the contrary, read in at least one coherent manner, the Constitution seeks a society in which democracy means far more than a formal adherence to the economic or social status quo. Loyal theorist Karl Klare has captured this vision of the Constitution as promoting a rich and broad view of constitutional democracy: 'In this enlarged optic, democracy includes conceptions of self-governance and human self-realisation that go beyond the traditional discourse of checks-and-balances and the trite division of government into legislative, executive and judicial branches. The Constitution introduces new governance relationships.'[19]

This reading resists the idea that the Constitution, no matter from where particular words or phrases in the text were borrowed, will reproduce a society wrenched from its African roots. To repeat, for us, the animating constitutional idea was, and should remain, the creation of a society based upon a new South African identity, which eschews the claim of white superiority in any form, or the concomitant idea that only Western ideas are to be employed to fashion the new society.

We need to admit that the conservative legal culture bequeathed to us by our colonial past and a regrettable poverty of legal imagination in too many cases have contributed to the lack of transformation of key legal rules, which continues to be an obstacle to substantive economic and social change. This must then lead to a discussion of the role of the law and courts in the attainment of this objective.

Lawfare is a central part of this discussion. As explained above, courts are an important and necessary site for accountability, and an instrument for realising the constitutional vision (the good side of lawfare). But they can and, indeed, have been abused by politicians precisely because they may be more decisive and effective than the messy, incremental processes of politics (the bad side of lawfare). So, while lawfare is a complex and contested concept, the manner in which the South African Constitution has envisaged the governance of the country mandates the courts to become partners with the other two arms of government in the reconstruction of society. In turn, that means that political, economic and social controversies will be fought out in the courts, which is indeed what the Constitution envisaged.

Conclusion

The key question that needs to be posed when we look at where we are and where we have come from is: how have we done so far as a democratic nation? For the critics of the Constitution, the answer, clearly, is not well enough. The critics suggest that the record supports their contention that, as inequality and poverty remain firmly entrenched, the privileges that whites gained from apartheid continue to be as entrenched as they were some 25 years ago. The standards employed to judge both academic and professional performance have hardly altered during the past two decades. At best, the Constitution has contributed nothing meaningful to the transformation of the economic or social structure of South African society and, at worst, it has helped reinforce the structures of society that were constructed over the 300 years of racist rule.

To evaluate this critical stance, we need to examine a number of issues that have come to the fore after at least a decade of state capture and lawfare, as well the legal fights to temper the consequences. There needs to be, first, a greater focus on the political context and, secondly, a critical examination of the role of courts in this process. In particular, we need to ask, have our courts over the past twenty-odd years grasped the radical challenges posed by the promises of the Constitution, as they would have been read by a community who were not trained in constitutional law? Put in a different way, has the constitutional idea as contained in the text – of a decisive break from the past, a fresh start by way of the construction of a non-racial, non-sexist democracy, based on freedom, dignity and equality for all – been vindicated, or has the country even begun its required journey in this direction without being hijacked or having lost its way?

Separation of powers is at the heart of the tension between the government and the judiciary, as described earlier. This prompts further questions: have the courts crafted a doctrine of separation of powers that facilitates this journey? How has the legal system, particularly our procedures (with the emphasis on access to the law by those for whom the Constitution made social and economic promises), as well as the structure and nature of the legal profession, served this set of objectives? Should we remain passive to the existing legal rules of access to justice? Why have we never duplicated the imaginative procedures adopted by other middle-income countries? Finally, how far have we travelled in closing the polarisation caused by the existing racial structures?

We pose some new answers to our current challenges in the concluding chapter of this book. Those answers draw on the lessons learnt from the cases described in the intervening chapters. These cases were chosen for three reasons. First, they remain relevant because they remind us of the limits of courts. Courts cannot fill the gap left by an executive or legislature or government that does not implement policy effectively and thereby transform South African society. The courts alone cannot lift South Africa unaided into the society prefigured in the Constitution: every arm of government, institution of state and active citizen must play their part.

Secondly, these cases warn us of how courts, too, can be captured – and eventually may be. Law can be (ab)used to legitimise political struggle, and delegitimise political opponents. The *Rivonia* trial and the charges filed, and dropped, against former finance minister Pravin Gordhan are products of the same drive by the executive. The Zuma trial is of a different hue – here serious criminal acts are alleged to have been committed, although Judge Nicholson's apprehension of the role played by politics cannot be discounted.

Finally, even in the dark days of apartheid, law was used by creative and courageous lawyers to restrain the arbitrary use of political power. The stories we tell, past and present, may help us understand the possibilities that a progressive cadre of lawyers might be able to realise and the limitations inherent in this exercise. Fundamentally, that leads to this question: how much more can be done today and tomorrow with the Constitution as our guiding source?

So, please, read more about why we chose the cases in this book, and we will catch up with you at the Conclusion, when we offer our answers to these questions.

2

WHY THESE CASES?

'If [the new constitution is a bridge and] this bridge is successfully to span the open sewer of violent and contentious
transition, those who are entrusted with its upkeep will need
to understand very clearly what it is a bridge from, and what
a bridge to.'[1]
– ETIENNE MUREINIK

During the long night of apartheid, courts were often sites of vigorous
political struggle. They were the places where different visions of South
Africa were presented to the public by the competing litigants – usually
the state against accused persons or applicants whose rights were at
stake.

Since 1994 and the beginning of constitutional democracy, similarly
significant contests have taken place in our courts. There is, however,
a major difference: litigation now takes place within the context of the
Constitution, which provides a vast range of rights for all who live in
this country.

This book seeks to examine some of the crucial cases in which battles
for justice in its various forms have been fought. It also provides an
explanation for how, 25 years into our constitutional democracy, it is the
courtroom, and not Parliament or the streets, to which this country has
primarily turned to defend democracy and our hard-won constitutional

institutions. In this sense, there is a stark and disturbing similarity between pre- and post-apartheid South Africa. Both periods have witnessed the existence of unaccountable forces imposing their will on the citizenry without a scintilla of regard for the rule of law. In the 1980s, it was the securocrats; over the past decade it was the Zuptacrats. But the result was the same: a parallel state was constructed in which (whether allegedly funded by the Guptas or the Watsons) the key business of government was conducted outside of the constitutional framework.

But, first, we must venture into the terrain of the theoretical and the conceptual, and consider the reasons why we have selected these particular cases that are analysed here, and the links between the old and the constitutional orders. These cases provide a useful background for the concluding comments in the book, where we move beyond the stories to speculate about the future of our constitutional democracy.

The cases

It was difficult to make the selection, but our primary reason for choosing the cases that appear here is that all of them contributed to a change – for better or worse – in the South African political landscape. In other words, they were chosen on the basis of their legal and political importance to South Africa at the time they were contested in the courts, and because of their implications for the nature and development of South African society, then and now.

There are, of course, many cases that assumed critical legal and political importance to South Africa at the time that they were litigated. The choice therefore proved to be very difficult, particularly in a one-volume work of this nature. Ultimately, we chose cases for which it can be truly said that the country held its breath awaiting the courts' decisions.

Legal cases are no more than stories. This may not seem apparent to some, in that laws are framed in arcane texts and legalese, or professional jargon, which the courts interpret and apply to the facts of the case. But cases take place within a particular political and moral context and the unfolding of the case and its outcome are essentially a narrative that directly affects the lives of individual litigants and, possibly indirectly, millions of citizens in this country.

The cases under analysis in this book are therefore stories that tell of our past, present and future. We have attempted to tell these stories without the legalese that complicates them, and with due recognition for the characters who have a role to play in them – i.e. the lawyers and judges who were responsible for the outcomes, and the litigants whose life experiences were the source of these cases.

When all of these (and similar) cases are considered together, they reveal a remarkable faith in the process of law, during the decades of determined efforts by successive racist governments to destroy the rule of law and with it, the failure to achieve a constitutional democracy for South Africa. When democracy finally came, a tangible faith in law's possibility appeared to have been rewarded.

Law and the government: When the past meets the future

During apartheid, the law created the very foundations essential to the construction of the system that allocated and denied rights and privileges on the basis of race. The cruelty of apartheid was maintained by volumes of laws and regulations. But, by their nature, laws can both promote and constrain the exercise of power. In other words, litigation can be used to undermine the law itself. Let us first examine law as a form of struggle during apartheid.

Many of the legal struggles discussed here were based on the idea that a law may be introduced by government to achieve a pernicious purpose, and yet also be employed by a resourceful litigant for an opposite end. Of course, the outcome could also depend on the approach to law of the judge before whom the case happened to be heard.

Take the case of Dullah Omar, later to become the first Minister of Justice in the democratic South Africa.[2] Omar was detained in 1985 without the benefit of a trial under a draconian piece of legislation called the Public Safety Act. His legal representatives argued that, unless the Public Safety Act expressly authorised the President to issue emergency regulations that included a denial of so important a right as the right to a trial, the regulations could not deny a detainee the right to make representations to the authorities as to why he or she should *not* be detained.

The majority of the court rejected this argument, holding that the president was granted the implied power to promulgate regulations that excluded the rights of detainees to make these kinds of representations. But, in a significant minority judgment, Judge Gerald Friedman insisted that a right as fundamental as that of being heard – when a person's rights to liberty are affected by an adverse decision – could be removed only by an Act of Parliament. A pro-executive judge might well be prepared to accept as law anything that the government called law, but a judge like Friedman insisted that the bedrock of law is the protection of the rights of citizens, and these, he argued, could be taken away only by an express legal provision, and not by reading an ambiguous text as negating the protection of rights.

In a country where the courts claimed adherence to the principle of the rule of law, certain judges took these claims seriously. But Judge Friedman was in a minority. From time to time, however, his approach did prevail. On occasion, the government was held accountable and this led to unexpected outcomes. Judges would read apartheid statutes in ways that revealed their open texture or ambiguity in their meaning. This would allow these judges to favour an interpretation that could produce an outcome that minimised the impact on the existing rights of individual citizens. They read the law to mean something other than the interpretation claimed by the government. In the early 1950s, the courts often adhered to this model of adjudication. In 1950, for example, the Appellate Division held that a regulation authorising racially separate railway coaches in circumstances where only black passengers were subject to criminal sanction for travelling in the 'wrong' coach was illegal because it promoted unequal and discriminatory treatment.[3]

This approach, as we shall see, became less common as the apartheid state gained strength. Nevertheless, the possibility of similar victories was never completely extinguished. Throughout the apartheid era, a contest between legal results that either preserved or destroyed people's rights was fought in the courts. In a work that heavily influenced a generation of progressive lawyers in South African to conceive of a legal theory that could justify human-rights litigation, English social historian EP Thompson, in his book *Whigs and Hunters: The Origin of the Black Act*, clarified the difference between a system of power that claimed adherence to the rule of law and one based on pure arbitrary power without any recourse to law. The key passage of his text reads thus:

> The inhibitions upon power imposed by law seem to me a
> legacy as substantial as any handed down from the struggles of

the seventeenth century to the eighteenth, and a true and important cultural achievement ... The notion of the regulation and reconciliation of conflicts through the rule of the law – and the elaboration of rules and procedures which, on occasion, made some approximate approach towards the ideal – seems to me a cultural achievement of universal significance ... I am not starry eyed about this at all ... I am insisting only upon the obvious point, that there is a difference between arbitrary power and the rule of the law. We ought to expose the shams and inequities which may be concealed beneath this law. But the rule of law itself, the imposing of effective inhibitions upon power and the defence of the citizen from power's all-intrusive claims, seems to me to be an unqualified human good.[4]

Thompson understood well that power worked through law but that the power holder was, on occasion, held accountable to a legal text that, given the nature of that text, was open to a litigant's interpretation. For this reason, governance under apartheid was sometimes vulnerable to challenges in the courts. Legal battles continued to rage throughout the period between 1948 and 1994. In most cases, the battle was fought without much success for the powerless. Sometimes, however, significant and surprising results were achieved. These victories were the product of many interrelated factors: the quality of lawyering, the ideology of the presiding judges, the political context in which the cases were fought, the intensity of the political struggle at that time and the nature of the factual and legal materials relevant to the particular case.

During South Africa's democratic era, legal battles have raged again, particularly in the decade of Zuma's government. There have been a plethora of cases that have gone to the heart of our political enterprise. From the expenditure on the President's private home in Nkandla to the challenge to key appointments – such as those of the NDPP, the COO of the South African Broadcasting Corporation (SABC) and the head of the Hawks – alongside a number of cases dealing with conduct in Parliament and the successful attempt to prevent a trillion-rand nuclear deal with Putin's Russia, the courts have been the site of ferocious political struggles, couched inevitably in legal language.

Law and strategy

Lawyers who understood the nature of law developed their litigation strategy to exploit the law's contradictions and to help create space for both political activity and the curbing of gross excesses of state power, all the while undermining the efficacy of government policy.

Former Chief Justice Pierre Rabie, who, as we shall later see, was the leader of an excessively executive-minded judiciary during the 1980s and whose court was described as having declared a war on law during the states of emergency of the 1980s, commented on the way in which lawyers, who brought cases in many different courts challenging the state of emergency declared by PW Botha in 1985, and again in 1986 and 1987, appeared to have coordinated their legal strategies.[5] And, to an extent, he was correct: those advocates who fought to uphold human rights certainly knew they were in for a ferocious fight and each case litigated was followed carefully by other litigators anxious to explore any possibility for a rights-based defence that emerged from previous encounters.

The adverse context in which these legal fights took place is well illustrated by the approach adopted by the senior judiciary, particularly the Chief Justice. Rabie presided over a court that was determined to reduce the space for any legal challenge to the government's repression. An interview conducted by Steve Mufson with Rabie, published in the *Sunday Star* of 3 May 1987, cast a bright light over this approach adopted by the overwhelming majority of the judiciary at that time:

> [Rabie] seemed unperturbed by the Government's encroachment on the rights guaranteed by Roman-Dutch common law; that is, rules of law inherited from our Roman-Dutch and English heritage and fashioned by our courts over a century to meet the perceived needs of the country. As far as Rabie was concerned, there was no question of more than one outcome in a case because, once Parliament enacted a law, 'It is the law,' he said. He viewed a Bill of Rights with scepticism and said that, in the United States, 'It has produced a bit of a shambles.' To him, the United States represented 'freedom run mad'.[6]

Rabie went on to tell Mufson:

We must be realistic. We have strangers coming in across the borders with bombs and mines. There is nothing in the common law to deal with a situation like that. The ordinary law of criminal procedure would require that a man be charged within 48 hours so that you can't question him any more after that. We must get information from people we arrest, especially when they are carrying weapons from the Soviet Bloc, otherwise we can't defend ourselves ... The situation in the country is pretty near that of a civil war. It is naive to think you can quell it by bringing people to court.[7]

Contrary to the likes of Rabie, who dominated the bench, there was a small group of exceptional judges who were prepared to listen to arguments about abuses of rights, and to read oppressive and racist legislation as narrowly as possible in order to give effect to the values of the common law.[8] According to their reading, the law, at its core, protected and promoted human rights, such as the freedom of the individual and the civil rights of all citizens. Lawyers continued to use Thompson's theory of law in their litigation strategies, knowing that some judges might see the law as having a curbing effect on unaccountable state power.

Challenging the state of emergency

An unusual example of this judicial approach, which demonstrates a belief in the possibility inherent in this form of litigation, occurred at a conference held in 1986. It was organised by Professor John Dugard, the then director of the Centre for Applied Legal Studies, an important human-rights institution within the University of the Witwatersrand. Dugard is truly one of the heroic figures of South African academia and a pioneer of human-rights jurisprudence in this country. He had organised the conference so that lawyers, both in practice and in academic life, could meet to discuss the possibility of legal challenges that could be mounted against the declaration of the state of emergency.

It was a time of great despair. The effect of the emergency had been to drastically circumscribe the space available for open political activity and dissent against government. Thousands of people had been rounded up and detained without trial. Chief Justice Rabie presided over the highest court in South Africa and had made his legal intentions clear. Vigilante organisations, whether directly or indirectly established by the government, and buttressed by the police and army, had taken charge of many black townships and crushed political opponents, all under the cover of national legislation that empowered the declaration of a state of emergency and consequent suspension of many legal safeguards.

It was not surprising, therefore, that the conference began in muted terms. At the conference, a judge who, more than any other, represented the possibility of an independent, courageous and principled judiciary had been invited by Dugard to give the keynote speech. He was Judge John Didcott. Imagine the situation: a sitting judge comes to Wits to give an address in an open forum to a group of progressive lawyers, no doubt infiltrated by a number of security-police spies. Didcott would have been aware of the risk he was taking in speaking so boldly in public: he could disappear if the government had its way. He reminded the lawyers present that there were available potential legal challenges to the emergency regulations. Didcott reiterated that it would be inappropriate for him to discuss the details of these avenues, as he wished to be available to sit as a judge in some of those cases.

It was an extraordinary call to legal arms – a judge appointed by the apartheid regime was urging the best of South African human-rights lawyers, through a brave, principled articulation of the innermost commitments of law, to be true to their calling. This speech was made at the very time that even the most progressive of South African lawyers were beginning to doubt the utility of their activities. Didcott was a special case on the South African bench. There were, however, other judges who were also prepared to adhere wherever possible to the underlying principles of the common law, including Gerald Friedman, Richard Goldstone, Ramon Leon, Johann Kriegler, John Milne and Laurie Ackermann.[9]

It is within this context of the contradictory qualities of law that the cases that were fought during the apartheid era and are discussed in this book are perhaps best understood. We arrived at 1994 with the possibility that law could promote a democratic enterprise. But this has proved more challenging than the optimism of 1994 led us to believe at that time. To probe this issue further, two concepts are critical to a full understanding: the constitutional bridge, and a working theory of adjudication, since judges are important builders of the bridge we have in mind.

The bridge

The history of litigation in South Africa before 1994 helps us understand the constitutional era that was born out of the legal rubble created by apartheid. The very form of constitutional democracy that took hold in South Africa after 1994 represented not so much a rupture of the old and a construction of the new, but, as human-rights activist and academic Etienne Mureinik wrote in a justly acclaimed article, the building of a bridge between a terrible past and the potentially liberating future:

> If the new constitution is a bridge away from a culture of authority, it is clear what it must be a bridge to. It must lead to a culture of justification – a culture in which every exercise of power is expected to be justified; in which the leadership given by government rests on the cogency of the case offered in defence of its decisions, not the fear inspired by the force at its command. The new order must be a community built on persuasion, not coercion.[10]

Mureinik saw the new Constitution as a bridge designed to transport a country away from a culture of authority to what he termed a culture of justification, that is, one where every exercise of power has to be justified by the power holder. Under apartheid, decisions of the government were based on instilling fear, which was, in turn, sustained by the 'force at its command'. Mureinik argued that leadership of government under the new Constitution had to rest on the 'cogency' – or persuasive quality – of the case that it offered in justification of decisions it made. The bridge would assist in the journey that society undertook to travel away from arbitrary and brutal exercises of power to decisions that could be subjected to debate, deliberation, public examination and, above all, justification.

The rich metaphor of the bridge needs to be extended beyond its use as offered by Mureinik. The bridge also represents the model of transformation that was followed in South Africa. There was no revolution, no violent rupture from the past. The old order was, in many instances, to remain, although the substance of the old would be changed in incremental stages. This path of negotiated evolution rather than violent, sudden revolution can be illustrated by the manner in which the bridge was constructed (see Chapter 7 for a detailed discussion of the concept of the bridge).

The constitutional bridge was to be created mostly by bridge builders who were fluent in the old legal traditions. Their construction was undertaken with the only tools in their possession, namely our inherited legal traditions, together with a constitutional mandate to engage in reconstruction of these traditions through the new text. Here we mean the inherited legal traditions, such as the structure of the bench (judges), the bar (advocates) and the sidebar (attorneys) – the form of the judicial institution in this country that was inherited from Britain with black gowns and frilly bibs, and much reference to 'M'Lord' and 'M'Lady' and to 'm'learned friend'.

The dominant conception of the common law is that of a timeless, universal body of truth inherited from the days of the Dutch occupation of the Cape. Through this, precedent retains its tenacious hold on progress as courts, in the main, follow decisions that were handed down in the distant past. A court is not free to decide a case without some constraint. An earlier decision by the higher court that set out some rule of law or interpreted a provision of legislation that is applicable in the case before the later court is now binding and therefore must be followed. All these legal rules and conduct form the traditions of which we speak. But it now becomes mixed with the new constitutional text and the interpretive moves of the courts in giving meaning to the new text. In this way, fresh legal material is manufactured, which, in turn, is employed in the construction of the legal 'bridge'. The Constitution is now the plan for our new society, the one we must all build to realise its vision.

Models of adjudication for a constitution

In addition there is the not insignificant matter of understanding the nature of judicial adjudication. As will be shown in the cases examined in this book, before 1994, the performance of the judiciary can be explained broadly by way of two models. Until the late 1950s, the courts, particularly the Appellate Division in Bloemfontein, were staffed by judges who were essentially libertarian: they distrusted state interference in the private lives of citizens. For them, the state was a nightwatchman that operated to guarantee the negative liberties of all citizens. After 1960, the courts in South Africa endorsed the law as a tool of social engineering by the state, regardless of the effect on individual freedom.

Neither of these models was suitable to the adjudication of a constitutional text that endorsed social democracy. That task requires a careful marriage between guarantees of negative liberty (freedom from state interference in individual choices) and positive obligations on the state to ensure the provision of a minimum level of services to all who live in the country. Judges would need to ensure that individual freedoms were supported by a stable, equitable socio-economic foundation. Whatever the chosen model of adjudication, change was clearly needed. Old styles of adjudication proved unsuitable for the new challenge of legal transformation.

The new role for the judiciary takes us back to the metaphor of the Constitution as a bridge from the past and now the plan for the new society, constructed by and with laws. As apartheid had built a legal system powered by race, the new democracy was to be created by laws sourced in the Constitution. Hence the vision continues to be constructed whenever Parliament enacts legislation: each new transformative statute is like another span in the bridge, another brick in the foundation of a new society.

This metaphor has further implications for our story: this construction is a process that never really ends. At best, the journey is a movement by society away from the past and in the direction of a community prefigured in a coherent reading of the constitutional text. That idea of community is never attained completely. The journey itself becomes an essential part of the transformative exercise. As the constitutional custodians, the judiciary therefore moves into critical focus.

The effectiveness of the judiciary

An important implication arising from the *Harris* cases, which dealt with the constitutional crisis of the 1950s, when the National Party government was determined to remove Coloured voters from the common voters' roll (see Chapter 3), is that when judges are isolated by governments and faced with negative public opinion, their role as potential instruments in the struggle to retain rights under attack, let alone in transformation, is truly limited. A constitution is not merely the sum of the provisions contained in its text: this text must be given life by the decisions of the courts. If the text constitutes the design of the bridge, the courts begin to build the bridge in terms of their particular conception of the design.

Of course, the construction of a constitutional bridge can only happen successfully if the community continually accepts the efforts of the court in building it. With this kind of acceptance, the legitimacy of the constitutional project – a bridge from the past, a design for our new society to be built – grows.

Legitimacy and efficacy are the very cement of the project. Efficacy means that the decisions of the courts are recognised and rendered effective by those in power. It is now commonplace to parrot the American constitutional theorist Alexander Bickel, who observed that the courts are the weakest arm of government, with no resident police force or army to enforce their orders.[11] The process of enforcement depends on the cooperation of the other arms of government. It is mainly the police who enforce court orders, if necessary, and the police are under the control of the executive. Efficacy is reinforced by legitimacy, meaning that the more the public respects and heeds the importance of court decisions, recognising that their content broadly reflects the moral convictions of the community, the more legitimate the courts become as an institution. In turn, this level of public regard develops into a form of public practice that does not take kindly to manipulation of the constitutional system.

The constitutional project requires support for the courts from the public, civil society and an independent media, to ensure that the other arms of government do not interfere with their work. The judiciary, therefore, needed a working legal theory to transform the existing legal system to now reflect the core constitutional values of freedom, dignity and equality. We will be able to assess the extent to which the courts have met that challenge after looking at their record of cases contained in this book. With this in mind, we turn to our selection of cases.

The Coloured vote cases
This book analyses a number of cases from both the apartheid past and democratic South Africa. In each of these cases, the stakes were enormous.

The three Coloured vote cases heralded the end of the liberal legalism that had flickered throughout the first part of the 1950s. With the decision in *Collins*, the last of this trilogy of cases, the South African legal system finally and definitively eschewed the idea that a common law, which placed the freedom of the individual at the centre of the legal enterprise, should trump legislation that took away these rights, save where the legislation in question made a denial absolutely clear. In the wake of the first two cases in the trilogy, the National Party responded to its legal defeats by altering the composition of the Appellate Division, so that its judgments would increasingly reflect the will of the (white) people of South Africa. Not only did this help give it eventual victory in *Collins*, but it also destroyed the last vestiges of a liberal court that may have challenged the executive.

In summary, these cases tolled the bell for the burial of liberal legalism, albeit of the weak kind that endured into the 1950s. Thereafter, it would be rare for government's race laws to be overturned by a court determined to preserve the rights of individuals, even those long existing in the common law of the country. By the time the final decision in the trilogy was made to approve the constitutional changes that disenfranchised the Coloured voters of the country, the National Party had gained control of the Appeal Court. Its campaign to alter the composition of the bench had borne fruit, which it harvested for more than two decades. Thus, the institution of an independent judiciary was seriously jeopardised.

Rivonia

Next up is the *Rivonia* case, a quintessential political trial, as defined by the Frankfurt School political scientist Otto Kirchheimer,[12] in that it adopts the form of criminal law to vindicate the existing social and political order by imposing criminal sanctions for the political actions of legitimate political opponents. In these ways, political acts designed to criticise the government or to organise opposition to government policy are subjected to a criminal censure. By the term 'censure', we mean an attempt by government to categorise political activity as nothing more than criminal conduct devoid of legitimate political purpose. After all, the courts impose severe sanctions on people convicted of criminal conduct. The possibility is then open for government to equate what it deems to be criminalised political conduct with, for example, common-law murder or robbery.

Rivonia was a trial of the political ideas of those leaders who represented the majority of the country. The state sought to present the leaders of the ANC as no more than a group of violent criminals. Of course, as in any political trial, the accused contested this attempt by the state to invoke a criminal censure with all the vigour that their testimony and legal team could muster. But the ultimate conviction of the accused held the possibility that South Africa's greatest leaders, including Mandela and Sisulu, could have been hanged. That alone was cause for the country to hold its breath. The trial also represents the story of a diminishing faith in the law. The defence lawyers were well aware of their limitations as they confronted a more confident, oppressive state and increasingly pro-executive judges. The scope for legal resistance had narrowed. *Rivonia* was not only about Nelson Mandela and the other accused, however – it was also about Bram Fischer, lead counsel for the accused, and his journey after *Rivonia* from being a leading senior counsel at the Johannesburg Bar to becoming a full-time revolutionary. In brief, it appears that, not long after the end of the trial, Fischer recognised that the existing legal system could hardly be employed meaningfully to effect significant social change.

Residence and relocation

Two other cases litigated during the apartheid era discussed in this book represented far more strategic and less defensive conceptions of litigation. In these cases, the law was used to curb the excesses of apartheid in key areas of state policy. Even before 1948, when the National Party came to power, influx control had diminished the freedom of movement of most South Africans on the grounds of race alone. By the late 1970s, literally hundreds of thousands of black South Africans had been made criminals in their own country by attempting to live with their families or work in urban areas from where they were barred by a system of laws designed to prevent their permanent residence in urban centres. Millions of people worked in exploitative conditions for the benefit of an economy controlled by the few. The system of influx control empowered government officials to treat millions of South Africans as pawns on a giant chessboard.

In this context, along came two tenacious litigants, Messrs Komani and Rikhotso, supported by the Legal Resources Centre (LRC), which had been established in 1979 by lawyers Geoffrey Budlender, Arthur Chaskalson and Felicia Kentridge as a law centre to represent the public interest, the first of its kind in South Africa. In two separate cases, the director of the LRC and future Chief Justice of South Africa, Arthur Chaskalson, managed to persuade a National Party-appointed Appellate Division that the administration of the apartheid pass laws was illegal. By the end of this litigation, the pass laws could no longer be properly enforced and the way had been cleared for black South Africans to live and work in urban South Africa. Not only did Veli Komani and Mehlolo Tom Rikhotso succeed in their quest to live legally where they had resided for years but the outcome justified the choice of a legal strategy during the height of apartheid rule where the very laws attacked in a conservative court had been designed as a main strut in the apartheid edifice.

Atrocities in incarceration

From the 1960s, the government employed a system of detention without trial to incarcerate its political opponents. As is the case today in the US and Britain, governments seek to bypass the law in their 'war against terror'. The South African government employed the justification of a 'communist onslaught' against its alleged 'civilised standard of life' to incarcerate people without any proof of an offence that could be tested by a legal system. The police were not prepared to be rendered accountable to even a generally sympathetic judiciary, which government had carefully appointed.

During the early 1960s, the system of detention began with incarceration without the authority of a court for a maximum defined period of 90 days. Within a decade, this period had been extended to indefinite detention. The cloak of secrecy and lack of accountability that was thrown over the system did not, however, prevent the regular publication of allegations of police torture of detainees. But it was only when a courageous district surgeon came forward to expose the atrocities committed by the police, invariably denied or covered up by government and rarely believed by the courts, even when they were confronted with detailed allegations of torture, that the sheer horror of the system was exposed to the nation through litigation.

The Wendy Orr case was a piece of strategic litigation designed to expose the system of detention without trial. The use of existing law and legal procedure to achieve this aim within the context of a state of emergency, where the country was controlled by the police, and not the courts, is a remarkable illustration of strategic human-rights lawyering.

These apartheid-era cases were part of a legal tradition upon which constitutional democracy during the late 1980s and early 1990s could be based. These cases showed that there was value in a rights-based legal culture and that the promise of a transformed jurisprudence had never been destroyed in its entirety.

Cases based on South Africa's Constitution

We have already spoken of the increasing practice of lawfare in South Africa over the past few years. We turn now to those cases discussed in this book that were litigated after the start of the country's constitutional democracy and in the Zuma era. These cases all illustrate the manner in which the bridge was constructed once the designs had been approved by the Constitutional Assembly. Each of these cases represented a challenge for the nascent South African constitutional project. On each occasion, the Constitutional Court, an institution created by the same new Constitution, was tested by the challenge of taking the law into uncharted territory, thus extending the bridge a little further towards the realisation of the society promised in the constitutional text.

The transition to democracy is never easy. The law, and hence the judiciary, can also be used by those who wish to subvert the new enterprise. The crossing of the bridge was challenged by opponents on both the left and right of the political spectrum. Here, two cases merit examination. When Louis Luyt, the president of the South African Rugby Football Union, challenged a government-appointed commission of inquiry into rugby, Mandela found himself summonsed by one of the most conservative judges in the country to explain why, as president of the country, he had appointed this commission. When the case went on appeal to the Constitutional Court, many judges of that court were impugned by Luyt, who called for their recusal, claiming that they would be biased against him. The *SARFU* case represented an attack by the old order on key instruments of the new democratic system of government. It is a story of political contest with a very different result from the previous time Mandela had appeared in court, at the *Rivonia* trial.

The left also resisted a key design of the bridge. Critical to the process of change was the Truth and Reconciliation Commission (TRC). The legislation that brought the TRC into existence guaranteed a process of amnesty for those who had committed and fully disclosed political crimes.[13] If they were granted amnesty, the Promotion of National Unity and Reconciliation Act granted applicants criminal and civil immunity. A number of families, including those of great South African leaders Steve Biko, and Griffiths and Victoria Mxenge, challenged the constitutionality of this provision. In what is now known as the *AZAPO* case, the Constitutional Court, palpably torn by the moral dilemma of the case, found that the postamble to the Interim Constitution had provided expressly for such immunity. Without this provision, the court opined that the construction of the bridge could have been blown up at its very inception. Hence the families had to lose their application.

Death penalty

The very first case heard by the Constitutional Court concerned the legality of the death penalty. The death penalty had been employed with increasing regularity in South Africa. Between 1978 and 1987, 1 218 people were hanged; in 1987 alone, the figure was 164. By the 1980s, the issue had become the subject of great political controversy. The death penalty was a punishment of first choice. As prominent political commentator Hermann Giliomee noted in 1988, '[a]lmost unnoticed, South Africa has got itself in a situation where it is hanging people at a rate which would cause even the most sordid banana republic to hang its head in shame'.[14]

In the late 1980s, South Africa experienced its own intifada. During this period of resistance, a number of apartheid bureaucrats who did the government's bidding in the townships were killed in the unrest. The state then employed the legal doctrine of common purpose to charge groups of people who were present at these killings with murder – the rationale being that as the 'mob' made common purpose with the unidentified killer(s), any member of the mob was guilty of murder. In a case that became known as the *Sharpeville Six*, the accused were convicted and sentenced to death. The application of the doctrine of common purpose enabled the state to obtain convictions without proving that any of the individual accused had been directly involved in the murder. The decision was upheld by the Appellate Division. Few decisions of this kind have prompted such discord. The lives of the six men were spared not only by way of a legal challenge heroically led by their counsel, Jack Unterhalter and Edwin Cameron (the latter now a leading member of the Constitutional Court), but primarily as a result of political campaigns that generated local and international pressure.

By 1990, the campaign against capital punishment had reached fever pitch as a result of cases like the *Sharpeville Six*. FW de Klerk, then the president, placed a moratorium on all executions. However, no agreement could be reached by the constitutional negotiators as to whether the death penalty should be declared unconstitutional. The decision was left to the Constitutional Court, which decided the matter in 1995, declaring capital punishment unconstitutional in the very first case argued before the court. The case of *Makwanyane* is not about the way that convicted murderers succeeded in their argument that the death penalty was unconstitutional. The accused hardly featured in the arguments before the court. Rather, in their judgments, the newly appointed justices of the court not only reflected on the history of the death penalty as a metaphor for a brutal history of government in which life and dignity, particularly of black South Africans, were not respected, but also asserted the importance of constitutional democracy and the vision the constitutional text held for the future of the country. The case was not about an individual criminal; it concerned the articulation of the core commitments of the new Constitution.

HIV/AIDS – Treatment Action Campaign

HIV/AIDS was among the most pressing social problems confronting democratic South Africa at its birth. Faced with a government that had steadfastly adopted policies that failed to fully acknowledge or address the problem, civil society, mainly through the Treatment Action Campaign (TAC), contested government's inaction with great vigour, courage, innovation and some significant success. As part of this campaign, in 2001 the TAC took the government to court to compel it to provide pregnant mothers with antiretroviral (ARV) drugs to prevent the transmission of HIV to their children. The case finally reached the Constitutional Court. The successful litigation by the TAC represented a victory in a new form of political trial. The Constitutional Court asserted that residents of this country could approach the court for basic goods and services, as promised in the Constitution, and could litigate to realise their rights to health and medical treatment, including access to ARV therapy. This case is a story of a new form of human-rights litigation in a democracy met by great official hostility where government initially indicated that it was not prepared even to abide the decision of the court.

Alix Carmichele

The Constitution and its centrepiece, the Bill of Rights, mandated constitutional scrutiny not only of the relationships between the state and the individual but also, where applicable, relationships between private actors. It also empowered the courts to extend the principle of accountability by the state to its citizens.

Alix Carmichele was subjected to a brutal attack by a man who should have been behind bars awaiting trial. Prosecution and police negligence had allowed him to roam free and confront Carmichele in the idyllic setting of Noetzie in the Western Cape. As had Komani and Rikhotso before her, Carmichele pursued her rights with great courage and tenacity, and she finally succeeded. Five court battles later, she had established an important legal principle: South Africa's law of delict[15] needed to be adapted, with the guiding spirit of the Bill of Rights, to entitle Carmichele and similar victims to successfully sue the state for damages as a consequence of its failure to protect them.

Same-sex rights

We also discuss the issue of same-sex marriages and other rights eventually extended to same-sex couples. In these cases, the Constitution was applied by the courts to uphold core constitutional values: the promotion of the dignity of the other and the protection of life for millions.

The case of same-sex marriages in particular, which preceded similar developments in many other democratic countries, pre-empted a political process that would have taken much longer. In a country in which homophobia is, sadly, alive and well, the Constitutional Court led public opinion and favoured our constitutional commitments to dignity and equality over the myopic bigotry of many within the country.

Al-Bashir and foreign policy

The al-Bashir decision, discussed in the Introduction and Chapter 12, shows both the possibility and the excruciating limitations of litigation and court orders to hold the executive accountable where it acts with impunity and in its self-interest. In short, the South African government flatly refused to comply with a court order. The case revealed how far the country had come from the time when Mandela fastidiously complied with adverse court orders. It was at the time the clearest indication of a rejection of the constraints that the Constitution imposed on the executive. At the same time, it also showed how South Africa had abandoned its human-rights-focused foreign-policy framework under the Zuma administration in a reorientation to self-interest masquerading as a new policy approach. The erosion of the country's status and moral authority on the global stage followed decisions such as the repeated refusal to grant a visa to the Dalai Lama in deference to Chinese objections.

State capture

The penultimate chapter on state capture, and the decisions in the spy tapes and Nkandla cases in particular, cover very recent instances of lawfare. They show the ongoing necessity to hold the executive and Parliament accountable, and the significant role of the judiciary, if we are ever to live in the South Africa promised in the Constitution.

Conclusion

All of these cases raised critical social and political questions; each affected many others who lived or live in South Africa; and each shows the contested nature of the law, as well as the different claims and visions of those who litigated these cases. Examining them may serve to tell some of our history and the inherent drama of the law. And that is one purpose of this book. But the deliberate linkage between the old and the new tells another, equally important, story: a constitutional democracy like South Africa is built on the former legal regime, either because the text of the Constitution responds to the old or because the old continues to haunt our attempts to move beyond it. More than that, the link reveals that constitutional democracy cannot be imposed – its values must be continually asserted and justified. The vision must be diligently and continually built. Indeed, this construction is the work of each generation, all guided by the Constitution.

3

WHO CAN RID ME OF THIS TROUBLESOME COURT?
The Executive v The Judiciary

'Fifty years after the constitutional crisis of the mid-fifties, our own understanding of the separation of public power, democracy and the legitimacy of courts is a matter of great public disputation.'[1]

– DIKGANG MOSENEKE, 23 October 2006

History has a curious way of repeating itself. The political storms of the past placed the judiciary at their very centre. More recently, the judiciary again has wrestled with controversies with wide-ranging political implications, including for the separation of powers. This pattern provides a valid reason to look back at the political turbulence of the early 1950s, and the courts' role in those stormy days.

On a hot summer's day, 20 February 1952, the finest legal minds of the Cape Bar congregated in the majestic courtroom of the Appellate Division of the Supreme Court, in Bloemfontein.

They had travelled from Cape Town to appear in a case that held massive implications for the last vestige of constitutional protection in apartheid South Africa: the right of South Africans racially classified as Coloureds to vote together with whites for Members of Parliament. Although the case had been brought nominally by a small number of individual voters, the challenge to the National Party's new scheme had been launched on behalf of a significant section of the population.

43

The seven samurai

The legal team assembled on behalf of the voters was led by Graeme Duncan KC, and included Harry Snitcher KC and Donald Molteno.[2] Duncan would later be described by one of his opponents in this case as 'one of the greats of the legal world over the past few decades'. At the time a truly dominant intellectual figure at the Cape Bar, Duncan was probably best classified politically as a Cape liberal. In contrast, Snitcher had been a prominent member of the South African Communist Party until 1948 and one of its leading intellectual figures. Whereas Duncan looked every bit the patrician lawyer, Snitcher was small and elf-like. Duncan may have been the team leader, but Snitcher was also an advocate of great legal skill and forensic shrewdness. He was one of the most eloquent lawyers, arguably the best of the last group of jury advocates.

The third member of the team was Donald Molteno. He had served as a so-called Native Representative in Parliament from 1937 to 1948. At one time, Molteno had been vice chairman of the Liberal Party. Later, he was to leave practice and become professor of public law at the University of Cape Town (UCT). In 1959 the newly formed Progressive Party employed his services to formulate its policy on qualified franchise, whereby black voters were required to meet certain requirements before they could be eligible to vote. For an erstwhile member of the Liberal Party, this policy was an exercise in expediency, in that it was clearly designed to soften the non-racial commitment of liberals in order to attract white votes. But it was a policy that, in part, was also faithful to the case that Molteno was about to fight in Bloemfontein.

The government team was led by Andrew Beyers KC. A large and seemingly avuncular individual, he had a most intimidating presence. Beyers first shot to prominence as the losing United Party candidate in the Oudtshoorn constituency during the 1938 parliamentary general elections. Unsuccessful in politics, he had enjoyed a successful practice at the Bar, which led to an appointment on the Cape Bench in 1956 and a speedy promotion to the Appellate Division in 1959. Shortly afterwards, he was appointed as the Judge President of the Cape High Court, a position he occupied until his retirement.

Whereas Beyers was a man of pronounced personality and sometimes humanity, Theo van Wyk KC, his team member for the state, possessed none of the latter. He was a formidable lawyer, though, which was evenly matched by a parsimonious and mean-spirited view of the world – a true apartheid ideologue. Van Wyk was later appointed to the position of Ad Hoc Judge at the International Court of Justice in The Hague. He, too, would become the Judge President of the Cape High Court. Unlike Beyers, Van Wyk never showed an inch of compassion when confronted by the inhumane consequences of apartheid.

The third member of the team was Dawid de Villiers, who was to take silk in 1954 and serve as an acting judge in 1959 and again from later that year to 1961. An outstanding legal mind, De Villiers declined a permanent appointment to the bench to concentrate, first, on legal and, later, commercial interests. In the 1960s, he was the leader of the South African legal team that argued the South West African case in The Hague. It was well known that the National Party was desperately keen to appoint De Villiers as a judge, as that would have made it likely for him to eventually become Chief Justice. He refused these offers and, instead, became the managing director of what we now know as Naspers. De Villiers was to become the political opposite of Van Wyk. In his later life, he embraced a non-racial South Africa with great enthusiasm. He returned to the Bar to argue a number of significant cases on behalf of people who had suffered the most under the grinding rule of the National Party he had so enthusiastically embraced in his earlier career.

The final member of the team was George Wynne. Like Beyers, Wynne had had an unsuccessful political career, in his case on behalf of the National Party. Later, he was to be appointed to the Senate and ended his career as a judge in the Eastern Cape. Apparently, he had been added to the team because some of his government clients thought he had a contribution to make – a view not shared by Beyers.

All these men had been to the Appeal Court many times before that occasion. But it is fair to say that, on 20 February 1952, they argued a case that was more important than any other they had undertaken during their distinguished legal careers. When the court convened on that day, it was to hear argument in a dispute that, in various forms, went on for five years and was to lead to a constitutional crisis of considerable proportion. The effect of this would be felt for the next four decades. This legal saga confirms the wisdom of our choice to constitutionally separate state and institutional powers, and cautions against any attempts to undermine that fine balance.

The nature of the dispute

To understand this case, we need to take a short historical detour. Before 1910, the voting laws for the Cape Colony permitted all males over the age of 21 to vote, providing each person was able to sign his name, and write his address and occupation. There were two further qualifications: ownership of property to the value of at least £75 or earnings of £50 a year. After 1910, changes to the electoral law permitted white women to vote subject to the same property qualifications that applied to white males. There was therefore a common roll, but not a common franchise. In 1936, black people were taken off the common roll in the Cape Province and given separate representation in Parliament. They were represented by whites. For a time, Molteno was one of these representatives. The Coloured community remained on the common voters' roll when the National Party won its electoral victory.

The principle of the common roll had been protected by Section 152 of the South Africa Act, the Constitution of the Union. That section provided that any law that sought to change the common voters' roll had to be passed by a joint sitting of the two houses of Parliament and by a two-thirds majority of the total number of members of both houses. The provision did not appear to be under any threat when South Africa celebrated the end of World War II. But on 26 May 1948, the National Party pulled off a stunning electoral victory aided by the electoral system, which, at that time, weighted votes heavily in favour of rural constituencies. The National Party and its allies won 79 out of the 150 seats in the House of Assembly. The fact that General Jan Smuts's United Party and its allies won 50.9 per cent of the vote – compared with 41.2 per cent for the National Party – was irrelevant. The minority party came into power and, with its victory, it was determined to engage in the implementation of its racist project.

One of its first steps was to consolidate its tenuous hold on power. In 1950 the National Party successfully introduced the Suppression of Communism Act, which outlawed the Communist Party and ensured the removal from Parliament of Communist Members of Parliament who had been elected to represent 'Cape natives'. This Act gave considerable power to the police to curb political opposition to the government. Over the next 40 years, the police would increasingly employ this and similar legislation to take control over civil society.

The National Party then turned its attention to the common voters' roll in the Cape, a province that was still significantly under the control of the United Party. In 1951, after a furious debate in Parliament, the National Party succeeded in passing the Separate Representation of Voters Act. As the law had stood before this Act was passed into law, all voters voted in the same constituency, whether white or Coloured. With the introduction of the Act, Coloured voters would be able to vote only in separate constituencies in which they were registered. That the National Party considered this Act to be important was crisply illustrated by a statement made by the then prime minister, DF Malan, when he responded to the possibility that the United Party would challenge the validity of the Act in court. Malan told Parliament: 'If the court should declare this Act of Parliament invalid ... it stands to reason that it would be a serious matter for Parliament and for the country. It would mean the undermining of Parliament's sovereignty; it would mean that the judicial authorities would assume powers belonging exclusively to a Legislature ...'[3]

The United Party ignored these threats and found four voters who acted as the plaintiffs in the case. The party could not itself bring the application against the constitutional change, so it needed to find individuals who would be affected by the new law and were willing to be used to initiate the case. The four men were Ganief Harris, a Malay bricklayer who lived in Woodstock, Cape Town; Edgar Franklin, a van driver who also lived in Woodstock; William David Collins, a Cape Town merchant; and Edgar Arthur Deane, a trade unionist and secretary of the Furniture Workers' Union. Collins and Deane were members of the Coloured People's National Union and they later became Cape Town city councillors.

Ganief Harris gave his name to this famous case, but in truth the litigants played little, if any, role in the proceedings.

The litigation was not launched without apprehension. Once relegated to the position of leader of the opposition after the electoral defeat of the United Party in 1948, Smuts began to concern himself with the possibility that the new government would change the Constitution in order to remove Coloured citizens from the common voters' roll. But, a few days after the election defeat, Smuts summoned prominent lawyer, successful entrepreneur and United Party spokesperson on Coloured affairs Abe Bloomberg to Pretoria to discuss the possibility of opposing such a move. Bloomberg was instructed to look into the legality of the National Party government's intentions. He briefed Duncan, Snitcher and Molteno, who were of the opinion that the Constitution could be changed only by a special majority of both Houses of Parliament.

Smuts remained uncertain, the opinion of senior counsel notwithstanding, so he approached Denis Cowen, a young law professor at UCT, who had written an article about the National Party's proposed legislation, which was published in the *Cape Times* in 1949 and later expanded into an academic paper that was published in 1951, 'Parliamentary sovereignty and the entrenched sections of the South Africa Act'. Smuts had read Cowen's article and invited the author to his suite at the Mount Nelson Hotel for a chat, where he probed Cowen over the possible success of a case based on his article. Smuts repeatedly asked Cowen if they had a good case, if they could win. But, ominously, he told Cowen that even if the case were won, the National Party would not rest until it had achieved its objective, even if it meant instituting a constitutional revolution by bypassing the authority of the courts. Cowen left the meeting with the clear impression of Smuts's conviction that a winning case may have heralded the end of the rule of law, as Smuts understood that concept.[4]

At the same time, the National Party obtained their own legal advice. Professor Ignatius Coertze of the University of Pretoria, who was, in his own words, 'a passionate supporter of the National Party', cautioned against trying to change the Constitution by way of a simple majority of both Houses sitting together.[5]

By the time the litigation was launched, Smuts had died. The new leader of the United Party, JGN Strauss, proceeded to ensure that Duncan and his team were briefed to challenge the manner in which the Constitution had been altered.

Harris I

Back to the courtroom in Bloemfontein. Ostensibly on behalf of the four voters, but, in substance, on behalf of a larger constituency of voters, Duncan rose to address the five members of the Appeal Court and argue that the Act was unconstitutional. He argued for some six hours and 15 minutes. Briefly, his argument was that Section 152 of the

South Africa Act remained in force even though in 1936, by way of the Statute of Westminster, the Union of South Africa had been granted a sovereign Parliament that was no longer under the control of Britain. Although South Africa was a sovereign state, nothing in the 1936 legislation indicated that the protection of the common voters' roll had to be altered by the abolition of a special majority. In essence, the voters' case was that if the constitutional protection of the Coloured vote had to be removed, it could be done only by a two-thirds majority vote of both Houses of Parliament.

Beyers and Van Wyk's arguments took even more time. Early on in his address, Beyers introduced a political note that underlined the government's entire argument: in his view, no country that emerged from a colony into a dominion,[6] and thus into a sovereign state, could claim to be sovereign unless it had a Parliament functioning in a bicameral manner, as did the British Parliament, which was free to pass a statute of any kind, in any manner it chose. In short, unless the legislature elected by the voters was completely sovereign, South Africa could not be considered to be a sovereign state. Over many hours, Beyers and Van Wyk sought to persuade the court to accept this proposition. But it became clear to the government team that, whatever precedent it had in its favour, Duncan's argument clearly held sway with the five judges.

A battle to postpone judgment

Before judgment could be handed down on 20 March 1952, interested parties had already intervened. The moderator of the Dutch Reformed Church in the Cape, Dr AJ van der Merwe, was the chair of the Central Committee of the Van Riebeeck Festival due to take place in April 1952, which was designed to commemorate the 300th year of the arrival of Jan van Riebeeck at the Cape. In January 1952, on behalf of the Central Committee, he had asked for an interview with Chief Justice Albert Centlivres. At this stage, the hearing had not yet taken place but perhaps Van der Merwe had some religious insight into the outcome of the case. He was concerned that the controversy that would inevitably surround the judgment would interfere with the celebratory mood the festival was designed to promote among white South Africans.

By the end of February, after the hearing, Van der Merwe had still received no response from the Chief Justice. He grew impatient and approached the prime minister, asking him to support a move that would encourage the court to postpone the handing down of judgment until after the Van Riebeeck celebrations. Malan wrote to Centlivres requesting a postponement of the judgment until after the conclusion of the festival. The Chief Justice informed Malan that courts could not deliver delayed judgments without the consent of the attorneys concerned. Pressure was now put on the attorneys for Harris and the other plaintiffs. On 18 March 1952, it was announced that judgment would be handed down on 20 March. Van der Merwe was disappointed. He had believed that a postponement would be obtained. A few days after the judgment was handed down, he issued a statement to the press, which sought to justify his earlier call for a postponed judgment. In this he released the correspondence between the Chief Justice and Malan. This prompted the Chief Justice to issue a statement setting the record straight and, in particular, emphasising that the court could not delay judgment without the consent of the attorneys concerned.

The judgment

In his comprehensive examination of this case, David Scher describes a less important but illuminating event leading up to the delivery of the judgment. Abe Bloomberg had acted as the United Party's attorney in the litigation. Shortly before the appeal, Bloomberg had had drinks in the private bar of Parliament with the government's senior counsel, Andrew Beyers. In his typically flamboyant fashion, Beyers was very confident of winning the case, and asked Bloomberg if he was prepared to place a bet on the outcome of the appeal. A £200 wager was concluded between the two men. When the appeal was lost by government, Bloomberg received a cheque for £200, together with a note, which read: 'My dear Bloomberg, herewith my cheque and best of luck. This is the easiest money you have ever won. I'm afraid I never even had a run for my money.'

In this assessment, Beyers was completely correct. The major difficulty that confronted Chief Justice Centlivres and his colleagues was an earlier decision of the court in *Ndlwana v Hofmeyer NO*, where the court had decided that, as the South African Parliament had become sovereign after the passing of the Statute of Westminster, the Appeal Court had no power to pronounce upon the validity of any Act of Parliament. The government lawyers had relied almost exclusively on this decision to contend that a South African court had no power to test the validity of legislation in South Africa after 1936. It was hardly a cavalier argument – after all, it had a 1937 precedent as support.

Chief Justice Centlivres refused, however, to follow the precedent set by the *Ndlwana* case. After a careful examination of that case, he found that the earlier court had not dealt properly with the question of whether the Statute of Westminster had by implication repealed the entrenched provisions, including Section 152, which contained a provision that a two-thirds majority of both Houses of Parliament was needed before the voting arrangements concerning Coloured voters could be changed.

Reading the judgment of Chief Justice Centlivres in the yellowing pages of a law report that is now more than half a century old, it is fascinating to find the level of detail to which the Chief Justice went to show that the 1937 decision had pronounced on a question of vital constitutional importance without the benefit of proper argument. Centlivres noted, by way of reference to the record of the *Ndlwana* case, that the appellant had argued for 55 minutes. Counsel for the respondent had argued for a quarter of an hour and the reply had taken but ten minutes. As the Chief Justice correctly noted: 'This short argument contrasts strangely with the argument in this case which lasted six days.'[7] In short, the decision had not been properly considered.

Once the Appellate Division had found that the *Ndlwana* decision was wrong, the government's case was fatally torpedoed. The entrenched clauses remained part of the Constitution. The Separate Representation of Voters Act had been passed by simple majority, with the two Houses of Parliament sitting separately. The constitutional guarantee of a mandated special vote by two-thirds of the members of both Houses of Parliament had not been followed. For this reason, the legislation had to be set aside.

The reaction

The government's reaction was swift and predictable. Malan gave a special statement to Parliament on 20 March 1952:

> The judgment of the Appeal Court ... has created a constitutional position which cannot be accepted. Neither Parliament nor the

people of South Africa will be prepared to acquiesce in a position where the legislative sovereignty of the lawfully and democratically elected representatives of the people is denied and where an appointed judicial authority assumes the testing right … it is imperative that the legislative sovereignty of Parliament should be placed beyond any doubt in order to ensure order and certainty.[8]

It did not take long for the government to come up with yet another legislative initiative in an attempt to implement its voting programme. On 22 April 1952, the Minister of the Interior, Dr Dönges, introduced the High Court of Parliament Bill. According to this bill, the power to review any order of the Appeal Court that invalidated a piece of national legislation would be vested in a special committee of Parliament composed of all members of the Senate and the House of Assembly, of whom 50 would constitute a quorum. It would be called 'The High Court of Parliament'. This 'court' would be served by a judicial committee consisting of ten Members of Parliament. The bill provided that the High Court was to be a court of law, the decisions of which were final and binding. The orders would be executed in the identical manner to those of the Appeal Court. Dönges told Parliament that this Act merely said that

> when a judgment has declared an Act of Parliament invalid, such judgment is subject to review by the elected representatives of the people. This court merely creates the opportunity whereby the elected representatives of the people express themselves clearly and unambiguously with regard to certain questions of the utmost importance. Those who oppose the Bill are begrudging the '*Volkswil*' [the will of the people].[9]

The National Party representatives again trumpeted the question of the will of the people, in reality meaning the will of the small white minority. HJ van den Berg, a National Party Member of Parliament, asked the House: 'Can you expect me to have any respect for a Constitution and for entrenched clauses in that Constitution which were entrenched against the wishes of the majority of the people of South Africa?'[10]

Harris II

The High Court of Parliament Act was passed on 3 June 1952. A judicial committee was then appointed. Four United Party members resigned from the committee. It had a quorum of six National Party members. Andrew Beyers QC, assisted by Dawid de Villiers, appeared for the applicants on an application to review the *Harris* judgment. No one represented the Coloured voters, but no matter, said Andrew Beyers, as he would not confine himself solely to his own case but place all possible points of view before the judicial committee. In what must have been one of the most unsurprising decisions ever to have been made by Parliament, or any tribunal for that matter, the judicial committee recommended the reversal of the decision of the Appellate Division that had declared the Separation of Voters Act invalid.

The High Court of Parliament then convened on 25 August 1952 to study the report of the judicial committee. The United Party boycotted the proceedings. As expected, the High Court of Parliament unanimously accepted the legal grounds set out by the judicial committee and declared the judgment and orders of the Appellate Division in the case of *Harris* to have been set aside.

Back went Harris, Franklin, Collins and Deane to court to set aside the High Court of Parliament Act, contending that it was invalid. The matter finally reached the Appellate Division on 27 October 1952. The same legal teams convened to argue before the same court. The high stakes were felt clearly by all the parties, including the two senior counsel acting for government, Beyers and Van Wyk. The voters' attorney, Pilkington-Jordan, wrote forcefully to United Party Leader JGN Strauss, lamenting the arrogance of the state advocates: 'Beyers again treated the Court with scant courtesy and both he and Van Wyk were thoroughly rude to Duncan. They really are monkeys in dinner jackets and the sartorial elegance of that garb does not in the least conceal the barbarian beneath ...'[11]

The tension between the parties notwithstanding, this time the dispute was far simpler. As Chief Justice Centlivres said: 'The approach to the problem before the court is to ascertain by looking at the substance and not merely the form of the Act whether the High Court of Parliament was in fact a Court of Law.' It was clear, said the Chief Justice, that the entrenched provision of the Constitution, namely Section 152, conferred on individuals the right to call on the courts to help them resist any legislative or executive action that contravened the entrenched sections of the Constitution. As the Chief Justice argued, 'These sections contain constitutional guarantees creating rights in individuals, the duty of the Courts, where the question arises in litigation, being to ensure that the protection of the guarantee is made effective, unless and until it is modified by legislation in such a form as under the Constitution can validly effect such modification.'[12]

His argument was that the Constitution provided individuals the right to approach the court for relief when their constitutional rights were infringed. There may not have been many rights under the Constitution but some remained, including the right of Coloured voters to be included on the common voters' roll. The question was whether the High Court of Parliament was really a court to which citizens could proceed should they be dissatisfied with the decision of the Appellate Division. Chief Justice Centlivres said that, whatever the High Court of Parliament might have been called by Parliament, it was still Parliament – and not a court. It may have been described as a court of law but this description could not alter the fact that, intrinsically, it was not a court of law, and it was courts that had to adjudicate on the Constitution.

The court was unanimous. The High Court of Parliament Act breached the Constitution and had to be set aside.

Certain members of the National Party knew that the advice given to Minister Dönges by Beyers, Van Wyk and the chief legal advisor to the government, DH Botha, had been poorly conceived. Dönges had been under great pressure to deal with the Appellate Division and, in desperation, had latched onto the opinions offered by his lawyers. That did not prevent the court from being blamed for the outcome. As former Springbok captain Dr PK Albertyn said, if one read the earlier judgment of the Appellate Division of 20 March 1952, it felt as if his team 'had played the entire match with the referee determined to cheat'.[13]

Whatever the reason, the National Party stopped short of using its High Court of Parliament to set aside the second *Harris* decision, which would unquestionably have created constitutional chaos. It had most certainly considered radical measures to restrict the independence of the judiciary. According to documents found in the papers of Eben Dönges, the National Party had contemplated initiatives ranging from compelling judges to sign a contract recognising the sovereignty of Parliament to only appointing 'Nasionale' candidates to the bench.[14] Paul Sauer, a senior member of the National Party, captured the sentiments of the governing party when he said in a well-published speech that it was 'undemocratic that six old men in Bloemfontein have the final say. Who is the boss – the six in Bloemfontein or you (the voters)?'[15]

Eric Louw, then Minister of Economic Affairs – and later to be a long-serving Foreign Minister, a service he fulfilled much in the vein of Nazi Germany's Joachim von Ribbentrop, in that he similarly sought to cultivate an aloof and urbane approach while defending brutal racism – was even more strident: 'Whenever these judges deal with cases involving "non-whites", they are inclined to view these cases within the context of their liberal outlook and convictions.'[16]

In a comment that revealed the racism that characterised apartheid South Africa, Louw went on to bemoan the fact that the judges in Bloemfontein were not prepared to accept that 'natives, due to a far lower level of civilisation and other inherent factors, could not enjoy the same civic opportunities as whites'.[17]

Dönges echoed the same racist bile, albeit indirectly, when he threatened that 'unless Parliament is convinced that its laws will not be invalidated, it will be obliged to employ American precedent and appoint only judges who have the same set of values'. He called upon the 'volk' to tell the judges in Bloemfontein that it was tired of the kind of 'legal cunning' the court had employed to subvert the will of the people.[18]

In the end, however, the government did not implement these strident legal changes immediately. Instead, it considered its position carefully and with surprising caution. Then, a few years later, it came up with a definitive legislative strategy to remove Coloured voters from the common voters' roll, at the same time ensuring that the overwhelming number of judicial appointments were filled by members of the National Party.[19]

We now turn to these developments to understand the final collapse of the legal challenge.

The *Collins* case

Three years had passed after *Harris* before the government introduced the Appellate Division Quorum Act. The new Act provided that, on the hearing of an appeal dealing with the validity of an Act of Parliament, a quorum of 11 judges of the Appellate Division was now required. In the earlier *Harris* cases, a quorum of just five had been sufficient – and they had been appointed under different political conditions. For the government, the gloves were now off: a bench of 11 allowed for reliable hands to be appointed. The government packed the court in preparation for a third challenge to its constitutional plans.

This change to the composition of the court was not the only reason for the government's optimism, however. The make-up of the court had also begun to change, owing to the retirement of key judicial figures and their replacement by reliable supporters of apartheid. By March 1955, Leopold Greenberg, one of the five judges who had sat on the *Harris* cases, had retired and in his place came Lucas Steyn, who had been a judge for less than four years. Before his appointment, Steyn had held the post of chief law advisor to the government, and in that capacity he had been part of the South African delegation to the United Nations. In 1950 he presented the government's case in the first advisory proceeding about Namibia before the International Court of Justice.

Steyn has been described by Edwin Cameron in an article that analyses his devastating contribution to South African law as someone who had

> a towering but parsimonious intellect; … he was a scrupulous but ungenerous judge; … his attempt to rid South African law of its unique and fundamental connection with English law was not only jurisprudentially and historically unjustified but ultimately quixotic; … he was an unfettered but – of his own volition – executive-minded judge and … during his term of office a legal temperature, already chill for the survival of human rights and the preservation of fundamental freedoms, turned several degrees colder.[20]

The government now had Steyn on its side. It may well have also had Henry Fagan. According to a letter that Dawid de Villiers sent to Prime Minister JG Strijdom on 19 November 1956, the government counsel were confident that, had he sat in the Harris case, Fagan would have decided in their favour.[21] But the other four judges, Centlivres, Van den Heever, Hoexter and Schreiner, were clearly a problem for the government, which did not want to fail a third time; hence the new strategy of expanding the court.

After its earlier reluctance to implement the crude proposals to strip the judiciary of its former independence, the government now moved decisively to pack the court with judges made in its own political image, using the 1955 Quorum Act. The Minister of Justice, CR Swart, told Parliament:

> The government intends to take steps … to reinstate the sovereignty of parliament. By the sovereignty of parliament we mean the state of affairs which obtained immediately after the 1937 decision … viz that Parliament can pass legislation without any limitation.[22]

Five further judges of appeal were appointed: De Beer, Judge President of the Orange Free State; Reynolds, Judge President of the Eastern Districts, together with his colleague Judge de Villiers; Judge Brink of the Free State; and Judge Hall of the Cape – reliable hands all. The government now felt it had put in place a court that would cause it no further trouble.

Next, the government passed the Senate Act, the purpose of which was to enlarge the Senate by granting greater representation to the larger provinces together with an increase in the number of nominated senators, the election of senators by a simple majority in an electoral college instead of by proportional representation and a dissolution of the existing Senate by the end of 1955. The enlarged Senate guaranteed the presence of many more National Party senators. When the two Houses of Parliament sat together, the National Party was now assured of the two-thirds majority that was needed to change the Constitution.

The government made no attempt to disguise its intentions to Parliament. In a speech on the bill, Dönges, said:

> The government cannot run away from its mandate … it has to take the necessary steps to carry out the mandate given to it. In the first place, it tries to do so by using its ordinary powers in the ordinary methods. However, if these do not succeed it has no alternative, if it is continuously thwarted and condemned to

ineffectiveness, than to use the reserve powers and the special methods given to it by the South Africa Act in order to carry out the will of the voters. ... In fact, it is the essence of a democratic government that it should use all constitutional means at its disposal to give effect to a mandate it received at an election.[23]

Strijdom was even more blunt: 'In the first place the object of this Bill and the legislation which will follow later is to put the coloureds on a separate roll ... The second aim of this Bill [is] to put the sovereignty of Parliament beyond all doubt in accordance with our interpretation of the Statute of Westminster and in terms of the 1937 decision of the Appeal Court.'[24]

The new court

Before we turn to the third challenge before the Appeal Court, mention must be made of the new court, which was to hear the final case in this saga.

The existing members of the Appellate Division had not been consulted about the new appointments. Oliver Schreiner proved to be the only member of the Court who remained faithful to the common-law principles that the court had steadfastly upheld in the earlier *Harris* cases. Writing to his wife on the new appointments, he did not disguise his disdain: 'I have little doubt that most of the cases will be decided fairly rightly – the job is not so difficult that every case calls for high quality, thank heaven. But it isn't going to be a court to be proud of being one's country's highest court. But we'll live through these interesting unattractive bounds – any rate in the long run the country is fairly certain to come right.'[25]

The senior judges' lack of regard for their new colleagues took on an odd spin over a game of bowls – or, rather, lack of it. There was a custom that judges of appeal would play bowls on Wednesday afternoons, when the court did not sit. There could have been no clearer condemnation of these new political appointments than a refusal to invite them to play bowls, as is apparent from another letter that Schreiner sent to his wife: 'I was glad to get your support for the view that we should be reasonably firm about extra-judicial associations with the newcomers. Whether there will be modifications over the years remains to be seen; but for the present, and especially with the most thick-skinned of them, it is clearly necessary to maintain a reasonable distance.'

Schreiner also made it clear what he thought of the intellectual capacity of the newcomers: 'There is the problem of dealing with the judgments of the new men – they take a good deal more working than do those of the old hands ... most of the burden falls on Albert [Centlivres] ... When one thinks of the number of people who believe that the additional judicial appointments must at least lighten the work for the seniors it makes one laugh a bit sourly.'[26]

This divided court heard argument on the Senate Act on 15 October 1956. There was only one appellant this time, William Collins. He was one of the individual voters who had appealed against the judgment of the Cape Supreme Court, which had given the government a taste of success when it upheld the validity of the Act. The debate between Graeme Duncan and the judges on the first day was far less interesting, however, than a remark made by one of the new judges, Eddy de Beer. Dawid de Villiers, on behalf of the government, had sought to attack the first *Harris* decision and invited the court to reconsider its validity. What he wanted was a fresh finding that the court had acted incorrectly in its first *Harris* judgment, when it set aside legislation duly passed by Parliament.

At some point in the hearing, De Beer said that he and the new judges had accepted their appointments only on the understanding that the *Harris* decision was not to be challenged. Suddenly, De Villiers withdrew his threat to attack the first *Harris* judgment. As Schreiner remarked to his wife:

> You can imagine, can't you, what a bombshell Eddy's announcement was. But can you picture people accepting the position on this court on condition that certain issues will not be raised before them? The inference is natural, that they were prepared to consider any other issues of a related kind and were consulted as to whether they felt prepared to deal with such issues. One assumes they were not invited to express their views in advance, but fancy any sort of talk of that kind, it just shows what we have come down to.[27]

Brink was the only other judge who told his colleagues that he had given a similar undertaking to the Minister of Justice, Swart.

Minister Swart sought to explain De Beer's bizarre but honest outburst when he addressed Parliament in January 1957.[28] He said that, when De Beer was approached to take an appointment on the Appeal Court, he had raised his difficulty with the court's decision in the first *Harris* case. Swart said that there had never been any intention of a conditional appointment, because the government did not impose conditions when appointing a judge, nor did the judge accept appointment on certain conditions. He had simply tried to help Judge de Beer with his personal problem, he said. This was one of the few occasions during the apartheid period when the public, had they paid attention, would have realised the extent to which direct political considerations played a part in the appointment of judges.

The judgment

Whatever the motivation of the government, its strategy finally bore fruit on 9 November 1956 when the Appeal Court handed down its judgment in the *Collins* case.

The majority judgment was delivered by Chief Justice Centlivres. He held that the House of Assembly and the Senate, sitting separately, could, by ordinary majority, reconstitute the Senate. Indeed, if the ordinary majorities altered the Senate so that it should consist entirely of government supporters, that too would be valid. It may have been that the Senate could not be abolished without using a special voting procedure, but that it could be reconstructed in the way the National Party had done did not make the legislation unconstitutional. Lucas Steyn, the government's pre-eminent legal Gauleiter, delivered a concurring judgment, the essence of which was that, whatever the purpose of the government in passing the legislation, this consideration was utterly irrelevant. The law had been passed legally and there was nothing that a court could do about such legislation. In keeping with the view articulated so often by the government during the entire crisis, Steyn found that the only sanction for passing such legislation was that the electorate 'would provide an adequate and more appropriate curb on the activities of Parliament'.[29] Decoded: so long as only white people voted, majority rule was clearly acceptable. The National Party would jealously guard the interests of the 'volk'!

Steyn had laid down the legal philosophy that was to remain dominant in the Appellate Division until 1994. So long as the law expressly empowered the executive, a court would not examine the substance of the law. Form, not substance, was the overwhelming test. Issues of justice, as protected in the common law, were of little concern.

In the second *Harris* case, the court had held that the High Court of Parliament was not a court but merely a group of parliamentarians constituting themselves as a court for one purpose, namely to subvert a court structure of which they did not approve. Here the substance, that is, the purpose of the legislation, was critical to the court's decision. But now it was significant only to Oliver Schreiner, who began by asking the question, was the body constituted by the Senate Act a Senate in substance and therefore a House of Parliament in the meaning of that word? If answered in the affirmative, this would be sufficient to pass the legislation. Theoretically, Schreiner maintained, Parliament could, by acting bicamerally, appoint or create any body whatsoever and call it a Senate. A court would be bound, if invited to do so, to enquire whether such body was really a House of Parliament. But that was to be myopic. It was impermissible to look only at the form of the Act. By looking at its purpose, he held that the revamped Senate was nothing more than a body devised by government lawyers to produce a sufficient majority to ensure that Coloured voters would be taken off the common voters' roll, and the Senate Act just a mechanism to obtain a vote in a joint session to take Coloured voters off the common voters' roll. Thus the new Senate could not be considered to be a Senate for the purposes of being a House of Parliament. The Senate Act was a legal fraud.

But Schreiner cut a lonely figure. The two other judges who had formed part of the two *Harris* judgments, Centlivres and Hoexter, were now part of the majority that upheld the government. Schreiner remained in splendid philosophical isolation. Writing to his wife he said: 'Strictly between ourselves, I've written a dissenting judgment but no one else agrees with me, so I must be wrong. It happens that way and one mustn't think the sky is going to fall because of the result of the appeal.'[30]

Edna Schreiner's response was insightful: 'It was amusing to think that the Government need not have gone to the expense of packing the AD [Appellate Division] with their minions.'[31]

It is interesting to consider why Judges Centlivres and Hoexter were not prepared to sign on to the Schreiner dissent and why, by contrast, Centlivres felt compelled to author the majority judgment. It seems possible that these judges knew the game was up. The court had changed: a majority of the court in favour of Coloured voters was no longer possible and, arguably of greater significance, the court was running heavily against (white) public opinion, which could be employed against the court to even more virulent degrees than had to date been the case. Better, then, to withdraw and live to fight another battle in the future.

Extra-parliamentary politics

There is another important part of the explanation. During the period in which the two *Harris* cases were decided, there was significant extra-parliamentary opposition from white groups, particularly in the form of the Torch Commando. This is not to underestimate the effect of the opposition of the majority of the population – on the contrary, those political forces ultimately changed the country. However, to the extent that the approach of the court was shaped by white opinion, opposition from these ranks proved influential.

Formed by ex-servicemen who had returned from World War II, the Torch Commando was described as 'the channel of expression of tens of thousands of disillusioned and frustrated men and women who were uneasy at the trend of events in South Africa. It particularly appealed to the returned soldiers and their families throughout the country.'[32] The group managed to obtain a paid-up membership of over 125 000 and initially drew vast crowds to its protests against the impending legislation. But it was a movement riddled with contradiction. As David Scher observed:

> The movement was fundamentally in harmony with South African social patterns and its members nurtured no incentive to revolutionary action. It certainly did not seek a frame of reference beyond that of protecting the Constitution against the attack of the Government. Their deep constitutional regard convinced many Torchers that their extra-party movement was incongruous in a democratic society. It was almost apologetically that Sailor Malan told his audience in July 1952 that the Commando was

not a permanent feature in the political life of South Africa and would, as soon as the need for it fell away with the return to power of the United Party, 'be dissolved like, morning mist'.[33]

By 1955, the movement was no more, and with it disappeared the last vestige of serious white opposition to the disenfranchisement of Coloured voters.

Does history repeat itself?

The constitutional crisis of the 1950s set a judiciary that had an established tradition of independence sourced in English colonial origins against a government determined to implement its own political programme without restrictions to constrain it and unfettered by judicial interpretation of existing law. This meant, as we have seen, that the National Party government grew increasingly intolerant of the judiciary, which it saw as subverting the will of the people. The fact that the National Party's racist vision of the world equated the 'will of the people' with the will of *white* people is irrelevant to this argument.

Fifty years later, and almost a decade into constitutional democracy, the ANC produced a statement that, save for the significant distinction that, this time, the governing party's conception of the will of the people embraced all South Africans, was astoundingly similar to the National Party's approach to the judiciary during the 1950s. In its annual statement of 8 January 2005, the ANC said:

> We need to ensure that all have equal protection under the law, and that all have access to the institutions of the state designed to protect and uphold their rights. We face the continuing and important challenge to work for the transformation of the judiciary. ... [W]e are also confronted by the similarly important challenge to trans-form the collective mindset of the judiciary to bring it into consonance with the vision and aspirations of the millions who engaged in struggle to liberate our country from white minority domination. The reality can no longer be avoided that many within our judiciary do not see themselves as being part of these masses, accountable to them, and inspired by their hopes, dreams and value systems. If this persists for too long,

it will inevitably result in popular antagonism towards the judiciary and our courts, with serious and negative consequences for the democratic system as a whole.[34]

This statement understandably provoked a public controversy, which died down briefly only to be resurrected when government introduced proposals to amend the Constitution. These proposals would have placed the administration of courts firmly under the control of the Department of Justice and introduced a Superior Courts Bill which made further changes to the manner in which courts were organised and increased the power of the Minister of Justice. If these proposals had been passed by Parliament, the most powerful judges in the provincial courts, the Judges President, would no longer have been appointed by way of the Judicial Service Commission, but by the President of the country.

The events of 50 years ago therefore provide a salutary warning of a continued possible threat to the judicial institution.

These proposals were not implemented, as it turned out. More than a decade later, the judiciary remains a resiliently independent institution. But, as the lessons of the 1950s have taught us, the threat to an independent judiciary is not a possibility that can be discounted, however remote the threats might appear.

Notwithstanding the proposed legislation of more than a decade ago, executive and legislative attacks on the judiciary have continued. To take but one extreme recent example, the Speaker of the National Assembly, Baleka Mbete, in July 2017 lambasted the judiciary, claiming that judges were often highly politicised, accusing some of them of being prejudiced against the ANC: 'When there is a case that affects someone from the ANC, these cases would find their way [into the courts] and if they end up in the hands of certain specific judges, forget it, you are going to lose that case. It has nothing to do with merit, correctness or wrongness. Some names pop up in their head already.' It was within this context that she noted that opposition parties 'seem to have a lot of confidence' that they would win in court.[35]

A further parallel to the events of 1950s – but one which backfired lamentably on the executive – was the refusal by former President Zuma to appoint Justice Dikgang Moseneke, the then sitting deputy Chief Justice, to the position of Chief Justice, in 2011. In the 1950s the failure to appoint Judge Oliver Denys Schreiner, the senior member of the Appellate Division, to the position of Chief Justice upon the retirement of Chief Justice Centlivres resulted a short while later in the elevation to that position of Judge LC Steyn – a tenacious supporter of apartheid. Ironically, Zuma's choice of Justice Mogoeng Mogoeng turned out to have had completely different results from what Zuma probably expected. Since promoted, Chief Justice Mogoeng Mogoeng has continued to enhance the independence and integrity of the judiciary, and delivered a number of judgments promoting constitutional values while eschewing any ill-conceived deference to executive authority that would have been to the obvious pleasure of the President who appointed him.

Our point is less to do with the individuals concerned – after all, there can be absolutely no comparison between the egregious deference to apartheid of LC Steyn and the principled independence of Mogoeng Mogoeng – but more with the fact that, in the 1950s, government had seen fit to refuse to appoint the most senior judge as Chief Justice because it did not consider him to be politically reliable. And there can be little doubt that there was a similar motive uppermost in his mind when Zuma refused to appoint Judge Moseneke to the top judicial job.

It is for this reason that judicial events of 50 years ago, dealing with the cases of the so-called Coloured vote, provide an ominous warning of possible threats to the judicial institution. When senior judges are called 'counter-revolutionaries' by influential members of the governing party, or it is claimed that judges are biased against the party, these outbursts recall the conduct of the ruling National Party during the 1950s, however distant the present threat may yet be on the political horizon.

Constitutional democracy is not something that is asserted: it is continuously defended by political action. Without this, it is possible that another chapter will yet have to be written about the removal of another troublesome South African court. Despite facing harsh criticism and enormous political pressure, the judiciary withstood the state-capture project relatively unscathed. Indeed, it was precisely this point that Zuma made at a speech he gave at the Walter Sisulu University in September 2018. He claimed that state capture was 'a politically decorated expression' and that all three arms of state (legislature, executive and judiciary) would have to be captured for it to be true that the state was captured.[36] An awfully clever argument …

4

THE RIVONIA TRIAL:
COMPETING VISIONS FOR SOUTH AFRICA

'The white state has thrown overboard every pretence of rule by democratic process. Armed to the teeth it has presented the people with only one choice, and that is its overthrow by force and violence.'[1]
– OPERATION MAYIBUYE DOCUMENT.

Today, Pretoria is a city that looks and feels like a part of the African continent. Take a walk at lunchtime down Thabo Sehume Street or Madiba Drive, until very recently Andries or Vermeulen street, respectively, and the transformation of the city from the apartheid military fortress of a few decades back is palpable. Forty years ago, however, Pretoria was the white capital of the Afrikaner kingdom. Huge white men, many bedecked with epaulettes issued by the police or the army, strode the streets of the city. Pretoria was the centre of apartheid power, its white inhabitants supremely confident of the future of their city and their country and the fortunes of their rugby team, the Blou Bulle (Blue Bulls).

It was into this citadel of repression, at the height of the power of the National Party, that the key leaders of the ANC were transported in 1963. They were being taken to a trial that sought to criminalise their political activity, whose aim was to establish a non-racial democracy. Specifically, this brutal clash of sworn ideological enemies took the form of a criminal trial.

The case became known as the Rivonia trial. As the government moved to destroy the ANC as a political organisation, the central command of the movement met regularly at Liliesleaf, a farm in Rivonia. The farm had been made available to the ANC by the Communist Party.[2] Ironically, this secret venue reflected privileged white South Africa. Liliesleaf Farm covered some 11.5 hectares in what is now the suburb of Rivonia on the northern outskirts of Johannesburg. In the early 1960s, Rivonia was no more than farmland, a far cry from the blocks of gated townhouses and marbled shopping malls that now characterise the northern suburbs of Johannesburg.

The farm was bought through a company that had been incorporated by the South African Communist Party. Legal records show that the occupants were a well-known architect, Arthur Goldreich, and his family, while the farming activities were supervised by Thomas Mashitane, who was a member of the Communist Party. These arrangements were designed to create a veneer of a normal family, with the Goldreichs purported to be the residents and Mashitane the foreman. The arrangement worked well for a while.

Initially, security around the farm was very strict, and few members of the ANC, other than the Central Committee of the Communist Party, even knew of its existence or the purpose to which it had been put. However, liberation struggle activist Ahmed Kathrada later wrote: '[A] number of us had started feeling uneasy about the continued use of the Rivonia farm. We were aware that the "need-to-know" principle had not applied to Liliesleaf for some time, and that far too many people – one of whom was Bruno Mtolo, a saboteur from Durban and leader of the Natal branch of the ANC's armed wing Umkhonto we Sizwe (MK) – had visited the farm.'[3] Mtolo's visit to the farm was to prove critical to the fate of its occupants, but more of that later.

On 6 July 1963, members of the high command of MK met at the farm to discuss a draft document that had been prepared by Joe Slovo. Lionel 'Rusty' Bernstein, like Joe Slovo a key member of the Communist Party, had raised strong objections to this document, which sought to alter MK's strategy from that of a sabotage campaign to guerrilla warfare. For Bernstein, the document was predicated on a completely inadequate analysis of the real balance of power in the country and had not taken sufficient consideration of the government's strength and MK's weakness.[4]

Absent from these central discussions was Nelson Mandela, who had already been in prison for some time. In 1962, Mandela had left the country using the identity of a certain David Motsamayi and travelled abroad for several months. During this trip, Mandela met up with the first group of MK recruits on their way to Addis Ababa for guerrilla training. Not long after his return to South Africa on 5 August 1962, Mandela was arrested and charged with illegal exit from the country and incitement to strike. He was in Natal at the time, on his way back to Johannesburg, posing again as David Motsamayi and now working as the chauffeur for a white theatre director and MK member, Cecil Williams.

On 7 November 1962, Mandela was convicted and sentenced to three years' imprisonment for incitement, together with an additional two years for leaving the country without a passport.

The document setting out Operation Mayibuye (the name given to a blueprint for armed resistance) envisaged a process of determining a date whereby, in preselected areas, trained and armed guerrillas would seek to join MK. These groups would catch the state forces by surprise, creating as much chaos and confusion for the enemy as possible. Before these operations could take place, the document explains, 'political authority would have been set up in a friendly territory with a view to supervising the struggle ... It is visualised that this authority would in due course of time develop into the "Provisional Revolutionary Government".'[5]

The ultimate aim of the plan was to ensure that an external guerrilla force would join some 7 000 armed men in four key areas to wage war on the South African government.

It was, as Anthony Sampson notes in his biography of Mandela,[6] a 'reckless and unrealistic scheme'. Among the ANC leaders, there was a clear divide. Govan Mbeki, Joe Slovo and Arthur Goldreich were enthusiastic proponents of the plan; Walter Sisulu, Ahmed Kathrada and other members of the high command, however, had strong reservations, and it was to debate these reservations that the leaders had gathered at the farm in July 1963. In Kathrada's opinion, the plan was almost naive in its scope and promise. But its architects had the advantage that the ANC leaders had been dispersed at the time, fleeing government repression.[7] There were many influential leaders of the movement who therefore did not have the chance to debate the plans and who would, in Kathrada's view, have resisted its adoption.

The security police, with the benefit of legislation that empowered them to detain political opponents without recourse to a court, had launched a ferocious campaign to destroy the ANC and the Pan Africanist Congress (PAC) by incarcerating their leaders after the Sharpeville uprising of 1960. So, by 1963, the police net was closing in on the high command of the ANC. Three months earlier, in April 1963, there had been a mass arrest of key members of the PAC and its military wing, Poqo. The Minister of Justice, John Vorster, told Parliament in June 1963:

> We dare not lose sight of the fact that we are still faced with the problem of the ANC and it is a very real problem because it is *par excellence* the organisation which has many more white brains at its disposal, not only overseas, but here as well ... the immediate danger is the ANC with its militant wing, the Spear of the Nation, and we are busy taking just as effective action against this organisation as we did with the PAC.[8]

On 11 July 1963, the police hit the jackpot. They raided Liliesleaf with the express aim of capturing Walter Sisulu, then the senior member of the high command. But they found far more than they had expected. When they arrived, a large group of key members of the ANC had congregated with Sisulu at the farm.

Kathrada maintains that neither the ANC nor the Communist Party ever found out who or what had led the police to Rivonia on that fateful day. Ironically, it had been decided that this was to be the last meeting at the farm because it was considered to have become too risky. Whatever the source of police information, white South Africa rejoiced at the arrests. Even that most liberal of newspapers at the time, the *Rand Daily Mail*, captured a feeling of relief among the white community when it carried the headline on 13 July 1963: 'Security swoop on Rand sparks huge investigation. Subversion: End Near. Arrests give new clues – police chief'.

The head of the Security Branch, the notorious Colonel Hendrik van den Bergh, proclaimed triumphantly: 'With these arrests the Security Branch has virtually smashed the various secret organisations which have threatened the safety of the state.'[9] Of those detained, Goldreich and Harold Wolpe, who had been arrested after the Rivonia raid, managed to escape the country by bribing a prison warder. Theirs is an extraordinary story but it is not for now. Nelson Mandela, already imprisoned, was joined in the dock by Walter Sisulu, Denis Goldberg, Govan Mbeki, Ahmed Kathrada, Lionel Bernstein, Raymond Mhlaba, James Kantor, Elias Motsoaledi and Andrew Mlangeni. In legal circles, the case was technically known as the *State v Nelson Mandela and Others* but it has gone down in history as simply the Rivonia trial.

All the accused were detained for 90 days without trial under the government's newly established security laws (of which more later in this book). Kathrada tells of police pressure on him to cooperate with the investigation. Displaying their usual combination of racism and antisemitism, the interrogators asked him if he wanted to go to prison 'for a bunch of k*****s and Jews'.[10]

Before their trial, they were permitted to meet their legal team. Bram Fischer, the team leader, and George Bizos were well known to them. Fischer was a leading member of the underground Communist Party and had been at many a meeting at Liliesleaf. As Kathrada wryly recalled, 'George was also well known to us because we were so often in trouble.'[11] The other lawyers, Arthur Chaskalson and Joel Joffe, were less known at that stage. The lawyers immediately set out the legal options but, for the accused, this was to be a political trial in which they would present a political justification for their actions.[12] But the accused were under no illusions: the legal case against them was immense and they faced the probability of the death sentence.

The opening of the trial

Even before the trial began, the attendant press coverage had ensured that the political temperature surrounding the trial would be raised. When it finally started on 9 October 1963, the *Rand Daily Mail* headline proclaimed: 'State alleges conspiracy planned on a military basis. Revolt, invasion, charges – eleven arraigned in more than 200 sabotage attacks.'[13]

The proceedings opened amid a massive police presence. Hilda Bernstein, wife of accused Rusty Bernstein, wrote of the way in which the police convoy swept through Pretoria's peak-hour traffic and drove into the court buildings, where policemen with Sten guns jumped out and surrounded the prison yard while the handcuffed prisoners were taken into cells below the court.[14]

The trial took place at the Palace of Justice in Pretoria, pictured on this book's cover. The building was constructed in 1897, a relic of the old Transvaal Republic and a magisterial landmark in the capital city. It is a splendid brown-brick building with an imposing flight of steps leading to the entrance. The external appearance of the building is marked by a symmetry of classical proportions, whose architecture is described as encapsulating 'centralised power and legal authority'.[15]

Of the internal appearance of the court, Hilda Bernstein said:

> The judge's bench is an elaborate pulpit of wood, carved and posted like an old-fashioned bed, at one end of the 60-foot court. He is enthroned there, dwarfed in his scarlet robes. On either side of this structure are beige curtains, draped and pleated from floor to ceiling, into which the voices of prosecutor, defending counsel and judge alike disappear and are lost. A huge-bladed fan, suspended on a long rod from the ceiling directly above the prosecutor's head, wobbles slowly through the summer days, imperceptibly stirring the thick air.[16]

The courtroom was segregated, with separate benches for white and black spectators. The benches reserved for white people accommodated members of the Security Branch and a few supporters of the accused. The rest were packed with family members and relatives of the accused. Winnie Mandela, who had already been banned and was not permitted to communicate with the public, was present but had to remain un-characteristically silent. Albertina Sisulu, recently released from jail, was also present.

On the opening day of the trial, the presiding judge, Quartus de Wet, was immediately faced with an application for a postponement. Bram Fischer, the lead counsel for the defence team, rose to request three weeks to thoroughly consider the indictment, being the description of the charges. This line of defence had an important precedent. Lawyers who had defended a larger group of ANC leaders in the treason trial of 1956 had material success in attacking the indictment. In that earlier case, the government had pressed charges against 156 of its political opponents, including many of the same men. The trial ended unsuccessfully for the government but only after five hard-fought years of litigation.

The thinking behind this line of attack was that, even during this bleak legal period, the law of procedure guaranteed a measure of fairness for the accused and the state was obligated to let the accused know in clear terms what case they were required to meet in court. The accused were entitled to object to the charge sheet on the basis that the charges set out were vague in describing all of the necessary particulars or that it failed to specify elements of the crimes for which they stood charged. When a court sustains such an attack, the state must be given a chance to remedy the charge sheet by amending it, failing which the charge has to be quashed and the accused freed.

In the Rivonia trial, the accused had not been charged with treason but with two counts of sabotage, the charge sheet alleging some 193 separate incidents under the Sabotage Act, a third charge in terms of the Suppression of Communism Act and a fourth, which concerned the financing of MK activities. But there were very few specific, detailed allegations to substantiate these charges. The indictment was a shoddy piece of work; Judge De Wet had no choice but to grant the postponement.

Back in court three weeks later, Bram Fischer rose again to attack the indictment. The atmosphere was now even more emotionally charged. The austerity of the legal process had given way to a political contest to be fought out in a courtroom. As the accused came up from the cells below the court by way of the dark stairwell, they gave the ANC raised-fist salute, and shouted out '*amandla*' (power), to which the gallery roared back '*ngawethu*' (it is ours).

Judge De Wet, who had been appointed to the bench in 1950, had risen speedily by judicial standards to become the Judge President of the Transvaal Supreme Court. Chaskalson believed De Wet was not a supporter of the National Party. Although his father had been prominent in the white opposition party, the United Party, he was apolitical, although he clearly harboured the racist outlook of most white people at the time.[17] De Wet looked down from his judicial throne. He was confronted with two lawyers of markedly different backgrounds, character and political vision. Fischer had been born in 1908 into the very core of the political and legal establishment that ruled South Africa throughout his life. His father, Percy Fischer, had been the Judge President of the Orange Free State, and his grandfather, Abraham Fischer, the Prime Minister of the Orange River Colony and later a member of the cabinet of the Union of South Africa. Fischer had been schooled at the prestigious Grey College in Bloemfontein and later at Oxford University. In 1940 he had joined the South African Communist Party and shot to prominence as one of its leaders. By the time of the trial, he was 55 years old and a barrister of considerable standing. A short, stocky man with striking grey hair and stern black glasses, Fischer was a quietly spoken, polite but very skilled barrister. His politics aside, Fischer comported himself in the best traditions of the English Bar – to this day, the exemplar for South African advocates.

But he was much more than just a talented counsel. Apart from his legal skill, Fischer was head of the Communist Party, banned by the National Party government in 1950. The party affiliates were among those who spearheaded apartheid's resistance, most of whom had been arrested at Rivonia. As an activist, Fischer was a critical part of progressive, non-racial resistance to the apartheid regime. As Chief Justice Ismail Mahomed said of Fischer in February 1998:

> Just occasionally in the life of a people, history produces a citizen the impact of whose life continues long beyond his physical demise to stimulate profound reflections on the complexity and the potential grandeur of our species and its unique need and capacity to formulate and to develop for itself a moral basis to regulate the interaction of its members *inter se* and between those members and the evolving environment which it inherits and generates. Such a rare man was Bram Fischer.[18]

One can only imagine the stress experienced by Fischer throughout the trial. Of this, Stephen Clingman, in his masterful biography of Fischer, wrote:

> MK had effectively been destroyed at Rivonia. Fischer realised that it was necessary to reconstitute the organisation even in a minimal form. As the Rivonia trial proceeded, he worked with David Kidson to reactivate Umkhonto structures, this while the *Rivonia* trial was proceeding! Bram's involvement at Rivonia meant that he had been observed by a number of people, including the black workers at the farmhouse, who were now to be called as prosecution witnesses. Any one of them, asked

to identify any individual in the courtroom they had seen at Liliesleaf, could have turned to Bram and pointed him out. For Bram to enter into the trial was in that regard an enormous, even life-threatening risk – and it was for this reason that when Rusty Bernstein first heard that he would be leading the defence, he turned to his co-accused and said, 'He deserves the Victoria Cross.' That was also the reason why, during the opening stages of the trial, when most of the farm workers were called to give evidence, Bram managed to be out of court, engaged in an arbitration which he freely admitted was 'hopeless', but which had the advantage of keeping him busy elsewhere.[19]

The prosecutor was a small bald-headed man with only a stub for a left hand, a legacy of an injury sustained while working in his father's butchery. Percy Yutar was born in Cape Town of parents who had come to South Africa from the Jewish ghetto in Lithuania, as had most of the country's Jewish community. He was fiercely ambitious. He became the first student in South Africa to be awarded a doctorate in law, in his case by UCT. The religious prejudice of the time meant, however, that this qualification did not assist him to move rapidly in the legal profession. Nevertheless, his ambition was all-consuming and he finally obtained an appointment as a junior state prosecutor. His willingness to work long and hard, and his indifference to the immorality of the apartheid system finally brought him the promotion he had craved for so long.

At the time of the Rivonia trial, Yutar was the deputy attorney general for the Transvaal, the second most senior prosecutor in the province. His experience of the virulent antisemitism that had confronted him earlier in his career prompted him to show to extravagant excess that he was a loyal Jewish South African. He proudly wore a signet ring in the shape of the Star of David and he was president of one of South Africa's largest orthodox synagogues. *Rivonia* now afforded the ambitious Yutar an opportunity to show how useful he could be to the government, and how loyal 'this Jew' could be to the country. The outcome of the trial was terribly important to his campaign to gain the ultimate prize: attorney general of the Transvaal. Yutar knew about Fischer's political affiliation, and during one adjournment he said to him that he 'had enough in his bag to put him away'.[20]

In its quiet and determined way, Fischer's attack on the indictment began to have an increasingly positive effect on Judge De Wet. Fischer pointed out that there was a great deal of generality in the manner in which the charges had been set out. This was particularly problematic because, if properly formulated, the charges would have clearly laid out allegations tying each accused individually to each charge. But, for example, Nelson Mandela had been charged with 156 acts of sabotage, all of which were alleged to have been committed while he was in prison.

Fischer argued for two full days in court. After he had completed his detailed argument, Dr George Lowen, who appeared for one of the accused, James Kantor, rose to address the court. Lowen was the very opposite of Fischer. He presented his address in a dramatic and emotional style, and was not afraid to use sarcasm. He spoke passionately on behalf of Kantor. Lowen was a German-trained lawyer who had participated in a number of trials of opponents of the Nazi regime before leaving as a refugee from Hitler's Germany. Understandably, he viewed this trial in similar fashion to his previous experience. He concentrated his arguments on the manner in which the state had treated his request for further particulars to the charges levelled against his client, Kantor. At one point, he told the judge: 'Take for example question 5. The answer given by the State was dash, dash, dash, exclamation mark' Judge De Wet replied, in what was now a clear indication of his attitude to the indictment, 'In my copy there are four dashes, Mr Lowen.'[21]

Yutar was in serious trouble with his indictment and he knew it. The case was not running well for the state. When he rose to answer the defence's submissions, his voice rose a number of octaves, almost to the point of a squeak, such was the level of his agitation. He implored the judge not to quash the indictment but, in his anxiety, he kept using the word 'squash' rather than the legal term 'quash'!

But the judge was having nothing of Yutar's plea. The indictment was clearly vague and full of generalisations, and contained insufficient particulars of the charges against each accused. The judge found for the accused:

When details are required of the dates when and place and manner in which each of the accused was alleged to have commenced acting in concert with the alleged co-conspirators, the reply is this is peculiarly within the knowledge of the accused. The accused are assumed to be innocent until they are proved to be guilty. And it is most improper, in my opinion, when the accused ask for particulars in regard to an offence which is alleged to have been committed to say to them, this is a matter which you know all about. That presupposes that he is guilty and he will not be told anything about the offence.[22]

The accused had won round one and were technically free, but the decision in their favour did not help them for long. They were immediately rearrested.

Joel Joffe, an attorney who had postponed his emigration plans to assist in the defence at *Rivonia*, recalls that, upon hearing the decision, Denis Goldberg bent down to kiss his wife. Warrant Officer Dirker 'grabbed him and hauled him off to underground cells,' said Joffe.[23] New indictments were prepared according to which the accused and 22 co-conspirators together with the South African Communist Party, the ANC and MK had committed sabotage by the employment of people for training in the preparation and use of explosives for warfare, including guerrilla warfare together with 192 listed acts of violence and destruction. It was also alleged that the accused had conspired to commit acts of guerrilla warfare, given assistance to military units of foreign countries which would invade South Africa and had generally participated in a violent revolution in South Africa. An additional count alleged that these acts were calculated to further the achievement of the aims of communism, and that the ANC was controlled and dominated by the South African Communist Party.[24]

Yutar rose to present his opening address to the court. The press had been well primed, with *Die Burger*, the leading Afrikaans daily newspaper in the Cape, running a double-page spread describing the state case in detail. Significantly, its header screamed: '*Rivonia* case: Goldreich and the others planned to build an armaments factory'.[25] The racist discourse of the newspaper could only see the Rivonia trial as that of the state versus a group of white miscreants leading a larger group of black followers. The readers of *Die Burger* were informed that the plan the accused had allegedly hatched was to manufacture sufficient explosives to blast Johannesburg sky high. *The Star*, the widely read Johannesburg afternoon paper, also carried a similar feature, entitled 'Reds backed revolt plan'. The report confirmed that behind the accused there was a 'vast communistic machine and organisation with all its manifold avenues of co-operation and assistance'.[26]

Yutar summarised the state's case against the accused as follows:

> The accused deliberately and maliciously plotted and engineered the commission of acts of violence and destruction ... The planned purpose thereof was to bring about in South Africa chaos and disorder and turmoil, which would be aggravated according to their plan by the operation of thousands of trained guerrilla warfare units deployed throughout the country at various vantage points. These would be joined in the various areas by local inhabitants, as well as specially selected men posted to such areas. Their combined operations were planned to lead to confusion, violent insurrection and rebellion followed at the appropriate juncture by an armed invasion of the country by military units of foreign powers.[27]

Throughout his address, Yutar continued to employ this form of emotive language designed to excite white fear. For example, he claimed that the state would 'show that the accused gloated over the first ...explosion ... and brought out a special poster of Umkhonto we Sizwe to mark the occasion'.[28]

This way, Yutar tailored his opening address not only to the judge, but also to the white electorate. When the legal teams arrived on 3 December 1963, the defence was surprised to see that microphones had been installed in the court for the purpose of broadcasting Yutar's opening address live on SABC radio. Yutar immediately enquired of the judge whether it was in order for his opening address to be broadcast. Judge De Wet looked particularly uncomfortable, saying that he had initially given instructions that the recording of the opening address could proceed 'in order to inform the public'. He went on to say that the position had now changed; although he never clarified how it had changed, he refused permission to broadcast Yutar's speech on the state-controlled radio.

This was a small but not insignificant victory. In general, the ability of the state to present its case without an immediate counter from the defence is a powerful mechanism by which to frame the case in the public mind. The public often assumes that the state's case is the truth. And by the time the accused have presented their case, which can occur only at the close of the state's case, public curiosity has waned and the damage against the accused has been done. In a political trial of this magnitude, Yutar would have wanted to use state-controlled radio to influence public perceptions and inflict as much damage on the accused as he possibly could during his opening address. By refusing him this, De Wet was at least intent on running a fair criminal trial and this afforded the defence another small victory.

The state's case

The state introduced 173 witnesses, 29 of whom had been detained without trial. Some of these witnesses had agreed to testify after great pressure had been exerted on them to give evidence against their former comrades. The key witness for the state was Bruno Mtolo, who had been a member of the ANC and the South African Communist Party, as well as a key figure of MK in KwaZulu-Natal. As was always the case with Yutar, he began leading the witness dramatically:

Yutar: Bruno, are you a saboteur?

Mtolo: Yes I was.

Yutar: Did you blow up pylons and other government property in Durban?

Mtolo: Yes I did.[29]

For three days, Mtolo told the court in considerable detail of the sabotage campaign of which he had been a part and his activities in it. This was critical evidence in support of the state case. After all, Mtolo was deeply connected to the ANC-led alliance. He had been an employee of the ANC-aligned union movement, the South African Congress of Trade Unions, and a close comrade of the leading ANC activist in Natal, Harry Gwala. He had first-hand knowledge of underground resistance to the government. And Mtolo served up that knowledge in vivid detail, building the state's case against the accused with personal recollections – and embellished with some inventive fabrication. Hence, as Hilda Bernstein correctly observed:

He [Mtolo], who spent three years as perhaps the most active saboteur in the country, one of the most energetic members of Umkhonto, incriminates everyone who has ever worked with him, everyone he has ever known in the ANC and Umkhonto, including his own brother who he identifies in court as one of the young men recruited by Umkhonto to be sent abroad for military training. He now accuses the men on trial for their lives of having lived in luxury.[30]

Mtolo described at length how Walter Sisulu had furnished his home with expensive items. Although they were false statements, the evidence was an important component of Mtolo's testimony. He sought to confirm the state's interpretation of the accused as violent, self-serving and greedy, and in his own book, he spoke of the selfish nature of the accused. Mtolo also raised the spectre of the ANC being dominated by the Communist Party:

I thought of the women who would be wearing green and black uniforms, instead of red and black because these people were not what they pretended to be. These were the leaders who, when I was sent to find out what steps were being taken to avoid the arrest of the youngsters for military training, told me, 'When soldiers are fighting these things should be expected.' They were the same people who made us and our families starve while they and their families were living in luxury.[31]

Yutar pressed this theme of greed and opportunism throughout the trial. In his closing address, he contended: 'It was tragic to think that the accused, who, between them, did not have the courage to commit in person one single act of sabotage, should nevertheless have incited their followers to acts of sabotage, guerrilla warfare, armed insurrection and open rebellion and ultimately civil war.'[32]

The defence's case

The approach adopted by the defence was made very clear at the outset in the way Nelson Mandela responded to the full charges: 'M'Lord, the government, not I, should be in the dock. I plead not guilty to all charges.'[33]

The strategy of the defence was not to deny responsibility for actions that they had indeed taken but rather to utilise every opportunity during the trial to explain their position and to put forward reasons for the political activity in which they had engaged. The trial was effectively a political forum: first, Yutar had presented the government's political programme, and now the accused were intent on exploiting the platform afforded by the trial to define and explain the nature of their political struggle.

Early on in the strategic discussions between the legal team and the accused, it was decided that Mandela would not give evidence as a witness but, rather, would address the court from the dock. In legal terms, this meant that any testimony he would provide by way of his address could not be challenged by the prosecution but it would have far less evidential weight in persuading the judge to bring in an acquittal.

Part of the defence strategy was to keep Yutar guessing as to the nature of the defence plan. That itself was not easy, as all consultations between the accused and the defence team had to take place in a hastily constructed room in the Pretoria prison in which the accused were held. Hilda Bernstein described the room as long and narrow, partitioned by a wooden counter down the centre and a row of bar stools on either side.[34] When the defence legal team first came into the room and found their clients seated on stools on one side of the counter, it was therefore as if they were consulting in something resembling an ice-cream parlour. Mandela captured this when, smiling politely, he said to his lawyers: 'What will it be today, gentlemen – chocolate or ice cream soda?'[35]

It was extremely difficult to consult in confidence because the room had been bugged, so that the recorded consultations could be analysed by Yutar and his legal team. This, of course, did have certain advantages. When the preparation for Mandela's evidence began, defence lawyers produced the voluminous record of the 1956 Treason Trial, where the state had failed to secure convictions of any of the 156 leaders of the Congress of the People, including Mandela. In essence, in that trial the state had sought to prove that the political programme of the Congress of the People, led by the ANC, being the Freedom Charter, was a call to revolution. The evidence led in that trial was clearly relevant to rebut the overall strategy of Yutar, being to portray the *Rivonia* accused as violent revolutionaries. The record of that trial ran to tens of thousands of pages. As a result, Yutar began to pore over these vast volumes as he worked on an anticipated cross-examination of Mandela. Of course, none of this record was ever used by the defence, but Yutar was not to know that until Mandela took the witness stand.

The defence team's turn to present their clients' case came on 23 April 1964. In his quiet style, Fischer outlined the case for the defence. In particular, he told the judge that the defence challenged the state's argument that the ANC was a tool of the Communist Party and that the objectives of the ANC were the same as those of the Communist Party. Fischer said that the defence would show that the leaders of MK and the ANC had decided to keep these two organisations entirely distinct, and that MK had never adopted the military plan known as Operation Mayibuye, which had been so central a plank of the state's case against all the accused.

Judge De Wet was visibly astonished by this opening statement and said almost disbelievingly: 'That will be denied?', to which Fischer replied:

> Yes, that will be denied. The evidence will show why it was hoped throughout that such a step could be avoided. The court will be asked to have regard to the motive, the character and the political background of the men in charge of Umkhonto we Sizwe and its operations; to have regard to the tradition of non-violence of the ANC; to the reasons which led these men to resort to sabotage in an attempt to achieve their political objectives, and why, in the light of these facts, they are to be believed when they say that Operation Mayibuye had not been adopted.[36]

When Fischer concluded his address, he informed the court that the defence case would begin with a statement from the dock by Nelson Mandela. Yutar, who had been preparing for weeks for the cross-examination of Mandela, was visibly shocked. In his best falsetto voice, he said: 'M'Lord, m'Lord, I think you should warn the accused that what he says in the dock has far less weight than if he submitted himself to cross-examination!' By now, Judge De Wet, who was notoriously short-tempered, had endured more than enough from Percy Yutar. Icily, he admonished the now almost hysterical lead counsel for the state: 'I think,

Mr Yutar, that counsel for the defence has sufficient experience to be able to advise their clients without your assistance.'[37]

Yutar's rather pathetic attempt at cajoling Mandela into being subjected to cross-examination having ended, Mandela rose slowly, a sheaf of papers in hand; he adjusted his reading glasses. Then, for hours, he explained to the court the political and intellectual background and development of his political ideas, his early commitment to nationalism and his conversion to non-racialism. He told the judge that it was wrong to suggest that the ANC had responded to the influence of foreigners and, particularly, communists: 'I have done whatever I did as an individual and as a leader of my people because of my experience in South Africa and my own proudly-felt African background, not because of what any outsider might have said.'[38]

Mandela's speech involved a direct challenge to the political authority of the government. He told the court: 'The government which uses force to maintain its rule teaches the oppressed to use force to oppose it … [Violence was adopted] not because we desired such a course, but solely because the government had left us with no other choice.'[39]

It is easy today, with the benefit of more than 50 years of hindsight, to gloss over the extraordinarily clear and direct challenge that Mandela laid down before the very heart of the South African political system, which had been fashioned over more than 300 years of racist rule. The press, the Security Branch agents who sat in court, Percy Yutar and his prosecution team, together with Judge De Wet, appointed as a Judge President by the National Party, all had to listen without interruption while Mandela contended that their fight was against 'real and not imaginary hardships', or, to use the language of the state, so-called hardships. 'Basically, my lord,' continued Mandela, 'we fight against two features which are the hallmarks of African life in South Africa, and which are entrenched by legislation which we seek to have repealed. These features are poverty and lack of human dignity, and we do not need Communists, or so-called "agitators" to teach us about these things.'[40]

Mandela then spoke of the long history of non-violent struggle that had been led by the ANC. He told the court: '[F]or a long time, the people had been talking of violence … and we, the leaders of the ANC, had nevertheless always prevailed upon them to avoid violence and to pursue peaceful methods. … [This] achieved nothing and … our followers were beginning to lose confidence in this policy.' He spoke of the violence perpetrated in 1957 on innocent women in Zeerust, who were ordered to carry passes, and the violence of the state-agent protests in Pondoland in 1960, when the government had attempted to introduce 'Bantu authorities' into those areas. He concluded: '[In 1961] I, and some colleagues, came to the conclusion that ... it would be unrealistic and wrong ... to continue preaching peace and non-violence at a time when the Government met our peaceful demands with force.'[41]

Mandela was coming to the end of his speech and to the part that had caused his lawyers grave concern. He wanted to end his exposition of his political ideology by saying: 'This was an ideal for which I am prepared to die.' His lawyers were concerned that this might provoke the judge to hang Mandela. He refused to leave these words out, but eventually agreed to insert the words 'if needs be' into the speech. He ended what Anthony Sampson has described as the most effective speech of Mandela's career,[42] with words that carried the central theme of the political struggle for the next 30 years, until the democratic Constitution of 1996 enshrined these commitments into law:

> During my lifetime, I have dedicated myself to this struggle of the African people. I have fought against White domination and I have fought against Black domination. I have cherished the ideal of a democratic and free society in which all persons live together in harmony and with equal opportunities. It is an ideal which I hope to live for, and to see realised. But my lord, if needs be, it is an ideal for which I am prepared to die.[43]

These words were uttered in a very quiet voice. When Mandela stopped speaking, silence descended upon the entire court. Even Judge De Wet appeared moved and, after what seemed an eternity, with an equally quiet voice, he turned to Bram Fischer and said, 'You may call your next witness.'

Nobel Laureate Nadine Gordimer has a different recollection of the speech:

> The address, after going through many changes, returned (I thought) to the simple verity of the second version, and read

much better than it was spoken: Mandela's delivery was very disappointing indeed, hesitant, parsonical (if there is such a word), boring. Only at the end did the man come through and when he had spoken that last sentence the strangest and most moving sound I have ever heard from human throats, came from the 'black' side of the court audience. It was short, sharp and terrible, something between a sigh and a groan.[44]

If Mandela's speech can be said to be the high point of the defence case, Gordimer was at least correct in her assessment of Walter Sisulu, whose performance she described as 'splendid … lucid and to the point'.[45] Sisulu, who was vigorously cross-examined by Yutar, gave a performance that was nothing short of remarkable. The contest was between a man of rudimentary formal education and one who had more tertiary qualifications than any other practising lawyer in the country at the time. Quietly but firmly, the short, bespectacled Sisulu asserted the very core of the morality of the ANC's political action, arguing that 'the African people like all oppressed people have got a moral right to revolt against oppression'.[46] As Kathrada said in his recollection of the trial: 'At the end of it all, Walter emerged from the witness box as cool, as calm and unruffled as when he entered it. Our lawyers and even the accused were amazed at his composure, his phenomenal memory and the masterly way in which he … acquitted himself.'[47]

One of the many mistakes Yutar made in court was to tackle directly the political issues underlying the trial. Normally, prosecutors would eschew such an approach and focus instead on the legal hurdles that need to be negotiated if the state is to be successful. But Yutar was determined to show the accused that their political ideology led only to violent crime. And, like many other white people, Yutar conflated academic qualifications with intelligence. This led him into tussles with Sisulu from which he emerged the loser.

While Sisulu was giving evidence, De Wet would reveal the dominant judicial mindset of the time. When Sisulu insisted that the 'masses' wanted the vote, the judge interrupted Yutar's cross-examination to ask Sisulu: 'Is that correct? You think they should have the vote, but how do you know that the ordinary Bantu about town wants the vote? … You only know that you think he ought to have it, but how do you know he wants it?' Sisulu exposed the judge's thinking with the reply: 'Well, I have not come across meetings where I have heard people saying, "No, we don't want the vote!" People always support the idea of the vote.'[48]

The judgment

The evidence was now at an end and both sides presented their arguments. At the end of arguments, the judge adjourned the case for three weeks to consider his verdict. The only true hope for the defence was that the judge had apparently accepted Fischer's argument that Operation Mayibuye had been nothing more than a proposed plan, and had not been accepted by the accused or the ANC, for that matter. Had that not been the case, a conviction would surely have led to death sentences for the architects of the plan, which called for mass production of explosives and an ambitious, widespread armed struggle.

On 11 June 1964, Judge De Wet returned to court to deliver his judgment. It took only a few minutes for him to read it out:

> I have very good reasons for the conclusions to which I have come. I don't propose to read these reasons. The verdict will be: Nelson Mandela is found guilty on all four counts; Walter Sisulu is found guilty on all four counts; Dennis Goldberg is found guilty on all four counts; Govan Mbeki is found guilty on all four counts; Ahmed Kathrada is found guilty on count two and not guilty on counts one, three and four. Lionel Bernstein is found not guilty. He will be discharged; Raymond Mhlaba is found guilty on all four counts; Andrew Mlangeni is found guilty on all four counts; Elias Motsoaledi is found guilty on all four counts. I do not propose to deal with the question of sentence today. My reasons will be made available in a statement.[49]

Mandela told his legal team that he, Sisulu and Mbeki had discussed with their colleagues the question of appealing against a possible death sentence, but had decided that it was politically inadvisable to do so. In other words, their trial would end once Judge De Wet had sentenced them.

Harold Hanson QC, a very senior member of the Johannesburg Bar, was then brought into the defence team to deal with the argument relating to sentence. Hanson was a large, ebullient man with a booming voice and a great talent for legal oratory. Chaskalson recalls Hanson as being a superb advocate, as good as anyone when it came to articulating legal argument in court.[50] It was considered prudent to employ a distinguished counsel, and one who was not known to be politically active. What is more, Fischer was under a great deal of stress at the end of this long trial of his comrades and friends. He regarded Hanson as a fine advocate with whom he was comfortable to leave the plea in mitigation. What was less known, however, was that Hanson had once been a member of the Communist Party.[51]

Hanson called one witness, the writer Alan Paton, best known for his novel *Cry the Beloved Country.* Paton was also the leader of the South African Liberal Party. Hanson asked Paton why he was testifying in this case – after all, it was a very brave move in the light of the hostility shown by the white authorities towards the accused and the vicious reaction that could be expected from government as a result of his testimony. Paton replied: 'Because I was asked to come. But primarily because, having been asked to come, I felt it was my duty to come here – a duty which I am glad to perform, because I love my country. And it seems to me, m'Lord with respect, that the exercise of clemency in this case is a thing which is very important for our future.'[52]

Paton went on to explain to the court how the failure of the peaceful political campaigns that had been pursued by the accused for decades had compelled them to the conclusion that there were only two alternatives left: to bow their heads and accept continued racist rule or to resist by force. Ominously, Judge De Wet interjected:

> There were many cases where people resisted and were convicted of high treason and executed. I have in mind the famous gunpowder plot in England. In the light of subsequent history, these people have legitimate grievances but they are not entitled to break the law by force. And what happens to people like that, historically, is that they get convicted of high treason and are condemned to death.[53]

It might have been expected of Percy Yutar to behave as prosecutors generally do in these cases – that is, to refrain from questioning Paton, who had appeared solely for the purpose of giving evidence in mitigation of sentence. The purpose of this evidence is just to provide the court with information and insight into the accused. It assists the court in balancing the interests of the accused with those of society when deciding on an appropriate sentence. Prosecutors generally allow this evidence to be presented without contest. Yutar was no ordinary prosecutor, however. He was running his own political trial.

He rose aggressively to cross-examine Paton, the introduction to his cross-examination setting the tone:

Yutar: Mr Paton, are you a communist?

Paton: No.

Yutar: Are you a fellow traveller?

Paton: I don't understand what a fellow traveller[54] is, but I understand your implication. No, I am not a fellow traveller.

Yutar: You are understanding my implications?

Paton: Correct.

Yutar: Do you share the aims and objects of the Communist Party?

Paton: Some of the aims I would share, such as the more equitable distribution of land and wealth, better economic opportunities.

Yutar: What don't you approve of in the Communist Party?

Paton: I disapprove entirely of their totalitarian methods which are adopted to bring about such changes.

Yutar: Do you disapprove of that?

Paton: Entirely.

Yutar continued to cross-examine Paton in great detail for reasons he had set out at the beginning: 'I propose to cross-examine this witness with your Lordship's leave. And I don't do so in order to aggravate the sentence, but in order to unmask this gentleman and make perfectly clear that his only reason for going into the witness box, in my submission, is to make political propaganda from the witness box.'[55]

The attorney for the defence, Joel Joffe, aptly described Yutar's cross-examination as 'a degrading exhibition … But the police at least enjoyed it, they tittered gleefully as this honest man, of undeniable courage, was smeared and demeaned by Yutar. Mr Justice De Wet, probably by reason of his own political prejudice, rather than of law, also appeared to be enjoying Paton's discomfiture.'[56]

The tension in the courtroom was almost tangible. The accused faced the prospect of the death penalty. At that point, only one man other than the judge knew for certain that this would not occur. He was Harold Hanson. Before he argued in mitigation of sentence, Hanson had gone to see De Wet. When he returned, he told Chaskalson, a member of the defence team: 'He is not going to impose the death sentence.' Chaskalson asked how he knew; Hanson replied: 'I asked the judge, who said: "Do not tell your clients but I am not going to impose the death penalty on them."'[57]

Obviously, neither the public gallery nor the accused could have known of De Wet's intention. But, as Chaskalson explained, there was no guarantee that the judge would not change his mind, so it was impossible for the defence team to tell their clients that there would be no death sentence. The possibility could not be ruled out for certain.

In court, Hanson gave an impassioned address about the need to recognise the political nature of the case. He reminded the judge of the struggles of Afrikaners earlier in the century. '[W]e in this country … understand well the struggle for national liberation. We understand its motivation, we understand it better than the people of any other land.'[58]

Unfortunately, but not unexpectedly, Hanson's plea fell on deaf judicial ears. In a soft voice, barely heard by the gallery, the judge began his decision and reasons for the sentence:

> I have heard a great deal during the course of this case about the grievances of the non-European population. The accused have told me, and their counsel have told me, that the accused, who are all leaders of the non-European population have been motivated entirely by a desire to ameliorate these grievances. I am by no means convinced that the motives of the accused were as altruistic as they wished the Court to believe. People who organise a revolution usually take over the Government, and personal ambition cannot be excluded as a motive.
>
> The function of this Court, as is the function of a Court in any country, is to enforce law and order, and to enforce the laws of the State within which it functions.

The crime of which the accused have been convicted, that is the main crime, the crime of conspiracy, is in essence one of high treason. The State has decided not to charge the crime in this form. Bearing this in mind, and giving the matter very serious consideration, I have decided not to impose the supreme penalty which in a case like this would usually be the proper penalty for the crime. But consistent with my duty, that is the only leniency which I can show.

The sentence in the case of all the accused will be one of life imprisonment.[59]

In his memoir, Kathrada captures the reaction of the accused:

He [Judge De Wet] spoke the crucial words 'life imprisonment' almost in a whisper, then hurried from court. A deep hush enveloped the courtroom, followed by an audible sigh of relief – not shock, as one would normally expect at the prospect of a life sentence but relief, because it was not a death sentence. We turned and smiled at the packed public gallery and Denis [Goldberg], I think, shouted: 'Life sentence!' The enormity and full implication of the sentence would sink in soon enough, but for that moment there was only jubilation that we were not going to be hanged.[60]

Conclusion

It is difficult to imagine how South Africa could have developed into a non-racial democracy 30 years later had Judge De Wet imposed the death sentence. He is long dead and there is no direct evidence as to what motivated him to impose sentences of life imprisonment, as opposed to the death penalty.

Later, in a rather distasteful attempt to reconstruct his image in the new South Africa, Yutar claimed he had saved the accused's lives by charging them with sabotage rather than high treason because, he said, 'his instinct was that the judge would not hang the accused for sabotage but only for treason'.[61] That reconstructed version of events is not supported by any available evidence. Kathrada, in an interview, justifiably poured scorn on Yutar's claim. In an interview in 1987 with Professor CH Albertyn, of Wits Law School, which fully justifies Kathrada's reaction, Yutar claimed that the difficulties encountered by the state in the earlier treason trial that ran between 1956 and 1961 were a significant factor in charging the accused with sabotage, which was easier to prove than treason.[62]

In an introduction to a right-wing journalistic account of the Rivonia trial,[63] Yutar argues that he consistently contended before the court that the accused had been guilty in 'a classic case of high treason'. However, he informed retired Judge HH de Villiers[64] that he had indicted the accused under the Sabotage Act, and not for high treason under the common law – this because of the treason trial, in which all the accused had been acquitted.

According to De Villiers, 'Yutar was concerned that because of the nature of the proof required by the common law, it was wiser to charge the accused under the Sabotage Act and not in terms of the common law of high treason.'[65]

George Bizos, at the time a junior counsel, who was a member of the defence team, took a different view. He has suggested that part of the reason for Judge De Wet's decision to eschew the death penalty was his own antipathy to capital punishment. Bizos remembers that De Wet had been deeply affected by a previous case in which he had sentenced an accused to death, only for the sentence to be commuted by the Governor General on advice from a state law advisor, who discovered that events after the trial had shown that a key witness had lied to the court.[66]

The fact that some judges, despite their fierce racism, were not in favour of the death penalty was known in South Africa and, hence, Bizos's explanation is very compelling. But there are other possible explanations. Nelson Mandela writes in his autobiography that the judge was not entirely immune from outside pressures, with foreign governments and institutions campaigning in favour of the accused.[67]

Of course, the judge would have been aware of the dominant white position. The National Party and its supporters were equally determined to see these key leaders of an organisation that they regarded as the greatest threat to continued white domination of the country removed permanently from society. Kathrada, however, was certain that intense international pressure, together with an internal political consideration, that by executing these leaders it would make martyrs of them, would have exerted significant influence on the judge. Bizos remembers a remark of Judge De Wet in which he told Fischer that the accused were receiving good press, a sure sign that the judge was aware of the overwhelming sympathy and support for the accused from the international community.[68]

For Judge De Wet, handing down a sentence of life imprisonment was the way in which he responded to these conflicting pressures. And this explanation finds some support in a book published shortly after the conclusion of the trial written by the same retired Appellate Division judge, Judge de Villiers, who was appointed by the National Party to the Appellate Division to deal specifically with the constitutional crisis documented in Chapter 3 of this book. Loyal to the white government, De Villiers attempted in his brief book to justify both the need for the trial and how it was conducted from a judicial point of view. Significantly, in the preface to his book, retired Judge President of the Natal Provincial Division, Francis Broome, wrote:

> Two recent overseas comments on the *Rivonia* trial indicate the need for a book like this. Both related to the sentence of imprisonment imposed by the presiding Judge instead of a sentence of death. One comment ascribed the Judge's leniency to government policy, the other to the pressure of public agitation. It is high time that the world realised the South African judiciary is independent and that its judges are not amenable to pressure from government, public or any other source.[69]

The manifest inaccuracy of the last sentence would seem to indicate the competing pressures that must have been felt by a judge whose default position was the maintenance of the then political system.

The verdict of even some of the conservative press was one of relief that the accused had not been hanged. *The Star*, for example, commented after the trial: 'They were foolhardy in the extreme, and might have had disastrous results for many besides themselves if it had not been nipped in the bud. They have reason to be thankful that it ended as it did and so have we all.'[70] Even the 'liberal' press supported the verdict. An editorial in the *Rand Daily Mail* argued that 'the sentences pronounced by Mr Justice De Wet in Pretoria yesterday at the conclusion of the Rivonia trial were both wise and just ... Would they have not been summarily shot ... [after a conviction for a similar crime] if this had been an Iron Curtain country??'[71]

These kinds of comments, however, also reflected the dominant white discourse, which Hendrik Verwoerd, the prime minister at the time, exploited to the full in a statement to Parliament and which won the enthusiastic endorsement of the opposition United Party. In his statement, he said:

> I want to state clearly and unequivocally that in this case we have not got to do with an opposition against the South African government's policy or the championship of the freedom and rights of people. We have to do with a Communist uprising which would have been brought about in South Africa ... should these Rivonia accused have succeeded, then a Communist-orientated government – whether white, black or mixed – would have been established.[72]

The South African government's few foreign friends appeared to adopt a view of pragmatic support for the sentence. Anthony Sampson relates that the British Ambassador to South Africa, Hugh Stephenson, informed the British Foreign Secretary, Rab Butler: 'We could be thankful that the judge did not give a death sentence because it means that a leader of the calibre of Nelson Mandela with his credentials enhanced by a term of imprisonment, should be available for the dialogue between black and white which must eventually take place in South Africa.'[73]

The evidence given by Paton and Stephenson's comments indicated that there were many outside the ANC camp who recognised presciently how important Mandela, Sisulu and the other leaders convicted in the Rivonia trial would be to a future South Africa. But, at the time, this was not how white-minority South Africa saw the picture. The prevailing attitude among the white population was well illustrated in an editorial that the *Sunday Times* ran:

> For the people of South Africa, the pervading lesson of Rivonia is that violence as a political weapon must be discarded once

and for all. Moral considerations apart, violence never stood a chance of success. Any reasonable assessment of the forces available leads to this conclusion. Meanwhile the damage done in the hardening of white attitudes is incalculable. The delicate mechanisms of human adjustment to change [have] been shaken loose, there are gears no longer in mesh.[74]

The judgment in the Rivonia trial was exploited by politicians to bolster attitudes against the ANC for more than two decades. This was best exemplified in PW Botha's so-called Rubicon speech in 1985, in which he said that there could be no negotiations with Mandela because he 'had planned violent insurrection, rebellion and the manufacture of a large number of bombs and grenades ... [and because] the crime of which Mandela had been convicted was in essence high treason punishable by death'.[75]

In her thesis on South African political trials, Professor Albertyn wrote that the Rivonia trial marked the end of a form of white-espoused liberalism. The trial had 'initiated a process of social amnesia, the beginning of the white memory of the ANC where the censures of violence and communism were merged into the public image of the ANC'.[76] Albertyn argues that the trial also 'marked the beginning of a process whereby whites failed to distinguish between violent and non-violent political action and all extra-parliamentary opposition was increasingly incorporated under the censure of violence. Together with this was a growing acceptance of the authoritarian methods against such opposition, as whites gave up liberal values of the rule of law and rights in favour of their own perceived interests and survival.'[77]

As white attitudes hardened, black political leaders in South Africa began to challenge, with growing intensity, the way in which their political struggle was censured as a violent, communist and criminal activity. Albert Luthuli, then leader of the ANC, said of the accused on the day they received their sentence:

They represent the highest morality and ethics in the South African legal struggle ... Their policies are in accordance with the deepest international principles of brotherhood and humanity: Without their leadership, brotherhood and humanity may be blasted out of existence in South Africa for long decades to come. They believe profoundly in justice and reason; when they are locked away, justice and reason will have departed from the South African scene.[78]

The immediate legal strategy employed by the defence in the Rivonia trial was to save the lives of their clients. That significant achievement was crucial to the future of the country. But *Rivonia* may also be viewed as a classic political trial, a contest about the censure of political activity that the state sought, with increasing desperation, to impose upon its legitimate political opponents. It took more than 30 years to remove this censure. After the Rivonia trial, South Africa experienced a speedy descent into a state of official lawlessness. The rule of law became honoured more in the breach than in the compliance. But 30 years after the completion of this key trial, constitutional democracy finally dawned in this country.

How legal values persisted over this period emerges in the chapters that follow. But before examining how certain legal values proved to be resilient during apartheid, it is necessary to remind ourselves that the concept of a political trial has not disappeared entirely from our contemporary horizon. During 2016, leading up to when he was fired in 2017, a relentless campaign was conducted against the then Minister of Finance, Pravin Gordhan. On 11 October 2016, with a great deal of fanfare, the otherwise somnambulant NDPP at the time, Shaun Abrahams, announced that he had issued summonses against Gordhan and two erstwhile senior members of SARS, Oupa Magashula and Ivan Pillay. Abrahams said that he was charging the three because they had committed fraud when SARS had paid R1.14 million into the Government Employees Pension Fund at the time of Pillay's early retirement.

This was clearly a political move designed to invoke criminal law to dislodge the sitting Minister of Finance, who was part of a group within the ANC that was resisting state capture by the Gupta family. Judiciously in the light of his subsequent conduct against Gordhan, EFF leader Julius Malema reacted immediately: 'All those who love our country and its constitution must occupy the streets of Pretoria in support of our democracy.'[79]

Abrahams, as it turned out, was forced to eat the humblest of legal pies when he withdrew these charges about three weeks later. It was clear that this decision had been prompted by widespread political protest – a united movement that recognised the political nature of Abrahams's attempt to wield the law against political opponents.

There are without a doubt huge differences between the Rivonia trial, which could have led to the deaths of Mandela and the other leaders of the ANC, and charges that have been pressed against Gordhan. But the point to take home from the more recent events is that attempts to exploit the law for political ends did not cease with the collapse of apartheid and the rise of democracy. They are still a possible risk that looms large on our political horizon.

5

THE CHALLENGE TO THE PASS LAWS: THE BEGINNING OF THE END

SELLERS: Can I see your ticket?

SEAGOON: I haven't got one.

SELLERS: You can't come up Blackpool Tower wi'out a ticket.

SEAGOON: Well, where can I buy one?

SELLERS: At the bottom.

SEAGOON: I'll go down and get one.

SELLERS: You can't go down wi'out a ticket.

SEAGOON: What am I supposed to do, jump off?

SELLERS: You can't jump off wi'out a ticket.

SEAGOON: (Megaphone) Oh hello folks. Trapped at the top of Blackpool Tower.

SELLERS: Wi'out a ticket.

... WITHOUT A TICKET. – From *The Goon Show: The Thing on the Mountain*, courtesy of the BBC

The border between tragedy and comedy is often porous. Peter Sellers and Harry Secombe captured the absurdity of the catch-22 logic of a bureaucrat confronting a citizen with ever-increasing obstacles in this scene from the 1950s BBC radio comedy, *The Goon Show*.

The system of South Africa's apartheid-era pass laws was based on a similar form of catch-22 logic but its purpose was egregious, arbitrary and cruel. Verwoerd and his predecessors, Hertzog, Smuts, Malan and

Strijdom, ran their own 'Goon Show' for the predominant benefit of an enthusiastic audience – a few million white South Africans – and to the incalculable human cost of a whole country. Theirs was a system of absurd logic that imposed unspeakable hardship on millions of South Africans.

For almost a half century, the lives of most of the South African population were stringently and brutally controlled by a complex web of legislation that formed the core of the apartheid structure. The system was built on four primary pieces of legislation that governed influx control; the denationalisation of millions of citizens who had 'Bantustan citizenship' conferred on them; an archipelago of labour bureaus designed to control the employment of black labour; and job reservation provisions that had the effect of excluding black people from being hired for specified kinds of occupations.[1] This system treated human beings as mere numbers, and hence stripped them of their identity and dignity. The treatment of the identities of black South Africans as irrelevant seems to have lived on beyond apartheid.

The irony of it all is that the major legal triumph over this web of inhumane laws is still known by the purported name of the plaintiff in the case, (Tom) 'Rikhoto', whose real name is Rikhotso.[2]

But before we look at this case, we must refer to the pass laws, and their legal intricacy and record of implementation.

Pass laws: The origins

The pass laws had a truly devastating effect on the rights of South African citizens. Between 1916 and 1984, something in the region of 1 770 000 black South Africans were arrested under a battery of pass laws and influx control regulations.[3] Most of them were prosecuted, the number of prosecutions during this period fluctuating from 89 to 1 482 each day. This intense level of criminalisation of a majority of our population took place in pursuit of the objective of racial segregation articulated by the Stallard Commission on Transvaal local government in the following terms: 'It should be a recognised principle of government that Natives – men, women and children – should only be permitted within municipal areas insofar and for so long as their presence is demanded by the wants of the white population and should depart therefrom when they cease to minister to the needs of the white man.'[4]

The National Party succeeded in developing an even more heartless form of influx control. A circular generated by the Secretary of Bantu Administration in 1967 captures the banality of this evil:[5]

It is accepted government policy that the Bantu are only temporarily resident in the European areas of the Republic, for so long as they offer their labour there. As soon as, for some reason, they become no longer fit for work or superfluous in the labour market, they are expected to return to their country of origin or the territory of the national unit where they fit in ethnically if they were not born or bred in the Homeland.[6]

Critical to the attainment of this objective was legislation that restricted permanent urban residence to those who had been born in a particular urban area and who had resided there since birth, and to those who had entered the urban area legally and resided there continuously for at least 15 years or who had worked for one employer for at least ten years. The spouse or child of a black man defined as a 'qualified person' was permitted to live permanently with him.

But segregation was not going to last forever. Enter Veli Komani.

In 1975 Veli Komani, a resident of Gugulethu, a township in Cape Town, launched an action for his wife, Nonceba Komani, to live with him in Gugulethu. With the benefit of the constitutional order that now prevails in South Africa, it seems almost unbelievable that, only about 40 years ago, a husband had to go to court to be allowed to live with his wife and, as we shall see, be advised that the case was by no stretch a 'winner'.

What Komani certainly would not have known was that his action would herald the beginning of the end of a central part of the apartheid system. Together with later legal action taken by Tom Rikhotso, who demanded permanent legal status as an urban resident, the lives of millions were about to change after decades of hopeless struggle against this brutal form of oppression.

Veli Komani had been employed by the same employer since 1960. By 1975 he was therefore entitled to reside permanently in the Cape Town area. He now claimed rights on behalf of his wife. When she came to Cape Town in 1974, Mrs Komani was given permission to stay with her husband for some 11 months. In April 1975, the authorities refused a further extension, contending that Komani lacked suitable accommodation for her in terms of the applicable regulations. In a nutshell, the authorities accepted that the law allowed a wife to stay with a husband who was qualified to reside permanently in an urban area, but only if she had permission, by way of a grant of a lodger's permit from the relevant housing authority. Obtaining this permit would prove impossible for Mrs Komani. After all, the applicable regulation was a masterpiece of legal mendacity: to obtain a permit, the applicant had to be lawfully employed. Without permission to be in the area, Nonceba Komani was hardly likely to obtain such employment, besides which the applicable section of the law gave her no such right, in the absence, of course, of the housing regulation.[7]

Mrs Komani was in the grip of the apartheid state's catch-22 – she could not gain employment without rights of residence, so she could not obtain a lodger's permit. Without a lodger's permit, she could not gain the right to live with her husband in the urban area of the Cape Peninsula.

Veli Komani went to the Cape Supreme Court in an attempt to break the deadlock. Curiously, he was represented by Advocate Charles Louw, a tenacious but conservative lawyer who, ironically, did much work for the police during this period. Komani's opponents were represented by a legal team that included the brilliant and highly eloquent Jeremy Gauntlett, later to become one of the leading human-rights advocates at the South African Bar.[8]

It took almost three and a half years for Komani to obtain a judgment, which upheld the refusal of the authorities to allow his wife to live with him. Judge Phillip Schock, a fine and hugely respected commercial lawyer, as eccentric as he was conservative, handed down the kind of judgment that characterised most apartheid jurisprudence – a rigid application of the text without consideration for the human implications of this interpretation, save when it adversely affected government interests. Hence, the judge held that, although the housing regulation effectively destroyed any right granted to Mrs Komani to live with her husband, it was nevertheless permissible for the government to insist that black women must comply with the relevant housing regulations.[9]

Komani was not prepared to give up the legal fight. But, after his attorney had filed an application for leave to appeal, the Legal Aid Board decided that Komani would receive no further funding for legal representation.

At this point, the Athlone Advice Office run by the Black Sash and the South African Institute of Race Relations,[10] which throughout this bleak and repressive period helped thousands of people whose lives were ruined by influx control, became involved in the Komani case. One of the stalwarts of the office, Noël Robb, sought to ensure the proper prosecution of Komani's appeal. Realising that the lack of funds might compromise the law firm that had acted so professionally and bravely for Komani in his application before the Cape Supreme Court, she wrote to Geoffrey Budlender, an attorney at the LRC.

It proved to be a stroke of genius. Budlender, then a junior attorney, had already acquired a national reputation as a human-rights activist. As a student, he had been an accomplished leader of the Students' Representative Council at UCT and, later, of the National Union of South African Students (NUSAS). In his capacity as head of the students' union, he had been on the receiving end of the then prime minister, John Vorster's, unique form of public abuse. Vorster had incorrectly informed the nation that Budlender was a failed medical student and smeared him as masquerading at the university as a student, while in reality, Vorster claimed, he was a political instigator. Only a leader of Vorster's ilk could have shown such interest in the academic record of a student leader.

Budlender's quiet and thoughtful manner disguises a remarkable firmness of principle and brave dedication to human-rights law. Robb's letter had therefore given Veli Komani access to the very best South African legal advice.

Both Budlender and Chaskalson, the director of the LRC, and one of the greatest advocates South Africa has ever produced, were concerned that earlier precedent might prove an insurmountable obstacle for the Komanis. In 1963 the Appellate Division, then on its way to a reactionary jurisprudential destination under Chief Justice LC Steyn, had decided that, to be ordinarily resident for the purposes of Section 10 of the Bantu (Urban Areas) Consolidation Act of 1945 ('the Act'), a litigant like Mrs Komani had to be lawfully resident, which, owing to her inability to obtain a lodger's permit, was not the case. Both men were understandably doubtful about the prospects of the Appeal Court changing its mind. There was, however, a legal option available to them: it was possible to argue that, since the 1963 case, the law had been changed and no longer required a dependant to obtain permission from the superintendent of the location before acquiring a right under the section. This change, it was hoped, might support the argument that ordinary residence did not mean lawful residence.

But consummate lawyers like Chaskalson and Budlender knew well that this line of attack was unlikely to succeed – a conclusion that proved accurate because the court had no compunction about dismissing this argument. Nonetheless, Chaskalson felt that the case may, at the very least, afford a long-term benefit, in that it would test the boundaries the court wished to maintain in policing this area of law.[11]

There was, however, a second argument that was to prove more decisive. Chaskalson had contended, in his heads of argument prepared in advance of oral argument and filed with the court long before the oral hearing, that the housing regulation was unreasonable. This law meant that women like Mrs Komani could never obtain residence rights as spouses, notwithstanding the wording of the section that allowed them to, because, even as a wife of a man 'who was qualified to reside in the urban areas', she could never obtain a lodger's permit. Without a lodger's permit, she could not be lawfully resident and hence she would have no right to live permanently with her husband. The *Goon Show* script had been cruelly applied throughout the country.

So, although a section of the Act appeared to give Mrs Komani the right to reside with her husband, a regulation (being a lower form of law) destroyed any possibility of the enjoyment of this right. Consequently, a husband and wife in the circumstances of the Komanis could never live as a family. Family life was thereby destroyed. The lawyers' legal attack was directed towards a result that was expressly authorised by the Act but subverted by a regulation, which, therefore, had to be contrary to public policy as represented by the Act of Parliament.

The case before the Appeal Court

The lawyers for Komani knew the formidable hurdles that awaited them in Bloemfontein. Nevertheless, they had some cause for optimism: the bench chosen to hear the case was favourable, with two of the judges being as liberal jurists as could be hoped for in a court in those days. Michael Corbett and Solly Miller were fair men, leaning towards the view that the common law still remained the basis of the legal system, rather than the racism of the apartheid legislation. Both were outstanding technical lawyers, respected by their more conservative colleagues. In addition, Chief Justice Frans Rumpff, a conservative lawyer, was reasonably fair. He had been one of the three judges in the treason trial of the late 1950s who had acquitted Mandela and the (initial) group of 155 co-accused in the main political trial of the ANC before *Rivonia*.

When the argument was heard by the court, the Chief Justice, a formidable, domineering man, leapt upon Chaskalson's argument that the housing regulation subverted the basic human rights of the Komanis. Chaskalson had contended that the Komanis were entitled to the basic human right of family life unless the law expressly negated that right. 'What human rights are you talking about?' was the Chief Justice's response. For him, the growing body of international human-rights law was of no consequence to a South African court.

The hostility to this line of argument was palpable. But, as Budlender later reflected, he had never seen a counsel so dramatically persuade a court during the course of oral argument. Chaskalson argued that, while South Africa did not include, at that stage, any of the international human-rights instruments in its legal system, the common law did recognise at root certain individual liberties and freedoms of the citizenry. And, gradually, Chaskalson began to get the court to accept his basic assumption: unless the law expressly removed a right, the citizen continued in his or her enjoyment of that right.[12]

Once that argument had been accepted, Chaskalson was able to press on. Now all five of the judges were listening intently to Chaskalson's distinctive, clipped delivery. The initial hostility from the bench was clearly on the wane. The key question for decision was, did a South African resident, even a black resident, enjoy residual rights to stay with his or her family, which could be taken away only by means of an express legal provision, or did such a person enjoy only the rights expressly conferred by law? This was a truly brilliant move by Chaskalson. He had shifted the debate away from a direct confrontation about human rights to the role of legislation in constituting the source of rights. A basic premise of the common law supported the idea of circumscribed government – that is, a citizen was permitted to act as he or she wished, save where an express law prevented or limited this freedom.

For the judges of the Appeal Court to dismiss this argument, they would have needed to reject it for the legal system as a whole. It had always proved conceptually problematic to use the common law to divide people on the basis of race – hence the need for a battery of racist legislation to subvert the idea of an individual legal subject as enshrined in the common law, which did not expressly recognise race. The Chief Justice must have known that he could not write a judgment of so dramatically racist a nature that the residue of common law applied only to white people. How would this be done and what would its effect be upon the limited but remaining legitimacy of the court?

Once the premise was accepted that rights needed legislative removal rather than the converse, the lawyers for the government were in trouble. Gerrit van Schalkwyk, a bald, cherubic man of few but measured words, who led Jeremy Gauntlett for the government, and who himself would later do sterling work as an advocate on behalf of the LRC, tried to argue that Section 10 of the Act conferred no right upon the Komanis to remain in a prescribed urban area, but rather gave those who qualified in terms of the Act immunity from prosecution. And the so-called 'right to remain' did not confer any right to reside in a particular place in a prescribed area, argued Van Schalkwyk. In short, the housing regulation could limit the already limited right, which meant that anyone who qualified under Section 10 could not be prosecuted for being in the area, and nothing more.

The court probed this argument with ever-increasing irritation because Van Schalkwyk had no answer to the basic premise developed by Chaskalson, being the absence of the provision of a law that prevented people like Komani from remaining in the urban area of Cape Town. Had the law not recognised some rights based upon birth and continuous residence? Van Schalkwyk provided no response and an exasperated Rumpff rounded on him with the terrifying force that he could and did bring to the bench. Budlender recalls thinking that the tide had truly changed when one of the judges, CP Joubert – a crusty, self-styled Roman Law purist who delivered a number of judgments that contained more Latin than English, and who had appeared to be asleep for much of the argument – suddenly asked Van Schalkwyk a question and, when no proper answer was forthcoming, rolled his eyes and returned to his position of repose.[13]

Chaskalson recalls that he was not truly confident when he completed his initial argument and that his opponents certainly considered that they were on the winning side by the first tea adjournment. They were laughing almost aloud at the difficulties Chaskalson had encountered from the bench. But Chaskalson also remembers Rumpff's irritation when Van Schalkwyk could not satisfactorily answer the bench's question and, by the end, he said, 'Rumpff had destroyed him'. At one point, Rumpff suggested to Van Schalkwyk that he felt the court was being 'led up the garden path'. Chaskalson expressed the hope that he was not leading the court up the garden path; Rumpff was at pains to assure him that that was not the case. At one point, Rumpff allowed himself a moment of existential humour. Chaskalson had contended that Komani and others in his position could not be regarded as temporary sojourners, to which Rumpff drily replied: 'We are all temporary sojourners, Mr Chaskalson.'

But the lawyers for Komani could not be too confident. Towards the end of oral argument, Judge Miller asked whether the argument on behalf of Komani did not ultimately turn on those legal rights negated by the regulations. When Chaskalson replied in the affirmative, but said it was unnecessary for the court to go so far to find for Komani, the court asked for further written argument on the point of whether the housing regulation was invalid because it appeared to negate the rights to reside in the urban areas granted in terms of the Act. This gave the team more time to refine this argument.

The judgment

When the judgment was finally delivered on 19 August 1980, the Chief Justice reviewed the history of residence in the urban areas by black South Africans from before the South African Union of 1910, concluding that there had been no absolute right to reside conferred by any legislation. But, focusing on a section of the Act that was not directly relevant to the case, he destroyed the argument that the government lawyers had used to justify the validity of the housing regulation.

The Chief Justice's reasoning went thus: Section 10(1)(*a*) of the Act provided a black person who was born and had lived continuously in an urban area the right to remain there on a permanent basis. Nothing in the Act nor in the history leading up to the Act indicated that this category of person had not acquired a right to so remain, yet if such a person did not possess the correct housing permit, he would have no such right. The right recognised by the Act could not be removed by a ministerial regulation, which, of course, is a lower form of law. Therefore, if the regulation sought to destroy a right, it was unlawful, not only in respect of Section 10(1)*(a)* of this Act, but generally. Consequently, the housing regulation had to be set aside.

With this decision, the regulation would no longer apply to Mrs Komani. She could now claim the right she enjoyed in terms of Section 10(1)*(c)*, as the wife of a man who was entitled to reside in the urban area.

Aftermath

It was a dramatic victory, a triumph for the lawyering of Chaskalson, Kentridge and Budlender, and for Komani's tenacity. It was also a remarkable and rather isolated example of the Appeal Court holding in favour of the liberty of the individual against the government. For almost two decades, the court had shown little enthusiasm for curbing the excesses of the government by asserting the importance of the common law in the process of interpreting ambiguous legislation. But, in this case, prodded by superb advocacy, the court revealed a surprising willingness to explore the contours of ambiguous legal language to the benefit of a lonely, individual citizen whose case, however, affected the status of millions of black South Africans.

Small wonder that the doyenne of the Black Sash, Sheena Duncan, proclaimed: 'This is the most exciting news we've ever had … The judgment actually makes nonsense of the whole house permit system. It means that no permits will be required except by persons who are not entitled to residence under the law.'[14]

Komani also had reason to feel optimistic. When he returned to the Langa pass office to ensure implementation of his court victory on behalf of his wife, he overheard a pass-law official saying, 'Now that k***** has won, it's all over – no one will need a pass.'[15]

But Piet Koornhof, the minister responsible for the pass laws, and a man who, early in his career, had written a doctorate at Oxford that showed the futility of much of the very apartheid enterprise that he spent the balance of his political career enforcing, had other ideas. He said that the court had ruled on only one case and in one province, and that it would be 'completely wrong to infer that a large-scale influx of wives and children' would now be possible, 'as each case [would] have to be judged on the facts concerned'.[16]

This time, as was usually the case when repression was to be increased, Koornhof was as good as his word. Within two weeks, the relevant government department (named the Department of Co-operation and Development – inappropriately, in light of the government's lack of commitment to integrity and honesty) issued a circular stating that, while a lodger's permit was not required for legal residence, nevertheless the Act was not affected by the court's ruling and hence people who did not qualify to be in an urban area had to obtain permission to remain.

So began a long and difficult process of forcing the government department to enforce the judgment. As Rick Abel documents in his superb study of this and other cases that characterised the apartheid period: 'Each case *was* different but only in the arbitrariness of official action. Applicants were asked to provide irrelevant documentation … told to obtain employment, or rejected because they were too old or had inadequate housing.'[17]

For almost five years after the *Komani* judgment had been handed down, government bureaucrats sought to subvert its effect. But, as they doggedly fought against the demands for humanity, another blow was to be struck against the pass laws.

The *Rikhoto* decision

One of the main obstacles facing black South Africans who wanted to obtain permanent residential rights in the urban areas was Section 10(1)(b) of the Act. As mentioned, this right was contingent on whether an applicant could show that he had worked for one employer for ten years on a continuous basis or had lawfully resided in the urban area for at least 15 continuous years. The problem was that permission was granted to work on a basis of 11 months each year, thereby forcing the employee to vacate the area during his 'leave' This way, the authorities hoped that a person could not prove to have continuously worked or resided for ten or 15 years.

It all hinged on how 'continuous' was interpreted; did it mean without any break, not even for a period of annual leave? If this question could be answered in favour of the applicant, the very structure of the pass laws would be significantly undermined. After all, it would then mean that a growing class of urban workers would gain permanent residence rights and, with the application of the *Komani* judgment, could then live with their wives and dependants. Some form of right to family life might then be restored.

The LRC in general and attorney Charles Nupen in particular were desperate to litigate in this area. Nupen was an ex-president of NUSAS, a person deeply committed to social and political change, and later to become the leading mediator of industrial and other disputes in the country. A victory would seriously torpedo the very structure of influx control.

Chaskalson urged caution and patience until the 'right' case could be found.[18] Finally, that case came along, and Nupen got his wish. Mehlolo Tom Rikhotso had worked for one employer from 1970 to 1981 when he came into contact with the Black Sash advice office. Like millions of black workers, Rikhotso had to take leave each year, and would return to his village in the homeland of Gazankulu. He was refused the right to permanent residence under Section 10(1)*(b)*, but could not understand why. The government's response was, unsurprisingly, predictable: Rikhotso was not entitled to permanent rights of residence because his yearly visits to Gazankulu broke the requirement of continuity. Each time he returned to Gazankulu, he was obliged, in terms of the regulations, to enter into a fresh 11-month contract with his employer. Hence he was deemed not to have worked for a continuous ten-year period.

The matter was taken up by the LRC. The case reached Nupen from the Hoek Street Law Clinic by way of a referral from Paul Kennedy, then a law student and later a silk at the Johannesburg Bar, who was approached by Rikhotso in March 1983. According to Kennedy's note to Nupen, Rikhotso told him that he had a lodger's permit, and that his name was not on the housing waiting list. Rikhotso expressed his concern that he would be removed from the house where he lodged, his lodger's permit would be cancelled and he would be forced to live in a hostel.[19]

The LRC brought an application for an order declaring that Rikhotso was entitled to remain in the urban area of Germiston. This time, the case was heard by a judge of the Supreme Court, Bryan O'Donovan, who was sympathetic to the problems faced by Rikhotso. Judge O'Donovan followed an earlier ruling by that great liberal judge of the 1950s, Oliver Schreiner (whom we met in Chapter 3) – namely that it was absurd to conclude that a person could never occasionally depart from where they lived in an urban area to gain rights under the section: the system of annual contracts was but a government requirement that did not detract from the conclusion that the intention of Rikhotso and his employer was that he be continuously employed. Arrangements for the renewal of his contract were concluded before he went on paid leave, the annual break was granted as leave and his absences from work for 'other causes' had occurred on isolated occasions only. 'The question is one of substance, not form.'[20] Judge O'Donovan thus concluded that Rikhotso had acquired rights to reside permanently in the urban area.

This was a major victory against a key part of the influx-control system. Koornhof's reaction, however, was that the record and judgment would now require careful study, an announcement that subdued the enthusiasm. As the *Sowetan* noted, 'People will continue being bulldozed out of their jobs, out of the towns and sometimes out of their minds. As usual, this will be done by petty officials who simply disregard or, even worse, are ignorant of such breakthroughs or changes to the law.'[21]

When the government decided to appeal Judge O'Donovan's decision, Rikhotso was more confident than most observers that he would win before the Appellate Division. He said that the highest court would uphold Judge O'Donovan because 'Johannesburg is just a town … And the Transvaal, it was a territory. But all the laws it was from Bloemfontein.' As Stephen Ellmann, who conducted an interview with Rikhotso, noted, for him, Bloemfontein was the site of the Appeal Court and therefore a kind of judicial 'head office' for the whole country. Its remove from the daily reality of ordinary South Africans made it appear a fairer tribunal than the lower courts, where they experienced racism on a daily basis.[22]

Almost two years after his initial victory, Rikhotso's case was argued on appeal. In the period before the appeal, as had been the case with *Komani*, the authorities did everything their obstructive minds could think of to subvert this hard-won right. In particular, they were determined to place as many obstacles as they could in the way of Rikhotso, whose simple intention was to ensure that his entire family could live with him. After all, if the victories in *Komani* and *Rikhoto* were taken together, that was the indicated result: the wife and dependent children of a person who had rights like Rikhotso could live with him in the prescribed urban area.

Within this uncertain context, Chaskalson and Karel Tipp, another of the supremely talented and principled lawyers off the NUSAS leadership production line, proceeded to Bloemfontein to defend the judgment of Judge O'Donovan. This time, their opponent was a more typical government lawyer, Renier Kruger, who had much experience in taking cases for government in order to ward off any gains occasionally made by the human-rights bar.

Kruger was a truly unimaginative lawyer and it showed in his argument. In essence, he repeated the arguments that had been rejected by Judge O'Donovan. Kruger pressed the point that Rikhotso had entered into a new contract each year and that no contract with a black employee could be concluded for longer than 11 months without official approval. Without this approval, as was the case here, there was no continuous employment, as required by the Act, he said. The judges had clearly been persuaded by Chaskalson's argument that the substance of the arrangement between employer and Komani was the key to the case. Kruger had no response to the question: 'Yes, we know the form of the arrangement as required by the regulations but what did the two contracting parties intend?'

This time, the court did not require further argument. The judgment was delivered by Judge Hennie van Heerden, an austere man but much respected for his intellect and who, unlike some Appeal Court judges at that time, was never accused of being influenced by the party's line. He decided the case purely on the point to which Kruger had no answer: Rikhotso may have not been able to show that he had entered into one unbroken contract for ten years but he had been employed continuously for that period by one employer. The breaks between each contract were treated by both sides as Rikhotso's right to leave. He therefore enjoyed, at the very least, a legitimate expectation that, at the end of the leave period, he would continue to be employed even if he was required, for regulatory purposes, to complete another formal contract. For this reason, he had met the requirements of the section and hence had acquired a right to reside in the urban area.

An interesting aspect of this judgment was a comment made by Judge Van Heerden to the effect that the sets of regulations, together with the battery of legislation that governed the system of influx control, were complex even for lawyers to navigate, and therefore posed a huge obstacle to those whose task it was to administer the system – and even more so to the millions whose lives were directly controlled by the system.

Yet, reading the judgment all these years later, one cannot but be struck by the irresistible simplicity of the reasoning employed by Judge Van Heerden on behalf of the unanimous court. So, the question immediately arises, why did it take so long for this argument to be raised and the result to be achieved? We shall return to some tentative explanation shortly.

The consequences

It was a major victory, not only for Rikhotso,[23] but also potentially for millions of black South Africans. As Chaskalson wrote after the judgment: 'The *Rikhoto* judgment enables migrants to take advantage of the provisions of s 10(1)*(b)* of the Urban Areas Act and by so doing to upgrade their employment opportunities and to create for themselves opportunities for a family life in the towns – a right which the administration boards and labour officers sought to deny them.'[24]

Chaskalson had expressed the consequences in his typically studied and measured fashion; the *Sowetan* captured the implication more bluntly: the judgment was a 'blow at a cornerstone of Government influx policies',[25] although the article warned that legislation would no doubt be introduced to reverse the court decision. The government appeared to understand the implications perfectly – Abel cites an unnamed government source as saying, 'Those rulings defeat the purpose of government policy. Contract workers were not meant to get Section 10 rights.'[26]

That implication was clearly considered by government. Along with its own supporters, others were also apprehensive about the consequences of the decision. The *Natal Mercury* typified the position of the 'moderate white': 'From the human aspect, the ruling should be a matter for rejoicing, since it opens the way for tens of thousands of black migrant workers to live permanently in the cities with their families. But it would be foolish not to temper one's gratification over the human benefits with some sober reflection on the practical consequences.'[27]

Similarly, the Afrikaans press warned of a black flood of new migrants into the urban areas. And Koornhof was under pressure from the breakaway Conservative Party, which advocated a 'pure' application of apartheid policy, as well as from his own supporters and part of the press. In Parliament, the Conservative Party's Frank le Roux attacked Koornhof for delaying government's response to the court's judgment: '[T]he Appeal Court in Bloemfontein passed the same judgment, almost word for word, as the Witwatersrand judgment. The question is what the Hon. Minister has done since September 1981 to counter the possibility of an unfavourable Appeal Court judgment.'[28]

The racist discourse that so overwhelmed white South Africans at the time[29] contributed to the fear of a massive migration of black citizens into the hitherto almost exclusively white urban areas. Koornhof was alive to this 'problem' and hence assured members of the Conservative Party that the government had no intention of 'throwing in the towel' as regards influx control.[30]

But outside pressure and increasing concern from industrialised capital created a measure of ambivalence, or at least caution, on the part of the government. Illustrative of industrial capitalism's approach was a statement made by Fred Ferreira of Ford South Africa:

> [C]ampaigns to pull tens of millions of rand out of companies doing business with South Africa could gather steam if the Government took this step [to override the *Rikhoto* judgment] … The Americans are certain to view an attempt to circumvent the judgment as an attempt to muzzle the courts … For this and many other reasons, I believe the Government would do well to implement the judgment.[31]

Koornhof, however, was not only aware of these pressures, but he also appeared to recognise the importance of the courts. He addressed Parliament in a rather different tone from how his predecessors, Louw, Sauer and Dönges, reacted to the *Harris* judgments: 'Whatever the judgment of the Appeal Court may be, a responsible Government will surely consider, in the first place what it can learn from that judgment and, in the second place be filled with pride that the courts in this country have built up a very good name world-wide … All we have to do is ensure that this finding is strictly adhered to.'[32]

This strategy of trying to use the legitimacy of the courts to its best political advantage in those relatively few defeats that the government suffered in the courts – without allowing them to circumscribe the government's racist vision – can be sensed in a further announcement from Koornhof:

> The government is obviously bound by the judgment. ... it is my duty to avoid at all costs that unrealistic expectations of instant accommodation in urban areas are not created in the minds of migrant workers and their families ... They have not acquired legal rights to demand a house in black urban residential areas ... squatting will not be permitted under any circumstances.[33]

Shortly after this announcement, Koornhof showed his hand. He introduced an amendment to the law, not to set aside the *Rikhoto* judgment but designed rather to make it more difficult for black citizens to employ the judgments of *Rikhoto* and *Komani* together and radically broaden the scope of the applicants' rights to reside in an urban area. The amendment revealed the plan: it applied solely to the wives and children of people qualified in terms of Section 10(1)*(b)*, the scope of which had been significantly extended by the courts in *Rikhoto*. The amendment stated that those wives and children who did not ordinarily reside with the qualified husband/father before 26 August 1983, the date of the commencement of the amendment, could reside with their husbands or fathers only in a house for which he had leasehold rights, a site or residential permit. A lodger's permit no longer applied. With the chronic shortage of suitable housing, such housing rights as leasehold or a residential permit were as rare as the proverbial hens' teeth.

The government's idea was clear. It could now claim that influx control by way of pass laws was no more and that it had abided by the two adverse court decisions. All it had done was to ensure that urbanisation took place in an 'orderly way' by ensuring that all who came to reside in the cities possessed 'proper' accommodation. In truth, government knew full well that the shortage of accommodation could effect exactly the same kind of injustice as the pass laws had.

The government had one final throw of the litigation dice. The issue around the meaning of 'continuous residence' for the purpose of qualifying for residence in an urban area had not been decisively determined in *Rikhoto*. Thus a certain Mr Mthiya was compelled to go to court because, in his case, he had taken more than a month's leave on three separate occasions. Like Rikhotso, he had worked for the same employer for more than ten years and had taken leave at the end of each separate contract term. But, on three occasions, the absence from work had been for periods of four, six and eight months. The Black Affairs Administration Board leapt at this. Unlike the case with Rikhotso, whose break from employment had always been for one month, the length of these three breaks was clear proof, argued the board, that there had not been an uninterrupted period of employment.

Again, Arthur Chaskalson went off to Bloemfontein, this time with Gauntlett as his junior counsel. The bench was hardly a liberal one, although the judgment was delivered by one of the finest private lawyers to grace the court during this period, Judge Erns Jansen. The judge appeared to have no problem with the argument that the lengthy absences were not decisive, in that there was an agreement that Mthiya would return to work on completion of personal business.[34] The court eschewed the formalism that had dominated its work for more than two decades to decide the case on the substance of an undefined agreement. Small wonder that one commentator observed that this decision 'put an end to the make-believe Alice in Wonderland attitude of regarding blacks who in fact live in urban areas on a permanent basis as not, in law, being there at all.'[35]

Assessment

Two key questions need to be answered. In the first place, why did a court which, since the Coloured vote cases, had been on a steady retreat from any liberal high-water mark of the early 1950s, hand down these two judgments? And, secondly, can it not be said, in the light of the bureaucratic insurrection against the *Komani* order in particular, and the subsequent amendment to the law after the delivery of the *Rikhoto* judgment, that the enthusiasm for these legal victories needs to be tempered?

The answers to these questions may well be interrelated. The entire saga of litigation from *Komani* to *Rikhoto* needs to be located in the very endemic contradictions of apartheid policy as racist rule entered its last decade. It has been correctly noted that the context of the *Komani* and *Rikhoto* cases did not resemble the earlier form of popular resistance to the pass laws that had characterised the Defiance Campaign of the 1950s. There were no strikes and no burning of passes, and, the Soweto uprisings notwithstanding, the government might have thought, with some justification, that repression had paid off, as it had in the 1960s and the consequent Rivonia trial.[36]

Komani and Rikhotso were single litigants, with no support other than that of the Black Sash and the LRC. There was no political campaign that powered the litigation,[37] and perhaps that makes the outcome even more surprising. The two judgments were not automatically enforced by the apartheid bureaucrats – it took many years for the *Komani* judgment, in particular, to be recognised and, even then, the government amended the law. But, eventually, the litigants and many others did obtain relief.[38] Later, the government resisted sweeping these judgments into irrelevance by passing laws to set them aside in their entirety, as had often been the case when the government suffered a rare defeat in court.

It is easy, with the benefit of decades of democratic hindsight, to question the importance of this litigation. But when these cases were launched, apartheid – its contradictions and the political effects of Soweto notwithstanding – was very much alive. Few would have predicted then that, within little more than a decade, the game would be up for the racist men and women who had governed with such confidence and for so long. These legal successes were therefore no small victories. They exposed the contradictions in the regulatory system of influx control and forced change, which, in turn, was to create conditions that, at least in part, gave rise to the growth in political resistance leading to the beginning of the process of capitulation in 1990.

That leads to the second question and the linkage already mentioned. When Koornhof, with his irritatingly mendacious enthusiasm, announced in 1980 that 'we can be, and are, well on the way to achieving in my country equality for all people before the law and equal chances and opportunities',[39] he was acknowledging that the policy pertaining to measures such as influx control had run its course.

In August 1978, the government-appointed commission of Dr PJ Riekert reported on its investigation into the problem of pass laws and the labour needs of the country.[40] The main tenet of the commission's proposals was that the approach to influx control should be changed from control of mere presence in an area to far tighter control (if that were possible) of accommodation in urban areas, as well as employment. This would eventually lead to a division between a core of permanent urban workers housed with their families and a reservoir of peripheral workers in the rural areas, where redundant, retired and sick urban workers would be sent when incapable of providing work or superfluous to the needs of capital.[41]

This cruel and cynical move came with its own contradictions. Once the numbers who were permanent residents grew significantly, many of whom were unionised workers, the potential for political activism became easier. Indeed, within a few years, political resistance, led by the United Democratic Front, had begun to change the very foundations of apartheid rule.[42]

Perhaps it stretches the story too far to argue that the victories in the Appeal Court led to the breakdown of the pass laws, but they did expose contradictions in the system, upped the cost of government's attempt at legitimacy if the judgments were expressly reversed and made it more difficult to fashion an effective control scheme.

But what about the Appeal Court and the results brought about in these judgments? The judgments in both *Komani* and *Rikhoto* read as relatively formalistic, technical approaches to the law. There is nothing in the judgments given by Judge Rumpff in *Komani* or Judge Van Heerden in *Rikhoto* that indicate any judicial disapproval of the system they were called upon to analyse. Abel notes that 'the courts took no cognizance of moral, economic, or political factors, resting their decisions exclusively on the narrowly legalistic ground that the regulations were *ultra vires* or misinterpreted'.[43]

That they approached the cases in this fashion is not surprising, however. Judges in South Africa, particularly during the dark years of apartheid, rarely articulated any normative premise upon which they based their judgments. But, as already discussed, the courts in these cases knew about the influx-control system and its consequences. In *Komani*, Chaskalson had framed the case in his address as concerning an egregious abuse of human rights.

The arguments raised went to the heart of the apartheid system, a point argued forcibly by government counsel. So the judges who, as a collective bench, had done very little to temper legislative or even executive excesses and who, through the results of these cases, fashioned a precedent that, beforehand, most legal commentators would have thought impossible to achieve, must be taken to have appreciated the consequences of their judgments.

So why would they have suddenly chosen to act in this fashion? Perhaps it may disappoint readers, but this book does not – nor do the authors consider that they can – advance one single, comprehensive reason for this process of adjudication. Some indications for an explanation are, however, possible. Arguably, no two influx-control cases had ever previously been litigated with the precision displayed by the legal teams in *Komani* and *Rikhoto*, nor had the Appeal Court ever been confronted in these kinds of cases with the quality of advocacy presented by Arthur Chaskalson.[44] Most cases are not won on advocacy alone, but, in rare cases, it does remain a powerful tool.

One must also remember that the policy instrument of the pass laws was, by then, no longer considered an essential mechanism for government to deal with what it perceived to be the problems of urbanisation. As discussed above, by the time these cases came to court, Riekert had already produced his report about the need to reconsider aspects of policy. For example, Riekert noted: 'The Commission is further satisfied that, although it will be possible … to apply influx control more effectively than at present, much of the bitterness and frustration caused by it can be eliminated.'[45] In similar fashion, Dr PJ van der Merwe, Director General of the Department of Manpower, said in 1979: 'It is hardly necessary to stress that the quality of life within black communities needs to be improved very substantially and very rapidly, in the interests of political and economic stability, the support for the free enterprise system by blacks, and economic growth and development.'[46]

The political and economic climate within which these cases were contested meant that the judges no longer operated in the age of racist certainty that had existed throughout the 1960s and until the Soweto uprisings of 1976. It is naive to suggest that a judiciary is impervious to the existing public discourse, even in the case of those who lived in Bloemfontein in the late 1970s, where, without internet access or email, and with only the local newspapers and the SABC, they were largely closeted from opposing thought.

In summary, a case was compellingly presented and argued. It raised troubling questions of a kind to which the political wisdom of the dominant party could not supply any easy answers. Part of the ruling class advocated significant changes to the very policy system that was being discussed in court. The cases could be disposed of on relatively narrow, technical legal grounds. This may not be a comprehensive explanation for these legal decisions, but all these considerations played a role in the eventual outcome.

Conclusion

Within slightly more than a decade of the Komani case being launched, South Africa had changed forever. Hence it is tempting, in the light of the subsequent dramatic developments, to reduce the importance of the litigation that was triggered when Veli Komani decided that the law should help him unite his family under one roof in the urban area where he lived and worked.

But, as has been illustrated in this chapter, these decisions hastened the end of a system that had cruelly governed the lives of black South Africans for almost a century. It made the task of the government more complex in its desire to revamp these legal controls, with its later changes creating more favourable grounds for political resistance.

Perhaps of equal importance, cases such as *Komani* and *Rikhoto*, thanks to the tenacious principles of the litigants, and the commitment, dedication and forensic brilliance of their lawyers, preserved more than a scintilla of the rule of law and therefore its potential importance for democracy. That preservation was to prove important in the manner in which the country became a constitutional democracy during the following decade.

The Komani and Rikhoto cases are not mere historical curiosities. Whenever government seeks to ram through policy that is irrational, notwithstanding public protest, litigation can, as it did in *Komani* and *Rikhoto*, significantly alter components of government policy that would otherwise lead to political or economic disaster.

Take, for example, the government's determination to implement a nuclear power scheme during the Zuma presidency. For a number of years, the President had championed the commissioning of as many as eight nuclear reactors, which would generate 9 600 megawatts of energy.

Considerable debate took place as to whether government could afford to implement such a large-scale nuclear scheme. However, the government ignored protests to the contrary, even from its own finance minister. In 2013 the Minister of Energy determined that South Africa would need 9.6 gigawatts of nuclear power and that it would be procured by the Department of Energy. A similar determination was made on 8 December 2016. On 20 September 2014, Zuma signed a document approving a Russian governmental agreement in relation to a strategic nuclear partnership, authorising the minister to sign the agreement, which was done the following day. On 22 September 2014, the Department of Energy and Russia's atomic energy agency (Rosatom) released identical press statements confirming a joint understanding of what had been agreed by the two governments and advising that the Russian Federation and the South African government had signed an international agreement to cooperate in respect of nuclear energy, and to install capacity of up to 9.6 gigawatts. Similar agreements were also then entered into with China and France in late 2014.

The government was impervious to political opposition to its ill-considered move. Earthlife Africa and the Southern African Faith Communities' Environment Institute, two non-governmental organisations, therefore approached the court challenging the decision. On 26 April 2017, Judge Lee Bozalek, with the concurrence of Judge Elizabeth Baartman, set aside the two determinations issued by the Minister of Energy that had laid the basis for the nuclear procurement deal. The court also said that the nuclear agreement signed between the South African and the Russian governments was unconstitutional and unlawful. In essence, this finding was based on the principle that the nature of the agreements concluded, in terms of Section 231(2) of the Constitution, required the approval of both Houses of Parliament. This had not happened and, accordingly, the agreements stood to be set aside for want of legality. Furthermore, the two determinations that had been made by the minister had, in the view of the court, far-reaching consequences for the country.

A rational and fair decision-making process was required from the National Energy Regulator of South Africa (NERSA), the recommendations of which would need to concur with the minister's proposed determination to prevent a fresh review. This judgment meant that

NERSA would have to adopt a procedurally fair process, giving affected persons the opportunity to submit their views and present relevant facts and evidence.

On what were clear procedural grounds, the court threw a massive spanner in the works of Zuma's nuclear deal. For, unlikely as it may now appear under the leadership of Ramaphosa, if government should ever seek to introduce a nuclear programme, it will have to ensure that NERSA conducts public hearings, and consider carefully the evidence provided. This will doubtless make it extremely difficult for government to provide justifiable reasons why 9.6 gigawatts of nuclear energy are required in South Africa, given the energy consumption and financial constraints of the country. A further review looms if government disregards the evidence.

In a similar way to what happened in *Komani* and *Rikhoto*, policy that could have had devastating financial and environmental consequences for South Africa was stopped by legal action, making it extremely difficult for government to resurrect the policy. The legal techniques might have been developed under the stress of apartheid but they are equally relevant when a democratically elected government decides to go rogue.[47]

6

EXPOSING DETENTION WITHOUT TRIAL

'The National Party is prepared to accept responsibility for the policies that it adopted and for the actions taken by its office bearers in the implementation of those policies. It is, however, not prepared to accept responsibility for the criminal actions of a handful of operatives of the security forces of which the Party was not aware and which it never would have condoned.'[1]

– FW DE KLERK

At the beginning of the second state of emergency, which was declared on 12 June 1986,[2] the *Weekly Mail* (now the *Mail & Guardian*) published a photograph prominently on its front page depicting a column of policemen armed with sjamboks and firearms, walking in formation down one of the main streets of Johannesburg. The caption read: 'The country is now in their hands.'[3]

This terrifying depiction of police power graphically captured the implications of the state of emergency. The police were the law, yet above and beyond the law. In reality, though, the creation of unaccountable police power had begun much earlier. Between 1960 and 1990, 80 000 South Africans were detained by the police without the benefit of a trial. During these three decades, South Africa had a parallel system of incarceration. Common-law criminals, including murderers and rapists, were imprisoned after a conviction by a competent court. Although many were arrested and then detained before the start of their trial, each had the opportunity to approach a court for bail. Violent criminals were entitled to legal representation, although, in many cases, the inexperienced lawyers who were appointed to defend these murderers and rapists in terms of a *pro deo* system should have been mandated to carry health warnings for their clients, such was their lack of preparation for dealing with complex trials. But, nevertheless, the trial took place in an open court and a conviction occurred after the presiding judicial officer had delivered a judgment setting out his or her reasons for both the conviction and the sentence. Once convicted, an accused had the right to lodge an appeal against the conviction and sentence.

In stark contrast, those 80 000 detainees were incarcerated at the whim of a police officer. Courts had only narrow powers to review these decisions, but even those powers were rarely exercised. All too often, courts committed jurisprudential suicide by limiting even the slim supervisory review powers that they held under the ordinary rules of common law. Detainees did not have the benefit of legal representatives who could argue that they had been detained illegally. The system allowed the police to incarcerate political opponents of the government. It is not surprising, therefore, that of the 80 000 who were detained, 80 per cent were released without any charge brought against them. Only 4 per cent of detainees were ever convicted of any crime.[4]

Mac Maharaj has provided a graphic description of his mistreatment in detention:

I was escorted to his office and told to strip naked. Told to put my penis on his desk. Then he took a policeman's baton and started to stroke it, without ever taking his eyes off me, and then he raised the baton and brought it whacking down on my penis. After that he paused; he threw questions at me, then left me in agony. When he saw my agony subsiding, he made me stand against that desk and put my penis there again. But this time he did not hit it immediately. He picked up his baton, raised it, and waited for the expectation of pain to capture me before he hit. And then a step further. When my penis was on the table and his baton was raised, he moved his arm, little jerking movements in slight flickers as though it was going to come smashing down, but it didn't. He watched me flinch; I cringed with the pain that was as real as if his baton had struck. And so it went on, a slight movement of his arm as if to strike, but no strike, driving me to a point where I was almost begging him to do it, to get it over with. But he could see that coming too.[5]

Maharaj's experience was not an isolated exception. Torture was systematically used against detainees. The TRC heard that about 22 000 detainees had been tortured and physically assaulted during their period of detention; some 73 detainees died while in detention.[6] For a long period, (white) South Africans were in denial about this parallel system of 'law', which was designed to crush legitimate political opposition to the apartheid regime. Many newspaper reports published research undertaken by various academics to inform the public of the nature and extent of police brutality.

It took a courageous young district surgeon to force the country to confront the reality of this systematic process of political repression. This chapter is about the story of that doctor and the legal team who helped her expose the reality behind detention without trial. The sheer intensity of the system employed for almost 30 years is itself powerful proof against FW de Klerk's defence to the TRC that torture and death were the work of just a few psychopaths who abused the criminal-justice system.

The first steps

Gilbert Marcus is a respected senior counsel. During his career, he has won many victories that have advanced the cause of human rights in South Africa. But, in this case, it was a cameo role played by Marcus that began a process of litigation that culminated in the exposure of some of the most notorious police practices employed in apartheid South Africa.

In 1985 Marcus received a telephone call from a friend, Kathy Orr. She told him that her sister, Wendy, a district surgeon in Port Elizabeth, was in urgent need of legal advice about a matter of great public importance. Marcus intuited the problems that Wendy Orr might be facing as a district surgeon. He knew immediately whom she should consult and referred her to Halton Cheadle. Cheadle, then in his mid-30s, had built a reputation as a leading labour-law attorney in South Africa.

As a result of his working with a number of hugely talented and coura-geous lawyers, including Clive Thompson, Fink Haysom, John Brand, Martin Brassey and Raymond Zondo, carefully planned litigation had ensured that a body of progressive labour law was under construction, which would help the independent trade-union movement create an industrial democracy in the midst of a racist autocracy.

Cheadle is one of the few lateral thinkers in the South African legal community. This gift, together with his great charm and prodigious energy, ensured that he had the ability to launch a series of significant legal challenges against crucial 'legal' components of the apartheid state. But few, if any, of his cases could have been as daring as the one that was to follow his meeting with Dr Orr. It brought into the public glare the very brutality that the government used to impose its undemocratic will upon any political opposition. To fully grasp the magnitude of this legally unfettered system of control, it is necessary to take a brief historical tour through its development.

The legal context of detention without trial

After World War II, the South African legal system became the subject of great international controversy, not only as a result of its race laws, but also because of its security legislation. Indeed, it was not the racist nature of the South African legal system but its repressive security laws that first prompted the UN Security Council to order mandatory sanctions against the member state when it directly imposed an arms embargo on South Africa.[7] This decision followed the death in detention of a great South African political leader, Stephen Bantu Biko, and a consequent security crackdown in 1977 in which 18 organisations and three newspapers were banned, 47 political leaders detained and a number of citizens subjected to various forms of restriction. Biko became the 45th person to die while being held by the police in detention.

Detention without trial had begun much earlier, however. In 1963, Section 17 of the General Law Amendment Act of 1963, commonly known as the '90-day clause', was introduced into the South African legal system. This provision authorised any commissioned police officer to arrest and detain in custody for up to 90 days any person whom the officer suspected of having committed or being about to commit certain offences, or being in possession of certain information. The detainee could then be held until the Commissioner of the South African Police had formed an opinion on whether he or she had satisfactorily answered all questions put during interrogation.

No one, save for a magistrate, had the right to visit the detainee or right of access to the detainee without the permission of the Minister of Justice or a commissioned police officer. The detainee was effectively cut off from the outside world – he or she had no right to consult a lawyer, or see family or friends.

Wide powers had been granted by Parliament to the executive to curb all forms of political opposition with the passing of the Suppression of Communism Act in 1950. But, even by these early 'standards' of unfettered executive contest, the 90-day clause introduced an entirely new dispensation. In a paper published in 1966, professors Tony Mathews and RCL Albino wrote:

> When Parliament introduced the 90-day clause, it brought something entirely alien into our legal system. The clause is foreign both to the spirit and traditions of South African law and to the Western ideas of freedom and government which we inherited, but which we have not treasured much in recent years. The origin of solitary confinement as a means of obtaining information and evidence is in itself an explanation of the alien taint it has in countries that know something of Western tradition.[8]

The cancer spread rapidly through the legal body, and the courts appeared to encounter legal or moral problem with these laws. In 1963 Albie Sachs (later to become a judge of the Constitutional Court, now retired), was detained under the 90-day clause. He brought an application to court to permit him and other detainees the same rights as prisoners awaiting trial, including the right to exercise and access to reading and writing materials. The Cape Supreme Court found in favour of Sachs. On appeal to the Appellate Division, Judge Ogilvie Thompson, in upholding the legality of detention without trial and the conditions in which detainees were held, determined that the purpose of detention without trial was to induce the detainee to speak. He therefore reasoned that a detainee like Sachs could not be considered the same as a prisoner awaiting trial. In any event, asked the judge, where would the boundary regarding a detainee's rights be drawn? He sarcastically wrote: 'In the present case we are concerned with reading matter and writing materials; but is a detainee who in happier days habitually enjoyed champagne and cigars entitled as of right to continue to enjoy them during his detention?'[9]

The court, presided over by Chief Justice Lucas Steyn, whom we encountered earlier in this book, and of which Ogilvie Thompson was a key member, had, once again, served the government well. The judiciary was complicit in the erosion of rights, in that it willingly, with a few notable exceptions, placed no legal barriers in the way of such unfettered police power. Increasingly, detainees were left to the (non-existent) mercy of the police. Judge Ogilvie Thompson got his reward: he became Chief Justice after Lucas Steyn's retirement in 1971.

By 1967, the 90-day detention period had been extended to one of indefinite detention without trial.[10] The Terrorism Act was the ultimate authoritarian tool. This Act's key provision was section 6, which empowered any officer above the rank of lieutenant colonel to order, without warrant, the arrest and detention for interrogation of any person who he believed had committed or intended to commit the offence of terrorism. The central phrase was 'offence of terrorism': the police powers of detention flowed from a belief that a detainee had committed, or was about to commit, an act of terrorism.

The definition of 'terrorism' was so wide that Tony Mathews suggested that 'without exaggeration, the crime is so broad that there is hardly a person who had not at some time committed it. With the enactment of this crime we have arrived at the position that the authorities, if they are determined, can bring home a charge of terrorism against anyone who is *persona non grata* with them.'[11]

Mathews illustrated the breadth of the definition of terrorism with the example of a senior police officer who had the power to arrest and detain, on an indefinite basis, the leader of the white opposition, De Villiers Graaff, because he had caused a traffic jam while moving from one side of the road to the other to sell a cake to a party supporter during the party's fundraising cake sale (hardly a terrorist act).

It was no exaggeration to say that the police were legally placed beyond any form of control or public accountability. Writer, artist and activist Breyten Breytenbach captured their enormous power when he wrote: 'There's nothing, there's … no power anywhere in the world that has any say over them. They can keep you for ever. They can put heavy hands on you. They can break you down. They may even go red in the face and really let rip.'[12]

As noted, the TRC received more than 22 000 statements from victims who alleged that they had been tortured by members of the security forces.[13] Infuriating as it is to now reflect on it, much of this would have been known to the white electorate, who chose to vote the National Party into power for five decades. Yet, if white South Africa was engulfed in a state of moral paralysis during the 1970s and 1980s, Dr Wendy Orr was about to prescribe an antidote to this condition, providing the means by which the conditions in detention could be exposed in the courts.

People could have found out if they cared

Today, it is difficult to find any defender of the system, as is evident from FW De Klerk's remarks cited at the start of this chapter. Yet, as noted, there was information readily available about these practices from the media and in academic research, most of it ignored. But courts held a measure of legitimacy – once accepted by a judge, allegations of torture were converted suddenly into a 'public truth'. The following is a short summary of the evidence that was available to the public, although, before the *Wendy Orr* case, it had little effect in shaping public reaction.

The TRC made reference to the study released by a group of doctors who documented that, between September 1987 and March 1990, 94 per cent of a sample of detainees had claimed either physical or mental abuse.[14] The study found that the beating of detainees was common practice and that half of those alleging physical abuse still showed evidence of the abuse on physical examination. An assessment of their psychological status found that 48 per cent of those detainees were psychologically dysfunctional.

It was consistently alleged over a 20-year period that detainees were subjected to forms of torture that included suffocation, including a wet bag secured over the head, forced electric shock, sexual torture and other manners of physical assault, as well as psychological torture and prolonged periods of solitary confinement.

The TRC concludes, in the clinical style that characterises much of its report: 'It is accepted now that detention without trial allowed for the abuse of those held in custody, that torture and maltreatment were widespread and that whilst officials of the former state were aware of what was happening, they did nothing about it.'[15]

As was evident from the early detention cases of the 1960s, the fact that this monstrous machine could be perpetuated was aided in considerable measure by the judiciary. As the TRC report continues:

> More distressing is the fact that many judges and magistrates continued to accept the testimony of detainees, despite the fact that most of them knew that the testimony had been obtained under interrogation and torture whilst in detention. In this way, the judiciary and the magistracy indirectly sanctioned this practice and, together with the leadership of the former apartheid state, must be held accountable for its action.[16]

In 1985 Don Foster, a professor in the Department of Psychology at UCT, published a report on the treatment of a large sample of detainees, in which he found that the vast majority had been subjected to the kind of torture techniques subsequently identified by the TRC. A vigorous publicity campaign was launched against this study, particularly in the pages of *Die Burger* and the *Cape Times*, by a number of academics, mainly from the University of Stellenbosch, who claimed that the report was unscientific and should not be trusted.

Professors Herman Crause, Diko van Zyl and Jacob van der Westhuizen kept up a barrage of pseudo-academic abuse in the press, claiming that the study was 'unacceptable science', in that, they argued, there was no control group (presumably, of detainees who were given champagne and cigars, as opposed to the wet bag), the detainees in the sample remained anonymous and the conclusions were not tested with the police before publication of the report.[17] In short, their critique was politics masquerading as science.

Retired Judge President of the Cape Supreme Court Judge Helm van Zyl joined the attack. For him, Foster's study provided ammunition to the country's communist enemies. He demanded to know the identity of all the detainees interviewed. He insisted that the courts offered all detainees protection.[18] We can only presume that the judge would have been happy to have the identity of all the detainees exposed to the police, so that they could be detained again, and with the courts completely ineffective in the supervision of police power.

Dr André Schulman, a medical doctor who at the time was a regular correspondent to newspapers, writing in defence of detention without trial, provided further support in numerous letters penned to the *Cape Times*. In one, he wrote:

> The effect of a 2.4 cm high front page headline announcing that the police subjected 83 percent of detainees to torture is to give stimulation and justification to those who want to commit real murder and torture on members of the police force and other 'collaborators' and to make the public less inclined to condemn them for these acts.

> Whether it is the scientific logic or the newspaper reporting which is at fault, a similarly prominent and emotive retraction is urgently needed.[19]

Brigadier Odendaal, a former Divisional Commissioner of Police, offered a quasi-official view:

> I have often been puzzled by some criminologists, because those I know haven't even seen the inside of a police cell, not to mention the slightest experience as to what goes on in the front lines of the battle against crime. In comparison, some of my men at Woodstock and other police stations can list a man's previous convictions just by looking into his face.[20]

White South Africans may have had their doubts about the nature of police conduct but the majority kept these to themselves. And the deaths continued. In the notorious John Vorster Square Police Station, the first death of a detainee took place in 1971. Ahmed Timol died while in police custody. The police claimed that he had jumped from a window on the 10th floor of the building while being interrogated (more of this case later in the chapter). Similar 'non-explanations' were provided for other deaths in detention in John Vorster Square. On 20 January 1977, Elmon Malele died. Police claimed that he had 'suddenly fallen down', hitting his head on a table, which caused a fatal brain injury. The following month, Matthews Mojo Mabelane died. This time, the police said the death had been caused by an attempt to escape: before they could react, Mabelane was already 'halfway' through an open window. On 5 February 1987, trade unionist Dr Neil Aggett was found hanging in his cell after 70 days of detention.

As resistance to apartheid increased, so did the numbers of people who were detained without trial. In 1985, some 2 436 people were detained in terms of section 29 of the Internal Security Act (the revamped version of section 6 of the Terrorism Act). According to the Minister of Law and Order, a total of 7 996 were detained from 21 July 1985 to 7 March 1986 in terms of regulations that had been promulgated under the Public Safety Act – that is, emergency regulations that had been passed during the mounting political resistance to apartheid rule in the second half of the 1980s.[21]

Wendy Orr: Preparing the case

When the young Wendy Orr met Cheadle on 3 September 1985, she had recently arrived in Port Elizabeth to work in the district surgeon's office after having completed her medical studies at UCT.

When Cheadle received the call from Marcus, he was also in Port Elizabeth, working in his capacity as a labour lawyer on behalf of the trade-union movement. He had travelled there to deal with cases to be brought by trade unions before the local industrial court. It was probably because of his well-known role as a prominent labour lawyer for the trade-union movement that the security police in Port Elizabeth did not consider that there was anything untoward about his presence. They probably presumed he was in the city to represent workers in an industrial dispute. Hence, their only interest would have been to obtain information about the proposed labour litigation. Had they known that this was but a side show, they would surely have increased their surveillance.

Orr's knowledge of police brutality was itself a reflection of South Africa's 'legal' system – where lawless police activity existed side by side with intricate administrative regulations. In keeping with South Africa's bureaucratic adherence to laws and regulations, there was a prison regulation that required each prisoner be examined by a doctor on admission, transfer and release. Prisoners who complained after they had been admitted or transferred had to be examined by a district surgeon, who was then obliged to record the complaint. If a prisoner complained of having been assaulted, the doctor was required to fill out a medical report and to complete progress reports on a prisoner's injury form. In August 1985, Orr had examined an average of 20 new emergency detainees each day. All these cases were subject to these prison regulations. On some days, she examined more than 200 detainees in a morning. It had become clear to her that, in the majority of cases where detainees complained that they had been assaulted, they presented symptoms consistent with their complaints.

As a medical student, Orr had not been politically active. Yet the ethical dilemmas confronting a medical professional working at the heart of this apartheid state-of-emergency machine troubled her greatly and she was now desperate to consult a reliable lawyer.

At their first meeting, she told Cheadle the entire story of her experience examining detainees. He realised that, for the first time, reliable evidence could be placed before a court to prove the extent of police brutality that was occurring as part of a system designed to maintain apartheid control.

Orr's medical reports had the potential to develop into a massive case. But, sensibly, Cheadle advised caution: if Orr wrote an affidavit documenting her observations, not only would she lose her job, but she would also be subjected to a great deal of pressure and harassment by the state. Her life would change dramatically and, in fact, would probably be endangered.

She asked for time to consider her position and, a week later, she contacted Cheadle again. She had decided that she was prepared to be party to litigation, a decision that had been taken with a great measure of anxiety and after careful consultation with her family and Marcus.

A big problem with litigation of this nature concerns the procurement of evidence. How can an allegation of torture against the police be proved? Normally, the case would turn on the word of the detainee against the official voice of the police. And a detainee would invariably be seen as an unreliable witness because, so the argument goes, the very fact he is a detainee makes him subversive and therefore keen to bring the police into disrepute.

In a case where the applicant seeks an order that will prevent the continuation of conduct that is alleged to be unlawful, litigation takes the form of an application, as opposed to a trial. The court is provided with sworn statements, or affidavits, made by the contesting parties. Only in exceptional circumstances does a court have the benefit of oral evidence given by witnesses. To have a district surgeon depose to an affidavit was a major advantage for Cheadle and his legal team. But obstacles remained. True, Orr could depose to an affidavit, but without documentary evidence to support her assertions, the state could deny these allegations, which, if true to the form of the courts at that time, might be enough to stave off any of the relief sought on behalf of harmed detainees.

The state argument would no doubt be the usual one: Orr was yet another tool in the hands of the communist-inspired onslaught against the South African government. There was no independent proof to support the wild allegations of a young and easily influenced district surgeon, no concrete evidence, and hence no relief from the courts. That had been the gist of the state's legal mantra and, for a long time, it had proved to be crushingly effective.

However, the Cheadle team then met with an amazing piece of luck. Orr's direct superior was Dr Ivor Lang, the assistant district surgeon for the Port Elizabeth area. Lang had built up a reputation as a doctor who appeared to act as a front for the security police, rather than as a medical practitioner who should have been primarily concerned with the welfare of his patients, rigorously adhering to the ethical responsibility of the medical profession. For example, in September 1977, Lang had examined Steve Biko on a number of occasions. He had disregarded the savage beatings and the serious injuries sustained by Biko. Even though there were medical tests showing blood in the cerebrospinal fluid, Lang issued a certificate in which he stated: 'I found no evidence of any abnormality or pathology on the patient.'[22]

Dr Lang's grossly unethical behaviour notwithstanding, the South African Medical and Dental Council exonerated him of unprofessional conduct, even in the face of massive protests organised by the medical faculties of the universities of Cape Town and the Witwatersrand. The pressure brought by some of these principled doctors finally bore fruit. In January 1984, the Supreme Court ordered the Medical and Dental

Council to reopen its inquiry into the conduct of the doctors who had examined Biko before his death. In July 1985, the court found Lang's superior, Dr Benjamin Tucker – who had authorised the police to transport Biko 470 kilometres in the back of a Land Rover, when he was suffering from serious injury – guilty of improper and disgraceful conduct. Biko had died shortly afterwards. Tucker was suspended for three months. (The council's appalling inability to grasp the sheer magnitude of Tucker's culpability meant that it suspended the three months' penalty for two years, knowing full well that Tucker was about to retire.)

Lang was found guilty of improper conduct, and was given a caution and a reprimand. But he was not about to take any further chances with his career when it came to the kinds of police brutality that had caused Biko's death. To cover himself, Lang now asked for every medical history card of each detainee to be copied. He instructed Orr to do this, which afforded her an unexpected opportunity to make two copies of 300 medical cards – one for Lang and another for her attorney, Cheadle.

The forensic advantage of this piece of luck can be seen in Orr's affidavit in support of the application that was to be brought before the court. The applicants sought an order preventing the police from assaulting or otherwise mishandling detainees. The dry legalese employed in Orr's affidavit to justify the order proved more damning than any emotive condemnation of the police and prison authorities, or of Dr Lang and the medical authorities responsible for detainees' health and welfare. The affidavit was truly a case of facts speaking for themselves. Orr said the following of the medical authority:

> On 5 September 1985, I was present when Dr Lang phoned his superior, Dr Krynauw. He is the regional director of the department of National Health in the Eastern Cape. Dr Lang informed Dr Krynauw that there were many detainees at St Albans who complained of police assault and asked him what he should do in this regard. After he had spoken to Dr Krynauw, Dr Lang told me that Dr Krynauw had said that all we should do was to make copies of all yellow cards of the detainees who had complained of assault and to keep copies in case any of the detainees should institute civil action against the department

of health. It seemed that Dr Krynauw was not at all concerned with the wellbeing of the detainees and that his only concern was to protect the department of health in the case of trouble.[23]

Cheadle's team now had the material to substantiate the allegations that were to be made by Orr. Confronted with this independent evidence, the state would encounter great difficulty contesting the allegations, although, as we shall see, the photocopies were not about to be put to immediate use.

Preparing the affidavits of the applicants (a number of ex-detainees), and particularly Orr's affidavit, proved to be a hazardous task. By now, the security police may well have been aware of Cheadle's presence. There was one alarming incident. A number of lawyers and their secretarial support had assembled to work on the application. Port Elizabeth is a small town and it is not easy to blend anonymously into the surroundings; hence the anxiety of the legal team. One evening, as they were having dinner at their hotel, one of the members of the team went to her room, to find papers and other possessions strewn over the floor. Their anxiety was that the security police had obtained some evidence of the impending application. Much to the relief of the team, however, it turned out that all the security police had taken were papers pertaining to the labour-law litigation that had brought Cheadle to Port Elizabeth in the first place.

After this initial scare, the police did not reappear – that is, until the night before the case was to be heard in court. Counsel for the applicants, Wim Trengove SC, recalls that a police armoured vehicle (a Casspir) had been parked that night outside the hotel occupied by the legal team. The occupants of the vehicle did not attempt to enter the hotel.[24]

Cheadle had had great foresight when he briefed Trengove, today widely regarded as South Africa's finest barrister, for this case. During this turbulent political period of the mid-1980s, Trengove had begun to build what would become a formidable reputation. Cheadle had first heard of Trengove earlier and briefed him in the Kannemeyer Commission, which had dealt with the massacre of members of the community in the Port Elizabeth/Uitenhage area. At that hearing, Trengove had also met Orr, Cheadle and others, like Haysom, who had all witnessed his forensic skills.

Trengove had proved to be a devastating cross-examiner of the police witnesses. Haysom, who later became Mandela's legal counsel, loves to tell the story of Trengove in action at the Kannemeyer Commission. A police officer had testified at some length, articulating the usual denial of police illegality. At about 12.40, the examination by the police lawyers ended. Judge Kannemeyer asked Trengove whether it would now be appropriate to take the lunch adjournment. Trengove insisted that the commission continue until one o'clock and that he be given the opportunity to begin his cross-examination. Within those 20 minutes, Trengove, with his staccato questioning, had reduced the police officer to a lying wreck. As Haysom came out of the court, he overheard the words of a police brigadier phoning headquarters to report on the morning's developments: *'Ons is nou in groot kak'* (now we are in deep shit).

With the affidavits prepared, the lawyers could now confidently launch an application to the Supreme Court. An application is made by way of a notice of motion accompanied by supporting affidavits and documentary evidence. A notice of motion sets out the relief the applicants seek in a case of this kind. In this case, an interim interdict was sought, in which the police were to be restrained from assaulting or threatening to assault a number of people who were listed in the documentation, any other person who was detained in terms of the emergency regulations and any person who would be detained in future in terms of the emergency regulations in the districts of Port Elizabeth and Uitenhage.

The legal team acted with shrewd insight when they chose not to accompany Orr's initial affidavit with any of the medical evidence in their possession. This was to avert the risk of triggering an investigation into how the copies of the medical records had been acquired by the legal team. The affidavit simply documented her experience as a district surgeon. It made no mention of the supporting medical records and files that were nevertheless in the possession of the legal team.

However, all Orr's allegations were sourced in the files that she had copied. Although Cheadle was understandably reluctant to employ this evidence for fear of exposing Orr to the very treatment that was the subject of the application, her affidavit itself told an astonishing and detailed story of police brutality, incorporating material that was captured in the medical records.

In some 50 pages, she described the experiences of numerous detainees who had suffered at the hands of their police interrogators. The following passages provide a flavour of the content of her affidavit:

A recent and rather bizarre case that comes to mind is that of Sicelo Gqobona, whom I examined at St Albans Prison on 18 September 1985. He was brought to the front of the queue of the sick parade that day because I was told the police were in a hurry to take him to the Louis Le Grange Police Station for interrogation that day. He complained of an upset stomach. He said that his stomach was upset because he had drunk petrol a week before. When I checked his record, I noticed that he had been in detention at the time. I asked him why he had drunk petrol and where he had obtained it seeing that he was in detention ... He said that he was being interrogated by the security police at the Louis Le Grange Police Station. In the course of his interrogation, I believe it was on Thursday 12 September 1985, they had forced him to drink petrol. He also said that they assaulted him, striking him in the face, and had trodden on his chest when he lay on the floor. By the time I examined him, his lips were very swollen and he had small lacerations on the inside of his mouth.[25]

Each case described in the affidavit takes the reader a step closer to the essence of police brutality. Of another case, Orr writes:

Of those detainees [whom] I examined on 16 August 1985, one case particularly comes to mind. He was a young man whose name I was subsequently able to trace in the drug register as Mbulelo Joseph Sogoti. He had weals from his shoulders to his buttocks. There were so many weals that I could not count them. They were superimposed upon each other. His wounds were fresh and he was in great pain. He was brought in to me in a wheelchair. He could not speak but his friends who brought him told me that he had been assaulted by the police. I prescribed bed rest and an intra-muscular injection of Pethilorfan (a very potent pain killer) and anti-inflammatory drugs. Whenever it is prescribed, it has to be recorded in a drug register kept at the hospital. It was by that entry that I was able to trace this man's name.

This case had a rather disturbing sequel. When I first examined the detainees, I specified that I required to see [Sogoti] again to review his case a few days later. He was, however, never brought to me again. I recently searched for a yellow [medical] card but found that it was missing. I then checked the prison register to see if I could find out what had happened to him. According to the prison register, he had not yet been discharged from prison. I asked to see him, but when his name was repeatedly called out there was no answer.[26]

Later in her affidavit, Orr makes mention of the yellow medical cards that she had extracted and copied:

[They] relate to the period from 22 July to 16 September 1985. There are 286 of them. As I explained above, they are obviously incomplete and there must have been more complaints than those. But even … at 286, the number of complaints is astronomical compared with the frequency of complaints of assault ordinarily received in prison. For instance, a few days ago I gathered approximately 200 newly admitted ordinary prisoners (prisoners not being held under the emergency regulations). Of those prisoners, only one had a complaint of assault. That proportion is typical of my experience in prison.[27]

When the police read this affidavit, they would, of course, not have known that each allegation was supported by documentation, particularly medical cards that had been copied by Orr.

As explained, the evidence placed before the court in this kind of case takes the form of an affidavit by the applicant, together with other supporting affidavits. The respondents (the police in this case) then have an opportunity to answer the allegations by way of their own affidavit (known as the answering affidavit). The purpose of the answering affidavit is to ensure that the respondents rebut the key allegations made by the applicant, in such a way that the court is faced with such contested evidence that it cannot justify granting any legal relief sought by the applicant. A person mandated to depose to the answering affidavit is required to state why the key allegations of the applicant have no basis either in fact or, arguably, in law.

Brigadier Schnetler, who deposed to the answering affidavit on behalf of the South African Police, might have thought that, without any objective evidence, Orr's allegations, together with confirmatory affidavits of detainees, would be dismissed by the court as nothing more than bold, unsubstantiated allegations. The line taken by Schnetler was to argue that the version of conditions of detention contained in the affidavits deposed to by Orr and other applicants was based on hearsay, and not on direct evidence, or that such a version could not be substantiated by any documentary evidence. But the details of the individual cases set out in Orr's affidavit forced Schnetler to refer to the very medical records that he believed would debunk Orr's claims of torture, but which, unbeknown to him, were already in the possession of Orr's lawyers.

This played straight into Cheadle's hands by giving him the opportunity to take advantage of a rule of court procedure whereby a party can demand copies of documents referred to by the opposition in their answering affidavit. In short, this rule means that, when Schnetler referred to medical records he alleged would illustrate that Wendy Orr was not telling the truth, the applicants could then request copies of those records so as to test the truth of the respondent's denial.

After reading Orr's affidavit, together with that of Brigadier Schnetler, the court was obliged to decide whether the rights of the various detainees, on all the evidence, were in jeopardy and, therefore, whether there was justification for an order preventing the police from committing assault or torture. Orr's evidence was obviously sufficient to persuade the court that there was a factual basis for the allegations that had been made. The court then granted what is referred to as an interim order, which prevented the police from acting illegally, pending a later hearing, when the court would then determine, on the evidence, whether a permanent order against the police should be granted.

Meanwhile, Orr and those detainees who were joint applicants could obtain a court order permitting them to obtain copies of all the medical records to which Schnetler had made reference in his affidavit. Now they could have copies of the records with the protection of the court, as the court had ordered that the applicant had a legal right to examine and copy any of the medical records referred to by Schnetler in his affidavit. Schnetler's defence was about to implode because the court could now be presented with documented proof to substantiate each allegation made by Orr in her initial affidavit. But we are running ahead of the chronology. We must return to the first application made to the court.

The detainees' case was supported by a detailed affidavit from a district surgeon, whereas the police's consisted of a set of bland and bare denials made by Brigadier Schnetler. Small wonder that when the parties went before Judge Eksteen on 25 September 1985, there was no basis on which counsel for the state could oppose the relief being sought by the applicants.

This relief, of course, had to be drafted into a court order. And, in this, Trengove understood the potential of the legal system. He embarked on an imaginative formulation of the draft order by inserting a paragraph into it, which Judge Eksteen granted. It provided that the officers in command of the St Albans and North End prisons in Port Elizabeth were instructed to read out the order to all detainees held at both prisons.

The officers in command of the two prisons complied with the order. They summoned the prisoners and detainees, and read the order out to them. The detainees, who had effectively been shut off from the outside world, listened in amazement as the prison officers read out a court order that restrained them from any form of assault. They cheered as the order was read out. Slowly, a change in mood and the power relationships occurred as the lengthy order was read out – to acclamation from the detainees and the consternation of the prison warders.

There was widespread press reaction to the court proceedings. The *Eastern Province Herald* of 26 September 1985 led with the story 'Doctor claims "daily abuse of detainees"'. The *Cape Times* editorial of 26 September 1985 captured the mood:

> The police can no longer brush off allegations about their treatment of detainees. Evidence is mounting that detainees are being systematically assaulted or tortured. The University of Cape Town's Institute of Criminology found last month that 83 per

cent of 176 former detainees had been assaulted and that physical torture of detainees was widespread. Without referring specifically to assault allegations, police denied that torture was used to obtain information from detainees. There have been numerous court cases recently in which detainees have alleged assault and brutality.

An article on this page today states the concerns of the relatives of those detained. Their views will only have been strengthened by the Supreme Court order granted in Port Elizabeth yesterday which restrained police from assaulting detainees in the Port Elizabeth and Uitenhage areas. An affidavit from a district surgeon backed by detailed allegations stated that detainees were systematically assaulted after arrest or during interrogation. ...

These allegations are horrifying. They warrant the suspension of senior police officers in the Port Elizabeth area. Together with similar allegations from other parts of the country they warrant a judicial inquiry into the maltreatment of detainees. If the allegations are found to have substance, the Minister of Law and Order, Mr Louis le Grange, should resign at last.

The whole shoddy system of detention without trial, which paves the way for such abuses, should be scrapped. The present system on available evidence results in the physical injury and sometimes the deaths of people who are in the care of the State. It does incalculable harm to the image of the police and to the prospects of a negotiated peaceful settlement in this country. It is a system South Africa should never have adopted and which it cannot afford to retain.[28]

The order granted by Judge Eksteen was, however, of a temporary nature. It allowed the police to file further papers and to approach the court in opposition to any final relief that might have been sought by applicants.

And, indeed, on 4 February 1986, the parties were back in court, this time in front of Judge Jones. In preparation for the hearing, Trengove had drafted heads of argument in which he noted: 'It is alarming that those assaults seem to have continued even after the interim order of the 25 September 1985.' So, notwithstanding the interim order and the widespread publicity, the police had simply continued with their practice of systemic torture.

Cheadle and his team had by now gained access to prison registers and various other documents housed in the prisons – these in addition to the medical records that they already had. Within a week, they had photocopied some 7 000 documents, which would be annexed to a 68-page affidavit deposed to by Dr Orr. The police may not have complied with the interim order of 25 September 1985, but the further legal action now exposed, in more detail, the forms of conduct that had become almost standard practice among the police towards detainees.

Judge Jones was faced with a massive amount of evidence on paper. In this kind of case, a judge may then have little option but to make an order that the disputes should be referred to oral evidence. This allows those witnesses who have deposed to contradictory affidavits to be cross-examined on their version of events. The judge made such an order. This meant that various parties would have to testify before the court about the conditions under which they had suffered at the hands of the police and to be cross-examined accordingly. The police witnesses would then be subjected to the withering cross-examination of Wim Trengove, never a pleasant prospect, particularly for officers who, as the record of evidence revealed, had lied continuously throughout this litigation.

The interim order restraining the police from any misconduct was extended to 17 June 1986. But, by then, the President had lifted the state of emergency, thus ending the emergency detentions. The applicants therefore, withdrew their case. However, in September 1986, Louis le Grange, the Minister of Law and Order, agreed to pay costs calculated at R22 262 000 without admitting any of the allegations. A year later, the police made a payment of R1.2 million to the victims of police violence and their families. Trengove recalls the joy of his clients at beating the oppressors. Even a local woman received R12 000 in compensation for police buckshot that had hit her in the buttocks!

Wendy Orr said she was pleased that the ex-detainees had 'received some form of compensation for all they [had gone] through'. However, she said she felt it would have been better had the case gone to court: 'None of the police involved has been disciplined … I feel angry that there are still doctors such as Ivor Lang who have not been disciplined and are still a party to the whole system.'[29]

Conclusion

The *Wendy Orr* case did not stop detentions or torture. A second state of emergency was declared on 12 June 1986 and, by the end of that year, about 25 000 people had been detained. During this period, a further 15 court applications were launched by 75 detainees regarding allegations of assault and torture. In 1987 a study by the National Medical and Dental Association revealed that some 89 per cent of a sample of 131 detainees claimed to have been beaten with fists, hands, sjamboks, batons and other blunt instruments.[30]

In June 1987, the National Medical and Dental Association called for an urgent investigation into allegations made by detainees at East London's Fort Glamorgan Prison that there was a marked lack of medical treatment. Similar action was initiated by detainees at Diepkloof Prison, Johannesburg.[31]

The pattern of detention and torture by the vast majority of district surgeons who 'administered' to detainees continued throughout the 1980s. The courts, save in a few notable cases, failed detainees miserably. The Appellate Division during this period supported the war against law by curbing any power of judicial review by which the police could have been held accountable.[32]

Viewed in this depressing light, the question arises as to whether any gains flowed from the immensely courageous action of Wendy Orr and the imaginative litigation strategy that ensured the legal success of the applications she brought to court.

The *Wendy Orr* application illustrates the complexity of litigation of this nature. As Rick Abel observes in his careful study of the *Wendy Orr* case: 'The application revealed the enormous disparity in the power of South African voices. Black victims … have loudly denounced police violence for decades. They have little access to media or courts, however, and less credibility with white audiences.'[33]

It took a determined and courageous district surgeon to make the courts listen to the cries of detainees who were overwhelmingly black.

But once her voice had been given judicial approval, albeit in the form of limited legal relief against the police, the practice of police brutality could no longer be denied. It was all very well attacking the police on the basis of academic research produced by the UCT Institute of Criminology, studies that could be attributed to 'left-wing academics'. But, once a court considered these allegations so serious that a court order against the police was granted, a denial of the practice became far more problematic. The system had been exposed in a court, and that was markedly more effective than academic research or reports in opposition newspapers. The manner in which the court orders were read to detainees shifted the power balance between captor and detainee. It emboldened others to use the courts to expose police brutality. Ultimately, the practice of detention continued for several more regrettable years. But the exposure of torture in the courts gave the evidence a new-found legitimacy. Significantly, the motley crew of pseudo-scientists, politicians masquerading as academics and white supremacists for whom any means to protect white rule was justified and who had incessantly attacked the UCT report fell silent as soon as the *Wendy Orr* case hit the press. Thereafter, no one had an excuse to use the defence that torture of detainees was not commonplace.

Returning to FW de Klerk's submission to the TRC in May 1997, in keeping with the National Party's overall argument before the TRC, De Klerk contended that the torture of some 20 000 people over a 30-year period was nothing more than the work of a few aberrant police officers. There can be no doubt that many of the most notorious security police officers involved in the administration of the system were cruel psychopaths. To be sure, had Mother Teresa policed the system, torture and physical brutality may not have taken place. Those who worked as security policemen were unlikely to be blessed with truly generous dispositions, even if many completed their week of torturing detainees by attending church services on Sunday mornings. But the fault did not lie with a few psychopaths: the pattern of torture revealed a systemic practice over 30 years. It was known to anyone prepared to read the accounts of detainees, whether in newspapers or in academic research; it was obvious to anybody who took the trouble to examine Wendy Orr's affidavit or the press reportage of the case. But the practice continued long after 1986. The system was the cause of the brutality, a system implemented and administered by the National Party. It is an insult to all of those who were brutalised by 30 years of detention without trial, in the manner described so compellingly by Mac Maharaj, to suggest that the sole cause of their suffering was a few aberrant psychopaths, like Rooi Rus Swanepoel.

The problem with the TRC is that, 20 years later, it appears that it has produced little in the way of truth, and even less reconciliation. Our past continues to haunt us. One influential critic has contended that the TRC understood violence as criminal, and not as political. It viewed the violence as being committed by individual perpetrators, who targeted individual victims. In this way, it limited the criminal responsibility of individuals to actions that exceeded political orders, actions that would have been defined as crimes even under apartheid law. The TRC, in short, failed to introduce a principle of accountability for violence that was enabled by apartheid law.[34]

The *Wendy Orr* case did not concern individual perpetrators, but a system, and that system was never fully interrogated by the TRC. A brutal history was therefore left to fester in the body politic without any response from government. More than 20 years after the TRC, the Pretoria High Court heard evidence following the reopening of the inquiry into the death of Ahmed Timol. A member of the South African Communist Party, Timol died in October 1971; he was said to have jumped from the 10th floor of the notorious Johannesburg Police Station in John Vorster Square (now the Johannesburg Central Police Station). As part of the systematic destruction of justice under apartheid, the 1972 inquest into Timol's death supported the story provided by the police to explain his death, and the magistrate held that Timol had jumped to his death on the basis of a South African Communist Party document that called on party members to commit suicide rather than risk betraying their comrades. This, according to the security police at the time, had been the guiding motivation for Timol's suicide. The document was, of course, never produced.

It was always assumed that the police had murdered activists such as Timol, and, 46 years after his death, an independent inquest was called upon to establish whether Timol had been murdered by the police. In his judgment, Judge Billy Mothle made the following general observation about the system and about detention without trial: 'The evidence further reveals the role of some carefully selected prosecutors, magistrates, and medical doctors who were complicit in the declaration of the so-called war against those opposed to the apartheid order. These persons betrayed and demeaned their respective oaths of office by participating in inquest proceedings that became a sham.' This, said the judge, concealed the 'atrocities' committed by the Security Branch and ensured that the judicial system found 'no one to blame'.[35]

At the 1972 inquest proceedings into Timol's death, notwithstanding proof of at least 16 injuries that Timol had sustained before 'falling to his death', the magistrate dismissed the argument that murder was involved as 'absurd'. Timol, he said, was a valuable find for the Security Branch, who desperately wanted to keep him. He concluded that Timol must have jumped out of the window of his own accord.[36] Insofar as the injuries were concerned, the magistrate proffered the explanation that they had been sustained in a 'brawl', during which Timol had been pushed around and had possibly fallen. In keeping with the disgraceful record of the judiciary before democracy, the magistrate found that although 'Timol was interrogated for long hours ... he was treated in a civilised and humane way'.[37]

The evidence that was led before Judge Mothle during the 2017 inquest confirmed exactly the opposite. Of significance was the testimony of a former member of the Security Branch, Paul Erasmus, who had joined the security police in 1977. His task was to produce propaganda material that would counter organisations and activists opposed to apartheid. His evidence, as summarised by Judge Mothle, included the following observation:

> Some magistrates, sometimes state pathologists and prosecutors, played along and ensured that culprits escaped justice. This protection of criminal activity and the part of the Security Branch also entailed holding mock trials where their witnesses would be coached and made to rehearse evidence. Some of the police would then be asked to role-play advocates questioning witnesses to enable them to avoid being adversely cross-examined.[38]

After evaluating a range of evidence provided by witnesses who had been detained, members of the Timol family, and lawyers and medical practitioners, Judge Mothle concluded that 'the security police [had] fabricated a version that alleges that Timol on his own, jumped out of the window of room 1026 at John Vorster Square to commit suicide'.[39]

Furthermore, the judge found that evidence given by former detainees and doctors presented a version of events not considered in the 1972 inquest, which proved that Timol, like other detainees, had been tortured to such an extent that he would not have been physically capable of propelling himself towards or throwing himself out of a window, as alleged by the police at the time.[40]

In considering all the evidence, the court found that 'detainees were subjected to beating and various levels of brutality', the least being a slap across the face. '[This] nevertheless remains an assault but not comparable to those who were hit with solid objects, punched and kicked … it would be more accurate to deal with the subject of ill-treatment or abuse of detainees under the rubric of torture, as it includes all forms of abuse visited on the detainees.'[41]

Had the magistrate in the 1972 inquest applied basic legal principles dealing with circumstantial evidence, he would have been compelled to accept that the overwhelming evidence showed that the only inference to be drawn from Timol's injuries was that they had been caused by his having been brutally tortured while under interrogation in detention.

The court found that there was no evidence supporting the view that the Security Branch had intended to commit murder, in the case of Timol. However, the police officers clearly foresaw the risk of murder occurring because of their brutal treatment and yet continued to act, appreciating that death might well occur.[42] In finding that *dolus eventualis* was the basis by which members of the Security Branch committed murder, the court found that Timol had sustained some 35 injuries before being pushed to his death, all of which demonstrated that, for the Security Branch, there were no boundaries when it came to perpetrating these acts of torture or showing contempt for human life. What's more, members of the Security Branch were very careful to remove Timol's body immediately from where he had landed to cover up their crimes. Significantly, one of his interrogators, Captain Johannes van Niekerk, had a record of brutality, including convictions for two counts of assault, in which a victim had died, and multiple complaints of serious assault and torture, including use of an iron rod and electric shock treatment.

In concluding his judgment, Judge Mothle said that the relatives of those who had died in detention should be given help to obtain the records and gather information, so that further inquests could be reopened.

The 2017 Ahmed Timol inquest shows, as did the evidence in the *Wendy Orr* case, that there was a level of systematic cruelty and barbarity perpetrated by the apartheid regime. Sadly, more than 20 years after the dawn of democracy, we have still only scratched the surface.

Lest this chapter be dismissed as concerning only the history of *Wendy Orr*, one particular legal case decided a long time ago, it is worth considering the following important statement made by Judge Mothle in concluding the Timol inquest:

> It is not ethical and proper on the part of a judicial officer to preside over or decide cases either out of fear, or in favour of a person, entity or institution, or an expectation of promotion or reward, or an advancement for some real or perceived interest. Judicial officers have to be loyal only to the Constitution and the cause of justice. Public officials and the administration of justice are enjoined by the law to justly guard against casting aspersions on the integrity of the judicial system by conducting themselves in the manner contrary to the oath of office. Such conduct has no place in a constitutional democracy.[43]

Given disturbing allegations in present-day South Africa about the ineptitude of certain public officials – those who do not administer justice without fear or favour when it comes to certain select individuals – this judicial statement is a universal warning whose significance extends way beyond any single historical legal case.

7

A BRIDGE OVER OUR TROUBLED WATERS?

– With apologies to SIMON AND GARFUNKEL

South Africa's transition from apartheid to a constitutional democracy occurred, in part, through the use of law. Democracy was also built in incremental stages, like bricks being laid one by one, rather than as a single major concrete structure being manoeuvred into place.

Two aspects of this transition are examined here. The first is the legal transition from an era characterised by oppressive legislation to one framed in terms of a democratic, rights-based Constitution. This was achieved through the mechanism of the Interim Constitution. The transitional arrangements set out in the Interim Constitution ensured that government would continue during the period leading up to the election of the first democratic government and that institutional integration would occur at all levels of government. Essentially, the transitional scheme foreshadowed the governmental, institutional and legal structures that would make up the future South African state. Most notable for our purposes was the creation of the Constitutional Court, an institution that was critical in helping transport South African society into an era of constitutional democracy, not least through its role in certifying the final Constitution.

The second aspect of the transition is the attacks that the transitional mechanisms, particularly the Constitutional Court and the TRC, were subjected to from both the left and right wings of the political spectrum. The left tested them with difficult cases brought by family members of anti-apartheid activists, including the family of Steve Biko, who challenged the TRC process, seeking their proverbial day in court. That case highlighted the difficulty of the new regime's efforts to reconcile the understandable urge for punishment and retribution with the necessary political reconciliation. One right-wing attack came in the form of the challenge to Mandela's executive authority brought by business tycoon, politician and former doyen of South African rugby, Louis Luyt.

The process of moving towards democracy

The political transition to constitutional democracy took place in highly managed stages.[1] Often accompanied by fraught political moments and, unfortunately, occasionally spilling over into violence, the transition was also prominently marked by the use of law. Politics alone was insufficient; law was needed to accomplish the shift in political power and government.

The beginning of South Africa's transition can be traced to mid-1989, when Mandela, who was then in Victor Verster prison, near Paarl, met the then president, PW Botha. Mandela acknowledged that it was 'in the national interest' for the ANC and the government to meet urgently to negotiate for the country's political future.

A month later, the ANC's lobbying efforts managed to ensure that the Organisation of African Unity (the forerunner of the African Union) and the UN adopted the Harare Declaration, which set out the basis for a transition to democracy, and that a representative and elected body drafted South Africa's Constitution.

In September 1989, PW Botha was replaced as head of state by FW de Klerk. At the same time, civil society organised a defiance campaign through a new umbrella body, the Mass Democratic Movement (which had grown out of the anti-apartheid organisation the United Democratic Front, which had been formed in 1983). A month later, several ANC leaders were released from prison. On 8 December, the Conference for a Democratic Future took place, during which about 6 000 representatives of the Mass Democratic Movement passed a resolution in favour of negotiations with the National Party government. This courageous endorsement of the path of negotiated transition set all South Africans to work on dismantling apartheid and choosing our shared, transformed future.

CODESA

Almost a year later, in November 1990, an all-party preparatory meeting took place, attended by 20 organisations and parties. The name given to this forum was the Convention for a Democratic South Africa (CODESA), and, importantly, it adopted the principle of sufficient consensus as the decision-making mechanism during its proceedings to settle disagreements. Unfortunately, minutes before the end of the meeting, the Pan African Congress walked out, accusing the ANC of selling out to the white minority.

Despite this, CODESA's first session on 20 and 21 December adopted a declaration of intent, which all parties, except the Inkatha Freedom Party (IFP) and the Bophuthatswana government, signed. The National Party confirmed, for the first time, that it would accept an elected constituent assembly provided that that body also acted as an interim national government. In February 1992, the National Party accepted the ANC's demand to form an interim government and that, in principle, a new South Africa should seek to be non-racial, non-sexist and democratic. A CODESA working group produced an initial agreement on general constitutional principles against which the Constitution would be tested when the time came to negotiate it. The agreement was an important milestone in the role that would be played by the Constitutional Court in certifying the final Constitution.

The agreement also settled the conflict between the ANC and the National Party over how the political transition would be managed. Whereas the ANC wanted the Constitution to be drafted and adopted after the first nationwide democratic election, the National Party wanted it completed before the country's electorate went to the polls. In a masterstroke, an agreement was reached whereby the parties would negotiate and adopt the principles against which the text would ultimately be evaluated. This way, these constitutional principles provided, in a sense, the first bridge over which the country travelled away from apartheid and towards a democratic constitutional state. Through this mechanism, the transition to a constitutional process was made possible.[2]

In March 1992 the National Party government held an all-white referendum to test support for the negotiation process; it received overwhelming support for reform. In the same month, the ANC proposed a two-phase interim government. The first phase would consist of the formation of a Transitional Executive Council (TEC); the second would begin after the elections and consist of the interim government and constituent assembly. The TEC would be multiparty in form and function alongside the existing Parliament. Subcommittees of the TEC, with executive powers, would be established for key areas of government.

At the beginning of May, the parties headed for CODESA II, the second plenary session, where the ANC hoped to achieve agreement on the proposed two-phase interim government. CODESA met on 15 and 16 May, but stalled on the question of the size of the special majority – as opposed to a simple majority of 50 per cent plus one vote – that would be required to adopt the final Constitution. Then, a massive setback occurred on 17 June, when more than 40 people were massacred during a march in Boipatong – a sign of the determined effort of reluctant and obstructionist groups to derail negotiations. Days later, ANC leaders met to discuss the massacre's implications: they reaffirmed a commitment to a negotiated settlement but broke off talks and accused the government of complicity in the attack. The ANC's Tripartite Alliance partners, the South African Communist Party and the Congress of South African Trade Unions (COSATU), launched a mass-action campaign on 15 July. The ANC sent a list of demands to De Klerk and, a few days later, the President responded by denying government involvement in the violence and refused to commit himself to majority rule. However, he also tried to reduce the political temperature by disbanding notorious battalions, banning dangerous weapons and agreeing to international monitoring.

Fishing for peace

At the beginning of September, the ANC chose its secretary general, Cyril Ramaphosa, to establish a channel of communication to replace bilateral meetings and allow contact to continue. Ramaphosa and Roelf Meyer, his National Party counterpart, promptly went trout fishing together. The importance of this relationship to the ultimate success of the negotiations should not be underestimated. It is also poignant to consider this in the light of today's brutal, racially divisive identity politics.

In fact, its significance was even discussed in Canadian political circles, as this quote from a speech given by a member of the Legislative Assembly of British Columbia shows:

I'd like to relate an anecdote that comes from Allister Sparks, who has written in *The New Yorker* about the silent revolution I spoke about earlier. He speaks of two young political men playing the same political position, but on opposite sides of the fence. The one on the white team was named Roelf Meyer, Deputy Minister of Constitutional Development. On the black team was Cyril Ramaphosa, Secretary General of the ANC and chief negotiator. Both men were invited by a mutual friend to do some fishing. Ramaphosa was an expert at fly fishing and offered to teach Meyer and his sons how to do it. Regrettably, as they were fly fishing, Meyer got a hook deeply imbedded in one of his fingers. The group returned home, where Ramaphosa's wife, who was a nurse, tried to remove the hook, without success. Finally Cyril intervened, seeing that Meyer was in some significant pain. 'Roelf,' he said, 'there is only one way to do this.' He poured him a glass of whisky and fetched a pair of pliers. He then took a firm grip on the hook and said: 'I've always wanted to hurt you Nats, but never as much as this.' And at that, Ramaphosa yanked the hook out. Meyer, relieved, looked up and muttered: 'Cyril, don't say I didn't trust you'.

Although the post-election period will be difficult, and many changes to come pose even greater challenges for South Africa, the centripetal forces that have brought South Africa this far appear stronger than those that would cause it to fly apart. The inescapable mutual dependency of black and white South Africans is what holds them together. It is the lesson of the fish hook. May we all learn such a lesson. Nkosi sikelel' iAfrika. God bless Africa.[3]

Demonstrating the tenuous and volatile nature of the political climate at the time, on 7 September 1992, soldiers in Bisho, Ciskei, opened fire on people who, as part of the mass-action campaign, were protesting against the homeland government. Although many died in this tragedy, it did mean that both sides returned to the negotiating table.

On 26 September, the two parties agreed on a record of understanding, addressing details of the transition, including the make-up of the

Constitutional Assembly, an interim government, the treatment of political prisoners, and hostels, dangerous weapons and mass action.

In the following months, the parties undertook bilateral negotiations and prepared for a planning conference to be held in March. On 4 and 5 March 1993, the planning conference on negotiations was held at the World Trade Centre in Kempton Park, near Johannesburg. In the cavernous hall, which was more suitable as an expo venue for launching new cars, but which had not been partitioned into offices and a negotiation chamber, delegates and advisors from 26 parties and organisations gathered – initially to pass a resolution for the resumption of negotiations.

On 1 April, the Multiparty Negotiating Forum of 26 participants – which also included several smaller parties, such as the PAC, the Conservative Party and the Afrikaner Volksunie party – met, and defined the issues to be dealt with at the multiparty negotiations.

Strains at the seams

However, crisis loomed yet again when, on 10 April, Chris Hani, the Communist Party leader, was assassinated by right-wingers Janusz Walus, a Polish immigrant, and former Conservative Party MP Clive Derby-Lewis. This tragedy prompted the ANC to call for negotiations to be speeded up.

In June, 27 April 1994 was chosen as the date for South Africa's first non-racial elections. The technical committee on constitutional matters was instructed to produce a transitional Constitution that set out the process and mechanics for the drafting and adoption of a final democratic Constitution by an elected assembly.

Then, on 25 June, Eugène Terre'Blanche and members of his Afrikaner Weerstandsbeweging (AWB) stormed the World Trade Centre. This ill-fated 'invasion' demonstrated the right wing's resistance to the negotiations – and the still-present threat of insurrection and civil war.

Tensions were also obvious from the stance of the IFP, which had proposed a federal constitution, which had been rejected at the negotiations. Eventually, after months of preparation, a summit between Nelson Mandela and the IFP's Mangosuthu Buthelezi took place to ease the IFP's concerns.

Three months later, the ANC and the National Party reached agreement on a Government of National Unity, a provision for two deputy presidents, the required percentage to elect a deputy president and the right to appoint cabinet posts. The National Party abandoned its claim to a veto over the decisions of the cabinet. On 16 November 1993, in a last-minute bilateral meeting between Mandela and FW de Klerk, agreement was reached on the final issues required to complete the Interim Constitution – a deal known as the 'six-pack' agreement. The Multiparty Negotiating Forum ratified the Interim Constitution on 18 November in the early hours of the morning.

In the meantime, however, violence between IFP and ANC supporters on the East Rand escalated to the point of civil war. In March 1994, Mandela and Buthelezi agreed to international mediation over the status of the former homeland of KwaZulu but the agreement fell apart before mediation could even begin. Bomb blasts in central Johannesburg and, on 28 March, the death of eight IFP marchers outside Shell House, the ANC's headquarters in the city, raised the temperature in the political pressure cooker.

In the same month, Ciskei and Bophuthatswana collapsed under the pressure of internal discontent. Terre'Blanche's AWB rushed to the defence of Bophuthatswana's leader, Lucas Mangope, but the AWB commandos were massacred. This folly was captured on the television news in an almost cathartic moment: black soldiers executing white racist terrorists. The right-wing myth of racial superiority was exploded on the television screens of the nation. The dangers of insurrection prompted General Constand Viljoen to establish the Freedom Front as a political party (on the promise of consideration of a white homeland) and join the list of candidates on the ballot in the upcoming elections.

Just days before the elections, agreement was reached through a Kenyan negotiator by all negotiating parties, including the IFP.

South Africa's first non-racial election was finally contested on 27 April 1994. It produced 400 leaders in the National Assembly and 90 in the Senate. In terms of Section 68(1) of the Interim Constitution, a joint sitting of these bodies formed the Constitutional Assembly, established on 9 May. Mandela was inaugurated as democratic South Africa's first president on 10 May 1994. The Constitutional Assembly worked within particular parameters towards the finalisation of a constitutional text. These constraints included the requirement of a two-thirds majority in favour for the adoption of the ultimate text, compliance with 34 constitutional principles agreed to in the Interim Constitution and the adoption of a new Constitution within two years. In June, the Constitutional Committee was established. This became the premier multiparty negotiating body in the Constitutional Assembly, led by Ramaphosa and Meyer.

By April the following year, several constitutional sticking points still remained: the death penalty, the lockout clause, the property clause, the appointment of judges and the attorney general, language, local government, the question of proportional representation and the bar against Members of Parliament crossing the floor. But, on 8 May, the final text was adopted and, from 1 to 11 July, the Constitutional Court's certification hearing was held.

Smoothing out a wrinkled text

The certification process permitted any political parties represented in the National Assembly to present arguments on whether or not the Constitution should be certified. This process – probably the largest hearing in South African legal history – involved at least 47 advocates representing 29 political parties, organisations and individuals. Among them were the ANC, the National Party, the IFP, the Democratic Party, the Conservative Party and the African Christian Democratic Party. COSATU, Business South Africa, the South African Agricultural Union, the Human Rights Commission and the South African Institute of Race Relations were among the organisations that made submissions. The court was required to test the text of the Constitution against the 34 agreed constitutional principles that had been negotiated early in the constitutional process and consider the arguments before it as to why it did, or did not, comply.

However, on 6 September, in the judgment *Ex parte Chairperson of the Constitutional Assembly: in re Certification of the Constitution of the Republic of South Africa 1996*, the court unanimously rejected certain clauses and ruled that the text adopted in May 1996 could not be certified. The court said the draft of the Constitution failed in several respects to satisfy the conditions thrashed out in multiparty talks. But it said the instances of non-compliance should present no significant obstacle to the formulation of a text that met these requirements. The court pointed to the Constitution's failure to entrench agreed fundamental rights, its failure to protect the independence of watchdogs, including a Public Protector and an Auditor-General, and to the reduction of provincial autonomy.

The Constitutional Assembly reconsidered the text and passed a number of amendments in sufficient time for the court to be able to certify the text that year. On 7 October, the parties reached an agreement on all eight clauses that had been rejected by the court. The assembly approved, with only one vote against, an amended Constitution for submission to the court on 11 October. The amended version contained many changes: some dealt with the court's reasons for rejection; others simply tightened up the text.

The Constitutional Court's second hearing began on 18 November. On 4 December 1996, in *Certification of the Amended Text of the Constitution of the Republic of South Africa, 1996*, it granted its unanimous approval. The judges found that the Constitutional Assembly had 'conscientiously' remedied the eight defective provisions. The court also dismissed 16 objections from the Democratic Party, the IFP and the province of KwaZulu-Natal, as well as the complaints of 18 individuals and interest groups.

The court certified that the text complied with the constitutional principles and it duly became the Constitution of the Republic of South Africa. It was signed by Mandela, as president, in Sharpeville on 10 December 1996 and came into effect on 4 February 1997. And so, the chief design for the constitutional bridge had been approved and adopted. Progress towards creating the society promised in the hard-fought text could now begin.

The Truth and Reconciliation Commission: A second bridge

Laudable though the creation of the Constitution was, there was much to be addressed in South Africa's new democratic society that could not be settled in a legal document. The tragic and terrible abuses and brutal excesses of apartheid had to be confronted. After the adoption of the Constitution, the relatively bloodless political transition that followed was due, in large part, to the political decision to create a TRC. This would be the process through which South Africa would discover, explore, confront and acknowledge its awful past. The TRC and its aims were to become the second bridge the country needed to build.

The Promotion of National Unity and Reconciliation Act 34 of 1995 provided for the creation of the TRC. The commission would be appointed by the President in consultation with the cabinet. The TRC was mandated to establish the complete picture of the gross violations of human rights committed between March 1960 (the time of the Sharpeville massacre) and 10 May 1994 by means of hearings and investigations that the commission would undertake. It was also charged with facilitating the granting of amnesty, the recommendation of reparations to the victims of human-rights abuses and the preparation of a report containing recommendations for measures to prevent any future violation of human rights.

The work of the TRC eventually included 140 hearings across the country, with about 2 400 victims who testified and the names of some 27 000 recorded. 'The final tally,' according to one 2006 news report, 'was 21 519 victim statements containing evidence of 30 384 gross human rights violations. The commission made more than 15 000 findings before it passed the baton to the government to follow up on recommendations ranging from redress to retribution, in the form of further investigation and prosecution.'[4]

Critical to the entire process envisaged by the Act was the amnesty committee. Staffed by three judges and two commissioners, this committee was empowered to consider applications for amnesty, which it could grant if satisfied that the applicant had committed an act that constituted a gross violation of human rights and had made full disclosure of all relevant and material facts, and if the act to which the application related was associated with political objectives and had been committed during the course of conflicts of the past. In terms of Section 20(7) of the Act, a person granted amnesty by the committee would not be criminally or civilly liable in respect of the act committed.

But the TRC process did not completely exclude the operation of the criminal-justice system. Prosecutions of those who did not apply for amnesty, or who were refused it, would be possible. And several prosecutions did take place. The most high-profile of these were the criminal prosecutions of apartheid apparatchik Eugene de Kock (aka 'Prime Evil') and the former head of South Africa's chemical and biological warfare programme, Dr Wouter Basson ('Dr Death'), and the plea bargain entered into by, among others, former Law and Order

Minister Adriaan Vlok for the attempted murder of Rev Frank Chikane.

The difference between the outcomes in the De Kock case (a successful prosecution and conviction) and the Basson case (acquittal after a trial lasting 18 months) starkly outlines the debate about which vehicle – a trial or a TRC hearing – ultimately revealed more of the details of the apartheid government's murderous methods. In essence, both processes searched for the truth and strove to establish 'what happened'. The TRC linked this, in its quasi-theological style, to forgiveness and cathartic confession, while, in general terms, retributive justice is the claimed goal of a trial. However, the TRC process has been criticised for producing a linear, 'just the bare facts' narrative that never grappled with or sought to explain the underlying pathologies and normative explanations for apartheid. Or, as Christodoulidis put it: 'It failed to re-write collected memories as collective memory.'[5] Individual narratives were never fused into a collective account of a brutal past.

In their book *Commissioning the Past*, Posel and Simpson perceptively explain how this happened:

> The limits of the 'history' written by the TRC in turn inhibit its 'cathartic' and 'healing' qualities. With its powers of explanation stunted, the TRC cannot produce a consensus about *why* the terrible deeds of the past were committed. The increasingly familiar refrain among white South Africans that apartheid was merely a 'mistake' for which no one was responsible, that somehow the system propelled itself impersonally, may be one of the more ironic, unintended consequences of the TRC's rendition of the past.

> To the extent that the [TRC's] report does venture into historical explanation, its consequences may once again be deeply ironic. The report's only answer to the question of why the country was subjected to such a violent and abusive past is itself in need of explanation – the prevalence and intensity of racism. But in the absence of an explanation for racism itself, the report fails to suggest any plausible grounds for transcending the racism of the past. If racism was part of the warp and woof of South African society, how can it be undone? The fact that it is

embedded in the social fabric is also a measure of its tenacity. If we do not understand the conditions under which racism was produced, reproduced and intensified in South Africa, taking account of its interconnections with other modes of power and inequality, such as gender and class, how can we transcend it?

In contrast, the trial records developed during the prosecutions of De Kock and Basson arguably offer more insight into the apartheid mindset. Taken together, of course, the TRC and parallel criminal proceedings have exposed South Africa's shameful past and made it increasingly difficult to claim the amnesia still so popular among white South Africans. These two trials require a brief examination.

De Kock

The 18-month-long criminal trial of Eugene de Kock – a 'marathon affair', in his words – clearly illustrates the implications of different types of solutions: prosecuting apartheid's foot soldiers, or those who executed its plans, while a political solution was found to deal with the handover of power by their commanders. As De Kock saw it, his trial was 'two years of betrayal',

> first by the state that gave me my orders, and then by my friends who lined up to testify against me.

> The state case ... turned out to be an attempt to find a scapegoat for the crimes of a repressive official apparatus whose tentacles reached right to the top – not only of the security forces, but also of the National Party government. I do not deny that I am guilty of the crimes, many of them horrible, of which I was accused. But I am not the only guilty one. The state chose to give indemnity from prosecution to many of my men simply so that a bulldozer of a case could be assembled against me – and in the process, allow other men just as guilty as I to laugh in the face of justice.

> But we at Vlakplaas [the farm, some 20 kilometres outside Pretoria, that served as the death squad's headquarters], and in the other covert units, are by no means the guiltiest of all. That

dubious honour belongs to those who assembled us into the murderous forces that we became, *and which we were intended to be all along*. And most of them, the generals and the politicians, have got off scot-free.[7]

The De Kock trial began on 20 February 1995 and saw 87 witnesses testify for the state. The prosecutor was Deputy Attorney General Anton Ackermann, together with a special team of investigators. Judge Willem van der Merwe, later to become a national figure when he presided over the rape trial of Jacob Zuma, adjudicated, assisted by two assessors. The trial record eventually reached 12 000 pages. De Kock faced 121 charges, including murder, manslaughter and conspiracy to murder.[8] He was convicted on 89 of these, and sentenced to serve two life sentences, plus 212 years, all to run concurrently.

As De Kock himself recognised, the trial was important for three reasons. First, as he put it, it was 'the first time that South Africans were made aware of what we in the security forces had been ordered to do; anyone who paid attention to the proceedings quickly realized the culpability of the generals and the government'. Secondly, 'the way in which the state chose to prosecute and portray me – as a common criminal, not a political one – was significant'. And, thirdly, 'one has to recall that what is now common knowledge about me and C10 [De Kock's special police unit] was mere speculation before my trial. Many pieces of evidence, stories and events exploded, as they say, like bombshells.'[9]

With respect to the second of these points, De Kock wrote that Ackermann had informed the court that the trial was not a Nuremberg-type hearing. On the contrary, he told the court, it was not political in nature but concerned criminality, and it would expose age-old sins: cold-blooded murder, theft, fraud and the perversion of justice.[10] One criticism of the trial was that it focused on 'purely individual criminal acts' rather than 'the question of structural and systemic crimes – the surrounding ideological/political philosophy, the setting up of Vlakplaas, and an administrative-executive system that directed De Kock'.[11]

Belatedly, in March 1996, De Kock applied for amnesty to the TRC but was denied it. Out of 7 115 amnesty applications made to the TRC, 1 154 got the nod and a further 150 people were granted partial amnesty.

But only 267 of these applicants were members of the South African security forces and, then, they were mostly police officers.[12]

The questions of guilt and remorse were not absent from De Kock's prosecution. Tellingly, De Kock's testimony in mitigation of sentence included the following statement: 'I cannot say how dirty one feels. Whatever we attempted in the interests of the country did not work. All we did was to injure people, to leave people with unforgivable pain, to leave behind children who will never know their parents. I sympathise with the victims as if they were my own children.'[13]

Accepting this sentiment at face value, and ignoring the self-serving circumstances in which it was made after his conviction, the trial leaves one with the uncomfortable but unavoidable conclusion that the TRC was neither the only, nor necessarily the best-suited, vehicle to expose the truth about what was done in the name of apartheid, or to achieve reconciliation.

Basson

Wouter Basson, a cardiologist and the former head of South Africa's chemical and biological warfare programme, named 'Dr Death' by the media, was prosecuted on 67 charges, including fraud, theft, drug possession and trafficking, as well as murder and conspiracy to murder. His prosecution was led by the same prosecutor, Anton Ackermann, who had headed De Kock's. Jaap Cilliers led the defence team. The trial began on 4 October 1999 and ended on 11 April 2002, following the testimony of 153 prosecution witnesses and a total of nearly 200 witnesses.

The trial record contains chilling testimony of assassinations through poisoning, painstaking research into lethal drug cocktails and the establishment of front companies through which millions of rands were channelled to fund, among other efforts, the notorious Project Coast (the 1980s top-secret chemical and biological weapons programme). Basson was also linked to the infamous assassination attempts on the lives of Frank Chikane and Dullah Omar. Despite the TRC's investigation into his activities and those of the chemical and biological warfare programme, and even though Basson appeared before the TRC hearings, he did not receive amnesty from that body but was criminally prosecuted.

However, this prosecution was a significant failure, severely hampered, as it was, by the legal rulings and attitude to the case of the presiding judge, Willie Hartzenberg. For starters, Hartzenberg refused to have assessors in the case. Usually, a judge can sit with two other people, who act as a sounding board for his impressions and assist in reaching decisions. But, here, Judge Hartzenberg, a highly competent and experienced judge, took the arguably surprising decision to sit alone, without assessors, who, at the very least from the point of public perception, could have assisted and provided a more demographically representative court trying the case – one in which the charges went to the very heart of apartheid's darkness.

In the first blow to the case against Basson, Judge Hartzenberg dismissed the charges relating to conduct outside South Africa on jurisdictional grounds and found that Basson was covered by the 1989 Namibian amnesty, which precluded prosecution of all security-force members deployed to the South West Africa/Namibia bush war. This meant that Basson could not be prosecuted for six of the most serious charges against him. These included the murder of an estimated 200 SWAPO[14] detainees injected with muscle relaxants before their bodies were thrown into the sea, a plan to murder Namibian administrator Peter Kalangula by smearing a toxic agent on the door handle of his car, and a plan to poison the water supply of SWAPO refugee camps located outside Windhoek with vibrio cholera.[15] Judge Hartzenberg also dismissed charges relating to the proposed murder of Ronnie Kasrils and Pallo Jordan while in exile in London, and the deaths of Gibson Mondlane in Mozambique and of Enoch 'Knox' Dlamini in Swaziland, in a rejection of the prosecution's argument that these plans were formed in South Africa.[16]

The remaining charges were all ultimately dismissed. However, in his 1 453-page judgment, Judge Hartzenberg made several typographical and major factual errors revealing, in the view of his critics, a less than thorough, and not impartial, weighing and consideration of the voluminous evidence before him: 'Apart from a slew of incorrect names (both of companies involved in the fraud charges and individuals, including some witnesses) there are several indications that the judge's attention might have wandered at times, or that he did not fully digest the significance of certain testimony.'[17]

In fact, at one point during the trial, Hartzenberg told an astonished courtroom that he was 'bored to death' with the presentation of evidence concerning financial dealings, fraud and theft. The acrimony between the bench and the prosecution, who perceived bias in his approach, also escalated to unprecedented levels during the trial. This prompted a recusal application (which was rejected) and culminated in the unusual step of prosecutor Ackermann placing on the record the 'untoward malice and hostility' displayed by the judge during exchanges with counsel in chambers.[18] In the end, Judge Hartzenberg's findings reinforced the perception created by other failed legal exercises that

> the top echelons of the former SADF appeared somehow to be above the law.[19] Coupled with the fact that the vast majority of CCB [Civil Cooperation Bureau] agents have still not been publicly named, that they have not been required to disclose details of their covert cross-border activities – or even all their operations inside South Africa – and that Project Coast's deepest and darkest secrets will almost certainly never be revealed, ... Hartzenberg's findings have, unfortunately, done far more to shield than shame those who can never answer truthfully when asked, as inevitably they will be, "So what did you do in the war, Daddy?"[20]

At the inevitable international press conference that followed his acquittal, Basson began his personal public rehabilitation, coupled with a return to private practice. As Burger and Gould observe, Basson argued that the millions spent on his prosecution could have been used to buy medicines that could save the lives of HIV-positive mothers and babies:

> In the most public of all forums, with the eyes of the world's media on him, the man who was only too willing to exchange his surgical scrubs and scalpel for the cloak and dagger of apartheid's CBW [chemical and biological warfare] spy, donned the mantle of human rights activist, appealing to the authorities in 'our hard-gained democracy' to reconsider priorities, use available funds effectively for the 'betterment' of the population, and decide what South Africans needed most: medicine or retribution.[21]

These two cases focused attention on the system's ability to deal with the past. The public disclosures that emerged from these trials brought South Africa closer to the truth of the systemic and calculated cruelty of the unparalleled system of apartheid than had the seven TRC volumes.

Perhaps presciently, and certainly understandably, the TRC mechanism did not meet with universal acclaim: this important bridge was attacked from the outset by litigants possessed of much moral authority who launched a gut-wrenching case.

The attack from the 'left'

In the case known in the law reports as that of the *Azanian Peoples Organisation (AZAPO) and Others v The President of the Republic of South Africa and Others*,[22] the families of key anti-apartheid activists who had been murdered during the apartheid regime, namely Steve Biko, Griffiths and Victoria Mxenge, and Dr and Mrs Fabian Ribeiro, together with AZAPO, brought an application to set aside Section 20(7) of the Act that established the TRC, which precluded prosecution in favour of amnesty. The applicants argued that the state was obliged under international law to prosecute those responsible for gross human-rights violations. As a result, Section 20(7) constituted a breach of international law, both customary international law (i.e. the collective body of historical practices between states) and international treaties law. In this case, the Genocide Convention of 1948, the International Convention on the Suppression and Punishment of the Crime of Apartheid of 1973 and the Convention against Torture and Other Cruel, Inhuman or Degrading Treatment or Punishment of 1984 were all relevant instruments of international law on which the application relied.

The applicants also argued that Section 22 of the Interim Constitution supported their case. That section provided that every person had the right to have justiciable disputes heard by a court of law or, where appropriate, another independent impartial forum. They argued that they had been denied that right. By operation of the TRC Act, they could no longer approach a court seeking, for example, civil remedies, such as damages or compensation arising out of the murder of their husbands, fathers, wives, daughters or sons. The TRC process displaced the families' entitlement to court-based relief into a very different truth-seeking and healing process. Did it deny them justice?

The government's lawyers countered these legal submissions by arguing that the Act followed directly on the post-amble of the Interim Constitution, which provided as follows:

> This Constitution provides a historic bridge between the past of a deeply divided society characterised by strife, conflict, untold suffering and injustice, and a future founded on the recognition of human rights, democracy and peaceful coexistence and development opportunities for all South Africans, irrespective of colour, race, class, belief or sex. ...

> In order to advance such reconciliation and reconstruction, amnesty shall be granted in respect of acts, omissions and offences associated with political objectives and committed in the course of the conflicts of the past. To this end, Parliament under this Constitution shall adopt a law determining a firm cut-off date, which shall be a date after 8 October 1990 and before 6 December 1993, and providing for mechanisms, criteria and procedures, including tribunals, if any, through which such amnesty shall be dealt with at any time after the law has been passed.

The government's argument was that the Constitution envisaged a process of amnesty and that the Act had merely implemented this constitutional mandate. The court was clearly confronted with a major moral dilemma. All the judges knew, or should have known, of the heroic sacrifices at issue. Many had been personally acquainted with the victims. To look these heroes' families in the eye and refuse the right to pursue a remedy against those who had murdered their loved ones in so callous and cynical a fashion represented a judicial task designed to elicit considerable angst. This is evident from the majority judgment of Judge Mahomed, in which he wrote: 'Every decent human being must feel great discomfort in living with a consequence which might allow the perpetrators of evil acts to walk the streets of this land with impunity, protected in their freedom by an amnesty from constitutional attack, but the circumstances in support of this course require carefully to be appreciated.'[23]

Our own interviews with those involved in the hearing confirm that the judges struggled with the dilemma posed by the case. Judge John Didcott, the judge with the most consistent human-rights record of any member of the judiciary who had sat during the apartheid era, was even more pugnacious and probing than usual on the bench. He tore into counsel for the government as he personally struggled to come to terms with the excruciating moral dilemma posed by the case and, in particular, the applicants.

The court understood the problem of justice as opposed to political settlement and, in particular was aware of the dilemma between the rights of individuals to seek redress for the egregious harms they had suffered and the political compromise designed to avoid a bloody revolution. To pick up again from the judgment of Judge Mahomed:

> The effect of an amnesty undoubtedly impacts upon very fundamental rights. All persons are entitled to the protection of the law against unlawful invasions of their right to life, their right to respect for and protection of dignity and their right not to be subject to torture of any kind. When those rights are invaded, those aggrieved by such invasion have the right to obtain redress in the ordinary courts of law and those guilty of perpetrating such violations are answerable before such courts, both civilly and criminally. An amnesty to the wrongdoer effectively obliterates such rights.[24]

Nevertheless, the judge offered as justification the existence of the amnesty, which enabled him to move beyond these problems and dismiss the application. The first response from the bench represented a serious stretch of the judicial imagination:

> The families of those unlawfully tortured, maimed or traumatised become more empowered to discover the truth, the perpetrators become exposed to opportunities to obtain relief from the burden of a guilt or an anxiety they might be living with for many long years, the country begins the long and necessary process of healing the wounds of the past, transforming anger and grief into a mature understanding and creating the emotional and

structural climate essential for the 'reconciliation and reconstruction' which informs the very difficult and sometimes painful objectives of the amnesty articulated in the epilogue.[25]

One is entitled to wonder whether this approach leads to a diminution of the moral weight of the abuses of human rights conducted under and by the apartheid regime and its human instruments, and to crimes being swept away on hopeful consequentialist speculation.[26]

The second justification offered by Judge Mahomed clearly revealed the pragmatism of the court in coming to its conclusion:

> Even more crucially, but for a mechanism providing for amnesty, the 'historic bridge' itself might never have been erected. For a successfully negotiated transition, the terms of the transition required not only the agreement of those victimized by abuse but also those threatened by the transition to a 'democratic society based on freedom and equality'. If the Constitution kept alive the prospect of continuous retaliation and revenge, the agreement of those threatened by its implementation might never have been forthcoming, and if it had, the bridge itself would have remained wobbly and insecure, threatened by fear from some and anger from others.[27]

The court had a clear understanding of its central role in the construction and preservation of the 'bridge'.

The attack from the 'right'

The TRC was not the only new institution to face a legal attack. The country's first democratically elected president and the newly created Constitutional Court were the next to come under fire – this time from the right of the political spectrum.

For many in South Africa, particularly among the white community, rugby is a religion. For them, it is therefore not a matter in which interference by government is welcome. However, the issue of non-racialism in rugby has been consistently on the political agenda since 1994. In 1997 former President Mandela appointed a judicial commission of inquiry to investigate the management of the internal affairs of the

South African Rugby Football Union (SARFU). The rugby union went to court seeking to invalidate this decision.

Two key arguments were raised in support of the application. Firstly, there was the allegation that Mandela had failed to invite SARFU to give its views regarding the purpose of the commission. Secondly, the question arose as to whether the President had not abdicated his responsibility for appointing a commission to the Minister of Sport, Steve Tshwete, and hence failed to appreciate that a presidential commission remained his sole responsibility.

The application was heard in front of an extremely conservative judge, William de Villiers, a man who early in his career had sought the exclusion of former Deputy Chief Justice, Dikgang Moseneke, from the Pretoria Bar. In an unprecedented move, the judge decided that the president should be summoned to give evidence before the court. And so it was that nearly 40 years after the *Rivonia* trial, Mandela found himself once again in the witness box in a Pretoria court.

The case was clearly an attempt by the 'old guard' to fight back against the very core institutions that underpinned the newly established constitutional democracy. An eminent senior counsel reported that he had been in the Pretoria High Court robing room when the announcement came through that the judge had summoned former President Mandela to give evidence. A huge roar of approval broke out from the assembled ranks of the Pretoria Bar: their man was giving it to this newly appointed president.

It is worth considering the remarkable decision by the President to choose to testify, when a claim of executive privilege (or the claim that a sitting member of the executive branch of government could not be compelled to testify) could have been used to avoid that spectacle. Interviews with those involved in the case confirm that Mandela was determined to demonstrate his belief that no one was above the law, that the law should be obeyed and that executive power should be held accountable through processes such as judicial oversight or consideration by the courts of the reasonableness of the executive's conduct.

But Louis Luyt's own account of former President Mandela's testimony reveals the deep acrimony and political manoeuvring that pervaded the proceedings:

Preferring to take the word 'stand' to its literal extreme, he refused a seat and stood up for the duration of his testimony. Observers in the business of myth-building described this as a gesture of respect for the court. I believe, however, that he did so to demonstrate his authority over the man seated on the bench. Mandela's refusal to use the customary 'Lordship' in addressing Mr Justice de Villiers and referring to him simply as 'Judge' supports this contention.

Referring to our questioning of the validity of his affidavit, which had prompted Justice de Villiers to subpoena him, Mandela told the court: 'I would never have imagined that Louis would be so insensitive, so ungrateful to say when I gave my affidavit [that] I was lying. Dr Luyt is a pitiless dictator. No leader can stand up to him. You cannot talk of democracy.'[28]

By the end of the trial, Judge de Villiers had, astonishingly, found not only that the President had failed to invite SARFU to make its views known before he appointed the commission, but also that the President's evidence in this regard could not be believed. In making a credibility finding against him, he also found that the President had abdicated his responsibility for the appointment of this commission. Inevitably, the case went on appeal to the Constitutional Court. Ultimately, that court overturned all the grounds on which Judge de Villiers had found for SARFU.

Far more significant, however, was the attack then launched by Dr Luyt on the Constitutional Court. Luyt claimed that he had 'a reasonable apprehension that every member of the Constitutional Court [would] be biased against him'. So he brought an application for the recusal of five of its members, namely justices Chaskalson, Langa, Kriegler, Sachs and Yacoob. He claimed that, 'after careful deliberation', he had decided not to include the other judges expressly in his application but to leave it to the conscience of each individual member of the court whether they should sit in the case. The scope of the recusal application was significant. If Luyt had been able to ensure that there were fewer than eight members of the court who could sit, no appeal would have been possible because the quorum of the court is eight judges.

The recusal application had much broader implications for the Constitutional Court's role in the new constitutional order. The stakes were high indeed. As one commentator noted: 'If allegations of past political affiliation and personal indebtedness by reason of appointment to the court were to hold sway, the Constitutional Court would effectively be paralysed. In virtually every case, the government is a litigant. Hence, it could always be argued that the kinds of factors raised by Dr Luyt would preclude a fair trial. The recusal application, therefore, was calculated to undermine the very status of the Constitutional Court as an institution.'[29]

Interestingly, and rather ironically in the light of subsequent attacks on the judiciary, the same type of claim – that the appointees to the court would be reliable ANC sympathisers – was made at the time by certain political commentators of different political positions. For example, historian RW Johnson alleged that the government could 'count on the sympathies of a large majority of the court'.[30] Meanwhile, respected progressive political analyst Steven Friedman asked, 'What happens to democracy when the right issues are raised by the wrong people?'[31] Friedman's argument was that 'serious questions' needed to be asked about the Constitutional Court's 'enthusiasm (or lack of it) for aiding citizens if doing so might cause offence to the majority party.'[32]

The specific grounds on which recusal of individual judges was sought were essentially of two types: that the judge in question was politically affiliated with the ANC or had personal relationships with office-bearers in the new executive. Luyt alleged that Justice Sachs had held a position of leadership in the ANC and that justices Langa and Yacoob had been members of the party.[33] However, all these judges had severed their ties with the ANC immediately upon their appointment to the court. Luyt alleged that, in addition to his party affiliation, Justice Langa's status as founder member of the Release Mandela Committee in Natal, his role as an advisor during the talks that led to the Groote Schuur and Pretoria Minutes, and his attendance at a 'personal dinner with former President Mandela at his house' were grounds for recusal.

As for Justice Kriegler, Luyt alleged, among other things, that there appeared to be animosity between him and his (Luyt's) attorney, that their own 'fairly close relationship in the course of which he on numerous occasions attended rugby matches at Ellis Park as my guest' had apparently ended and that perceived sarcasm in his questioning at an earlier hearing in the appeal raised concerns of bias.

Luyt also raised questions about Justice Chaskalson's representation of former President Mandela at the *Rivonia* trial, and of his former wife on various occasions; his role as advisor to the ANC during the constitutional negotiations; former President Mandela's attendance at the wedding of Justice Chaskalson's son; and a dinner he had attended that had been held in honour of Justice Chaskalson when he left the Legal Resources Centre, which he had served with great distinction.

The flavour of Luyt's objections is captured in his truly appalling attack on Justice Sachs, the basis of which is set out in the judgment of the court:

> Perhaps the most inappropriate allegation made in the whole of this unfortunate application is that relating to the severe injuries which Justice Sachs suffered in Maputo at the hands of South African security forces. As is well known, Justice Sachs lost his right arm and sight in an eye in consequence of a bomb placed under his car. The allegation that Justice Sachs would by reason thereof be biased against the fourth respondent or in favour of the President reflects adversely on those who make that allegation and provides no basis for recusal. This is a tasteless allegation which is rejected. The less said about it the better.[34]

The recusal application failed. This was a result that Luyt described, in his inimitable way, as 'about as surprising as hearing that the All Blacks had beaten Japan'.[35] But this case was critical for another reason as well. It revealed the anxiety that this new Constitution, with its lofty ambition for a non-racial, non-sexist and truly free society, would penetrate far into the intimate personal sphere of South African citizens. This reach would mean the critical analysis of personal areas such as language, religion, sexual orientation, marriage and, yes, even sport. As Luyt saw it, 'the government continues to march relentlessly towards greater control of every facet of our lives'.[36] A more recent example, which confirms that the same kind of anxiety has not dissipated with time, is the controversy and subsequent complaints of human-rights violations that ensued after the Forum for Black Journalists excluded white journalists from an off-the-record briefing by the then recently elected ANC president, Jacob Zuma, in February 2008.

The *SARFU* case also held fundamental implications for the court and its legitimacy and in terms of the outcome of the main attack on the president of the republic. It is obvious that legitimacy and credibility are the main currency of any court and that the highest court in the land must be held to the highest ethical standards, and be unimpeachable, in order to have any real (moral) authority. The appearance of bias would have been fatal to a young court's authority and a society's acceptance of its decisions.

The perception of the highest court as biased, whether in favour of a political party or incumbent government or political faction, and not as impartial and loyal only to the values and principles of our constitutional democracy, holds deeply troubling consequences, particularly for a critical institution in our democracy. It is clear that the mere establishment of the Constitutional Court and its operation have alone been insufficient to lift it into legitimacy in the minds of South Africans. A study conducted in the 1990s by James Gibson found empirical support for this view:

> In most established political systems (and especially in the United States), courts draw far more loyalty from ordinary citizens than do parliaments. Parliaments are often tainted with all the unsavory business of democratic politics – compromise, partisanship, log-rolling, and so on – that people find displeasing … Courts, on the other hand, usually shroud their proceedings in secrecy, presenting a public image of solemnity, dignity, and reasoned and impartial decision making. Nothing could be more different from the way in which parliaments are typically portrayed (for example, as having notorious and unruly question periods). That the South African Constitutional Court attracts no more loyalty than the Parliament suggests that the Court has been unable to differentiate itself, that the image of the institution as doing something quite different from the other branches of government, and in a different way, has not yet penetrated the consciousness of the South African mass public. Failure to establish itself as a strictly legal institution has impeded the growth of the legitimacy of the Constitutional Court.[37]

This failure to set the Constitutional Court, as an institution, above politics, removed from the fickle and capricious nature of that arena, provided the licence for increasingly common attacks on the court and the broader judiciary in the fraught political climate of the Zuma years. Public support for an institution whose role is unknown to, and therefore unappreciated by, most South Africans simply cannot be expected. But it is critical to the success of our constitutional democracy. As former Chief Justice Langa said in a 1999 speech:

> The integrity of the judiciary is fundamental to peace, justice and security in any country. This imposes a heavy responsibility on judges and magistrates to function in a manner that sustains such integrity. Judges are accountable. They do not work in secret or behind some bush. They have to give reasons for their judgments and these are available for scrutiny and analysis by higher courts and by the public ...
>
> But a good judge needs appropriate judicial space within which to work. In the exercise of our judicial function, we are answerable only to the Constitution and the Law. An environment must exist wherein the judges can dispense justice impartially, without fear or favour. That then requires that government and the public respect the independence and integrity of the bench.[38]

It is to part of the record of the Constitutional Court that we must now turn, and in particular to three cases where it faced the burden of dealing with the need for transformation.

8

A BREAK WITH THE PAST,
A VIEW OF THE FUTURE

'[A]s long as almost 90 per cent of people who commit murder
in South Africa are never apprehended, prosecuted and convicted, individuals are unlikely to be deterred from committing
murder regardless of the punishment imposed on the 10 per-
cent who are in fact caught and convicted. Instead of discussing
the re-introduction of the death penalty, the time might well be
better spent findings solutions for the bizarrely low conviction
rates for murder and other serious crimes.'[1]
– PIERRE DE VOS, 23 November 2016

Life and death. An eye for an eye. State-sanctioned murder. A necessary
deterrent. Cruel and inhuman punishment.

Few legal issues promote as passionate or divisive a debate as that
surrounding the use of the death penalty. Scan the letters to the editors
of South Africa's newspapers on any given day and, invariably, there
will be a call for the reintroduction of the death penalty to 'deal with'
the prevalence of violent crime in this country. Politicians and the public
alike regularly make public appeals for a referendum on the issue. To
these people, the death penalty is an essential crime-fighting weapon
that has become unavailable since the abolition of capital punishment
by the Constitutional Court in a judgment delivered on 6 June 1995.

The court's decision holds significance for South Africa beyond the

173

issues of crime and punishment. As seen in the preceding chapters, certain lawsuits transcend their facts and assume an importance far beyond the immediate dispute because of their significance for society at large. *State v Makwanyane* was such a case. Not only was it the first case chosen for hearing by the new Constitutional Court, but *Makwanyane* also represented a foundational moment, a line drawn in the sands of South Africa's history marking the start of a new legal era.

The court's judgment embodies this dramatic change. Unusually, each of the 11 judges wrote a judgment concurring with the main judgment written by the president of the court, Arthur Chaskalson. Each judge set out reasons for supporting the decision to abolish the death penalty. These judgments are striking in how they differ from most court judgments, which laboriously recount the facts of the case to be decided. Here, the details and factual background as to how its protagonists – Themba Makwanyane and Mavusa Mchunu – came to be sentenced to death are all but absent. These men appear to be irrelevant to the decision, appearing only fleetingly in Justice Chaskalson's main judgment. Their stories and role in the case are dealt with in a meaningful way only by the judgment penned by Justice Kate O'Regan. Before 1994, it is likely that these men would have ended their lives on the gallows. Neither Makwanyane nor Mchunu are sympathetic figures. They were callous murderers convicted of a quadruple homicide from a botched cash heist ambush and robbery, in which Volkskas Bank employees Cornelius Havenga, 22, and Petrus Pretorius, 63, and police officers Matthys Thompson, 23, and Robert Goddard, 22, were all shot dead.[2] The importance of so-called social impact litigation in the new constitutional era is well demonstrated by the litigation process in this case. Renowned senior advocates Wim Trengove and Gilbert Marcus were approached by the Bar Council and accepted the case as a vehicle to challenge the constitutionality of the death penalty.[3] A plaintiff was needed – someone who was sentenced to death under the old penal system. The Department of Correctional Services was contacted and the names of prisoners under a death sentence were requested. These happened to be Makwanyane and Mchunu. By this bureaucratic coincidence, these men gave their names to one of the most important cases in post-apartheid South Africa. They never even met the lawyers who would argue to spare their lives before the hearing of the appeal.[4]

The 11 judges bore the clear mark of the new society under construction: most had fought long and hard for the end of apartheid. Some had been intimately involved in the drafting of the Constitution, including the 'right to life' clause, and negotiations for South Africa's transition to a constitutional democracy. In fact, five of the judges were on the public record as abolitionists and none were on the record as being in favour of capital punishment, making the job of counsel arguing for the retention of the death penalty a truly uphill battle.[5] This was confirmed at the hearing by an intervention made by Acting Judge Sydney Kentridge, the legendary senior counsel, widely regarded as the finest lawyer never to have become Chief Justice of South Africa. Among his many important cases, Kentridge had led the team on behalf of the Biko family at the inquest into the death in detention of the struggle leader. He interrupted his colleagues' barrage of questions from the bench to request that the retentionist camp's counsel be heard 'in your own words and in your own time'. This was an unsubtle judicial hint to his colleagues, Ismail Mahomed and John Didcott, to afford counsel a chance to develop his argument. The two then remained relatively silent for a few minutes.

Kentridge admitted in an interview with the authors that he and some of his fellow justices did not find the case as easy as one might expect.[6] Primarily, this was because counsel for the retentionists raised some thoughtful arguments, described below, that required careful consideration and deliberation before they could be rejected. But the case was also difficult because of the court's awareness of the political stakes and the importance of its treatment of the death penalty in building a new South Africa.

These stakes were confirmed on the day before the hearings began. The Constitutional Court's first president, Chaskalson, informed the audience who attended the opening ceremony of the court that the first case to be heard by the court concerned the vital question of whether the state had the right to take the life of a convicted person. During his inauguration speech in which he officially opened the Constitutional Court, the first democratically elected president, Nelson Mandela, had noted that the last time he had been in a court was to find out whether he and his co-accused in the *Rivonia* trial would be sentenced to death. The significance of the decision three decades earlier to imprison, rather than execute, Mandela was surely not lost on those in attendance. Mandela then went on to say, 'Today I rise not as an accused but on behalf of the people of South Africa, to inaugurate a court South Africa has never had, a court on which hinges the future of our democracy.'[7]

But before we return to this landmark case, it is necessary to embark on a brief excursion through the history of capital punishment.

History of the death penalty[8]

The question of capital punishment has bedevilled most societies. It is a punishment as old as human history and has seen the convicted beheaded, forced to walk the plank, burnt at the stake, crushed by heavy stones, mauled by ferocious beasts, crucified, drawn and quartered, disembowelled and dismembered. In more recent times, states have used the guillotine, noose and gallows, firing squad, electric chair and lethal injection to apply the ultimate penalty.

In 1752, British judges could order posthumous tarring and chaining of corpses to increase the horror for onlookers, apparently hoping to enhance the claimed deterrent effect on potential wrongdoers. In 1783, James Boswell proposed that 'convicts should be hanged without hoods that the distortions may be seen'. In an ideal world, he argued, criminals would have their heads publicly smashed open with an iron mallet, before being jugulated with a machete and hacked apart with an axe. He noted that attendance at public executions of criminals was for enjoyment, not deterrence. Even debtors were liable to end their days for nothing more than indebtedness: after 60 days in prison, their failure to repay their creditors was punishable by execution or enslavement, at the choice of the creditor. In fact, if a debtor owed more than one creditor, he could apportion the debt among the creditors by having them collectively tear him limb from limb. In Roman penal law, an individual who had killed his parents was beaten with rods until blood was drawn, then drowned in a sack containing a dog, a cock, a monkey and a snake.

Public executions were common worldwide until the 19th century, when politicians began to become concerned that, on one hand, the raucous ritual of the gibbet would lead to its becoming unpopular, and, on the other, 'popular disgust' would soon lead 'to the entire abolition of capital punishment'. Hangings then took place behind prison walls and away from public viewing, arguably increasing popular support for the death penalty because the physical horrors of execution were no longer witnessed by the public.

Prussia was the first European state to end public executions, relocating beheadings away from public view in 1851. Russia and the Austro-Hungarian Empire next abolished the death penalty.

But, as widespread as the gory practice of capital punishment may have been, there is another trend that can be identified – the move towards the abolition of capital punishment as societies develop and democratise. With the notable exception of the US, where the continued appetite for executions can be explained, at least in part, as a function of that country's religious and puritanical past, and resulting religious and conservative world views, the death penalty has largely been abolished throughout the world in the last century. By the end of 2017, 106 countries had abolished the death penalty for all crimes and 142 countries had abolished it in practice.[9]

Even in those countries that retain the death penalty, the circumstances in which it is available have been reduced and circumscribed, as in its abolition for minors or mentally ill offenders. When coupled with the rise in forensic technology, such as DNA testing, which has been frequently used to clear convicted prisoners on death row through the diligent efforts of law students and public-interest lawyers worldwide, resistance to the use of the death penalty is common.

Justifying the death penalty

The trend to abolition notwithstanding, the death penalty retains significant popular support. The 'hang 'em high' lobby apart, there are rational justifications presented for its retention. Two main arguments have been used to justify the capital punishment of criminals. First is the principle of retribution, embodied in popular discourse in the idea of 'an eye for an eye', which essentially institutionalises and legitimises the desire to avenge the acts of criminals. Proponents argue that the accused's own actions 'brought this on themselves'. Hence, retributive justice promotes a theory that proportionate punishment is morally acceptable as a response to crime. Only a proportional response to a crime represents just punishment, it is argued. Critics of this argument suggest that it requires the state to sink to the level of criminals and makes the state 'no better than them'. Retribution, obviously, precludes the possibility of an individual's rehabilitation during his incarceration, given his death.

Second, advocates of the death penalty claim that it is a deterrent to future criminal activity. Although heavily disputed, this argument boils down to 'if they know they might die for it, they might not do it'. However, extensive studies around the world have demonstrated that the availability of the death penalty has little or no conclusive deterrent effect on criminal activity.[10] But, even if one were to accept the deterrent effect of the death penalty, it begs the question of whether an alternative punishment, such as life imprisonment, would not serve as an equally effective deterrent.[11]

But, clearly, the most vexing problem with the administration of capital punishment is the irreversibility of the death penalty in the event that the conviction was the result of an error. A study in 2000 by researchers at Columbia University of 5 800 capital convictions from 1973 to 1995 found serious errors in 68 per cent of them.[12] The horror of an innocent man or woman being executed for a crime he or she did not commit means that even supporters of the death penalty can only conscionably hope that it is carried out in the absence of any reasonable doubt as to the guilt of the accused.

The death penalty in South Africa

Historically, the death penalty was part of the law governing South Africa from the days of its control by the Dutch East India Company. Here, executions were also public affairs, often accompanied by disembowelling, dismemberment or 'breaking' on a wheel (when the body was stretched from opposite sides). In fact, the 17th-century executioner received separate payments for such additional services – eight *rixdalers* for decapitation or hanging, twelve for breaking limbs, six for strangling, two for scorching, six for quartering and hanging up the pieces and four for chopping off a hand.[13] One wonders how this scale of payment for these gruesome services was determined! By the end of the 18th century, such 'accessory torture' had been abolished, although public execution was still practised until late in the 19th century.[14]

The Criminal Procedure and Evidence Act 31 of 1917 provided for a mandatory sentence of death for murder, except where the perpetrator was younger than 16 or was a woman who had murdered her newborn child. The courts could exercise mercy, however, and this resulted in a reprieve for many.[15] Later, during apartheid, the death penalty was used to punish a wide range of offences, including murder, robbery and housebreaking with aggravating circumstances, sabotage, 'undergoing training or obtaining information abroad to further communism, and furthering economic and social change in South Africa by violent means', 'participation in terroristic activities', kidnapping and child-stealing, and rape.[16]

By the late 1980s, after South Africa had declared numerous states of emergency, the Society for the Abolition of the Death Penalty, Lawyers for Human Rights and other civil-society organisations challenged the death penalty and urged reform. Government repeatedly affirmed its commitment to the death penalty but indicated it was 'receptive' to proposals to reform capital punishment. Minister of Justice Kobie Coetsee, in remarks to Parliament on 27 April 1989 (five years to the day before the historic elections ending apartheid), identified reforms for consideration, including abolition of the mandatory death sentence for murder, creating an automatic right of appeal to the Appellate Division once a capital sentence was passed, and some extension to a judge's sentencing discretion.

Needless to say, black South Africans suffered the harshest consequences of the apartheid state's imposition of the death penalty. Judicial bias played a significant role in a number of cases. For example, between 1947 and 1966, no white offender convicted of the rape of black women was executed. In damning contrast, 122 black offenders convicted of the rape of white women were hanged during the same period of time.[17] This racial bias was often exacerbated by the accused's poverty, resulting in inadequate legal representation for capital cases. Accordingly, the death penalty's arbitrary imposition was often the result of ineffective counsel, overeager prosecution, judges willing to ignore irregularities in evidence and a lack of procedural safeguards.

During the nearly eight decades in which statistics were maintained, 4 226 executions were carried out in South Africa. In the 57 years between 1911 and 1968, 2 323 executions (an average of 40 per year) took place. However, in the 20-year period between 1968 and 1988, 1 904 people were executed (an average of 95 per year). In 1987 alone, 164 people were executed, the largest number ever hanged in one year.

The total number of executions in South Africa for the ten-year period 1980 to 1989 was 1 219. During the same period, the total number of death sentences handed down in South Africa (excluding Transkei, Bophuthatswana, Venda and Ciskei) was 1 842.[18]

By the early 1990s, the death penalty was restricted to the crimes of murder, treason committed in wartime, robbery with aggravating circumstances, kidnapping, child-stealing and rape. It was discretionary, not mandatory, and could be imposed only when the judge was satisfied that 'the sentence of death is the proper sentence' following a consideration of any facts in mitigation or aggravation of sentence.[19]

As shown in academic studies, the discretionary nature of the death sentence meant that the 'personal disposition towards capital punishment of the individual judges played a critical role in where, in cases where the death sentence was a competent verdict, it was imposed'.[20] The highly problematic consequence of this finding was that the identity of the judge presiding over a capital trial was a major factor in whether a conviction would carry capital punishment. Or, as Angus and Grant frame the issue, 'Judges are not *automata* and we do not suggest that they ought to make decisions mechanically. It is, therefore, inevitable that personal attitudes will play a role in judicial decision-making and result in differences in sentencing. But, where life and death are at stake, such inconsistency cannot be tolerated.'[21]

This personal discretion, and its inconsistent outcome, was vigorously defended, however, by the Deputy Judge President of the Transvaal Provincial Division at the time, Judge David Curlewis. In correspondence responding to the Angus and Grant study, Curlewis said:

Only an *ignoramus*, or a person with little regard for the truth would deny [that judicial attitudes towards the death penalty play a material role in imposing or not imposing that sentence]. ...

The above fact does not lead to people who do not deserve to die being sentenced to death; it leads to people who should be sentenced to death escaping the death penalty. ...

Let me make my meaning plain. A person who deserved to hang was more likely to get the death sentence from me or my ilk than (at random) my brothers Roux, MacArthur, Van Schalkwyk, Nestadt, Goldstone or Gordon. The reason is that these judges are at heart abolitionists for one reason or another.

There's nothing wrong with this. After all, the present Chief Justice is an abolitionist, and beliefs are to be respected. But obviously, and for that reason, they cannot be sound on the imposition of the death penalty.

The answer to this problem (until the Government does away with the death sentence) will be clear to the authors: for the good of the community and for the peace of mind of such judges, they should not sit on capital cases.[22]

Curlewis argued, notwithstanding, that this was an unsatisfactory state of affairs, given how highly the legal system prizes predictability and certainty.

As apartheid came to its final chapter, the imposition of the death penalty became a highly politicised issue. This is best exemplified by the case of *State v Safatsa and Others*,[23] known more commonly as the *Sharpeville Six*. Here, six people were each sentenced to death for the murder of the Deputy Mayor of Lekoa by a mob. Judge Wessel Human imposed the death penalty on the six defendants despite the acceptance that none of their actions had causally contributed to the death of the victim.

However, the doctrine of common purpose – according to which, if two or more people, having a common purpose to commit a crime, act together to achieve that purpose, the conduct of each of them in the execution of that purpose is imputed to all the others[24] – was used to cure the otherwise fatal deficiency in the evidence presented by the prosecution. These sentences were upheld by the Appellate Division and the pending executions attracted an international campaign for clemency, supported by calls for sanctions if the executions took place. Initially, the government obdurately supported the decision of the Appellate Division. The Deputy Minister of Information, 'Slim' Stoffel van der Merwe,[25] said that to hang a criminal has a demonstrative effect, 'namely that crime is punished'.[26]

In the end, though, the government bowed to the political pressure.

The Sharpeville Six were saved from the gallows by presidential reprieve – but not before South Africa's judiciary and system of 'justice' had taken substantial flak, enduring criticism and international scorn for the prospect of imposing capital punishment. The negative perceptions of the highest court at the time, the Appellate Division, were captured in the following criticism of the appellate judgment in a work devoted to the case: 'The cost of this narrow judgement was potentially incalculable … The cries for justice would henceforth only be answered where property rights were at stake. Life and liberty would count for nothing. And the worst was that this retreat was not forced upon the court by a dictator.'[27]

So it was that the escalation in executions during the 1980s coincided with the political turmoil engulfing the country at the same time and, when welcome political change came, the issue of the death penalty was not spared either.

First, a moratorium on the death sentence was announced in a watershed speech by President FW de Klerk at the opening of Parliament on 2 February 1990. De Klerk announced that all executions were suspended and that every sentence of death passed but not yet executed was to be reviewed. The import of this radical change to the punitive regime in South Africa, and its appropriate announcement in one of the most significant political speeches in our history, was captured by Etienne Mureinik:

> A leader committed to breaking that cycle [of systematic racial oppression and execution] could have found no better way to start than by suspending the hangman. Had we continued to treat it as routine to break human necks in batches of seven, the season of violence would have had to linger. Every hanging has proclaimed the value of violence, and every hanging has affirmed the contempt for the personhood of people upon which apartheid depends. It had become impossible in this country to pledge peace and humanity without noticing the role of the death system, and undertaking to do something about it.[28]

Then, death row prisoners were afforded an automatic right to appeal to the Appellate Division. This was a significant change because any litigant, including people sentenced to death by a trial court, would otherwise have to request or apply for leave or permission to appeal. Now, there was a right of appeal. As Mureinik explains, this was significant not only because it recognised the unique position of such persons but also because it acknowledged that 'the entire approach to punishment for murder' had until then 'been erroneous'.[29]

Finally, the death penalty was to be limited to 'extreme cases'. This too recognised that the use of capital punishment in South Africa had exceeded all justification and was disproportionate to any acceptable rationale.

The gallows were last in operation on 14 November 1989 and it is a tragic fact that executions took place just a few months before the moratorium hardened into reprieve and reprieve into abolition.[30]

For many opponents of apartheid, the execution of Eastern Cape ANC leader Vuyisile Mini in 1964 made it clear that the death penalty was used for overtly political purposes. Its suspension, and then ultimate abolition, marked another step towards the establishment of a constitutional democracy and the recognition of every person's dignity and humanity. It was therefore an issue that would inevitably confront the negotiators for a new Constitution.

Death penalty and a constitutional South Africa

As explained in the previous chapter, during CODESA, negotiators from political parties representing all South Africans convened. Delegations from across the governmental and political spectrum began negotiating the creation and design of a transitional government and the first representative democratic state for all South Africans. The issue of the death penalty was understandably fraught and controversial. In fact, despite countless days of discussion and several draft provisions, no consensus could be reached by these political negotiators on whether the death penalty would continue into the new South Africa.

The Interim Constitution provided for a right to life. This unqualified formulation was the result of the multiparty negotiations at CODESA, but also showed how the negotiators could not agree on the question of the death penalty and decided instead to leave the issue up to the new Constitutional Court. In contrast, other bills of rights often qualified the right to deal with capital punishment, abortion or euthanasia, creating the textual space in which to permit, or prohibit, each of these. But

South Africa's right to life was wholly unqualified and therefore gave no guidance on whether it could be limited to allow for the imposition of the death penalty.

Critical to an understanding of how the Constitutional Court resolved the question of the death penalty in particular, and to constitutional litigation generally, is a grasp of the workings of the so-called limitations clause. Every right enshrined in the Constitution could be limited by a law of general application (in other words, something that was not a mere political policy statement but a properly enacted piece of legislation or rule of the common law). Any legal limitation of a constitutional right required proof from the state that such a limitation was justified. A limitation was only permissible under the Interim Constitution's limitations clause to the extent that it was reasonable and justifiable in an open and democratic society based on freedom and equality, and did not negate the essential content of the right in question. In other words, a court was required to make a two-stage enquiry: first, was the right in question limited by the conduct at issue? Secondly, was this limitation justified? The constitutional debate about the death penalty therefore turned less on an answer to the question of whether the death penalty breached the right to life: the key issue was whether it could be properly justified.

So it was that, when the tall, angular, balding figure of senior counsel Wim Trengove rose in mid-February 1995 to address the Constitutional Court in its first case, the issue could not have been more stark. Life or death. Or, more precisely, whether the South African government would continue to impose the death penalty, by hanging by the neck until dead, on criminals convicted of the most serious crimes.

From 15 to 17 February 1995, the new Constitutional Court heard argument regarding the constitutionality of the death penalty. The precarious and novel nature of this new apex court was reflected in the temporary nature of the court, which was then housed in the rather inauspicious setting of an office complex in Braamfontein. This was before the Constitution Hill precinct had been constructed. The argument was held in a corporate environment without the traditional wood-panelled walls of a courtroom. There were no grand staircases leading to a 'legal palace'. The teams of distinguished counsel took the lift to the second floor, sandwiched between the first floor, which housed the offices of

American Express and the third floor, occupied by a firm of attorneys.

But, despite the setting, the importance of the moment cannot be overestimated, and the novelty and unprecedented nature of the proceedings cannot be exaggerated. Counsel even confessed to a palpable sense of nervousness on both sides – both from themselves and the bench – at this first hearing. And there was no precedent for any of the new court's procedures or protocol: what robes the judges would wear, what order they would sit in on the bench, how they would be addressed by counsel – or even what the procedure would be for organising oral argument.

The 11 judges had held a meeting to discuss these elementary practical and logistical details. At this meeting, they decided to be addressed as 'Justice so-and-so', in line with the American judicial tradition, instead of the traditional, and gendered, 'm' Lord' or 'm' Lady' (which is still used today to address judges in many high courts). On the question of how the judges should be seated, they decided against seniority of tenure, which would have placed Richard Goldstone first. Laurie Ackermann's wise, if self-serving, suggestion to sit in alphabetical order was also rejected, as was arranging themselves by chronological age. In the end, the judges decided that they would not sit in any particular order – although the Chief Justice was to sit in the centre, with his deputy to his right.

The judges of the Constitutional Court also chose unisex robes, embodying equality. Their robes are green and therefore strikingly distinct from the English-style black robes worn by judges in the civil courts or red when dealing with criminal matters. Unlike the robes of senior counsel, the justices' gowns are not made of silk (which provides the colloquial term for a senior counsel) to symbolise the fact that not all of the judges are drawn from the ranks of silks. Unlike the vast majority of judicial appointments drawn exclusively from the ranks of senior counsel, the first court included three professors of law.

The parties to the case themselves embodied the changing political dispensation: the applicants, represented by Wim Trengove, and the national government, represented by veteran human-rights advocate George Bizos SC, were both in favour of abolishing the death penalty. It was the attorney general of the Witwatersrand, represented by Klaus von Lieres und Wilkau SC, who argued for its retention. Several amici curiae, representing the viewpoints of abolitionist civil-society organisations, the police and the Black Lawyers' Association, also argued to assist the court in deciding this most contentious of cases.

The main argument advanced by the abolitionist parties was that the death penalty violated sections 9 (the right to life) and 11 (the right to be free from cruel, inhuman and degrading punishment) of the interim Constitution's Bill of Rights. As Chaskalson, the president of the court, summarised in his judgment:

> The principal arguments advanced by counsel for the accused in support of their contention that the imposition of the death penalty for murder is a 'cruel, inhuman or degrading punishment', were that the death sentence is an affront to human dignity, is inconsistent with the unqualified right to life entrenched in the Constitution, cannot be corrected in case of error or enforced in a manner that is not arbitrary, and that it negates the essential content of the right to life and the other rights that flow from it. The Attorney General argued that the death penalty is recognised as a legitimate form of punishment in many parts of the world, it is a deterrent to violent crime, it meets society's need for adequate retribution for heinous offences, and it is regarded by South African society as an acceptable form of punishment. He asserted that it is, therefore, not cruel, inhuman or degrading within the meaning of s 11(2) of the Constitution.[31]

A press report of the day covered the retentionist position accurately:

> The camp fighting for the death penalty includes the SAPS [South African Police Service] and the State, represented by Witwatersrand Attorney-General Klaus von Lieres. They are supported by a private citizen, retired civil engineer Ian Glauber, who has formulated a well-considered, multi-pronged argument.
>
> Glauber posits that murder committed as a result of emotional distress should be separated from murder committed by criminals who have no personal, emotional or psychological links with their victims. The latter, he says, deserve mandatory death

sentences. He also disputes the claim that the death penalty fails as a deterrent, saying only the most brazen and stupid would not be deterred by such a fate. Glauber further argues that the primary objective of the Constitution is to protect the fundamental right to life of the innocent victim and not the perpetrator. On the irrevocability of the death sentence, he says that given the laws of evidence and conduct of the process, particularly capital cases, there tends to be an extreme unlikelihood of an innocent person being erroneously convicted. Glauber says that references in the Bible and Koran to death penalties repudiates claims that it is against the word of God.[32]

Both the judges and counsel were probing the scope and limits of constitutional litigation, testing in particular to what extent public opinion could inform the debate around the meaning of a constitutional right. The court was having none of this populist discourse, however. It was determined to set out as clearly as possible its conception of the Constitution, the rule of law and the role of the Constitutional Court in its interpretation and administration without bowing to popular views.

Newspaper reports at the time recorded some of the comments from the bench:

> White-haired and bearded with penetrating eyes, Natal judge, John Didcott, is terrier-like in trying to tear apart the pro-death-sentence arguments. Justice Didcott snaps that he does not see why the Constitutional Court should have to pay attention to public opinion, however strong, and which may be 'ill-informed' or 'based on a fallacious belief'. Besides, says the judge, paying attention to public opinion is the job of the legislature and not the judiciary, which is there [to] interpret existing laws.[33]

The judges did not entirely hide their differences from the public gaze. At one point, Justice Albie Sachs, who had been a somewhat controversial appointment,[34] asked his first question of George Bizos. Before Bizos could say a word in response, both Justices Didcott and Mahomed fired questions at the bemused Bizos. Justice Didcott told him not to answer Justice Sachs's question, which, in his view, was hardly relevant. Bizos was reduced to asking the presiding judge, 'Who, Justice Chaskalson, must I answer first?'

As Von Lieres returned to the argument of the significance of public opinion, citing pro-capital-punishment sentiments expressed to the Constitutional Assembly chairman, Cyril Ramaphosa, at a meeting in the Cape, he drew an outburst from Justice Johann Kriegler, to 'play the ball and not the man', arguing that 'one incident in Paarl does not a national public opinion make'.[35] Even Bizos, on behalf of the government, canvassed the pro-retention public opinion. In his typically colourful way, he read from newspaper clippings and letters to the nation's editors with such catchphrases as 'Hang 'em high!' He too was admonished from the bench that these references were irrelevant to the case before the court. Unusually for the tenacious Bizos, who is not one to allow judges to disturb his flow of argument, he quickly changed tack.

In response to these submissions, the court carefully explained in its judgment the critical difference between its role and that of the legislature, or Parliament. It is worth quoting the main judgment at length on this point:

> The Attorney General argued that what is cruel, inhuman or degrading depends to a large extent upon contemporary attitudes within society, and that South African society does not regard the death sentence for extreme cases of murder as a cruel, inhuman or degrading form of punishment. It was disputed whether public opinion, properly informed of the different considerations, would in fact favour the death penalty. I am, however, prepared to assume that it does and that the majority of South Africans agree that the death sentence should be imposed in extreme cases of murder. The question before us, however, is not what the majority of South Africans believe a proper sentence for murder should be. It is whether the Constitution allows the sentence.
>
> Public opinion may have some relevance to the enquiry, but in itself, it is no substitute for the duty vested in the Courts to interpret the Constitution and to uphold its provisions without fear or favour. If public opinion were to be decisive, there would

be no need for constitutional adjudication. The protection of rights could then be left to Parliament, which has a mandate from the public, and is answerable to the public for the way its mandate is exercised, but this would be a return to parliamentary sovereignty, and a retreat from the new legal order established by the 1993 Constitution. By the same token, the issue of the constitutionality of capital punishment cannot be referred to a referendum, in which a majority view would prevail over the wishes of any minority. The very reason for establishing the new legal order, and for vesting the power of judicial review of all legislation in the courts, was to protect the rights of minorities and others who cannot protect their rights adequately through the democratic process. Those who are entitled to claim this protection include the social outcasts and marginalised people of our society. It is only if there is a willingness to protect the worst and the weakest amongst us, that all of us can be secure that our own rights will be protected.

This Court cannot allow itself to be diverted from its duty to act as an independent arbiter of the Constitution by making choices on the basis that they will find favour with the public.[36]

The judgment

The judgment issued by the Constitutional Court struck down the death penalty in South Africa. It also announced that things would never be the same in the country and proclaimed the new normative view grounded in the Constitution. The judgment was influenced by the personal and cultural backgrounds and experiences of the judges, by the acceptance of traditionally African concepts, such as ubuntu, and by the court's recognition that this judgment would describe and set the course for the new South African constitutional democracy. George Bizos captured the importance of the court's impressive judgments when he observed that the decision had been taken to strike down a central component of the country's penal regime after an application by two accused who 'were almost beyond redemption'.[37]

The judgment is significant for its engagement with and reliance on comparative law – in other words, comparing the state of law in countries around the world. It is also striking for its rejection of public opinion on the death penalty. This was an assertion of the court of a constitutional project that rejects being bound by the inevitable fluctuations of such opinion.

Arguably, the most powerful case for the retention of the death penalty is the deterrent argument – that criminals would be deterred from committing crimes if they carried the death penalty. Yet, this relies on three assumptions, none of which survived the careful scrutiny of Justice Chaskalson, who authored the main judgment. First is the assumption that those who are criminally inclined will pause and change their intended criminal course of action because of the possibility that the gallows will exact retribution. This ascribes a degree of rationality to the depraved that is, unfortunately, unwarranted.

Secondly, before capital punishment is imposed, a criminal must be detected, apprehended, successfully prosecuted and linked to the crime, and then a court, and usually an appellate court as well, must satisfy itself that the death penalty is warranted. So, even when the death penalty was available as punishment for a particular category of offence, it was not always imposed by the court. Given South Africa's truly dismal performance at detecting, apprehending and prosecuting criminals, the sentencing stage is usually never reached. Therefore, a criminal in South Africa, it was argued, is unlikely to be deterred by the possible punishment, when the chances are is that the essential prosecutorial steps to the gallows will never be taken.

Finally, the deterrent argument assumes that a criminal will be deterred by nothing less than the death penalty. It therefore seems as if death-penalty proponents assume that the alternative to the death penalty is no punishment at all or punishment that can never deter. The court's decision makes it abundantly clear, however, that the alternative to capital punishment is a term of life or long-term imprisonment. Clearly, a rational person would be similarly deterred from criminal conduct by the prospect of decades in the hospitality of the Department of Correctional Services, in prison conditions that are truly dire.

The court therefore chose to assert its authority and unique role in the South African legal system with this most controversial of issues. It seized this opportunity to define the new constitutional order in a bold stroke. The judges' appreciation of the historic moment is clear throughout the judgment. Its tone shows that the new court, and the society it would help create, was a very clear break with the apartheid past where state power was abused in the worst possible way by depriving its citizens of their humanity, dignity, personhood and life itself. This sentiment was captured in Justice Didcott's judgment when he stated, simply, that 'the wanton killing must stop before it makes a mockery of the civilised, humane and compassionate society to which the nation aspires and has constitutionally pledged itself'. The judgment also describes the nation-building and transformational project then under way in the country.

The court held that the constitutional prohibition on cruel, inhuman and degrading punishment must be construed in the historical context of the Constitution, as well as in light of other related fundamental rights provisions in the Constitution, specifically the rights to life, dignity and equality. The right to be free from cruel, inhuman and degrading punishment must also be realised in a way that secures the full measure of its protection for individuals.

The court also recognised the political context that placed the question of capital punishment before it and acknowledged that it had been the subject of vigorous, though inconclusive, debate during the multiparty negotiating process. This failure to resolve the issue in the drafting process led to the Solomonic solution that deliberately left the determination of the constitutionality of the death penalty to the Constitutional Court. Rather than being an abdication of responsibility by the negotiators, this was a recognition of the limitation of the multiparty negotiations and that the decision should be left to an institution fluent in the new South Africa's language of human rights.

Interestingly, while many of the judgments mentioned ubuntu and its inherent respect for each person's humanity and dignity, only the judgment of Justice Sachs dealt in any meaningful way with the question of how the death penalty was treated under African vernacular, or customary, law. Sachs argued that

> the materials suggest that amongst the Cape Nguni, the death penalty was practically confined to cases of suspected witchcraft, and was normally spontaneously carried out after accusation by the diviners. [Academic John Henderson] Soga says that the death penalty was never imposed, the reasoning being as follows:

'Why sacrifice a second life for one already lost?'[38]

Summary execution sometimes followed assaults on wives of chiefs or other aggravated cases, but were otherwise unknown, as most criminal conduct was usually dealt with out of the property of the accused.

> [O]ffences were considered to be against the community or tribe rather than the individual, and punishment of a constructive or corrective nature was administered for disturbing the balance of tribal life.[39]

Sachs was the only judge who tried to anchor the rejection of capital punishment in any norm or bedrock principle, such as ubuntu. This is important because the other arguments (the deterrent effect and retribution) are consequentialist in nature, meaning that the death penalty should be declared unlawful because all justifications offered for its existence cannot be sustained. However, if a new method of execution that did not constitute cruel, inhuman or degrading punishment were conceived, that basis for opposing the death penalty might then fail. Similarly, if a new scientific study confirmed unequivocally the deterrent effect of the death penalty, that argument would also fail.

Given this reasoning by the court, the question of the legality of the death penalty could be revisited in the future if further and better justification can be produced. Only a foundational, moral basis to reject capital punishment as abhorrent and hence contrary to a defined norm, standard or value that could not be revised would escape this fate. Justice Sachs's consideration of the issue in African vernacular law and his reach towards a foundational value that rejects capital punishment are therefore critical because they offer a possibility of rejection of the death penalty that is immune to any impugned or contested scientific data. Accordingly, Sachs found that the vernacular law's 'rational and humane adjudicatory approach is entirely consistent with and re-enforcing of the fundamental rights enshrined in our Constitution'.[40]

The reaction
Public reaction was divided, as expected. For example, Rabbi David Hoffman of the Progressive Jewish Congregation said he was 'very sad'

for the families of victims of prisoners on death row, and asked: 'Is this decision really compassionate for the innocent and the victims of crime in our society?'[41] Angry letters flooded in to the nation's newspapers, complaining to the effect that the right to life applies only 'to those who are found guilty of murder. It certainly does not apply to the law-abiding citizen or the victim'.[42]

Other South Africans cautiously welcomed the decision but demanded that such criminals should serve the longest possible sentences, including life imprisonment without parole, and that they should be trained to serve their victims' dependants, thereby relieving the state of a financial burden.[43]

At the time, the Gauteng premier, Tokyo Sexwale, seemed to share the view of many analysts who claim that the futility of life for prisoners serving life imprisonment (lacking, as it does, any hope of release, incentive for good behaviour or prospect of rehabilitation) is worse than being killed by the state when he said that he hoped that Chris Hani's killers, Janusz Walus and Clive Derby-Lewis, two of the more infamous death-row inmates, 'would grow thin with worry' in prison. 'In their porridge and in their coffee, they must see nothing but Comrade Hani's face,' he said. Sexwale added that it had been suggested to him that the two be hanged in public in the 80 000-seat FNB stadium outside Johannesburg.[44]

The then Justice Minister, the late Dullah Omar, an outspoken death-penalty abolitionist, assured 'a nation crying out for the death penalty that if prisoners were spared the gallows by the court, they could spend the rest of their lives behind bars – with no remissions of sentence.'[45]

South Africa's last hangman and his assistant retired on 8 June 1995, following the scrapping of the death penalty by the Constitutional Court. Both men had been on full pay since the last executions in 1989 and were pensioners by the time of the court decision that ended their livelihood. At the time, 453 prisoners were on death row. Bizos was appointed to spearhead the review of their sentences and lead the process of determining each of their fates.

On the question of what to do with these prisoners, FW de Klerk (then deputy president), called for clemency to be granted to them, because 'the slate must be cleaned'; he urged the debate to focus on 'whether we want to have this in future, in a country where there is a high incidence of crime'.[46]

The Constitutional Court ordered that the death sentences of these prisoners had to be set aside and substituted with appropriate alternative sentences. Two years later, Parliament passed a law providing for such substitution. On 25 May 2005, the Constitutional Court was called on to pronounce on the constitutional validity of that law and expressed its dismay that, ten years later, 62 people remained under the sentence of death. The court therefore extended its supervisory jurisdiction and began a process in which a series of reports were filed with the court, detailing extensively the status of the process and offering explanations and reasons for the continuing delay of substituted sentences. Each report occasioned a judgment from the court, issuing further supervisory orders. By 15 September 2005, 40 people were still on death row, but that number was reduced to 28 by 7 November and to nine by 15 February 2006, and the process was completed by 28 July 2006. Sentences were typically substituted with life or long terms of imprisonment.

This successful use of the court's supervisory powers showed the opportunity lurking in future cases to press political and social progress. The added weight of the court's supervision increased the political momentum to address the problem. As we turn to consider the strategic lawyering of the TAC in the next chapter, we will see once again this potential for the judicial branch to oversee the implementation of policy required by the Constitution.

Conclusion

Through *Makwanyane*, the democratic will of the new South Africa was exerted in a significant and profound way. Like the landmark cases during the apartheid regime described earlier in the book, *Makwanyane* provided a clear indication of the power of law and the role of courts in shaping a country and society. In contrast to the apartheid courts, however, this case also shows the Constitutional Court as a constructive instrument, articulating and creating a new relationship between the state and its citizens.

One thing is clear from *Makwanyane*: a constitutionally sourced process of litigation, argument and decision could result in an outcome unimaginable just a few years before, when apartheid seemed a permanent feature of South African society. *Makwanyane* also showed that the individual and personal histories and experiences of the judges who decided it were a factor in the final decision. In this case, all of the judges had a clear and common understanding of the role played by the death penalty in apartheid South Africa. The judges understood their bridge-building role, thereby offering the possibility of courts being as dynamic and reflective of their political context as any other institution of government. The appointment of outstanding jurists with constitutional imagination had made an immediate impact.

The other important aspect of the decision was its rejection of majoritarian rule, or at least popular opinion, in favour of fidelity to the enumerated constitutional principles and values, regardless of their popularity with the broader society. The court rose above populism to enforce law and assert constitutional values despite the lack of popular support for such a decision.

Tellingly, though, the fact that one subsection – providing for the death penalty as a competent punishment for treason committed in wartime – remains on the statute books demonstrates that the issue of the death penalty may well be revisited at some time in the future. For this reason, the consequentialist nature of most of the reasons advanced by the court for its decision in *Makwanyane* is troubling, since they do not provide a comprehensive and permanent answer to the question of why capital punishment should be prohibited in South Africa's constitutional state.

It is obvious that the death penalty is the starkest exercise of power that a government has to regulate its citizens' lives, by literally depriving them of life. If one also accepts that the courts embody the morality and social mores or norms of a society and that particular community's view of justice, then how courts deal with the criminal defendant accused of the very worst and most repugnant crimes is an illustration of that society's view of itself. It also points to the possibility of rendering state sovereignty accountable to values that are not within the reach of transient power. The first judicial act in building South Africa's transformed society was performed by the Constitutional Court in a decision on a fundamental question for any just government: the range of state power over a citizen – that is, when will it deprive a person of life? Viewed in this way, the judgments in *Makwanyane* represent a sizeable part of the foundations upon which the constitutional bridge must be erected.

9

ACTIVISM, DENIALISM, SOCIO-ECONOMIC RIGHTS (AND BEETROOT)

'We cannot afford to allow the AIDS epidemic to ruin the realisation of our dreams. Existing statistics indicate that we are
still at the beginning of the AIDS epidemic in our country.
Unattended, however, this will result in untold damage and
suffering by the end of the century.'[1]

– ETIENNE MUREINIK

The South African government's policy choices on HIV/AIDS in the
Mbeki era were controversial; they were also an example of socio-
economic rights-based lawfare. That these choices landed up in court
was inevitable; that the resulting legal war was waged over innovative
constitutional clauses that the ANC had ensured were part of the
Constitution was a great historical irony.

The inclusion of socio-economic rights in the Constitution, such as
access to adequate housing, sufficient food and water, social security
– and healthcare services – was the subject of intense debate during
the constitutional drafting process. Legal academics joined the fray. The
debate essentially grappled with the unease generated by permitting an
unelected judiciary to grant socio-economic rights to litigants; this was
weighed against the alternative: leaving the realisation of those rights
to, arguably, the greater unpredictability of the political struggle.
Essentially, if these rights are included in the Constitution, they are then

justiciable (i.e. subject to judicial processes) and their holders can approach the courts for relief based on the text of the Constitution. Opponents of this view argued that these rights should rather be established by the political processes of mobilisation, lobbying, and legislative and executive action. They held that society cannot have judges running the country and making key distributional decisions in place of the elected and executive representatives of the people.

The former view – that of the proponents – won out, and socio-economic rights were included in the Constitution. In a hugely influential article written in 1992, Etienne Mureinik spoke of the importance of the courts being able to review policy choices rather than make them, using an argument that was rather prescient: 'A court might likewise intervene if the annual budget appropriated funds to build a replica of St Peter's, or perhaps a nuclear submarine, before the rights of education promised by the Constitution had been delivered.'[2]

As this chapter shows, these constitutional rights may not have been employed to challenge the purchase of submarines but they were used to successfully challenge the then government's response to the HIV/AIDS epidemic that has been devastating South Africa.

Denialism and dissident science[3]

More than five million people were living with HIV in South Africa around the birth of the new South Africa.[4] As in other parts of the world, the virus was first identified in the white homosexual community, but it was later discovered among black South Africans, and is now present throughout South African society and in all communities.[5]

Following the unbanning of the ANC, consultation between government and other health officials resulted in the formation of the National AIDS Convention of South Africa in 1992. An eight-member drafting team, including two of the women who would hold the post of health minister after apartheid, Nkosazana Dlamini-Zuma and Manto Tshabalala-Msimang, produced a National AIDS Plan a year later.[6] This was adopted by the Government of National Unity in 1994.[7] However, despite this promising beginning, national AIDS policy faltered during the Mandela presidency, sacrificed to other goals, such as restructuring the healthcare system and emphasising basic or primary healthcare services.[8]

Mandela made no major public statement about AIDS until three years into his presidential term, and then to an international audience in Davos. As Hein Marais powerfully summarises the position, '[m]easured minute-by-minute during his presidency, Mandela probably spent more time with the Spice Girls and Michael Jackson than he did raising the AIDS issue with the South African public'.[9] In an interview with the BBC, Mandela later admitted that he had faced resistance from audiences when he mentioned AIDS and that he had been warned that to talk about it might lose him the next election: 'I wanted to win and I didn't talk about AIDS.'[10]

Writer and sociology professor Xolela Mangcu attributes this omission on the part of the President 'mainly to the fact that Mandela found it awkward to talk about sexual issues, and was apparently discouraged from doing so by members of his own party'.[11] Regardless of its explanation, this failure of Mandela's political leadership at a time when HIV prevalence was rising sharply in South Africa drew criticism from Edwin Cameron, South Africa's AIDS-activist judge: 'He more than anyone else could through his enormous stature have reached into the minds and behaviour of young people ... A message from this man of saint-like, in some ways god-like, stature would have been effective. He didn't do it. In 199 ways he was our country's saviour. In the 200th way, he was not.'[12]

Health Minister Dlamini-Zuma made other mistakes. There was the *Sarafina II* scandal, where European Union funding was allocated to, and wasted on, a play intended to raise awareness of AIDS. A furore also broke out around government support for Virodene, a claimed antiviral medication made from antifreeze, or dimethylformamide, which resulted in the purging and mass resignation of personnel at the South African Medicines Control Council.[13]

In 1998, the health minister further undermined the government's response to HIV/AIDS by suspending projects aimed at preventing HIV transmission from mother to child (known as mother-to-child transmission prevention, or MTCTP) through the use of ARV treatment.[14]

Later, with Mbeki as president, the South African government's HIV/AIDS policy veered increasingly off course, abandoning internationally accepted science, and headed into the dark terrain of AIDS denialism.[15] Perhaps the nadir of the Mbeki administration's health policy was the fact that the government disputed that HIV causes AIDS. The government was also reluctant to accept that ARV therapy worked and dismissed offers of assistance from the pharmaceutical companies, in the form of price reductions for ARVs and generic drug production. As recently as March 2016, Mbeki continued to pen open letters justifying his stance on the epidemic and government's (non-) response to it.[16]

The inclusion of so-called denialist scientists[17] on the Presidential AIDS Advisory Panel drew heavy criticism. In his typically acerbic style, the cartoonist Zapiro captured the madness of providing such a platform for these views in a cartoon published on 16 March 2000, showing the Mad Hatter announcing to former 'President Mbeki's Select Advisory Panel of International AIDS Experts' – consisting of Dr Strangelove, the Nutty Professor, Dr Jekyll, Dr Seuss, the Pool Doctor, Dr Doolittle, Dr Alban, Professor Calculus and Doctor Khumalo – that 'there is no causal link between HIV and AIDS'.

Mbeki's denialism was crisply summarised in his comments to the 13th International AIDS Conference held in Durban in 2000. He told the assembled scientists, activists and medical professionals: 'The world's biggest killer and the greatest cause of ill-health and suffering across the globe, including South Africa, is extreme poverty.'[18] In later public statements, Mbeki asked Parliament: 'How does a virus cause a syndrome? It cannot really, truly. I think it is incorrect from everything I have read to say immune deficiency is acquired exclusively from a virus.'[19] He repeated this view in newspaper articles and interviews locally and internationally. When *Time* magazine pressed him on whether he would acknowledge a link between HIV and AIDS, he replied: 'This is precisely where the problem starts. No, I'm saying that you cannot attribute immune deficiency solely and exclusively to a virus.'[20]

Mbeki's Minister of Health, Tshabalala-Msimang, courted controversy of her own making, claiming that HIV had been scientifically engineered by the world's ruling elite to reverse the explosive population growth of the mid-20th century.[21] She also urged AIDS sufferers to consume beetroot, garlic, lemon, olive oil and African potatoes to boost their immune system.[22]

The Mbeki government asserted that the white and, to use the government's term, 'Western' attitudes to its denialist position on HIV/AIDS were racist. This point of view was captured in a document said to bear Mbeki's electronic signature, but believed to be authored by former cabinet member and ANC Youth League President Peter Mokaba, which trumpeted:

> Regardless of the fact that the scientific proof is hard to come by, nevertheless the conviction has taken firm hold that sub-Saharan Africa will surely be wiped out by an HIV/AIDS pandemic unless, most important of all, we access anti-retroviral drugs. This urgent and insistent call is made by some of the friends of the Africans, who are intent that the Africans must be saved from a plague worse than the Black Death of many centuries ago. For their part, the Africans believe this story, as told by their friends. They too shout the message that – yes, indeed, we are as they say we are! Yes, we are sex-crazy! Yes, we are diseased! Yes, we spread the deadly HI Virus through our uncontrolled heterosexual sex! In this regard, yes, we are different from the US and Western Europe! Yes, we, the men, abuse women and the girl-child with gay abandon! Yes, among us rape is endemic because of our culture! Yes, we do believe that sleeping with young virgins will cure us of AIDS! Yes, as a result of all this, we are threatened with destruction by the HIV/AIDS pandemic! Yes, what we need, and cannot afford, because we are poor, are condoms and anti-retroviral drugs! Help![23]

In a letter dated 4 September 2006 addressed to Mbeki, 82 concerned HIV scientists from all over the world, with prestigious credentials, captured the poverty of the government's response to the epidemic and the danger of the AIDS-denialist view:

> To deny that HIV causes AIDS is farcical in the face of the scientific evidence; to promote ineffective, immoral policies on HIV/AIDS endangers lives; to have as Health Minister a person who now has no international respect is an embarrassment to the South African government. We therefore call for the immediate removal of Dr Tshabalala-Msimang as Minister of Health, and for an end to the disastrous, pseudo-scientific policies that have characterised the South African government's response to HIV/AIDS.[24]

But the final word on the government's failure to address HIV/AIDS goes to Stephen Lewis, the UN Special Envoy for HIV/AIDS in Africa, who concluded the 2006 International AIDS Conference in Toronto by saying:

> South Africa is the unkindest cut of all. It is the only country in Africa, amongst all the countries I have traversed in the last five years, whose government is still obtuse, dilatory and negligent about rolling out treatment. It is the only country in Africa whose government continues to propound theories more worthy of a lunatic fringe than of a concerned and compassionate state. Between six and eight hundred people a day die of AIDS in South Africa. The government has a lot to atone for. I'm of the opinion that they can never achieve redemption.[25]

Clearly, it is well beyond the scope of this chapter to document the many shifts, details and developments that have marked South Africa's HIV/AIDS policy. It is hoped that the preceding pages show how politicised HIV/AIDS treatment became, and how the views of government and AIDS experts were so divergent that treatment reached an impasse. Something had to give to break the deadlock.

Campaigning for treatment

Leading the opposition to the government's response to the issue was the Treatment Action Campaign, founded on World AIDS Day, 10 December 1998. At its head was Zackie Achmat, who cut his political teeth as a community organiser in Mitchells Plain and later in the Marxist Workers' Tendency, a pro-poor socialist faction of the ANC. Achmat lives openly with HIV.

The TAC began as a part of the government-sponsored National Association of People Living with HIV/AIDS. In the hope of greater effectiveness, it broke away the next year to become an independent organisation.

Among the TAC's stated objectives are to promote and sponsor legislation to ensure equal access to social services for and equal treatment of all people with HIV/AIDS.[26] To this end, the TAC sets out to challenge, by means of litigation, lobbying, advocacy and all forms

201

of legitimate social mobilisation, any barrier or obstacle, including unfair discrimination, that limits access to treatment for HIV/AIDS in the private and public sectors.

Achmat confirmed in an interview with the authors[27] that the TAC consciously and deliberately chose to pursue parallel strategies of law and politics to achieve its objectives. Therefore, mobilisation, lobbying and education were complemented by strategic litigation. The litigation was also tailored to focus on narrow issues. This approach not only exploits the spaces available for change, but also creates the political and social conditions necessary for change. This context-creating political work needs to come before, during and after the institution of any related litigation because launching a case without this supporting political work would be dangerous. The TAC chose to campaign around the MTCTP issue 'not simply as a medical problem, but a human rights issue'.[28]

The case

ARV treatment, such as the drug nevirapine, given to HIV-positive mothers, administered in this case in a single dose, is an essential aspect of preventing the further spread of HIV. According to publications issued by the TAC and the AIDS Law Project in July 2001,

[a]t least 30 of every 100 HIV-positive pregnant women in South Africa will transmit HIV to their babies. This is called mother to child transmission. It mostly happens during delivery, but may also occur while the baby is in the womb or after birth during breastfeeding.[29]

The nevirapine prevention regime consists of a single dose of 200mg given at the onset of labour, and one dose of 0.6mls nevirapine syrup given to the newborn within 72 hours of birth.[30] Where medically indicated, it can drastically reduce and all but immunise the infant against transmission of the HI virus. By 1998, it was estimated that up to 70 000 HIV-positive babies were born every year, with resultant increases in infant mortality rates.[31]

Between 1999 and 2001, the TAC held a series of meetings with the two ministers of health who were in office during that time to press for the provision of ARVs. It mobilised demonstrations, delivered to the President a petition signed by 50 000 people and ran campaigns calling on the manufacturers of the required drugs to reduce their prices. At first, these efforts were relatively well received and prompted government action. For example, the Gauteng Health Department moved aggressively to establish five sites at which MTCTP programmes were introduced.[32] However, as the grip of so-called AIDS denialism tightened and the pseudoscience of AIDS dissidents gained traction within the executive, the government's policy and action on MTCTP came off the rails. The health minister and president publicly aired views that the toxicity and possible side effects of ARVs were reasons to avoid their use.[33] As Mark Heywood, co-founder of the TAC, explains,

> on 5 April 2000 the Minister of Health, Dr Tshabalala-Msimang, made a speech to Parliament that had all the hallmarks of 'dissidentese'. Raising reasonable concerns about a number of deaths of adults on therapeutic drug trials that appeared to be associated with daily Nevirapine use as part of a combination of anti-retroviral drugs, she confused these deaths with use of the same medicine for preventing intra-partum HIV transmission – despite the knowledge that it requires only one dose to mother and child and the fact that there were no reported adverse safety events concerning its use in MTCT.[34]

Over the next few months, the government seemed to accept nevirapine in the light of encouraging clinical trials in Uganda. In response, the TAC backed off from its demands, pending the outcome of a local trial.[35] However, the government's next steps – notably, Mbeki's failure to mention HIV as a specific challenge facing Africa in his opening speech to the International AIDS Conference held in Durban in July 2000, and the government's declining of an offer of five years' free supply of nevirapine from its manufacturer – made it clear that waiting for political resolutions was probably going to be futile.[36]

The TAC again contemplated legal action to force access to the necessary treatment for MTCTP. It was joined in its drive for MTCTP action by, among others, Save Our Babies, a campaigning group of paediatricians founded by Drs Haroon Saloojee and Ashraf Coovadia.

Following the formal registration of nevirapine with the Medicines Control Council for MTCTP purposes on 18 April 2001, the TAC assembled its legal team, comprising Geoff Budlender, attorney and director of the Legal Resources Centre Constitutional Litigation Unit, and advocates Gilbert Marcus SC and Bongani Majola.[37]

The TAC's first letter of demand was sent to health minister Tshabalala-Msimang and the nine provincial Members of the Executive Council (MECs) for health, seeking explanations for the failure to make treatment available throughout the country's public health sector. At the time, ARV provision was limited to two pilot sites per province, one urban and one rural. These pilot sites provided a comprehensive complementary programme, which included counselling, information and education around critical issues, such as breastfeeding. The effect of the programme structure was that, if a patient went to one of the two provincial pilot sites, ARVs could be obtained. But if a patient was unable to access one of these sites because she could not physically go to them, and she could not afford the cost of private healthcare and had to resort to the public system outside of these sites, she would be denied this critical treatment.

Although it was obviously more desirable to have drug treatment bolstered by the other aspects of the programme, it was plainly undesirable to deny necessary drugs altogether.

Tellingly, the nine provinces differed drastically in terms of their ARV roll-outs. For example, while eight of the provinces claimed that their efforts were restricted to the pilot sites, the Western Cape planned to provide ARV treatment programmes in all of the province's healthcare facilities. As Heywood explained:

> This early disjuncture between the provinces was to be the undoing of the government's legal case. By offering an example of what could be done, it created a moral pressure on other provinces to extend their programmes beyond the artificial boundaries of the pilot sites. Hereafter a divergence developed, sometimes openly, sometimes covertly, between those provinces who saw it as part of their constitutional duty to expand prevention programmes, and those who apparently did not.[38]

While the government responded to the TAC's concerns about the structure of the pilot programmes by reiterating its concerns about drug safety and efficacy, and the need for further research, the TAC, joined by other civil-society organisations, challenged the reasonableness of this policy in an application filed in August 2001. The respondents in the application were the Minister of Health and the provincial health MECs. The Western Cape was later dropped from the case, given its acquiescent approach to the ARV roll-out.

Two issues in one

There were essentially two issues in the case, which are related to each other as a result of the structure of the Bill of Rights. The first was government's overarching duty under sections 7(2) ('The state must respect, protect, promote and fulfil the rights in the Bill of Rights') and 8(1) ('The Bill of Rights applies to all law, and binds the legislature, the executive, the judiciary and all organs of state') to implement the rights expressly guaranteed in the Bill of Rights, including specific healthcare rights. These were the right of every citizen to public health care and the right of children to be afforded special protection. These are expressed in sections 27 ('Everyone has the right to have access to ... health care services, including reproductive health care ... The state must take reasonable legislative and other measures, within its available resources, to achieve the progressive realisation of each of these rights') and 28 ('Every child has the right ... to basic nutrition, shelter, basic health care services and social services').[39]

This umbrella duty then leads to the second issue arising out of these provisions: whether government is constitutionally obliged to plan and implement an effective, comprehensive and progressive programme for the prevention of MTCT throughout the country.

The government opposed the application on two grounds: that the relief sought was unaffordable and that nevirapine posed health risks, which required further research. Although admitting that the drug had been registered with the Medicines Control Council for MTCTP purposes, the government's legal papers expressed doubts about its safety and raised the prospect of drug resistance in the future, which would be 'catastrophic for public health'.[40] The government also raised the flag of impossibility by arguing that nevirapine was most effective when provided as part of a counselling, testing and educational programme, focused, in particular, on breastfeeding practices (to prevent HIV transmission through breastfeeding) and ensuring access to infant milk formula. Such a programme, it argued, was impossible due to resource constraints.[41]

In response, the TAC filed replying papers replete with expert affidavits challenging the government's representation of the scientific evidence for nevirapine's safety and the question of resistance, as well as evidence of the health department's budgetary and resource capacity to roll out its provision.

The fact that the high political stakes of the TAC's challenge to the government's public-health policy on MTCTP were clearly felt by both sides was confirmed by counsel in interviews, as was the high level of acrimony displayed by both parties. The possibility of political interference in the case was also raised. The South African Human Rights Commission applied to be an amicus curiae. This followed the commission's investigation of a complaint filed by Costa Gazi, a doctor from the Eastern Cape, who accused the Minister of Health of manslaughter for failing to provide MTCTP measures. However, the commission abruptly withdrew its application to assist the court. Subsequent media reports revealed allegations that the government's senior counsel had contacted the commission's chairperson, Barney Pityana, and that the President's legal advisor had approached another member of the commission to discuss its involvement in the case. According to these reports, an internal discussion resulted in a 5:4 vote to withdraw from the case. The commission denied that political pressure had caused its change of heart, stating that 'the decision to withdraw was based on the fact that we had nothing new or additional to contribute to the TAC case'.[42]

Judge Botha in the High Court

The application was heard amid the charged atmosphere of rallies and marches organised by the TAC, building up to an all-night vigil by some 600 TAC volunteers outside the courthouse. The hearing was packed with TAC members, journalists, medical professionals and members of the public, who were curious about this most high-profile of cases.[43]

The judge who heard the case was Chris Botha, ironically the son of a true apartheid ideologue and former Minister of Bantu Affairs – but his personal background was no obstacle to Judge Botha's capacity for making a progressive judgment. In his judgment, issued on 14 December 2001, he found in favour of the TAC and decided that the government's policy on MTCTP was not reasonable. Judge Botha required that nevirapine be provided when its prescription was medically indicated and ordered that the government was under a duty to both develop and implement an effective, comprehensive, national programme to prevent or reduce mother-to-child transmission of HIV.

The judgment was both praised and attacked. The *Sunday Times* published an editorial noting that '[t]he outcome shows that even strongly dominant political opinion cannot stand in the way of a Constitution that is supreme. Every child born free of HIV as a result of this week's decision will be living proof of the wisdom our society showed in opting for this form of democracy.'[44]

However, some legal academics argued that the judgment showed the judiciary as blurring the line between its role and that of the executive, and overstepping the mark. This criticism boiled down to a claim that 'government policy is a political creature and this is why it is governments that make policy, not judges. The remedy for unpopular government policy should rightfully be political, not legal.'[45]

This line of argument was used by the health minister when she announced the filing of an application for leave to appeal directly to the Constitutional Court on 18 December 2001, seeking clarification of the jurisdictional boundaries between executive policymaking and judicial review. At the same time, the TAC's lawyers launched an application to execute the part of the judgment ordering nevirapine to be made available where there was capacity to do so. They argued that further delay came at the unacceptable cost of newborn lives. Ordinarily, the initiation of appellate proceedings suspends the operation of any court order. However, the TAC's legal team argued that implementing the court's order before the appeals were finalised could save ten newborn lives in South Africa a day.[46] The government did not deny this claim.

Politically, provincial unity on the issue began to splinter after the judgment, with the premiers of Gauteng and KwaZulu-Natal announcing that their MTCTP programmes would be expanded.[47] This was echoed in Mbeki's opening of Parliament speech and later interviews, when he indicated that 'provinces with the resources to extend the programme should not be delayed by provinces that did not have the resources'.[48] However, the health minister distanced herself from these statements and was thus christened 'Dr No' by *The Star* newspaper.[49]

On 1 March 2002, the government's application for leave to appeal and the TAC's application for an execution order were heard by Judge Botha. He ruled in favour of the TAC, finding himself 'unable to formulate a motivation for tolerating preventable deaths for the sake of sparing the [government] prejudice that cannot amount to more than organisational inconvenience'.[50]

The government then sought leave to appeal the decision on the execution order to the Constitutional Court. This application was again heard by Judge Botha, who refused leave to appeal. In response, the government sought leave to appeal directly from the Constitutional Court. Heywood argues that this was 'a failure of legal strategy' because, 'although the legal issues that the Constitutional Court had to decide were narrow, and different from those it would consider in the appeal, these could not be approached without consideration of the actual issues, including the rationality of the MTCT policy.' The result, said Heywood, was that the government had created a situation that allowed the issues 'to be aired in the highest court in the land, a month before the dates set for the full appeal'.[51]

Heywood reported that, during the hearing,

> the Constitutional Court judges frequently appeared to be at a loss as to why government was so fiercely opposed to the execution order. In answer to a question from Chief Justice Chaskalson about how infants would suffer from being provided [with] a potentially life-saving drug, the government's advocate, Marumo Moerane SC, referred to 'drug resistance'. When asked by Justice Madala whether government had documented any adverse events resulting from the use of Nevirapine in the past 11 months, Moerane answered 'no'. Yet, when Justice O'Regan later asked precisely what harm would be caused by the execution of the order, his answer was that there was 'potential for great, great harm'.[52]

On 4 April, the Constitutional Court refused the government's application for leave to appeal against the order of execution, which prompted a newspaper headline 'YES, you will, Dr No.'[53]

The minister, for her part, made regrettable comments to the media in which she indicated that she might decide not to abide by the court's decision, apparently claiming that new information on the drug's safety required caution. In a television interview with SABC News on 24 March 2002, Tshabalala-Msimang was asked whether she would be prepared to follow the court's decision:

> Minister: My own view is that the judiciary cannot prescribe from the bench – and that we have a regulatory authority in this country that is interacting with the regulatory authority FDA of the USA and I think we must allow them to assist us in reaching conclusions.
> Interviewer: Mmm, so you think it's inappropriate that this is in court, but nevertheless it's there. Will you stand by whatever the court decides?
> Minister: No, I think the court and the judiciary must also listen to the regulatory authority, both of this country and the regulatory authority of the US.
> Interviewer: So you're saying no?
> Minister: I say no. I am saying no.[54]

The Minister of Justice at the time, Penuell Maduna, rushed to assure a startled public that the government had 'no intention of circumventing the courts. ...We stand ready to abide by the final decision of the courts on the execution order.'[55] Yet the health minister's remarks underscored the discomfort apparently felt by the executive about the judiciary's oversight role. They also exposed the contours of their resulting challenge to the separation of executive, legislative and judicial powers structured by the Constitution.

The Constitutional Court hearing

At the time of the hearing in the Constitutional Court, the posture of the matter had changed in significant ways from when it was before the lower court. Government accepted that something more had to be done to roll out the treatment programme: the allocated budget had been increased accordingly, and three provinces were already at 100 per cent coverage in their roll-outs. One therefore has to wonder why the government persisted in the appeal. The health minister had backed down politically and appeared to have conceded the flaws in the policy, given the adjustments made to it. Nevertheless, the government doggedly persisted in the appeal.

The atmosphere at the hearing was tense. Counsel for the government, Moerane, spoke of the emotional judges who gave him a hostile hearing. It was plain that politics had percolated through the court's walls and informed the Constitutional Court's view of the appeal. It also was clear that the judges were affected by the broader context in which its decision would be received. This was a major challenge to the executive of the republic. Yet the court appeared emboldened to take on the executive branch knowing that public opinion, including international opinion, was against its policy.

There was also palpable tension between the legal teams. The matter had been characterised by a lack of cooperation and a strategic approach that saw every possible technical or procedural point being taken. This all served merely to delay and frustrate progress on the matter – and increase its cost.

As an aside, one of the toughest strategic choices faced by legal teams in such high-stakes and high-profile cases is simply which battles to fight. While technical or procedural arguments may whittle down the case or gain some tactical advantage, they are often not taken up so as not to blur the focus on the main issue(s) in the case. So, adversaries will often agree to condone some non-compliance with the rules of procedure by the other side so as to get the matter heard in the most focused way.

Obviously, fatal flaws cannot be ignored. But, often, given the client's desire to litigate the issue in the full glare of publicity and exploit the political moment of a public hearing before a court, encrusting the case with unnecessary legal points obscures the real issue or the 'big picture'. The lawyers therefore need to understand the client's agenda with the litigation because such cases are rarely just about the law. The TAC legal team spoke of the government's legal team adopting a singularly obstructive, technical approach. It appeared that the 'big picture' was not uppermost on their agenda.

The atmosphere inside the court was only heightened by the TAC's decision to mobilise: 'stand up for your rights' marches took place in Johannesburg, Cape Town and Durban on the first day of argument, 2 May 2002; more than 5 000 people marched to the Constitutional Court. The court was also packed with HIV/AIDS activists and health workers, and the media had the hearing well covered.

The judgment

On 5 July 2002, judgment was handed down by the court. Contrary to its practice of identifying the judge or judges who authored a judgment in which other members of the bench concur, this time the Constitutional Court handed down its unanimous judgment authored by 'the court', as it did in other politicised cases, such as the *Schabir Shaik* appeal. This was plainly an assertion of its role in executive oversight and demonstrated the judges' appreciation for the critical political importance of their decision. Turning to the government's policy and executive pronouncements, the judgment found that the policy did not pass constitutional muster, in that it failed to ensure 'reasonable' access to healthcare services in a way that reasonably took account of competing pressing social needs.

It is a somewhat unusual judgment because it covers the science and medicine of HIV/AIDS, ARVs and treatment options in a considerable amount of scientific detail. This was a bold move given the AIDS denialism that polluted the corridors of power at the highest level. In most judgments, the recounting of the relevant facts is usually fairly uncontroversial and merely a necessary part of explaining the later reasoning of the court when it applies the law to that particular set of facts. While parties to litigation often have competing versions of the facts, by the time the matter reaches an apex court, the facts are often fairly settled. Their interpretation and significance is where the contest will remain. But here, the act of recounting the science in question was a political gesture: accepting mainstream scientific explanations and theories on HIV/AIDS and the options available for its treatment meant a rejection of denialism, scientific dissidence and alternative views of the epidemic's cause, progress and required treatment.

The tone of the judgment reveals that this case was a no-brainer on the factual issues. It also represented a deliberate assertion of the court's institutional integrity and the mechanism of justiciability through which questions of executive policy were susceptible to judicial review and evaluation. But the court was not about to run head-first at the executive edifice. Instead, it developed its own conception of deference to the executive's powers – one that seeks to marry the mandate of the text with the political realities confronting the 'weakest arm of government'. In other words, the court outlines the acceptable approach to the questions in the case but allows the executive to determine how to follow this approach.

The court's interpretation of so-called socio-economic rights was built on a series of cases that had arisen before the TAC case. First, in *Soobramoney*[56] and, later, in *Grootboom*,[57] the Constitutional Court developed the requirements that government policy must be reasonable, tackle the plight of the most vulnerable first and navigate a course between reasonable measures and available resources.

This 'reasonableness' approach was chosen in preference to the so-called 'minimum core' conception of such rights. The latter view would require a court to determine the minimum content, or minimum core, of each right and then evaluate the government's policy to ensure that this was satisfied. However, this approach ignores the resources and other constraints on government and requires the court to set policy, rather than allow it to be set by other branches of government. This strays outside the usual court's expertise. Politically, the minimum-core approach is problematic because it is so definitive and prescriptive. In contrast, the reasonableness approach allows government to decide on the nitty-gritty content of a policy and its implementation, and requires only that this be reasonable in light of the factors to be considered and the other demands on government's resources. To an important extent, it also recognises the weakness of a state that has battled to transform from one serving a few million white people to a democratic state that caters for the needs of the whole population.

So, the court recognised that its pronouncements on policy had budgetary and political consequences, and hence the polycentric nature of such decisions. It also accepted that 'besides the pandemic, the state faces huge demands in relation to access to education, land, housing, healthcare, food, water and social security. These are the socio-economic rights entrenched in the Constitution, and the state is obliged to take reasonable legislative and other measures within its available resources to achieve the progressive realisation of each of them. In the light of our history, this is an extraordinarily difficult task.'[58] In its judgment, the Constitutional Court defined itself out of the policymaking process by stating that

> [c]ourts are ill-suited to adjudicate upon issues where court orders could have multiple social and economic consequences for the community. The Constitution contemplates rather a restrained and focused role for the courts, namely, to require the state to take measures to meet its constitutional obligations and to subject the reasonableness of these measures to evaluation. Such determinations of reasonableness may in fact have budgetary implications, but are not in themselves directed at rearranging budgets. In this way the judicial, legislative and executive functions achieve appropriate constitutional balance.[59]

The court's judgment in this case therefore reads far more pragmatically than some of its others. Gone are the lofty ambitions and idealistic tones of *Makwanyane* (see Chapter 8). Instead, this is the grime and guts of political process or, rather, what happens when political policy goes wrong.

Public opinion

The judgment raises the question of whether there can be a legal victory in such a case without political pressure framing the issues. Put another way, was this case a slam dunk for the Constitutional Court because the government had already accepted – or been forced to accept – that its policy must change under sustained critical political pressure from the TAC, the media, international commentators and other members of civil society?

Overall, the government's capitulation stands in welcome contrast to its earlier response in *Harris* to the Appellate Division's rejection of its policy choices (see Chapter 3). Although the health minister's ill-advised comments that she would not abide by the decision of the court may reveal an insider's view of where power should lie, ultimately the government yielded when it was clear that its policy was indefensible.

Another interesting comparison is how, in this case, the court was bolstered by public support for its position, whereas, in *Makwanyane*, the court discounted public opinion that ran contrary to the stance it wished to adopt. This interplay between public opinion and the court's decision making reveals that the bench is not isolated from politics and popular views. But, instead, it chooses when to follow and when to resist prevailing opinion. This awareness of political context and of how its decisions will be received explains, to some degree, the court's general reticence and incremental approach. It is then left to apex courts to take radical steps on pressing issues.

A weak remedy

Despite its assertiveness in finding the government's policy unreasonable, the Constitutional Court was not as bold as Judge Botha when it came to the remedy ordered. The question was whether, in addition to declaring the policy unreasonable, the court would also exercise its supervisory jurisdiction – through a structural interdict that would require regular report-backs on progress in line with the court's judgment. The order made by Judge Botha included a structural interdict requiring the appellants to revise their policy and to submit the revised policy to the court to enable it to satisfy itself that the policy was consistent with the Constitution. The Constitutional Court rejected this remedy, although it demanded immediate action to be taken by government. And it displayed a sense of irony – some might even consider it humour, others sarcasm or naivety – when it said that the government 'has always respected and executed orders of this Court. There is no reason to believe that it will not do so in the present case'.[60]

Two explanations present themselves for the court's refusal to impose the structural interdict and to constrain itself to a pronouncement on constitutional validity. First, the political winds had shifted and the policy had been revised, making court supervision less necessary (although contempt proceedings were called for in December 2002 against the health minister and MEC for Health in Mpumalanga).[61] The judgment acknowledged that during the course of the proceedings, the state's policy had evolved and was no longer as rigid as it had been when the proceedings had begun.[62]

Secondly, the court was ultimately reluctant to wade into matters of so-called polycentric policymaking. Recognising that the demands on government were diverse and immense, and that the effect of the court's order could be to divert resources away from other areas pressing for attention, the court left such decisions to the policymakers.

In argument, counsel for the government raised issues pertaining to the separation of powers, which are relevant to explaining the court's remedial choice in two respects. First, the government urged deference by the courts to decisions taken by the executive concerning the formulation of its policies. And, secondly, the government argued that a limited order was most appropriate where a court finds that the executive has failed to comply with its constitutional obligations. In the judgment, the court appears to have accepted the import of the second argument but found, in the first, that deference must yield to justiciability. In the words of the judgment, '[i]n so far as [judicial oversight] constitutes an intrusion into the domain of the executive, that is an intrusion mandated by the Constitution itself'.[63] The court therefore recognised the principle of the separation of powers but only as long as that separation does not detract from the supremacy of the constitutional role of the court.

The TAC case made it clear that government was accountable – to the courts, to the Constitution and, through both of these, to the citizenry it serves. But it also revealed the weakness of litigation in achieving political and social goals. Delay, expense and often imperfect outcomes accompany litigation. This is why it is seldom successfully used in isolation from politics. In the crisp words of Geoff Budlender, the judgment was 'simply the conclusion of a battle that TAC had already won outside the courts, but with the skilful use of the courts as part of a broader struggle'.[64]

10

A SPECIAL RELATIONSHIP[1]

'Family, good friends, cigarettes and anger.'

– ALIX CARMICHELE, when asked what sustained her in her 13-year
fight for justice.[2]

Carol Burgers, her partner and children were holidaying in Plettenberg
Bay. On Sunday 6 August 1995, they decided to enjoy a walk along the
beach by the secluded town of Noetzie. A tranquil and beautiful hamlet,
Noetzie is an isolated spot 12 kilometres from Knysna, as one heads
towards another popular holidaymakers' paradise, Plettenberg Bay. To
get there, a dirt road passes through the forests that mark the area and
leads to the beach. A handful of homes, only two of which are used
by year-round residents, are the sum total of Noetzie.

Burgers's group were startled to see a woman rushing towards the
beach, clutching her left arm and bleeding. They initially thought she
had been bitten by a dog. But, as they rushed to help her, Alix Carmichele
told them that she had been attacked by a man named Francois Coetzee.
She also said that he was out on a pending rape charge and that her
close friend, Julie Gosling, had repeatedly urged the police to apprehend
Coetzee because he was a danger to the community. Gosling arrived
shortly afterwards, to find her friend sitting, covered in blood. About
two hours later, an ambulance arrived to attend to the injured Alix.

Coetzee handed himself over to the police after the attack. Unfortunately, this was not the first time he had attacked a woman in the area. His crimes prompted litigation that would last more than a decade that sought to secure recognition of the constitutionally mandated duty of the state to prevent violence against women.

Francois Coetzee, 21 years old in 1995, was unemployed and lived with his mother in Noetzie. Born in Knysna, he was the eldest of six children. His father, Daniel, had left the family when Francois was nine. Annie Coetzee, his mother, worked as a domestic worker for Julie Gosling. Gosling edited a local Knysna classified newspaper, *Action Ads*, and was occasionally assisted in the business by Annie.

Coetzee was a troubled child. Court records show how, as an early adolescent, his mother became aware that he was accused of molesting young girls. Hoping that there was some medication available that could control these urges, she consulted the family doctor about her son's behaviour but was told that he was too young for any medication. Given what would follow, one can only wonder what tragedy could have been averted had there been some earlier intervention to address Francois's inappropriate urges.

Beverley Claassen

Coetzee's grandmother lived in Hornlee, near Knysna. Next door lived Beverley Claassen, who was 25 when she was assaulted by Coetzee in 1994. He had climbed through her bedroom window and into bed with the sleeping Beverley. He touched her on her legs and waist, and pulled her underwear down. Beverley woke up and screamed, scaring Coetzee, who scampered back out through the bedroom window.

Coetzee later acknowledged at trial that his 'leg and hands were not where they should have been' and claimed that he was looking for somewhere to sleep, and that he thought he was outside his grandmother's house. He was convicted of housebreaking and indecent assault. The magistrate found that he should not be sent to prison, taking into account that this was his first conviction, and that he was a young man who had testified, in mitigation of sentence, that he wished to finish his matric and further his studies at the University of the Western Cape. The magistrate found that Francois might have been drunk on the night in question, but that he was nevertheless responsible for his actions. He was therefore sentenced to 18 months' imprisonment, suspended for four years, and to a fine of R600 or six months' imprisonment plus 12 months' imprisonment suspended for four years. His mother paid the R600 fine, and he was never incarcerated.

Eurena Terblanche

Nearly a year later, in March 1995, Coetzee attempted to rape and murder another female neighbour, Eurena Terblanche, who was 17 at the time. Terblanche was in matric at Knysna Secondary School, as was Coetzee, and they knew each other. Coetzee had played dominoes at Eurena's house. On the evening of 3 March, a dance was held at the Hornlee Hotel, which Francois and Eurena both attended; he offered to walk her home, and she accepted because she knew him.

As subsequent evidence would show, on the way home, Coetzee persuaded her to accompany him on a detour, claiming he wanted to visit a friend of his. At first reluctant, she agreed. A little further on, he stopped and asked her what she was going to give him in return for walking her home. Terblanche thought he was joking, and laughed it off. Coetzee then tried to kiss her; when she resisted, he wrestled with her. Grabbing her by the neck, he kicked her legs from under her and threw her to the ground, then punched her, kicked her and sat on top of her. She struggled, but eventually passed out as he hit, kicked and throttled her. He told her to shut up and, during the attack, said that he wanted to kill her.

When she came to, Eurena felt wet between her legs. She was found wearing only a T-shirt, and her denim trousers and shirt were lying next to her. But her panties were not there. Her arms had been pressed underneath her and her legs were a little open. At the time she had passed out, she had been fully clothed.

She fled to the home of people she knew and told them about the attack, then, together with some neighbours, went home to her mother, Doreen. The police were called and Doreen told them that Coetzee had raped her daughter. The police reported that Francois was already in custody, having been arrested at the Hornlee Hotel. He had apparently returned to the hotel where he asked staff to call the police, saying he had murdered a girl. They disbelieved him but made the call; when the police came, they arrested him for being under the influence.

Terblanche was examined by a district surgeon and then provided the police with a statement about the attack. As Coetzee had been convicted in September the previous year on charges of housebreaking and indecent assault on Beverley Claassen, he had become known to members of the Knysna community. Her mother told the police about Francois's earlier conviction for the attack on Beverley Claassen, which the duty officer noted in the investigation diary, thinking it may be relevant to the question of bail.

Following further interviews with Eurena, and an inspection of the crime scene, the investigating officer handed over the file to the prosecutor handling Francois's appearance in court on 6 March. The investigating officer appears to have made no effort to ascertain the details of Francois's earlier conviction, and recommended that he be released on a warning. The prosecutor followed this recommendation, and Francois was released and returned to live with his mother in Noetzie.

More warnings

A day or two later, Doreen Terblanche visited her friend Julie Gosling, because she knew that Gosling employed Francois's mother in her home and business. She told Gosling of the attack on her daughter and of Coetzee's earlier conviction for the attack on Beverley Claassen.

Distressed at this news, Gosling went to see the police to ask why Coetzee had been released on a warning when it seemed reasonable to predict that he would commit a similar crime again – it was just a matter of time. She was told to discuss her concerns about his release with the senior public prosecutor, Dian Louw, whom Gosling knew. Gosling told Louw that she was afraid that Coetzee would attack again. Louw told her, however, that there was nothing that could be done – until he broke the law again.

Coetzee's own mother was worried about the likelihood of her son repeating his criminal conduct, and feared that he may harm himself too. She discussed these fears with a relative of hers, who was also a sergeant in the police service, as he was giving her a lift home. When they arrived at her house in Noetzie, they discovered that Francois had in fact attempted suicide. He had tried to hang himself with his necktie, and had consumed all the pills in the house before slashing his wrists. He was rushed to hospital and treated, after which he returned home.

Coetzee tried to commit suicide three times following his attack on Eurena Terblanche.

The next day, he was interviewed by prosecutor Louw. Coetzee admitted to her that since the age of ten, he had suffered uncontrolled sexual urges. He had molested his cousin, would masturbate after becoming aroused on seeing women in bathing suits and otherwise masturbated frequently. Louw noted his previous conviction and recorded his sense that, when he attacked women 'it was as if a "superhuman, unnatural" force got hold of him' and he then committed a deed that he was not even aware of. 'His friends had started calling him "the ghost".' He requested that he be sent to Valkenberg, a psychiatric hospital in Cape Town, and asked that he should not be kept in jail before he was sentenced.[3]

Coetzee was referred to Valkenberg Hospital for 30 days' observation of his mental health. He returned to Knysna for a court appearance on 18 April 1995, where a report was handed up concluding that, despite a troubled past, he was mentally fit to stand trial. He was charged with raping Terblanche, a count to which he pleaded not guilty. The case was postponed for hearing until early May. Again, the presiding magistrate was not informed of Coetzee's earlier conviction and he was released on his own recognisance and warned to appear in court at the next hearing.

Coetzee told the inspector who accompanied him back to Knysna from his stint at Valkenberg that he knew that he had 'done something wrong'. He told him that he was reading the Bible, that he knew that he would receive a jail sentence and that he had decided that he was going to study while he was in jail.

Alix Carmichele

While out awaiting trial, Coetzee struck again. As would emerge in later legal proceedings, one morning towards the end of June 1995, Alix Carmichele, a freelance photographer from Knysna and close friend of Julie Gosling, awoke after spending the night at Gosling's home to find Coetzee snooping around the house and trying to push the window open. Carmichele confronted him; he told her he was looking for Gosling. Shaken, Carmichele called Gosling and told her about the incident. Gosling said that Coetzee's explanation was inconceivable because he could have clearly seen that her car was not at the house.[4] At Carmichele's request, Gosling went to the Knysna charge office and reported the incident. From Gosling and Carmichele's evidence, it appeared that Coetzee was stalking Carmichele.

Again, Gosling was referred to prosecutor Louw. Gosling reportedly told Louw that she had to do something about Coetzee: 'I said, "Dian, you've got to do something about this guy, there must be some law to protect society, not necessarily me or people at Noetzie", and she said to me that there was nothing she could do.'[5]

On 2 August 1995, Gosling and Carmichele again raised their fears about Coetzee with Louw. Louw claimed to be powerless to do anything about him – until Coetzee broke the law again.

Four days later, on 6 August 1995, as the Burgers were walking on the beach at Noetzie, Carmichele had gone to Gosling's home. It was late morning. She had arranged to meet her friend there for a braai. She noticed an open window in the house, which struck her as unusual because Gosling was fastidious about locking up. Carmichele let herself in and went to play with Julie's dogs outside. Ten or fifteen minutes later, she went back into the house to use the bathroom.

As she would later tell the police in her statement:

As I was walking towards the bathroom, a man who I recognized as Francois Coetzee jumped out in front of me. He held a pick handle above his head. He struck me once on the head and I fell onto my knees. The blows that followed were directed at my head and face ... he struck me once again with the pick handle. I noted that he reached for a knife, which he had between his teeth and in his mouth. He spoke to me, calling me by my name and ordering me to turn around onto my stomach. That is when I noticed my left arm hanging uselessly and quite obviously broken ... The knife was still in his mouth and he shouted at me through clenched teeth ... he dragged me by my clothes into the passage, still holding the pick handle and the knife. ... By this stage, I was lying on my left side, when he suddenly threw the pick handle to his right into the passage and took the knife from his mouth. Standing over me, astride my body, he stabbed me with the knife. He lunged at me forcefully, stabbing at my heart region, on my left breast. The blade of the knife bent as it hit my breast bone and the blade buckled. I knew he intended to murder me by the crazed look in his eyes, therefore I kicked out at him with both my legs. He seemed surprised. He fell back and I tried to grab the pick handle, but I realized he was recovering quickly so I made a dash for the already open double doors … Holding my broken arm, I dashed through the doors leading out to the deck and ran out onto the beach, towards people.[6]

On 11 September 1995, Coetzee represented himself at the trial on charges relating to Eurena Terblanche. After emotional testimony from both Terblanche and Coetzee, he was found guilty of attempted rape and sentenced to seven years' imprisonment.

On 13 December 1995, Coetzee stood trial in the Knysna regional court for the attack on Carmichele. He was convicted of attempted murder and housebreaking, and sentenced to an effective term of imprisonment of twelve and a half years. He was incarcerated in Malmesbury Prison. In a depressing later development, Coetzee violently assaulted a female warder in Malmesbury Prison in 2006.

Round one

Carmichele later described to a journalist how 'with each operation (to mend the broken bones in her arm),' she became 'more angry'. She asked herself why it had happened to her: 'It didn't have to happen to me; if only the police and prosecutors had done their jobs properly.'[7]

She was introduced to Perino Pama, an attorney who practised in Knysna. She retained him to launch a lawsuit aimed at holding the state accountable for its failure to prevent Coetzee's attack on her. Like other cases in this book, the *Carmichele* case was the product of the extraordinary good fortune of having both a determined litigant and a committed attorney who was willing to fund the case without payment, and who was up for the fight, which would drag on for years and years.

As Carmichele recognised and explained in media reports, the same system that had failed her, had also failed to protect a desperate lost soul from himself: despite his handing himself over after attacking his second victim, despite his telling a state prosecutor that he could not control himself around women and despite his attempting to commit suicide while out on a warning, the state had let Francois Coetzee go free. 'A grave injustice has been done to Francois,' Carmichele said. 'Perhaps if they'd heeded his calls for help, he could've been rehabilitated. Now he'll spend most of his youth in jail. It's a wasted life.'[8]

Carmichele instituted proceedings in the Cape High Court for damages against the Minister for Safety and Security and the Minister of Justice and Constitutional Development. She claimed that members of the SAPS and the public prosecutors at Knysna had negligently failed to comply with a legal duty they owed to her to take steps to prevent Coetzee from causing her harm. Carmichele initially claimed R177 315.49 for her medical expenses, lost income and other damages.

When the trial started on 4 September 1997, Carmichele was represented by advocates Terry Price, an experienced member of the Port Elizabeth Bar, whose previous career as a police officer and prosecutor was invaluable, and Deon Erasmus. 'Fef' le Roux SC, a seasoned counsel from the Cape Bar, and his junior, Ranjan Jaga, acted for the state. Judge Dayalin Chetty presided. He had been appointed to the Cape High Court after a successful career as a silk, or senior counsel, in the Eastern Cape, and had earned himself a well-deserved reputation as a thoughtful, careful and hard-working jurist.

Procedurally, the issues of liability (was the state responsible for the attack on Carmichele?) and damages (if so, how much was she entitled to as compensation?) in the case had been separated. This meant that they would be determined in stages. Without a finding as to liability, there would be no need to lead evidence establishing damages.

The case opened with evidence from the sergeant who had received Eurena Terblanche's report of her attack and who had noted Coetzee's previous conviction for the Claassen assault, thinking that it may be important to the prosecutor for bail purposes. The next witness was Doreen Terblanche, who confirmed that she had told the police when reporting the attack on her daughter that this was Coetzee's second attack on a local woman. She also testified that she had told the police this because she did not want Coetzee released from custody. After he had been released, Coetzee went to the Terblanches' home. Doreen told him she did not want him there and called the police; he ran away. When the police arrived, she told them that if Coetzee ever set foot on her property again, she would 'burn him until he was well-done' and how unhappy she was that he was not in custody.

The magistrate from Knysna, Kevin von Bratt, who had released Coetzee after the attack on Terblanche and who had referred him to Valkenberg for observation, took the witness stand next. He confirmed that the prosecutor had not made him aware of Coetzee's previous criminal conduct. Tellingly, he also confessed that the enactment of the Interim Constitution had shifted the approach to bail from a burden on an accused person to convince the court of his entitlement to bail, to an emphasis on the personal freedom of the individual. The practical effect of the new constitutional regime was that accused persons were released from custody more easily and readily.

Annie Coetzee then testified. She described how the attack on Carmichele was the culmination of her son's tragic life and how she had thought for a long time that 'there must be something wrong with him if he does these things'.[9] She confirmed that he was known to her neighbours and employer in Noetzie, and that he had sometimes helped Gosling with chores, such as carrying and fetching.

Carmichele told the court that she knew about Coetzee's problematic personal history and his earlier attacks on local women. She confirmed that she had felt threatened by him, despite his slight build, and that both she and her friend Gosling had told the prosecutor, Louw, about how they feared that he was a danger to them. She also described the attack itself and said she believed that Coetzee had wanted to rape her during the vicious assault.

In an unusual development, Carmichele's attorney in the case, Pama, was next up to testify. Pama was needed as a witness to introduce the handwritten notes made by Dian Louw, the prosecutor, as evidence in the trial. There was an awkwardness here, the result of the parochial Garden Route community of Noetzie and Knysna, because Pama and Louw knew each other socially. Pama said that Louw never had a bitter word for him concerning the case and he was determined to make a case about how the system had failed his client, rather than about the prosecutor's shortcomings.

(Louw has since left the legal field and is now a practitioner in body-stress release. But one can only speculate on whether the inevitable stress caused by this case may have prompted her to choose a career change.)

At the close of the case, the state moved to dismiss Carmichele's claim. On 1 November 1997, Judge Chetty granted this application, in what is known as absolution from the instance, meaning a finding that has the effect of ending the trial – namely, that there was no evidence from which the court could reasonably find that the police and prosecutors had acted wrongfully. In addition to dismissing the case, the judge ordered her to pay the legal costs, including the costs of two counsel, incurred by the state. Carmichele had failed to convince the court that it was reasonable to expect that the state should have prevented the harm caused to her by Coetzee or that it was under a duty to do so.

This enquiry into the reasonableness of the state's action considers the convictions of the community, or the collective moral and social norms and standards observed and expected by our society of its members. These convictions are embodied, in the first instance, in the Constitution. In particular, an individual's constitutional right to the safety and security of his or her person is implicated. In this case, the state's 'action' was in fact its inaction, or an omission to act on the warnings received about Coetzee. In the words of Pama, 'One is, generally speaking, entitled in law to "mind one's own business", but this does not apply to the state. It is not entitled to mind its own business. Its very purpose is to mind the business of others.'[10]

If Carmichele could establish that the state had negligently failed to prevent the harm caused to her, the question of the suitable remedy would then arise: the 'so what?' question. As a victim of violent crime, she was in a different position from other kinds of victims. For example, imagine that a bureaucrat fails to perform some duty, and this causes someone financial loss. The remedy is to compensate for that loss with a payment equivalent to the amount due if the bureaucrat had done his or her duty. As a victim of crime, however, Carmichele cannot have her body restored to its pre-assault state. But she can be compensated financially for the loss or damages suffered. These would include her medical expenses and lost income. This remedial solution would serve to create an incentive for the state to ensure that its functionaries perform their duties satisfactorily. It also distributes the burden of the loss resulting from the incident across the community, rather than it having to be borne by the crime victim alone.

Part of this question of liability is whether Carmichele needed to establish that there was a 'special relationship' between herself and the state, giving rise to a particular risk against which she, in particular, should be guarded. Although one could see that the repeated warnings about Coetzee established some sense of a relationship, and a direct one at that, ultimately no special relationship was needed. In other cases, municipalities have been held liable, for example, for potholes in their sidewalks into which pedestrians have fallen, resulting in injury, and for rocks falling onto roadways. In none of these cases has a 'special relationship' between the state and the pedestrian or road user been required. Carmichele argued that hers was a case analogous to these scenarios. To the extent that a 'special relationship' was required, there was such a relationship between women and the state, given that the former required the assistance and resources of the latter to protect them against violent sexual predators.

Judge Chetty noted that neither Carmichele nor Gosling had laid a charge of trespassing against Coetzee from the earlier incident when he was snooping around the Gosling residence, and emphasised Magistrate Von Bratt's testimony that accused persons were regularly being released on bail at the time. Relying on English case law, which is beyond the scope of this chapter to debate, the judge found that the state had not acted unreasonably or unlawfully, and dismissed the case. Round one to the state.

Round two

Three weeks later, Carmichele applied for leave to appeal Judge Chetty's judgment to the Appellate Division (now called the Supreme Court of Appeal) in Bloemfontein. The judge granted her leave to appeal, but that appeal was also dismissed, again with costs. It was now a dispiriting 2–0 to the state.

The only issue considered by the court in Bloemfontein was 'whether the failure on the part of [the state] to ensure that Francois was not allowed out on bail or a warning, but incarcerated pending his trial, constituted a breach of a legal duty'[11] that was owed to Carmichele. Advocate Andrew Breitenbach, assisted by Advocate Terry Price, argued the appeal for Alix; the same legal team represented the state as before. Breitenbach is today a senior counsel, who has written several thoughtful articles in the area of administrative law in South African academic journals. He is a highly respected public lawyer, and once he was on brief, it was clear that the court was going to be confronted with sophisticated constitutional arguments relating to the need to develop this area of law to grant relief to victims like Carmichele.

Interviews conducted by the authors confirm that the legal team knew that politics would enter into this stage of the case. The case was throwing the spotlight not only on the role of the court in holding other branches of government accountable, but also on the court's approach to cases of gender violence. The issues to be decided would have far-reaching consequences and the potential to alter radically the relationship between the state and those it should protect from violent crime. It goes without saying that any step towards creating greater accountability for the impact of crime on South Africa would not be taken lightly.

Unfortunately, the five white male judges who presided over the case seemed out of touch with the dramatic shift in judicial attitude required by a constitutional democracy. The judgment is striking in its failure to even consider the effect of the Constitution, or to engage at all with the constitutional imperative to develop the law to accord with the rights and obligations set out in the Constitution. It was as if the appeal court wanted to insist that private law – that sphere of law that concerns individuals' status and relationships – was somehow immunised from the legal impact of the enactment of the Constitution. This marked reluctance to engage with the constitutional issues of the rights of women to the state's protection of their physical integrity, safety and security, clearly presented by Breitenbach in his argument, foretold the disappointing judgment. Unsurprisingly, the court dismissed the appeal, with costs. It found that the state did not owe Carmichele a duty to prevent Coetzee's release from custody, that the prosecutor was under no obligation to oppose his release, and that the state and Carmichele were not in a 'special relationship'.

Pama reported feeling decidedly depressed at the judgment, believing the case was over. Being very conscious that they had now lost twice, Pama described feeling as if he had received a 'black eye' from the Cape High Court and a 'broken nose' from the Appellate Court: 'I could not help feeling that the Constitutional Court would cut my head off.'[12] However, when Breitenbach recommended that they appeal to the Constitutional Court, Carmichele showed the resolve and determination that had marked her whole approach to the case and agreed to press on.

Round three

Carmichele approached the Constitutional Court for relief. Following argument on 20 March 2001, the court handed down its judgment on 16 August 2001. Authored by justices Ackermann and Goldstone, the judgment at last handed victory to Alix Carmichele.

One of the country's leading advocates, Wim Trengove SC, joined Carmichele's legal team for this round of the fight. Her Constitutional Court case was also bolstered by argument from the Gender Research Project of the Centre for Applied Legal Studies (CALS) at Wits School of Law, argued by Advocate Janet Kentridge. Not only did this boost the Carmichele team's morale, demonstrating that they were not alone in their fight, but the CALS submission generalised the case beyond Alix Carmichele and connected it to the broader struggle for women's human rights and gender equality in South Africa. As the CALS submission framed the issue: 'Sexual violence and the threat of sexual violence goes to the core of women's subordination in society. It is the single greatest threat to the self-determination of South African women.'[13]

The case was important for another reason: it marked a step along the road in terms of developing South Africa's law in line with the Constitution. The common law – that body of law established historically and subsequently drawn upon in cases as binding – must be developed in a way that takes account of the Constitution, especially the Bill of Rights. It cannot atrophy and become like an insect preserved in amber; it must grow organically as required by the demands of constitutional democracy. In this case, the constitutional rights to life; respect for and protection of the dignity, freedom and security of the person; personal privacy; and freedom of movement were all up for question. The delictual common law on what constitutes a duty of care and negligent conduct in such circumstances was now a work in progress. Old principles must be revisited and shaped to conform to constitutional imperatives. As the Constitutional Court judgment set the issue:

> Section 39(2) of the Constitution provides that when developing the common law, every court must promote the spirit, purport and objects of the Bill of Rights. It follows implicitly that where the common law deviates from the spirit, purport and objects

of the Bill of Rights the courts have an obligation to develop it by removing that deviation.[14]

For this reason, the Constitutional Court specifically noted that neither of the two earlier judgments in the case – by the High Court and the Appellate Court – had taken account of the relevant provisions of the Bill of Rights or the consequent obligation to develop the common law in light of the Constitution. On the merits of the case, the Constitutional Court dealt with the claim against the police separately from that against the prosecutors. On both legs, however, the Constitutional Court found that a duty existed to do far more to prevent violence against women.

The Constitutional Court judgment was significant for at least two reasons: it was the first time that the court had asserted the importance of the new constitutional normative framework, and it extended this framework, which now needed to be applied by judges in deciding disputes in the area of private law. It also refused to defer to the Appellate Division's view that private law and in particular the law of delict (claims for a civil wrong) were unaltered by the Constitution.

Pama, who was unable to travel to Johannesburg for the handing down of the judgment, reports that when he got the call from his correspondent attorney who had attended court, he raced to the top of the staircase in his Knysna law offices, bellowing, 'We won!' An emotional Pama called Carmichele and the other members of the legal team to report their victory. The result attracted massive media coverage – probably because it was some rare but welcome good news in the fight against crime.

Round four

The win in Braamfontein on 16 August 2001, nearly four years after the trial had started in Cape Town in September 1997, did not mean the end, however, of this now marathon matter. The case was referred back to the High Court in Cape Town where the trial continued on 7 March 2002, with the same legal teams that had appeared in the Constitutional Court. In effect, the reversal on appeal by the Constitutional Court of Judge Chetty's grant of absolution from the instance meant that that a new order replaced it – the application for absolution was denied. This meant that the respondent, the state, was required to begin its defence of the claim in the continuation of the trial. The state called the police officers and prosecutor as witnesses. Prosecutor Louw conceded that her decisions not to oppose Coetzee's release on his own recognisance on 6 March 1995, and again after his return from Valkenberg, on 15 April 1995, were mistakes. The police officers called to testify confirmed that they were aware of Coetzee's earlier conviction and had other knowledge of his deviant past, but had bungled and should have passed on this information effectively.

The testimony of the main investigating officer, in particular, revealed why Trengove is considered such an outstanding trial lawyer. Inspector Klein, in the police service in Knysna since 1985, was closely cross-examined on what little he had done to ascertain the details of Coetzee's previous conviction for indecent assault. Klein claimed to have spoken to Mrs Coetzee on 5 March 1995 in Hornlee about her son, testifying that she had told him that Francois was a good boy, a father figure in their home, that he contributed to their household expenses, had passed matric and wanted to study further. She testified that Coetzee should be released on his own recognisance because she did not have any money for bail. However, she denied ever having had any such conversation about her son with Inspector Klein.

To corroborate this conversation, Klein had relied on an entry in his police pocket book. An entry, squeezed between the other entries on page 16, and running over the fold in the middle onto page 17 (instead of continuing on the next line on page 16), recorded 'Noetzie MAS 26-03-97'. Trengove put it to Klein that this entry was fabricated and had been inserted after March 1995 in order to bolster the evidence of his investigation.[15] Klein denied this – he claimed that this was the way he made notes in his pocket book.

However, no other entries appear in this fashion in the pocket book. Moreover, this conversation should have occurred on 26 March 1995, but the date recorded in the pocket book is two years later, in 1997. The final nail in the coffin of this testimony's credibility was that Klein recorded an MAS case number in this entry, testifying that this was the case number for the case against Coetzee for the assault of Eurena Terblanche. However, other police testimony confirmed that the system of numbering cases with MAS began only in April 1996.[16] Prior to that, cases of this type would have borne an 'MR' case number (*misdaadregister*, meaning crime register). The case number for the Terblanche assault was MR-26-03-95. It was therefore clear that Inspector Klein had tried to bolster his evidence, plugging the hole where a proper investigation of Coetzee's prior criminal conduct should have led the police.

Judge Chetty delivered a new judgment, finding the police and prosecutor jointly and severally liable to Carmichele for the damages she had suffered as a result of the attack, and ordered the state to pay her legal costs. This new judgment, in a nutshell, found that the police and prosecutor's conduct fell short of the standard requiring that they act with care and diligence. Carmichele's lawyers had finally established the state's liability for Coetzee's attack on her. In the ordinary course, the matter would then have proceeded to considering what damages, if any, had been caused and what compensation, if any, should result.

Round five

However, three months after the restart of the trial, on 3 June 2002, the state applied for leave to appeal this latest defeat. Carmichele's affidavit opposing this application described how she was 'dumbfounded' by this development. She said:

> At the hearing in the Constitutional Court, one of the Justices said that he did not want to see this case 'yo-yoing' through the South African legal system. It would be most unfair to me for this to happen. The whole ordeal has left me feeling tired and now despondent once again. I cannot understand what benefit an appeal will bring to the [state]. This case should not be dragged on for years with no resolution or closure and ultimately a waste of taxpayers' money.[17]

It is worth considering why the state chose to appeal Chetty's judgment. It makes one wonder whether the state's legal advisors had read the Constitutional Court's judgment, which made it clear that the Constitution was there precisely to come to the aid of claimants like Carmichele. Did they simply choose to pursue the appeal because that avenue was procedurally available to them?

In any event, Judge Chetty refused leave to appeal, and the state then applied directly to the Appeal Court in Bloemfontein for leave to appeal. Leave to appeal was granted; the appeal was heard on 3 November 2002. In November 2003, the court that had previously found against Carmichele confirmed her victory.

Despite finding for Carmichele, this hearing, unfortunately, further underscored the journey still to be undertaken before the judiciary comprehends and becomes sensitive to the traumatic position of survivors of violent sexual assaults. At one point in the hearing, Judge Louis Harms, the most senior member of the bench who presided that day, commented that only 'attempted rape' by Coetzee had been established here, and that Carmichele's specific injuries were 'superficial' (notwithstanding the multiple surgeries required to repair them). He then commented on Coetzee's actions, to the visible discomfort of his judicial colleagues, saying that 'if we grade this as rape cases go, it merits less than five out of 10'.

The judicial reference to rape was strange, in that the case turned on an attempt to murder, and not rape. However, in Judge Harms's judgment, it is clear that he was interested in this question, as he referred in detail to the question of rape in his judgment: 'Neither Court found that Coetzee [had] attempted to rape the plaintiff, something alleged by her in the particulars of claim. There was also no finding that the assault had been indecent or committed with an indecent intent.'

The judge went on to say: 'The thought of rape had, no doubt, crossed the plaintiff's mind because she knew Coetzee, she had been told that he had a previous conviction for rape, she believed that he had raped Ms Eurena Terblanche and she and, especially, Gosling believed that he was a menace to society who should be behind bars. But all this does not mean that any indecent intention on the part of Coetzee was established on a balance of probability.'

It is presumably for this reason that during argument, Judge Harms raised the issue of rape in this judicially crudest of manners.

Admittedly, his colleague, Judge Ian Farlam, hastened to add moments later, 'I don't know how you rate rape. But if you put attempted rape with attempted murder, it becomes very serious indeed.' He added, 'Your danger to society does not depend on whether there was penetration or not.'[18] This exchange revealed troubling judicial thinking that prompted journalist Carmel Rickard to take Judge Harms's attitude to task:

How could any judge think of 'grading' rape, of actually assigning a value to its severity? What does that say to the woman involved about her ordeal and how it is viewed by society? … I kept asking myself these questions, but there was another even harder one: if these words had shocked me deeply, how would the woman who had actually lived through the experience be feeling if she had been here? How would she feel about the ability of judges to understand the impact of her trauma? What would happen to her confidence that the legal system could ensure that she and other women are taken seriously when they report and describe a sexual attack?[19]

Judge Harms earned himself the dubious 'Mampara of the Week' award from *Sunday Times* columnist Hogarth with the comment:

Hogarth is loath to test the patience of court officers such as Judge Louis Harms by honouring them in this space. But Judge Harms had made a very strong case against himself as reported elsewhere … He was applying his mind to an [earlier] case where a man had attacked a woman, sat on her, punched her in the face, bit her, then dragged her some way before knocking her head, threatening to kill her and throttling her until she was unconscious. Then he pulled off her clothes and attempted to rape her before leaving her for dead. So, what did the good judge have to say about these grotesque violations? 'if we grade this as rape cases go, it merits less than a five out of 10', said he. As judges go, two out of 10.

Judge Harms's comment cannot be simply dismissed as insensitive. It also reveals the tragic and infuriating fact that South Africa's courts are so mired in the torrent of cases caused by the very worst criminal conduct, that degrees of reprehensibility present themselves. Only by comparing cases can courts make some sense of the facts before them in any particular case and deliver appropriate judgments.

An anecdote from this appellate hearing bears repeating, demonstrating some of the challenges of this litigation.[20] At one point during Trengove's argument, Judge Harms commented to him that his cross-examination had troubled the court, given that it used inappropriate and offensive language, and seemed to infuse Coetzee's attack on Carmichele with a sexual element. As the court adjourned for lunch, the judge provided counsel with the page reference to the cross-examination that had so offended the court. Distressed at this, and unsure what the learned judge could have been referring to, Trengove reviewed the record of his cross- examination. There, a question had been put to a witness, dealing with what Coetzee had said to Carmichele while he held her leg as she lay on the floor. Accoding to the transcript of the testimony, he had said: '*het oor en oor vir haar gesê dat sy moet hom naaï*'. This was a most unfortunate typographical error. It should have read: '*het oor en oor vir haar gesê dat sy moet omdraaï*'.[21] After the lunch adjournment, a relieved counsel could advise the court of this mistake.

In the end, Judge Harms, notwithstanding the public criticism, wrote an important judgment on behalf of the court, confirming that Carmichele was owed a duty by the state, that such duty had not been met and that the state's appeal should be dismissed, with costs of two counsel. Round five to Alix.

But how many more rounds ...?

Having taken her fight to five courts over 13 years, Carmichele had still not recovered any compensation for her injuries. She returned to court in April 2008, armed with revised and updated expert evidence detailing the basis for her compensation claim. This process of evaluation by her own and the state's experts, including a psychologist, psychiatrist, industrial psychologist, orthopaedic surgeon and physiotherapist, meant that she was forced to relive the traumatic attack and its impact on her life. She told an interviewer in October 2007 that she had been 'dissected like a rat to determine how much [the state] has to pay. I had to reveal my deepest, darkest secrets, my most private thoughts and feelings. Now everything I think or feel is in a report and will be in the public domain.'[22] This humiliating and invasive experience of the legal system is not uncommon for survivors seeking justice and compensation.

In September 2008, Judge Roger Cleaver awarded R673 772 in damages to Carmichele. This was supposed to cover past medical expenses, past loss of income, her loss of earning capacity, future medical expenses and general damages. Sadly, this parsimonious amount was unlikely to cover the true costs of pursuing justice for 13 years.

In interviews with the authors, Alix recounted her disappointment with the legal system. She described the immense discomfort of having her private physical and emotional space intruded upon during the countless hours of examination by expert doctors and the state's lawyers, and of being exposed to humiliating cross-examination during her two days on the witness stand at the damages trial. During this, she was questioned at length on items in her bank statements ranging from how much she spent on groceries to insinuations that she hid income. The way the legal system exacts evidence and proof from victims of crime is defective and undignified. It takes years, and much cost, to sue for justice, while it also spawns more conflict.

Not only did Alix have to recount the horrific experience of the assault (which the state's counsel downplayed by referring to it as a 'scuffle' throughout the hearing), but she also had to defend her life choices in minute detail. Her decisions to end personal relationships, relocate or accept work – each had to be explained and justified. In the sense that the victim becomes re-victimised by the law, Alix Carmichele is not alone, nor is she likely to be the last to suffer this way.

On a national level, the levels of violent crime, including incidents of sexual assault on women, remain horrifically high. While *Carmichele* is undoubtedly a triumph and has radically changed the law, it also reveals the limitations of using law alone to secure redress and prevent the mistakes here. In fact, millions of rands of claims brought by victims of crime are believed to be pending against the state using the *Carmichele* precedent. From this, one can deduce that she was one of many failed by law-enforcement in South Africa. Indeed, this fact only compounds the sense of disappointment for Carmichele. All of this fight would be 'worth it' or justified in some way if her case had radically changed the situation for other victims of crime. But it did not. While the legal precedent may open another avenue for accountability, true justice and fair compensation remain illusory. It all seems the proverbial hollow victory, and confirms the incremental and imperfect way in which the legal system seeks to deliver justice. One can also conclude that this avalanche of claims speaks far more about the failure of our institutional crime fighting than the undeniable success of one lawsuit to provide a legal avenue for compensation to victims of crime. This is illustrated yet again in crime statistics released in Parliament.

The 2017/18 annual report tabled by the SAPS in Parliament showed that 317 475 convictions were recorded in all criminal courts: 890 in high courts, 24 976 in regional courts and 291 609 in district courts, with an average conviction rate of 94.7 per cent, which the SAPS claims is a modest performance improvement.

However, 920 911 dockets were submitted for decision. In view of the conviction rates, the question arises as to what happened to the other 600 000 or so dockets. This is not clear from the data and information presented in the 2017/18 report.

Regional court prosecutors received 119 234 dockets for a decision, but just 18 940, or roughly 15 per cent were prosecuted. Prosecution was declined on 43 298 dockets, while 57 270 were returned for further investigation, according to the 2016/17 annual report. The numbers for district prosecutors showed that of the 777 196 dockets received for a decision, just 91 687, or about 12 per cent were brought to court. A total of 253 710 dockets were returned for further investigation – and in 430 363 cases, or 56 per cent prosecution was declined.[23]

However, determined as we are to end on an optimistic note, it is worth remembering that the Constitutional Court judgment certainly did open the way for others to follow Carmichele's hard-beaten path to justice. Two cases in particular demonstrate how Carmichele's case takes us further along the bridge to Mureinik's culture of justification.

First was the case of *Van Eeden v Minister of Safety and Security*, decided on 27 September 2002 by the Supreme Court of Appeal. Ghia van Eeden sought damages in delict from the state for the injuries and loss she suffered as a result of sexual assault, rape and robbery by one André Gregory Mohamed in August 1998. In the words of the judgment, Mohamed was

> a known dangerous criminal and serial rapist who had escaped from police custody in Durban on 22 May 1998. Mohamed escaped from police cells, where he was being held for an identification parade, through an unlocked security gate. At the time, he was facing no fewer than 22 charges, including indecent assault, rape and armed robbery committed in the

Durban area. Within six days of his escape, he resumed his sexual attacks on young women, this time near Pretoria.[24]

Van Eeden was one of Mohamed's victims in this latter series of attacks and, like Carmichele before her, initially had her claim dismissed by the trial judge, since he was bound by the Supreme Court of Appeal's decision in the first *Carmichele* judgment (see 'round two' above). However, by the time the Supreme Court of Appeal heard the appeal, the Constitutional Court's decision in *Carmichele*, overturning the former court's judgment, had been delivered. The Supreme Court of Appeal therefore had the opportunity to engage immediately and directly with the newly evolved common-law understanding of the state's duty to prevent crime in light of the constitutional normative framework. The Supreme Court of Appeal therefore found that the failure by the state to prevent Mohamed's escape gave rise to delictual liability to the subsequent victim of the crime committed by this man.

The second case to consider was that of *N K v Minister of Safety and Security*,[25] decided by the Constitutional Court on 13 June 2005, and, like *Van Eeden*, the case benefited from the exceptional lawyering of Trengove. This case also involved a claim to recover damages in delict from the Minister of Safety and Security for the harm suffered by a claimant (identified by her initials as 'NK') as a result of being raped and assaulted on 27 March 1999. In the words of the court's summary of the judgment,

> Her assailants were three uniformed and on-duty police sergeants. Ms K, who had had an argument with a boyfriend with whom she had been out for the evening was looking for a telephone to call home when she met the police officers at approximately 4 o'clock in the morning. They offered her a lift home which she gratefully accepted. Thereafter they took her to a deserted place, raped and abandoned her. The three policemen were subsequently convicted of rape and kidnapping, and sentenced to life in prison by the Johannesburg High Court.[26]

Judge O'Regan wrote the judgment for the unanimous court considering the vicarious liability of the Minister for Safety and Security for these police officers' conduct. She concluded, as set out in the court's summary of the judgment, that

> although it is clear that the policemen's conduct constituted a clear deviation from their duty, there nevertheless existed a sufficiently close relationship between their employment and the wrongful conduct. Three factors lead to the conclusion that the Minister is liable: First, the fact that the policemen bore a statutory and constitutional duty to prevent crime and protect the members of the public – a duty which also rests on their employer (the Minister); secondly, the fact that the applicant accepted an offer of assistance from the policemen in circumstances in which she needed assistance, it was their duty to supply it and it was reasonable of her to accept assistance; and, thirdly, the fact that the wrongful conduct of the policemen coincided with their failure to perform their duties to protect the applicant.[27]

The judgment emphasises that the Constitution mandates members of the police to protect community members and that for this mandate to be performed efficiently, reasonable trust must be placed in members of the police service by members of the public.

All of these cases, and the many others that followed, show how law can be used to expand the meaning and reach of the common law, and to ensure constitutional justice for the many South Africans who remain victims of crime. Unfortunately, this precedent has not altered the fact that the country faces a truly massive crime wave or that the justice system is alienating, frustrating and unsatisfying for many of its litigant users. Nor has it apparently created sufficient incentive for the state to dramatically enhance its law-enforcement and crime-prevention resources. But it must surely be at least a step in the right direction.

11

GAY MARRIAGE: FROM POSSIBILITY TO REALITY

'It was because the majority of South Africans had experienced the humiliating legal effect of repressive colonial conceptions of race and gender that they determined that henceforth the role of the law would be different for all South Africans. Having themselves experienced the indignity and pain of legally regulated subordination, and the injustice of exclusion and humiliation through the law, the majority committed this country to particularly generous constitutional protections for all South Africans.'[1]

– JUSTICE EDWIN CAMERON

Before 1994, South African law contained numerous homophobic provisions. But, during the CODESA negotiations, the political parties agreed to a Constitution that became the first in the world to explicitly outlaw discrimination based on sexual orientation. Viewed against the country's history, it was a surprising but most welcome development.

The common-law definition of marriage in South Africa, which dates from when the Cape was colonised by the Dutch East India Company, manifestly discriminated against same-sex couples. More recently, in 1905 the Chief Justice of the then Transvaal, James Rose Innes, said: 'Marriage is a union of one man, one woman, to the exclusion, whilst it lasts, of all others.'[2]

This position remained unchanged until the constitutional negotiations, which culminated in the Interim Constitution, which was passed in 1994.

The reasons for the National Party's acceptance of an anti-discrimination clause in the Constitution, which included sexual orientation as one of the prohibited grounds, have never been made clear. To be sure, though, the legal experts on all sides who assisted the various political parties were significantly influenced by the carefully argued and erudite memorandum of Professor Edwin Cameron, who later as a judge of appeal authored the judgments in *Fourie* and *Kevin Botha*. This document, which eloquently argued for the inclusion of such a clause, was written on behalf of a non-governmental organisation (NGO), the Equality Foundation, and was intended to guide the constitutional negotiations.

There is an illuminating story of late-night negotiations concerning the inclusion of sexual orientation as a provision in the anti-discrimination clause. Kobie Coetsee, the then Minister of Justice, was a man not well known for his clarity of language – in either English or his home language, Afrikaans. Late into the night, Coetsee was objecting, in an obscure way, to the inclusion of this provision in the anti-discrimination clause. Finally, the ANC negotiators realised that his objection was based on the argument that a clause that outlawed discrimination against sexual orientation would allow for a constitutional attack on the crime of bestiality. One of the ANC negotiators then put it to Coetsee that, while he might be worried about the sexual activities of some of his voters, the ANC had no such problems. A roar of laughter broke the tension and, with it, the deadlock. That was the last serious objection raised against the provision.

The road to *Fourie*

A series of cases followed the inclusion in the Constitution of the anti-discrimination clause based on sexual orientation, which were designed to secure recognition of the rights of gays and lesbians. In 1999 a challenge was brought against the criminalisation of private consensual sexual acts between gays and lesbians. In this dispute, known as the 'sodomy case', the Constitutional Court had no difficulty in finding that the crime of sodomy had to be struck from the body of South African criminal law. UCT academic Pierre de Vos wrote reflectively on the court's break with the past and of the possibility recognised in this judgment: 'It is difficult to overstate the power of the rhetoric in [this] case. In a way no court in the world has ever done, the Constitutional Court rejected the very basis of different treatment of gay men and lesbians by rejecting the notion of normal and abnormal sexuality ...'[3]

A year later, the Minister of Home Affairs was brought before the Constitutional Court to defend the discriminatory impact of a provision in the immigration laws that afforded special protection to permanent residents who were engaged to marry South African citizens, while ignoring the rights of same-sex life partners in the same position. Finding this discrimination to be constitutionally impermissible, Justice Ackermann said of the legislation:

> The message is that gays and lesbians lack the inherent humanity to have their families and family lives in such same-sex relationships respected or protected. It serves in addition to perpetuate and reinforce existing prejudice and stereotypes. The impact constitutes a crass, blunt, cruel and serious invasion of their dignity. The discrimination, based on sexual orientation, is severe because no concern, let alone anything approaching equal concern, is shown for the particular sexual orientation of gays and lesbians.[4]

The next case involved Kathy Satchwell, a judge of the Johannesburg High Court. She successfully took the Minister of Welfare and Population Development to court on behalf of herself and her partner, arguing that the exclusion of a provision for a pension to the surviving same-sex partner in a statute was discriminatory compared to the potential provision of a pension for the surviving opposite-sex spouse – in this case, of a judge.

Later, the Constitutional Court held that the provision in childcare legislation that confined the right to adopt children to married heterosexual couples, to the exclusion of same-sex couples, conflicted both with the principle of what was in the best interests of the child and the inherent right to dignity of same-sex couples.

Fourie

Finally, in 2005, the big kahuna arrived before the courts – the right of gay and lesbian couples to be married. The case of *Fourie* concerned a constitutional challenge to the common-law definition of marriage and to a provision in the Marriage Act that preserved the institution of marriage exclusively for heterosexual couples. As the introduction to the Constitutional Court's judgment explains, this case involved two female partners:

> Finding themselves strongly attracted to each other, [they] decided to set up home together. After being acknowledged by their friends as a couple for more than a decade, they decided that the time had come to get public recognition and registration of their relationship … Like many persons in their situation, they wanted to get married. There was one impediment. They are both women.[5]

The complaint of the applicants, Adriaana Fourie and Cecilia Johanna Bonthuys, was that the law excluded them from celebrating their love and commitment to each other in marriage, and that the law shut them out, unfairly and unconstitutionally, from this union. This exclusion, they contended, came from the common-law definition, which states that marriage in South Africa is a 'union of one man with one woman, to the exclusion, while it lasts, of all others'.[6]

Neither the Supreme Court of Appeal nor the Constitutional Court encountered any judicial difficulty in finding that same-sex marriages required legal recognition. The differences between the judges turned on the role the courts should play in making the necessary amendments to the existing marriage laws. And these approaches have important implications for the way in which courts initiate social change through their judgments.

Judge Edwin Cameron, in the majority judgment of the Supreme Court of Appeal, and Justice Kate O'Regan, in a minority judgment in the Constitutional Court, held that the common law should be developed to read into the law the necessary words that would, with immediate effect, permit same-sex couples to marry. By contrast, Judge Ian Farlam, in a minority judgment in the Supreme Court of Appeal, and Justice Albie Sachs, on behalf of the majority of the Constitutional Court, held that the resolution of this extremely sensitive issue should be deferred for one year to allow the legislature time to consider the question and craft an appropriate legislative solution.

The difference in approach between Cameron and O'Regan on one hand, and the majority of the Constitutional Court on the other emerges clearly from the following passages in their judgments. Justice Cameron writes:

> The task of applying the values in the Bill of Rights to the common law thus requires us to put faith in both the values themselves and in the people whose duly elected representatives created a visionary and inclusive constitutional structure that offered acceptance and justice across diversity to all. The South African public and their elected representatives have for the greater part accepted the sometimes far-reaching decisions taken in regard to sexual orientation and other constitutional rights over the past ten years. It is not presumptuous to believe that they will accept also the further incremental development of the common law that the Constitution requires in this case.[7]

In contrast, Justice Sachs, on behalf of the majority of the Constitutional Court, said:

> This is a matter that touches on deep public and private sensibilities. I believe that Parliament is well-suited to finding the best way of ensuring that same-sex couples are brought in from the legal cold. ... It is my view that it would best serve those equality claims by respecting the separation of powers and giving Parliament an opportunity to deal appropriately with the matter. In this respect, it is necessary to bear in mind the different ways in which the legislature could legitimately deal with the gap that exists in the law. ... Parliament should be given the opportunity in the first place to decide how best the equality rights at issue could be achieved. Provided that the basic principles of equality as enshrined in the Constitution are not trimmed in the process, the greater the degree of public acceptance for same sex-unions, the more will the achievement of equality be promoted.[8]

The appropriate role of the judiciary

The difference in approach between Justice Sachs on the one hand and Justices Cameron and O'Regan on the other reflected the sensitivity regarding this important question. Something similar happened in the United States, and an understanding of what occurred in that country helps frame the key issues that emerge from this legislation in South Africa.

On 18 November 2003, the Massachusetts Supreme Judicial Court found in a 4–3 ruling that, as the Massachusetts Constitution confirmed the dignity and equality of all persons and forbade the creation of second-class citizens, it was impermissible to deny a marriage licence to same-sex couples. Fittingly, the majority opinion was written by Chief Justice Margaret Marshall, born in South Africa. Marshall had been a prominent member of NUSAS in the 1960s at the time when the student union had invited Robert Kennedy to tour South Africa in the teeth of heated opposition from the National Party government.

In her opinion, Marshall wrote: 'Our obligation is to define the liberty of all – not to mandate our own moral code.' To the argument that a same-sex marriage might cause harm to the institution of marriage, she responded:

> Here, the plaintiffs seek only to be married, not to undermine the institution of civil marriage. They do not want marriage abolished. They do not attack the binary nature of marriage, the consanguinity provisions, or any of the other gate-keeping provisions of the marriage licensing law. Recognizing the right of an individual to marry a person of the same sex will not diminish the validity or dignity of opposite-sex marriage, any more than recognizing the right of an individual to marry a person of a different race devalues the marriage of a person who marries someone of her own race. If anything, extending civil marriage to same-sex couples reinforces the importance of marriage to individuals and communities. That same-sex couples are willing to embrace marriage's solemn obligations of exclusivity, mutual support, and commitment to one another is a testament to the enduring place of marriage in our laws and in the human spirit.[9]

This decision invoked both enthusiasm and ferocious opposition. Within hours of the decision's announcement, the then Massachusetts governor, Mitt Romney, held a press conference and denounced the ruling, calling for a constitutional amendment to reserve marriage to opposite-sex couples. Some have suggested that the election of George W Bush in 2004 was partly due to the controversy caused by this decision.[10]

But, as in South Africa, the impetus towards the legal recognition of same-sex marriages also grew in America, culminating in a 5–4 decision in favour of the legality of same-sex marriage by the US Supreme Court. On 26 June 2015, in *Obergefell et al v Hodges*,[11] Justice Anthony Kennedy, writing for the majority, found that there were four distinct reasons why the court had to recognise the right of same-sex couples to marriage. First, there was a right to personal choice regarding marriage that was inherent in the concept of individual autonomy. Secondly, the right to marriage was fundamental because it supported the two-person union in its importance to committed individuals. This principle applied equally to same-sex couples. Thirdly, the fundamental right to marry safeguarded children and families, and drew meaning from the related rights of procreation, child-rearing and education. As same-sex couples also had children and families, they were deserving of this safeguard. Finally, Justice Kennedy said that marriage was a 'keystone of the nation's social order' and that there was no difference between same- and opposite-sex couples with respect to this principle. Consequently, preventing same-sex couples from marrying placed them at odds with society and denied them countless benefits of marriage. It also introduced instability into their relationships without any justification.[12]

The majority opinion elicited ferocious dissent from Justice Antonin Scalia. Rather callously, Scalia began by saying, 'The substance of today's decree is not of immense personal importance to me. The law can recognise a marriage or whatever sexual attachments and living arrangements it wishes and accord them favorable civil consequences, from tax treatment to rights of inheritance.' However, he went on to say:

> It is of overwhelming importance … who it is who rules me. Today's decree says that my Ruler and the Ruler of 320 million Americans coast-to-coast is a majority of the nine lawyers on the Supreme Court. The opinion in these cases is the furthest extension

in fact – and the furthest extension one can even imagine of the Court's claimed power to create 'liberties' that the Constitution and its amendments neglect to mention.[13]

Scalia went on to say that, before this decision, public debate over same-sex marriage had 'displayed American democracy at its best'. For him, the outcome of this debate depended on the democratically elected legislatures in the country. If the constitutional text did not expressly strike down a practice that had been adopted for a very long time, it was not for the courts, but for the democratically elected state legislatures, to make the decision. For this reason, he denounced what he considered to be 'a naked judicial claim to legislative, indeed super-legislative, power – a claim fundamentally at odds with the country's system of government'.[14]

The appropriate role for the judiciary

Ironically, in the sense that Scalia did not share his legal philosophy, this is exactly the same position taken by Justice Sachs. By the time that same-sex marriage was legally recognised by the US Supreme Court, American public opinion on the matter had reached almost 60 per cent approval level.[15] However, it is unlikely that same-sex marriage would have been recognised throughout the US given the power of individual states.

This, of course, was not a problem that confronted South Africa. The South African Parliament voted on 14 November 2006 by 230 votes to 41 in favour of the bill allowing the same civil-marriage and civil-union rights for same-sex couples as those enjoyed by opposite-sex marriage partners. The Civil Union Act came into force on 1 December 2006, making South Africa just the fifth country in the world and the first in Africa to legalise same-sex marriages. It is a matter of pride that, at the time of writing, South Africa remains the only African country where same-sex marriage is constitutionally recognised.

But the decisions of Scalia and Sachs, on the one side, and those of Cameron and O'Regan on the other, raise the need for a profound debate concerning the role of the judiciary in a constitutional democracy. The key question, which has been explored in this book, is the extent to which the judiciary is entitled to intervene in controversial social, economic and political disputes. Or, put differently, when the judiciary decides cases of fraught political, economic or social import, the debate hinges on whether it has overstepped the boundary between its competence and that of the democratically elected legislature. It is a debate to which we shall return in the conclusion.

The conception of family life and significant others that was vindicated in the cases reflected on in this chapter is a middle-class, heteronormative one: the rights of two parents, spouses, with duties of support, and obligations towards each other, were recognised in a domestic context. This privileges a particular stereotype and it was a fight to extend it to same-sex couples. However important and significant this fight, it must also be recognised that the daily existence and lived experience of the LGBTQI[16] community in South Africa is often a much more basic struggle for survival. The experience of what is termed 'corrective rape', murders motivated by prejudice and hatred, and assaults (verbal and physical) is the grim reality of too many in South Africa. And the irrational rage and anger unleashed by the film *Inxeba*, a gay love story that 'tackles tradition, sexuality, masculinity and what it means to be an outsider', according to its creators, were appalling and sobering. The backlash to the movie was often couched in justificatory terms referencing a claimed lack of respect for Xhosa culture. There was intolerance evident in the controversial call for the film to be classified as adult pornographic material. This highlighted a, perhaps deliberate, intolerance for the values of equality espoused by our Constitution, which embraces all ideas, expressions and life choices.

While pension benefits, adoption and civil unions may now be available by law, the struggle for true acceptance continues.

12

THE GREAT ESCAPE

'I accept, in the light of the earlier discussion of head-of-state immunity, that [in implementing its obligations under the Rome Statute], South Africa was taking a step that many other nations have not yet taken. If that puts this country in the vanguard of attempts to prevent international crimes and, when they occur, cause the perpetrators to be prosecuted, that seems to me a matter for national pride rather than concern.'[1]
– JUDGE MALCOLM WALLIS

In 1993, former President Mandela wrote an article for the journal *Foreign Affairs*, in which he promised that South African foreign policy would be based on 'our belief that human rights should be the core concern of international relations' and that the country was 'ready to play a role in fostering peace and prosperity in the world we share as a community of nations'.[2]

As President, Mandela emphasised that South Africa intended to become a responsible global actor in terms of a policy based on the centrality of human rights and international relations, the promotion of democracy worldwide, the primacy of justice in respect of international law, the peaceful resolution of conflicts, and the prioritisation of African interests and concerns in policy choices.

Later, during the Mbeki era, concern began to mount over South

Africa's attitude to the relationship between human rights and foreign policy, largely as a result of the approach that South Africa had taken towards the Zimbabwean crisis, as well as the position that it took as a member of the UN Security Council, and the UN Human Rights Council in particular, in its refusal to support UN proposals for sanctions against Zimbabwe or any action against Iran's human-rights abuses.

Therefore, within ten years, the Mandela commitment to human rights as a pillar of South Africa's foreign-policy decisions had been honoured more in the breach than in the observance. By the second decade of democracy, South Africa appeared to favour authoritarian governments on the continent, such as Swaziland and Zimbabwe. Paradoxically, it supported Resolution 1973 of the United Nations Security Council, which authorised the 2011 NATO intervention in Libya, contradicting the African Union's position calling for an African political solution. In 2014 South Africa appeared to very reluctantly support a resolution passed by the UN Human Rights Council to combat violence and discrimination based on sexual orientation and gender identity.

In 2009 South Africa declined to issue a visa to the Dalai Lama to participate in a conference. This decision was widely condemned as betraying a commitment to human rights in order to appease China in a bid to attract foreign investment. Barbara Hogan, then a cabinet minister, took the unusual step of saying, 'My government is dismissive of human rights ... they should apologise'.[3]

Significantly, although Hogan was criticised for failing to adhere to traditional cabinet collective responsibility, not only was she not forced to resign, but she was made part of the cabinet in the newly elected government under Jacob Zuma. Initially, it appeared that the new government was intent on returning to the Mandela doctrine, particularly when it protested in August 2009 against the unlawful detention of then Burmese opposition leader Aung San Suu Kyi and expressed its concern about the situation in Sri Lanka, adding its voice to the call for an independent investigation into the Sri Lankan government's conduct during the civil war with the Tamil Tigers.

However, the disdain for a foreign policy anchored in human rights which had characterised the Mbeki government made itself felt again when the Zuma government adopted an equivocal approach to gay rights at the UN Human Rights Council, and later, with even greater force, in its attitude to the arrest of Omar al-Bashir, a decision that marked a complete retreat from the Mandela doctrine and its promise of the early 1990s.

The president of Sudan, Omar Hassan Ahmad al-Bashir, is a hugely controversial figure. He came to power in a coup in 1989 by ousting a democratically elected government. During a violent civil war, he was accused by the Justice and Equality Movement, together with the Sudanese Liberation Army, of neglecting Darfur and oppressing non-Arabs. An armed insurgency began that led to the deaths of between 200 000 and 400 000 people.[4] On 21 March 2005, the UN Security Council referred the Sudanese situation to the ICC.

On 14 July 2008, the Chief Prosecutor of the ICC, Luis Moreno Ocampo, alleged that al-Bashir bore individual criminal responsibility for genocide, crimes against humanity and war crimes which had been committed in Darfur since 2003. He accused him of having 'masterminded and implemented' a plan to destroy three non-Arab ethnic groups in the region, and charged him on counts of murder, rape and deportation. Pursuant to the court's decision, the first arrest warrant was issued on 4 March 2009 by the Pre-Trial Chamber, indicting al-Bashir on these crimes. In this way, al-Bashir became the first head of state ever to be indicted by the ICC.

The warrants were forwarded to all countries that were parties to the Statute of the International Criminal Court (known as the Rome Statute), including South Africa. When the warrants were forwarded to these countries they, as signatories, were obliged to ensure that al-Bashir would be surrendered to the ICC in the event that he came within any of these jurisdictions.

Al-Bashir in South Africa

Al-Bashir's infamy may be located in the turbulence of Sudan, but in 2015 he became Exhibit 1 in the case against the South African government and its complicated relationship with the rule of law and the required compliance with the orders of the ICC. In June 2015, al-Bashir arrived in South Africa to attend the African Union Assembly of Heads of State. The Southern Africa Litigation Centre, an NGO, brought an urgent application on Sunday 14 June 2015 before the Gauteng High Court in which it sought an order declaring that the failure to take steps to arrest al-Bashir was in breach of both the Constitution and South Africa's international obligations, and a further order to compel the South African government to cause al-Bashir to be arrested and surrendered to the ICC to stand trial.

The government managed to procure a postponement to 11.30 on Monday 15 June, so that it could prepare affidavits to oppose the application. Of considerable importance was that the High Court, on the Sunday, had been alive to the possibility that al-Bashir may leave the country before the court had an opportunity to hear the matter, and thus escape arrest. For this reason, it made an order prohibiting al-Bashir from leaving South Africa until a final decision had been made. The government was therefore directed to take all necessary steps to prevent him from leaving before then.

The hearing before the High Court

On Monday 15 June 2015, the Judge President of the Gauteng High Court, Dunstan Mlambo, constituted a full bench of three judges, over which he presided. Although during the postponement process, it was indicated that the hearing would begin at 11.30, the government asked for a further extension because its affidavits were still not ready. The hearing was then set to start at about 13.00. The court sought assurances from counsel leading the case for the government, William Mokhari SC, that al-Bashir was still in the country. Mokhari informed the court that, according to his instructions, al-Bashir remained in the country and this assurance was repeated during the course of argument.

After hearing argument, the court issued an order at around three o'clock that the failure of the South African government to take steps to arrest al-Bashir, was a breach of the Constitution and therefore invalid, and that the government was now to be compelled to take all reasonable steps to arrest al-Bashir without its own warrant and detain him, pending a formal request for his surrender from the ICC.

What the judges did not know at this time, however, was that journalists had already received reports from midday on the Monday that al-Bashir had departed or was about to depart from Waterkloof Air Force Base. This information proved to be correct because a Sudanese aircraft took off from Waterkloof at 11.15, and among its passengers was President al-Bashir.

The timeline before the High Court

When the court convened at one o'clock on 15 June, it heard argument from both Advocate Isabel Goodman, acting on behalf of the Southern Africa Litigation Centre, and Advocate Mokhari. As argument confirmed before the court, journalists in the court were convinced, on the basis of their sources, that al-Bashir had arrived at Waterkloof and may well already have left the country. Mokhari continued to assure the court that, based on the instructions that he had received from his clients, this was not the case and therefore a real live dispute confronted the three judges. After hearing argument, the judges retired to their chambers to consider their position. Shortly before the judges returned to court, Mokhari approached Goodman and insisted that she accompany him so that he may speak to the judges, as it would have been highly improper for him to try to communicate with judges without the presence of opposing counsel.

Judge President Mlambo was understandably not prepared to entertain any discussion outside of an open court and insisted that the judges resume the hearing and that any submission or information that Mokhari wished to impart should be done in open court. After this order was handed down, Mokhari – who, according to an affidavit deposed to by the Director General of the Department of Home Affairs, had been informed 'shortly before the order was made' that al-Bashir had departed – then informed the court that al-Bashir 'had flown the coop'.

Goodman, evaluating the position with an understandable measure of caution, insisted that the court direct government to file an affidavit explaining the precise circumstances of the departure of al-Bashir. The director general's affidavit, which he offered in response, is a work of much wonder. In it, Mkuseli Apleni confirmed that al-Bashir had left on a flight from the Waterkloof Air Force Base on the morning of 15 June 2015. Apleni claimed that al-Bashir's passport had not been among those shown to officials of the Department of Home Affairs at the air force base. According to the director general, the passports of passengers on board a 'VIP flight' would be presented to the immigration officer by a representative of the foreign state on the VIP flight accompanied by a protocol officer from the Department of International Relations and Cooperation. It appeared that neither of these two officials we had been provided with a passenger list. The practice in such cases was that passengers would not personally appear before the immigration officer. He or she would simply check the passports that were handed in for applicable endorsements and visas, and then scan and stamp the passports. The passports would be handed back to the representatives of the foreign state of the VIP flight in the presence of the protocol officer and the flight would then be considered cleared for departure from an immigration point of view. The director general confirmed that the immigration officials working at the Waterkloof Air Force Base were aware of the court order that had been handed down by the court on 14 June 2015. They checked to see whether any of the passports belonged to al-Bashir, concluded that they did not have his passport and, made no further investigation, and the VIP flight was consequently authorised for take-off.

The reaction

It was hardly surprising that, when the Supreme Court of Appeal later evaluated this affidavit, Justice Malcolm Wallis described the explanation as to how the plane was allowed to travel, the court order notwithstanding, as 'risible'. Judge Wallis said in his assessment of the government's explanation:

> Senior officials representing government must have been aware of President Al Bashir's movements and his departure, the possibility of which had been mooted in the press. In those circumstances, the assurances that he was still in the country given to the court at the commencement and during the course of argument were false. There seem to be only two possibilities. Either the representatives of government set out to mislead the court and misled counsel in giving instructions, or the representatives and counsel misled the court. Whichever is the true explanation, a matter no doubt being investigated by the appropriate authorities, it was disgraceful conduct.[5]

Deputy ANC Secretary General Jessie Duarte took a different line from the disingenuous affidavit deposed to by the director general. She said that it was 'unfortunate' that South Africa had to disobey the court order: 'It's unfortunate that we actually had to disobey a judge's order to comply with an international obligation that we have. ... I think the country made the right choice. You do not make the choice to arrest a sitting Head of State on your soil ever.'

Duarte said that the African Union Constitution obliged member states to support the decision of its Peace and Security Council – one of which was to defer for a year the bringing of charges against al-Bashir.[6]

The party's secretary general, Gwede Mantashe, went further in developing this line. He argued that the affair hinged on whether South Africa should subsume its relationship with the continent to 'other superior multilateral Western institutions'. He said, 'Africa is not inferior, not a junior to European-based institutions. We cannot juniorise Africa.' Justifying the decision on political grounds, Mantashe said that, had South Africa arrested al-Bashir, it could have faced isolation, and its soldiers stationed in several African countries would have been at risk. He argued that if the South African authorities had arrested al-Bashir, the country would be 'the pariah state in the continent'. At its core, he argued, this affair was 'a serious political matter', in that South Africa could not isolate itself from the continent.[7]

Mantashe went on to say that court rulings against the government had become a worrisome trend. Once the judiciary had become politicised and began to debate rules of Parliament, he said, 'it means one arm of government [exerts] authority and virtual powers over another arm of government'.[8] Warming to his theme, Mantashe told viewers of TV actuality programme *Carte Blanche* that there was 'a drive in sections of the judiciary to create chaos for governance'.[9]

As well as these arguments along pragmatic political grounds, the government also raised legal arguments in justification of its conduct. Deputy Minister of Justice John Jeffery told Parliament that, as a head of state, al-Bashir had diplomatic immunity in terms of the Diplomatic Immunities and Privileges Act of 2001. In general, state parties are obliged to comply with the request by a court for surrender or assistance if a person who is subject to an arrest warrant is found on their territory. However, Jeffery referred to Article 98(1) of the Rome Treaty, which provides that a court may not proceed with a request for surrender or assistance which will require the requested state to act inconsistently with its obligations under international law in respect of the state or diplomatic immunity of a person or property of a third state unless the court can first obtain cooperation of that third state for the waiver of immunity. Relying on a range of international law cases, Jeffery insisted that there were precedents that supported the government's argument that heads of state enjoy immunity. Thus, in his view, the government had not acted illegally in its decision to allow al-Bashir to fly out of South Africa after the conference.

Jeffery sought to bolster his argument by claiming that, even if the legal arguments raised by government were not particularly persuasive, the ICC was not the kind of court South Africa had 'signed up for'. The court had deviated from its mandate and allowed itself to be influenced by powerful non-member states, he claimed:

> We signed up for a court that was going to hold human beings accountable for their war crimes – regardless of where they were from, We perceive it as tending to act as a proxy instrument for these states who see no need to subject themselves to its discipline, to persecute the African leaders and effect regime change on the continent. It is being used as a court against Africa ...[10]

Allowing al-Bashir to escape was therefore justified, at least in the eyes of government, on both legal and political grounds.

The legal fight

When the matter was initially heard by a full bench of the Pretoria High Court, the Southern Africa Litigation Centre argued that the only basis on which the government could seek to avoid its duty to arrest and surrender Bashir would have been if he enjoyed some form of diplomatic immunity from arrest or from the jurisdiction of our courts. On the basis of the questionable advice of the then Chief State Law Adviser, Enver Daniels, government contended that there was an agreement between it and the African Union Commission in terms of which South Africa had agreed to host the summit, and that Clause 1 of Article VIII of the General Convention on the Privileges and Immunities of the Organisation of African Unity meant that South Africa was required to accord 'members of the commission and staff members, the delegates and other represen-tatives of inter-governmental organisations attending the meetings, the privileges and immunities, which are set forth in the convention. It was significant that no reference was made to heads of state, as the government argued. The convention extended privileges and immunities including immunity from arrest or detention to 'representatives of Members States, to the principal and subsidiary institutions as well as to the Specialised Commission of the African Union ... while exercising their functions and during their travel to and from the place of meetings'.[11]

Government contended that, if this set of provisions were read together with Section 5(3) of the Diplomatic Immunities and Privileges Act[12] and Section 231(4) of the Constitution, the Minister of International Relations and Cooperation was empowered to publish a notice in the Government Gazette providing immunity to all delegates and attendees of this summit. On this basis, government's approach was the following: 'Cabinet collectively accepted and decided that the South African Government as the hosting country was first and foremost obliged to uphold and protect the inviolability of President Bashir in accordance with the AU terms and conditions and to consequently not arrest him in terms of the ICC arrest warrants whilst attending the AU summit.'[13]

As one commentator noted, any respectable lawyer would realise that these arguments were tendentious in the extreme.[14] For a start, the Organisation of African Unity Convention had not been made part of South African law in terms of section 231(4) of the Constitution. It was not binding on South Africa, and therefore the personnel of the African Union did not automatically enjoy privileges and immunities in South Africa. As the court said, failure to ratify the convention represented a clear choice by the legislature not to confer blanket immunity on African Union staff and officials who attend meetings, and certainly not on President al-Bashir.[15]

A ministerial notice could not solve the problem by suddenly providing al-Bashir with immunity, which otherwise he would not have possessed. Furthermore, any sensible reading of the Rome Statute would have informed the reader that there was an express provision that heads of state do not enjoy immunity under its terms.

But these absurd legal arguments put up by the government paled into insignificance when the factual questions were posed by the court. In particular, the court asked, 'How was it possible that President Bashir would, with his whole entourage, travel from Sandton to Waterkloof

Airbase, without any of the respondents' knowledge?' There is only one answer that could be reasonably inferred: the government had deliberately flouted South African law.

For this reason, the court concluded:

> A democratic state based on the rule of law cannot exist or function if the government ignores its constitutional obligations and fails to abide by court orders. A court is the guardian of justice, the corner-stone of a democratic system based on the rule of law. If the State, an organ of State or State official does not abide by court orders, the democratic edifice will crumble stone by stone until it collapses and chaos ensues … Where the rule of law is undermined by government it is often done gradually and surreptitiously. Where this occurs in court proceedings, the court must fearlessly address this through its judgments, and not hesitate to keep the constitutional obligations to administer justice to all persons alike without fear, favour or prejudice.[16]

Off to Bloemfontein

The legally pathetic arguments put up by government to the full bench did not deter it, however, from appealing the judgment to the Supreme Court of Appeal. It reinforced its legal team by appointing one of South Africa's leading counsel, Jeremy Gauntlett SC. Now a new argument was developed: the Diplomatic Immunities and Privileges Act provided a head of state with immunity from the criminal and civil jurisdiction of the courts of South Africa.

In handing down judgment on 15 March 2016, Judge Malcolm Wallis, on behalf of the court, was not prepared to be persuaded by any of these desperate last throws of the legal dice. He referred to the manner in which the South African legislature had passed the so-called Implementation Act, which ensured that the Rome Statute became part of South African law. For this reason, this Act had to enjoy priority over previous legislation. It stood to reason, where legislation dealing generally with a topic such as immunity was contrasted with a specific statute, such as the Implementation Act, the latter had to be read so as to exclude immunity in relation to international crimes and the obligations that South Africa had expressly undertaken when becoming a signatory to the ICC.[17]

Given the government's churlish attitude to the Rome Statute, the following passage of the judgment is of considerable significance:

> I accept, in the light of the earlier discussion of head of state immunity, that in doing so South Africa was taking a step that many other nations have not yet taken. If that puts this country in the vanguard of attempts to prevent international crimes and, when they occur, cause the perpetrators to be prosecuted, that seems to me a matter for national pride rather than concern. It is wholly consistent with our commitment to human rights both at a national and an international level.[18]

Expressed differently, the court was saying that South Africa's Constitution promotes human rights and a human-rights perspective on the world. The courts, as the custodians of the Constitution, will not support an executive that seeks to aid and abet a war criminal evading accountability and justice for his victims.

It was for this reason that the court took the unprecedented step of stating that either the representatives of the government had misled the Gauteng Court or the representatives had themselves been misled by government. Either way, it was 'disgraceful conduct'.

The political response

The ANC did not take this adverse decision lying down. Mantashe claimed that the court had not adequately considered the effects on the country's interests had it arrested Bashir. ANC MP and then chairperson of the National Assembly's Portfolio Committee on Justice, Mathole Motshekga, said 'We are dealing with a situation where the West wants us to implement the concept of justice without looking at our realities and therefore we will support the position of the ANC that our membership of the ICC should be reviewed.'

And that was not all. Mantashe went on to say 'there is a drive in some courts to create chaos for government'. The ANC also complained about 'an emerging trend in some courts of a judicial overreach'. Former Deputy Chief Justice, Dikgang Moseneke, was mentioned in the context of a speech that he had delivered concerning the nature of the Constitution and the powers granted to the executive. In this connection, Blade

Nzimande of the South African Communist Party said, 'We liberated this country ... we are never going to ask for permission from forces who were never with us in the trenches', referring to members of the judiciary.

Chief Justice Mogoeng called for a meeting with the heads of courts, saying: 'Judges, like others, should be susceptible to constructive criticism; however, in this regard, criticism should be fair and in good faith. Importantly, the criticism should be specific and clear. General gratuitous criticism is unacceptable.'[19] In a response to an extraordinary statement to policemen who were told by the head of the Hawks that certain judges 'colluded with people to produce certain judgments', the Chief Justice said: 'There have been suggestions that in certain cases judges have been prompted by others to arrive at a predetermined result. This is a notion that we reject. However, in a case in which a judge does overstep, the general public, litigants or other aggrieved or interested parties should refer the matter to the Judicial Conduct Committee or the Judicial Service Commission.'[20]

The stand-off eventually led to a seven-hour meeting between Zuma and certain of his ministers on one side, and the Chief Justice and senior members of the judiciary on the other. They ultimately arrived at an agreement on ten key points, which were aimed at ensuring mutual respect in their dealings.[21] That the al-Bashir judgment and the reaction to it by the ANC had led to this meeting was described by some as 'historic' and 'epoch-making'.[22] However, former Constitutional Court Judge Zak Yacoob may have been more accurate when he warned about private meetings and smoked-filled rooms between the judiciary and executives:

> The conversation between the courts on the one hand and the legislature and the executive on the other is of a different kind. It is not about branches of government talking to each other privately and secretly to obtain a common understanding of the needs of our country. The executive and the legislature on the one hand and the judiciary on the other should indeed talk to each other. But they do so in a specialised, structured way.[23]

Whatever the merits of this kind of meeting, the Chief Justice earned great plaudits for defending the judicial institution against unbridled and unsubstantiated attacks. But Yacoob's point remains: the structured conversation between the judiciary and the executive is not always understood by the executive or the legislature as anything more than an opportunity for warning shots to be fired in the direction of the judicial institution.

The upshot of the al-Bashir case is that it shows that South Africa has travelled a long way – though in reverse – from the halcyon days of our early democracy, when the executive understood the nature of a constitutional democracy in the fullest sense of the word. Recall the Constitutional Court's judgment in *Executive Council, Western Cape Legislature v President of the Republic of South Africa*,[24] in which the court found that Parliament had acted beyond its authority in purporting to delegate law-making capacity to former President Mandela. On national television, Mandela said that he abided by the ruling and respected the court, albeit that he disagreed with the contents of its decision.[25] By contrast, it is unlikely that the meeting that took place between Zuma and the Chief Justice will be the last word between the executive and the judiciary, particularly as the judiciary is called upon to adjudicate an increasing incidence of lawfare that has exploded in our country.

The government response to a legal defeat

The meeting between Zuma and the Chief Justice notwithstanding, the government was determined to have the last word on the role of the ICC in South Africa. In October 2016, Minister of International Relations and Cooperation Maite Nkoana-Mashabane announced: 'The Republic of South Africa has found its obligations with respect to the peaceful resolution of conflicts at times are incompatible with the interpretation given by the International Criminal Court.'[26]

This was followed by a statement made by the Minister of Justice and Correctional Services, Michael Masutha, who rather optimistically concluded that South Africa's plan to leave the ICC would enable the country to negotiate peace and conflicts in Africa more effectively: 'South Africa is hindered by the Rome Statute in ICC, which compels the country to arrest officials who also have diplomatic immunity.'[27]

As a result of the government's decision to withdraw from the ICC, Masutha announced that an application for leave to appeal against the decision of the Supreme Court of Appeal would be withdrawn and that a bill proposing the repeal of the Implementation Act would be tabled in Parliament.

Nkoana-Mashabane then signed a notice of withdrawal to give effect to this decision, notwithstanding an undertaking by the Minister of Justice that Parliament would have a say. Her statement read:

> In 2015 South Africa found itself in the unenviable position where it was faced with conflicting international law obligations which had to be interpreted within the realm of hard diplomatic realities and overlapping mandates when South Africa hosted … the [African Union summit] from 7 to 15 June 2015. … South Africa was faced with the conflicting obligation to arrest President al-Bashir under the Rome Statute, the obligation to the AU to grant immunity in terms of the Host Agreement and the General Convention on the Privileges and Immunities of the Organisation of African Unity of 1965 as well as the obligation under customary international law, which recognises the immunity of sitting heads of state.[28]

In its explanatory statement as to its decision, the government said that the Implementation Act of 2002 and the Rome Statute of the ICC 'compel South Africa to arrest persons who may enjoy diplomatic immunity under customary international law but who are wanted by the International Criminal Court for genocide, crimes against humanity and war crimes and to surrender such persons to the International Criminal Court. South Africa has to do so, even under circumstances where we are actively involved in promoting peace, stability and dialogue in those countries.'[29]

Withdrawing from the withdrawal

In a legal move that paralleled the litigation launched against the British government for seeking to exit the European Union without first obtaining parliamentary approval, the Democratic Alliance (DA) and the Council for the Advancement of the South African Constitution, (CASAC) adopted the view that, in terms of Section 231(2) of the Constitution, the government could not exit the ICC solely by way of executive action. The country's commitment to the ICC had been enshrined in legislation passed by Parliament: as it had been parliamentary action that had got the country into the ICC, it was therefore only Parliament that could take the country out of the ICC. In short, the argument was that only Parliament could repeal the Implementation Act. As has become fairly common practice in contemporary South Africa, government had appeared to obtain extremely questionable legal advice. (Cannot the taxpayer obtain a refund for such poor legal recommendations, we wonder?) The dispute finally landed up before three judges of the Pretoria High Court.

Government's argument was that, in the first place, the national executive, and not Parliament, has the primary role in international relations, including the conclusion of treaties. The legal requirement of a prior approval by Parliament is not explicitly stated in the Constitution, nor should it be inferred from or read into the Constitution. Furthermore, because the original function for concluding treaties is not that of Parliament but of the national executive, parliamentary approval should be required only for a treaty to become binding; the agreement to conclude a treaty remains the function of the national executive. Ratification by Parliament means no more than formal confirmation of consensus expressed by the executive.

On this tendentious basis, government argued that the undoing of a treaty was also a power that lay exclusively within the domain of the national executive and did not need parliamentary approval. Parliamentary approval relates solely to the binding effect of a concluded treaty. Much as concluding a treaty is a core function of foreign relations, which is within the competence of the national executive, the cancellation of a country's obligations under a treaty was also a constitutional competence given solely to the executive.

A unanimous bench of three judges disagreed. The essential reasoning of the judgment was captured in the following passage:

> As the Constitutional Court explained in *Glenister II*, a resolution by Parliament in terms of s 231 (2) to approve an international agreement is a positive statement ... to the signatories of the agreement that Parliament, subject to the provisions of the Constitution, will act in accordance with the ratified agreement. Therefore the approval of an international agreement in terms of s 231 (2) creates a social contract between the people of

South Africa through their elected representatives in the legislature, and the national executive. That social contract gives rise to rights and obligations expressed in such international agreement. The anomaly that the national executive can, without seeking the approval of the people of South Africa, terminate those rights and obligations, is self-evident and manifest.[30]

In summary, on 22 February 2017 the court found that the executive required prior parliamentary approval to bind South Africa to an international agreement, and there was no reason why a withdrawal from such an agreement should be different. The executive did not have the legal power to deliver a notice of withdrawal from the ICC without obtaining prior parliamentary approval.

CASAC was particularly keen to extend the relief sought. It wanted the court to entertain a substantive challenge about whether it was legal to withdraw from the Rome Statute. Here the court was particularly careful in the demarcation of its judicial role: 'That decision [to withdraw] is policy-laden, and one residing in the heartland of the national executive in the exercise of foreign policy, international relations and treaty-making, subject, of course, to the Constitution.'[31]

The difference between this outcome and so many other reversals suffered by the government in recent times is that, for once, the government abided by the decision of the High Court. It did not seek to appeal the order. It notified UN Secretary General António Guterres that because of the High Court decision, to the effect that withdrawing from the Rome Statute had been found to be unconstitutional and invalid, it formally revoked its withdrawal.

This decision was followed by a briefing note prepared by a number of eminent jurists, including former Constitutional Court judges Laurie Ackermann, Richard Goldstone, Johann Kriegler, Yvonne Mokgoro, Kate O'Regan and Zak Yacoob. As Justice Yacoob had stated when South Africa joined the ICC, the country had made that choice on the basis that

some human rights violations are so gross, so bad, so punishable, that no leader, even if he or she was a state leader at the time, should be able to get away with it. And that is actually the question. Are there human rights violations that are so gross, that *nobody*, whatever their situation, should be allowed to get away with them? That is the essential moral issue that we as a country have to get to terms with once again.[32]

In this spirit, the ex-judges' briefing note contended that Africa needs the ICC. The issue of immunity for heads of state is a red herring because only the al-Bashir case before the ICC raises this question. Although the South African government had suggested that serious international crimes could be prosecuted by an African regional court, the briefing note pointed out that there was no regional court in Africa that could handle such a case, and the prospects of one being established in the short to medium term remained dim.

Conclusion

The ICC saga, triggered by the visit of President al-Bashir, became a barometer of the health of South Africa's human-rights-based leadership and governance. Leaving aside the ill-advised legal advice that must have encouraged the government to litigate, the generosity shown to al-Bashir and the government's negative reaction to the ICC are most revealing. As Yacoob made clear, a significant retreat has taken place by South Africa from the commitment to human rights that it embraced twenty-odd years ago, which was so central to the spirit that propelled the introduction of the Constitution. Courts heroically defended the constitutional ramparts against an ever increasing series of attacks on the core democratic enterprise that was launched with enthusiasm and expectation more than two decades ago. But government has, at best, shown a lukewarm attitude to the human-rights enterprise.

Faced with a determined executive onslaught, the judgment of the Pretoria High Court represents, arguably, the furthest that a court can journey in its attempt to defend the principle of legality. Although the court found that the executive did not have the legal powers to withdraw from the Rome Statute unilaterally, with regard to its *decision* to withdraw, the court noted: 'There is nothing patently unconstitutional, at least at this stage, about the national executive's policy decision to withdraw from the Rome Statute, because it is within its powers and competence to make such a decision.'[33]

This judgment highlights a concern articulated throughout this book

– that there is a division between the legal and political terrains and, on the latter, the courts must be very careful how and where they tread.

The upshot was that the executive required prior parliamentary approval before it could implement so radical a decision as to withdraw from the Rome Statute. This falls clearly within the principle of legality, and hence the competence of the courts. But whether the executive can initiate a policy decision to withdraw from the Rome Statute – as long as it adheres to proper legal procedure – is an entirely different question. This is a line that the courts cross with potentially great cost to the judicial institution because it becomes weakened where it ventures into overtly political terrain. And this is the problem posed by the increasing prevalence of lawfare in South Africa: there is a danger that the courts could be lured into political territory to the great detriment of the continued legitimacy of the judicial institution.

This is not to say that the effect of a court decision to hold government accountable does not have significant political ramifications. In this particular case, South Africa revoked its memorandum to the UN on its intention to withdraw from the ICC; it cancelled the parliamentary process that had been put in motion after the court had ruled that the withdrawal was unconstitutional and invalid. And an ensuing ANC discussion document of 2017 with regard to the ICC was somewhat more measured than had been the case with previous versions. It stated:

> The [Rome] Statute and the unbalanced manner in which the western powers prefer it to be implemented does not give due regard to fundamental issues of the need to strike a balance between peace and justice.[34]

African States are signatories to the Rome Statute. However in the recent past they have raised concerns about the manner in which the Rome Statute is implemented without due regard to the continent's efforts to address issues of conflicts and peace, some of which are lasting legacies of colonialism. It is therefore fundamental that, the AU and its member states urgently finalise efforts to enable the African Court on People and Human Rights to discharge its expanded mandate.

Significantly, this document made no mention of withdrawal from the ICC. This omission shows that the decision by the courts to prohibit an executive-led withdrawal had a clear effect on government policy.

The doctrine of separation of powers is an enigmatic idea, but central to any interpretation of it is the notion that the judiciary is tasked with the role of overseeing that all branches of the state and its organs act within the law.

As American constitutional scholar Alexander Bickel noted many years ago, the judiciary has no police force nor army to command, and is therefore the weakest arm of government. But its power is derived from a legitimacy sourced in its function as a custodian of the core values of society, as enshrined in law.[35] Hence, when it delivers a judgment that insists that the executive cannot act outside of legal boundaries, its decision has consequences, particularly when civil society is active in the dispute giving rise to the litigation.

Viewed in this context, lawfare may have positive consequences, albeit on a limited terrain.

13

'STATE CAPTURE' (NOUN)

The construction of a parallel state utilising existing organs of state, state-owned enterprises and constitutionally mandated institutions for corrupt objectives, primarily by deploying leaders to those organisations that display a firm commitment to subverting accountability or diverting them from their lawful mandates and a resolute determination to ignore the consequences of their conduct for the people they serve.

– MICHELLE LE ROUX and DENNIS DAVIS

'What is a state capture? I am sure very keen to know. ... They can't just make it sound so important and big, this state capture. ... It's all fake and political, just to paint black a particular family and individuals.'

– JACOB ZUMA, 13 November 2017, on ANN7 TV NEWS

The Zuma era is defined by the state capture project. His cabinet was filled with the unqualified, the incompetent and the indifferent. Organs of state that were designed to deliver on the constitutional promise were diverted from their mandates into a project of enrichment for the connected. State-owned enterprises were the primary targets of capture, their lucrative monopolies and enormous budgets an obvious target for theft, dressed up as preferential procurement policies and supplier development programmes. The label of these purportedly inclusive economic policies applied a veneer of respectability that was used to justify the looting and silence critics. Key to the success of this heist was ensuring the impotence of institutions that carry a constitutional mandate to hold accountable those who do not uphold the rule of law and to prosecute those who break the law.

The Constitution was designed to promote accountability and transparency through some of the key institutions it created, namely the judiciary, Parliament, the NPA and the Public Protector, working together with other organs of state, including anti-corruption units and SARS.

Of course, no institution exists just on paper. Its leaders and staff determine whether it does its job. Implementation is the result of commitment from those at the top and throughout the ranks to their respective mandates to promote accountability, uphold the rule of law and perform the constitutional function imposed on each institution. Each is an actor with a specific and important role to play.

But state capture shows how offices can be occupied by mutinous officers who display contempt for their constitutional responsibilities. Let us consider each of the institutions that played starring roles – some as the villains, some as the heroes – in the state-capture project.

Parliament

Section 55 of the Constitution requires Parliament 'to ensure that all executive organs of state in the national sphere of government are accountable to it and to maintain oversight of the exercise of national executive authority ... and any organ of state.'[1] Yet Parliament was somnambulistic until the political winds changed, firstly in 2014 with the arrival of the Economic Freedom Fighters, then in 2016 with the loss of major metros to the opposition DA and in the last two years as parliamentary committees finally woke up to inquire of the executive and organs of state how wholesale corruption and governance collapse had occurred on their watch.

Multiple motions of no confidence brought by the opposition parties were tabled, debated and all defeated by the governing party's majority. In the final days of the Zuma administration, parliamentary committees into state-owned enterprises and other sites of state capture were eventually convened, enthralling viewers as they watched their elected representatives finally discover their job descriptions. Cabinet ministers and senior executives were finally challenged and asked to explain how billions had been raided as blind eyes were turned to the plunder.

But despite this last-minute spring into action, Parliament has largely been dismal at holding the executive accountable. Ministers were able to dodge committee hearings with dubious excuses, and nothing happened. Vigorous and compelling speeches were made in the National Assembly, and nothing happened to smug and seemingly untouchable members of the executive.

The impotence of this key arm of government has been diagnosed as being the result of South Africa's party-political and electoral system, a point to which we return later.

Suffice to say, our legislature's inertia and inability (or unwillingness) to hold the executive accountable meant that resorting to lawfare was inevitable. And it was not the only institution to fail in its constitutional mandate to uphold the rule of law, ensure accountability and promote the constitutional vision.

National Prosecuting Authority

The NPA is a 'single national prosecuting authority' with 'the power to institute criminal proceedings' and which 'exercises its functions without fear, favour or prejudice'.[2]

Since before he took office as president, Zuma has been in jeopardy of facing criminal charges. In August 2003, the then NDPP, Bulelani Ngcuka, announced his intention to charge Schabir Shaik on counts of corruption involving allegedly corrupt payments to Zuma, but stated that he would not charge Zuma.

In June 2005, Shaik was convicted of corruption in relation to payments made to Zuma. On 20 June 2005, Vusi Pikoli, the then NDPP, indicted Zuma on charges of corruption. On 31 July 2006, the matter was called for trial on two corruption counts, which mirrored the two corruption counts on which Shaik had been convicted. But the NPA was not ready to proceed with the trial, so the matter was struck from the roll.

In December 2007, Mokotedi Mpshe took a new decision to indict Zuma on 18 main counts of racketeering, corruption, money laundering, tax evasion and fraud. The indictment was, for the most part, based on the same subject matter that had been dealt with in the Shaik trial. Advocate

Mpshe had been appointed as acting NDPP following the removal from office of Pikoli after the latter had been suspended by former President Mbeki (for his efforts to prosecute police commissioner Jackie Selebi) in 2007 and later removed by Parliament and President Motlanthe in 2008 following the Ginwala Inquiry into his fitness to hold office.

In September 2008, Judge Chris Nicholson set aside the indictment decision taken by Mpshe on the grounds that it was not an independent decision and was tainted by political interference. In January 2009, the Supreme Court of Appeal overturned that judgment, leaving the decision to charge Zuma intact. On 6 April 2009, Mpshe decided to withdraw the charges against Zuma. Later that month, the DA brought proceedings to review and set aside the decision of Mpshe to withdraw the charges against Zuma.

On 29 April 2016, a full bench of the Pretoria High Court reviewed and set aside Mpshe's decision to withdraw the charges against Zuma. Zuma's attempts to appeal that decision to the Supreme Court of Appeal have now failed.

In the meantime, back at the NPA, Mpshe had been replaced by Menzi Simelane – until 2012, when he too was removed after his appointment was declared invalid by the Constitutional Court.

Nomgcobo Jiba then took over as acting NDPP until she was replaced by Mxolisi Nxasana in October 2013. Jiba continues to be embroiled in legal proceedings after having been struck off the roll of advocates following adverse character findings against her, as well as fraud and perjury charges related to her unlawful authorisation of racketeering charges against former KwaZulu-Natal Hawks head, Johan Booysen.

Nxasana was removed from his office by then President Zuma less than two years after his appointment, seemingly due to his independence, which appeared to surprise Zuma, and replaced by Shaun 'the Sheep' Abrahams, who, throughout his tenure, surprised no one, instead eschewing any vigorous prosecution of those implicated in corruption.

Public Protector

The Public Protector must 'investigate any conduct in state affairs, or in the public administration in any sphere of government, that is alleged or suspected to be improper or to result in any impropriety or prejudice' and 'to take appropriate remedial action' regarding that misconduct.[3]

Modelled on the Scandinavian ombud, the Public Protector is supposed to resolve complaints and disputes about public service misconduct with wide, flexible remedial powers. The Public Protector can mediate and conciliate disputes, bringing about creative, affirming resolutions to complaints and disputes, or refer them to the appropriate law-enforcement or other authorities if no resolution is possible.

The reader can be forgiven for being unable to name the first two office-bearers of this powerful and important institution: Selby Baqwa and Lawrence Mushwana. The former was singularly forgettable and wholly absent from political life, while the latter's greatest achievement was the R7 million golden handshake he received on departure, given that 'throughout his term of office, Mushwana [was] accused of succeeding only in protecting the ANC from the people, instead of protecting the people, as his mandate required'.[4]

Thuli Madonsela was appointed Public Protector in 2009 by Zuma. This was the first of two appointments made by Zuma who are widely considered to have surprised him with their diligence, determination and dedication to delivery on their constitutional mandates. The other was Chief Justice Mogoeng Mogoeng, appointed in 2011. A recognition of these 'mistakes' and a commitment to not repeating them were seemingly revealed during the parliamentary processes to select Madonsela's successor. In the build-up to those hearings, many assumed Judge Siraj Desai was the executive's frontrunner to replace Madonsela. But this proved to be a cunning decoy. The actual preferred candidate, the unimpressive and dependably compliant Busisiwe Mkhwebane, sailed through with support from all political parties except the DA.

Scorpions and Hawks

The Directorate of Special Operations (the Scorpions) was an independent agency combining investigative and prosecutorial expertise within the NPA mandated to prosecute organised crime and corruption. It was disbanded in January 2009, following former President Mbeki's recall and during the caretaker presidency of Kgalema Motlanthe, and replaced by the Directorate for Priority Crime Investigation (the Hawks), located within the SAPS.

The Scorpions' demise followed the adoption of a resolution at the ANC's December 2007 Polokwane national elective conference (which elevated Zuma to the top job in the party and eventually the state) for the ostensible reason that a unit of this kind should not be independent of the police.

In reality, however, the Scorpions were crushed because of the enthusiasm with which they investigated corruption allegations against high-profile office-holders, which had involved raids on certain of Zuma's properties two years earlier. Zuma, deputy president at the time, had said that the Scorpions were worse than the apartheid-era police force and that they had investigated him 'from head to toe'. When the Scorpions insisted they were following the law, Zuma said, 'You've got to change that because it's a wrong law.'[5]

Once he had become leader of the ANC, that change was swiftly achieved by the Zuma administration, despite heroic litigation undertaken to challenge this move by businessman Hugh Glenister.

South African Revenue Service

SARS became an autonomous organ of state in 1997 with the mandate to collect and administer all revenue collection from taxpayers. SARS is an essential institution, since it collects the funds that are then deployed by the state to provide housing, healthcare, education, infrastructure and every other essential component of economic growth and development. Its compliance and enforcement activities, especially when Pravin Gordhan was commissioner, ensured that tax revenue growth exceeded macro-economic growth, an indication of its effectiveness.

This trend reversed, however, once Tom Moyane was appointed SARS commissioner by Zuma.[6] Moyane was reportedly the highest-paid director general in the public service while at Correctional Services. In 2017 the Special Investigating Unit announced a probe into a controversial tender awarded during his term. He also attracted attention as a member of the four-person panel that was set up to investigate why the Waterkloof Air Force Base had been used by the Gupta family in 2013 as their private landing strip. The panel exonerated Zuma and blamed low-level functionaries for this disgraceful episode. Bruce Koloane, chief of state protocol, was rewarded for being the fall guy with an ambassadorial posting to the Netherlands.[7]

Within two years of Moyane's appointment as SARS commissioner in 2016, more than 55 group executives and other senior staff members had left SARS, and there were widespread allegations about SARS protecting not only Zuma, but also alleged criminals, such as Mark Lifman.[8] Its enforcement activities (which fuelled the so-called 'rogue unit' narrative peddled by *The Sunday Times*) were a key theme in the state-capture saga. Weakening the detection and enforcement capacity of SARS, coupled with the strange treatment of tax collection and administration (making it both more difficult and less effective), hobbled an institution that would otherwise have played a critical role in revealing and preventing some of the looting.[9]

Judiciary

Only the judiciary lived up to its constitutional mandate in the Zuma era. Deluged with cases challenging the state capture project, seeking to hold the executive accountable, demanding that office-bearers perform their functions rather than maintain their loyalty to Zuma and the endemic spread of corruption under his term of office, the courts held firm. Some of the key political controversies over the past decade should have been foreseen, but in some cases the volume and intensity of the litigation over political and governance failures through this period caught us by surprise. Here is lawfare, red in tooth and claw. To recap, since 2008, the following cases, all associated with Zuma or his administration, have been through or are still winding their way through our courts:

- Zuma/Thint/Thales – regarding the legality of search warrants relating to the arms deal and the admissibility of evidence (including the infamous encrypted fax)
- A complaint to the Judicial Service Commission regarding an attempt by Judge President Hlophe to influence two Constitutional Court judges in the same case
- Menzi Simelane's fitness and propriety for appointment as NDPP
- The Hawks cases brought by Hugh Glenister challenging the demise of the Scorpions and their replacement with a less independent anti-corruption unit
- The challenge to the appointment of Berning Ntlemeza as head of the Hawks on the basis that he had previously been found to have conducted himself in an unfit and improper way
- The application to set aside the agreement that removed Mxolisi

Nxasana as NDPP and ended his efforts to clean up the NPA, and led to his being replaced by Shaun Abrahams

- The applications to strike senior prosecutors and alleged Zuma supporters advocates Jiba and Mrwebi from the roll of advocates and thereby disqualify them from employment at the NPA
- The failure of the President to comply with the Public Protector's recommendations, including his obligation to repay state money spent on improvements to his homestead at Nkandla
- The demand for reasons for the cabinet reshuffle in March 2017, in which Zuma removed several cabinet ministers, with Pravin Gordhan and Mcebisi Jonas the most high-profile casualties
- The challenge to the expulsion of the EFF by the Speaker of the National Assembly following the turbulent state of the nation address in 2015
- The 2013 demand by then leader of the opposition in the National Assembly, Lindiwe Mazibuko, that the Speaker schedule a motion of no confidence in the President
- The setting aside of the unlawful initiation of the nuclear-procurement process
- The cases dealing with the legality of the appointment of Hlaudi Motsoeneng at the SABC
- The suspension of eight journalists and editors from the SABC for refusing to comply with controversial editorial policy
- The failure of the Department of Social Development to replace Cash Paymaster Services as the vehicle for the payment of social grants
- The failure to arrest President al-Bashir despite the fact that a warrant had been issued by the ICC
- The challenge to the decision to drop criminal charges against Zuma taken by then acting NDPP, Mokotedi Mpshe
- The related application to gain access to the so-called spy tapes relied on for that decision
- The aborted charges against former finance minister Pravin Gordhan relating to the operation of the so-called 'rogue unit' and alleged contraventions of the National Strategic Intelligence Act
- The application by former finance minister Gordhan regarding the closure of the bank accounts of the Oakbay group of companies
- The related demand by Gupta-owned Optimum Coal Mine that the

Financial Intelligence Centre's certification of its receipt of 72 suspicious transaction reports be set aside

- The President's review of the Public Protector's recommendation in her *State of Capture* report that a commission of inquiry be appointed by the Chief Justice
- The review of the *State of Capture* report by ministers Des van Rooyen and Mosebenzi Zwane
- The aborted interdict applications to prevent the release of the *State of Capture* report by the Public Protector
- The challenge to the Speaker's powers to block cellphone signals in Parliament
- The Constitutional Court case seeking a secret ballot for the August 2017 motion of no confidence in former President Zuma
- The EFF's Constitutional Court case seeking the impeachment of former President Zuma
- The disciplinary proceedings against those held responsible for the Waterkloof landing of the Guptas' wedding guests
- The review of the arms deal commission of inquiry (the Seriti Commission)
- The challenge to the appointment of Robert McBride as head of the police watchdog, the Independent Police Investigative Directorate
- The disputes regarding the dismissal and pending prosecution of senior SARS employees, including Ivan Pillay, Johann van Loggerenberg and Andries Janse van Rensburg, as a result of the so-called rogue unit reports
- The fraud and other charges (dropped eventually) against Pravin Gordhan for the early retirement of his deputy at SARS, Ivan Pillay
- The cases involving former Hawks boss Anwa Dramat and top cops Shadrack Sibiya and Leslie Maluleke pertaining to the so-called 'Zimbabwe rendition' incidents
- The controversies surrounding the status of crime intelligence head Richard Mdluli
- The steps taken to force the President to sign the Financial Intelligence Centre Amendment Act
- The urgent attempts by Gupta-linked Vardospan to obtain banking licences for Habib Bank
- The contest over control of the VVIP terminal between the

Oppenheimers and the Guptas, implicating then Home Affairs Minister Malusi Gigaba

- The Marikana civil claims and pending criminal prosecutions (of the strikers, not the police)
- Litigation to return the fees earned by McKinsey and Trillian for work ostensibly done at Eskom
- Various disciplinary and employment disputes relating to Gupta lieutenants and associates, such as Matshelo Koko, and other managers of state-owned enterprises, such as Siyabonga Gama at Transnet
- The battle over the R30 million payment to Brian Molefe from Eskom
- The disputes over the financing of the Gupta plane
- The Estina/Vrede dairy scheme and the ongoing review by the Public Protector of this corruption saga
- The battle between the Asset Forfeiture Unit and the Guptas regarding funds frozen that are said to be the proceeds of crime from the Estina dairy scheme
- The criminal charges brought and provisionally withdrawn regarding the Estina saga
- The criminal charges laid by now Minister of Public Enterprises Pravin Gordhan against the EFF's leaders
- The tit-for-tat charges laid by EFF leader Julius Malema against Gordhan alleging that Canadian bank accounts held millions of dollars in bribes, and other allegations regarding Gordhan's daughter's business career
- Various applications brought by Moyane regarding the Nugent Commission of Inquiry and the disciplinary charges against him arising from his time as SARS commissioner, all aimed at keeping his position

It is an extraordinary list of cases for the courts to handle – and it is probably incomplete. Indeed, the near-daily jaw-dropping revelations at the various commissions of inquiry into state capture, SARS, the Public Investment Corporation and the fitness for office of senior prosecutors supplement this list and lend a political context to what was really going on in most of them. It is impossible to tell each of these stories here, so we have chosen to focus on three that illustrate the arguments made in the rest of this book. These are, first, the 'spy tapes' case, then the review of the Public Protector's Nkandla report and, finally, the impeachment case.

Spy tapes

The so-called spy tapes case against Zuma relates to his attempts to avoid and delay prosecution on 16 charges of corruption, fraud and racketeering connected with the so-called arms deal. The arms deal scandal was revealed in September 1999 by firebrand PAC MP Patricia de Lille, who raised concerns in Parliament about the arms deal and revealed a dossier that was said to detail the corruption.

In November 2002, the *Mail & Guardian* revealed that Zuma was being investigated in connection with the arms deal. In August 2003, then NDPP Bulelani Ngcuka announced that there was a prima facie case against Zuma, but that it couldn't be won.

This reluctance to prosecute did not extend to Zuma's benefactor and co-accused, Schabir Shaik. Judge Hilary Squires found Shaik guilty of two counts of fraud and one of corruption in the KwaZulu-Natal High Court in Durban in May 2005. Squires found Shaik had a corrupt relationship with Zuma.

Shortly following this decision, then President Mbeki 'released' Zuma from his duties as deputy president. Thus began the succession battle settled at the ANC's elective conference in Polokwane in 2007, from which Zuma emerged victorious. However, in December 2007, the Scorpions charged Zuma with corruption, fraud and racketeering, arising from the arms deal.

These charges were dropped in September 2008 after Judge Chris Nicholson granted Zuma's application to have the charges dismissed. Nicholson also agreed with his argument that there were signs of a conspiracy in the timing of the charges.

Days after the Nicholson judgment, the Zuma-led ANC 'recalled' Mbeki and he resigned as president. However, in 2009, the Nicholson judgment was set aside on appeal, but shortly thereafter acting NDPP Mokotedi Mpshe announced that the NPA would drop the charges against Zuma in any event.

Explaining that decision, Mpshe referenced taped telephone conversations between Scorpions head Leonard McCarthy and Ngcuka, who at one stage said to McCarthy, 'You made my day,' after finding out that Zuma would be re-charged. The phone conversations constitute the so-called 'spy tapes'.

A decade-long court battle followed between the DA, the NPA and

Zuma. First, the DA sued to get their hands on the 'spy tapes' and then, after their attempt succeeded, they went to court to have Mpshe's decision declared irrational, as this would lead to a possible Zuma prosecution.

Eventually, in October 2017, the Supreme Court of Appeal dismissed Zuma's and the NPA's appeal. In December, Zuma's faction lost the ANC's elective conference when Ramaphosa was elected ANC president. He then had to make representations to NDPP Shaun Abrahams as to why he shouldn't be prosecuted. However, in the new political climate, Abrahams announced that Zuma's prosecution would proceed.[10]

To date, that prosecution has not taken place. Indeed, further lawfare is pending, with applications to permanently stay the prosecution, including on the ground that the matter has been much delayed.

That 2017 decision by the Supreme Court of Appeal to dismiss Zuma's appeal was the result of a concession in the course of argument by Zuma's counsel, which made it impossible to persist with the appeal. For the same reason, the NPA's enthusiastic support for the then President's appeal skidded to a necessary halt.

So let's look more closely at the Supreme Court of Appeal's decision. It opens by quoting TS Eliot – 'the recurrent end of the unending'.[11] Something that ends, but doesn't end aptly, contextualises this long-drawn-out affair, or, as the court put it more prosaically, a 'litigation saga that has endured over many years and [involving] numerous court cases'. The court said:

> It is doubtful that a decision in this case will be the end of the continuing contestations concerning the prosecution of Mr Zuma. Minutes into the argument before us, counsel for both Mr Zuma and the NPA conceded that the decision to discontinue the prosecution was flawed. Counsel on behalf of Mr Zuma, having made the concession, with the full realisation that the consequence would be that the prosecution of his client would revive, gave notice that Mr Zuma had every intention in the future to continue to use such processes as are available to him to resist prosecution. The South African public might well be forgiven for thinking that the description at the beginning of this judgment was coined to deal with the prosecution or latterly, more accurately, the non-prosecution of Mr Zuma.[12]

The sudden and dramatic change of stance in the course of argument of the appeal arose when Zuma's counsel had to concede that the decision to discontinue his prosecution was liable to be set aside as irrational, given the existence of a *prima facie* case against his client. The court concluded that the contortions within the NPA about when to charge Zuma (before or after the Polokwane conference) 'had no bearing on the integrity of the investigation of the case against Mr Zuma and did not impact on the prosecution itself'.[13] As the court put it:

> It appears ... to be inimical to the preservation of the integrity of the NPA that a prosecution is discontinued because of a non-discernible negative effect of the timing of the service of an indictment on the integrity of the investigation of the case and on the prosecution itself. There is thus no rational connection between Mr Mpshe's decision to discontinue the prosecution on that basis and the preservation of the integrity of the NPA. If anything, the opposite is true. In these circumstances discontinuing a prosecution in respect of which the merits are good and in respect of which there is heightened public interest because of the breadth and nature of the charges and the person at the centre of it, holding the highest public office, can hardly redound to the NPA's credit or advance the course of justice or promote the integrity of the NPA. ... [14]

> [I]t beggars belief that the present regime at the NPA, on its own version of events, saw fit to defend Mr Mpshe's decision as being rational. For all these reasons I can find no fault with the reasoning and conclusions of the court below that the decision to discontinue the prosecution was irrational and liable to be set aside. A question one might rightly ask is why it took so long to come to the realisation at the eleventh hour that the case for both the NPA and former President Zuma had no merit.[15]

The point about the spy tapes decision is how it revealed the Stalingrad-style litigation strategy that had been deployed by Zuma and his legal team for more than a decade – a strategy waged on trying to avoid prosecution (his 'day in court', which Zuma sometimes claimed to yearn for) by spending many other days in court (and many millions of our taxpayer rands) pursuing appeals, resisting applications, running indefensible arguments until the final moments when their implausibility and error were revealed, and then collapsing. It is a strategy that continues to avoid prosecution thanks to other pending litigations – and an NDPP seemingly happy to sit on the sidelines. A further opportunity to make representations was afforded to Zuma, followed by a review of the decision to pursue prosecution and an application for a permanent stay of prosecution. That application had yet to be decided at the time of writing. And no trial has yet begun – despite the prosecutorial team confirming that they are ready to run and have hundreds of witnesses lined up to testify. Perhaps only turning off the funding tap to the lawyers who have acted for Zuma will bring an end to the Stalingrad strategy.

The saga also demonstrates the ease with which the integrity and effective operation of the NPA were destroyed thanks to some key appointments at the top of that organisation. The ranks of diligent and committed prosecutors were rendered inert once political will evaporated in the top job. In contrast to the efforts of NDPPs such as Pikoli and Nxasana, the sheepish leaders of the NPA under Zuma not only prevented prosecution of key players involved in corruption (see anyone mentioned in the #Guptaleaks trove of *prima facie* evidence of fraud and corruption), but also abused their office by pursuing criminal charges against figures seen as opposed to the state-capture project – the charges brought, and later dropped, against Gordhan being a prime example.

Nkandla

Certain values in the Constitution have been designated as foundational to our democracy. This in turn means that as pillarstones of this democracy, they must be observed scrupulously. If these values are not observed and their precepts not carried out conscientiously, we have a recipe for a constitutional crisis of great magnitude. In a State predicated on a desire to maintain the rule of law, it is imperative that one and all should be driven by a moral obligation to ensure the continued survival of our democracy. ... And the role of these foundational values in

helping to strengthen and sustain our constitutional democracy
sits at the heart of this application.[16]

These words of the Constitutional Court explain what was at stake in
the so-called Nkandla case.

In March 2014, the then Public Protector, Advocate Thuli Madonsela,
released a report titled *Secure in Comfort*, in which she investigated
allegations of improper conduct or irregular expenditure relating to security
upgrades at former President Zuma's private residence, located in Nkandla,
KwaZulu-Natal. She found that Zuma had derived undue and unlawful
benefit from the irregular deployment of taxpayer funds relating to various
security features, including the infamous 'fire pool', amphitheatre, visitors'
centre, kraal and chicken run (regarding which more later). She directed
that a calculation of the value of this benefit should be made, and that a
share be demanded from Zuma to #PayBackTheMoney.

Her report was submitted to Parliament, given its role to ensure compliance with the remedial action required by its duty to hold the executive
accountable. But, for more than a year, the President and the National
Assembly ignored the Public Protector's report and recommendations.

The ANC used its majority in Parliament to set up an *ad hoc* committee
to examine the report; the committee exonerated the President. It also
examined a report commissioned by the Minister of Police, Nkosinathi
Nhleko, into the security upgrades. This report was memorably released
accompanied by a video displaying the merits of a fire pool in a staged
firefighting exercise with operatic backing music ('*O sole mio*') and
featuring firefighters using equipment that resembled hosepipes.[17]

Nhleko, drenched in flop sweat as he cued the video that accompanied
his report, was not alone among our public servants who would be
called upon to degrade themselves in defence of the 'fire pool'. Nhleko
explained that 'the security and fire practitioners found that it has been
established the fire-fighting capability at the residence of the President
in Nkandla is not up to the required standards as per the national fire
regulations. This is caused by, among others, the low water pressure
from the main water supply as well as insufficient and/or inadequate
fire-fighting equipment.'[18]

Several other politicians also found interesting ways to justify the
construction of the R3.9 million swimming pool and defend the President,

including ANC Youth League national coordinator Magasela Mzobe, who said, 'Zuma didn't ask for a swimming pool – he is busy running the country.'[19] In addition, we were told that the pool was:

> a water resource that can be utilised to fight fires.[20]
>
> – Chairman of the parliamentary committee into Police Minister Nathi Nhleko's report CEDRIC FROLICK.

(When Frolick was asked about the infamous fire pool, he initially said that it was a 'recreational facility' and then quickly backtracked to say that it was indeed a fire pool.)

> There are no fire extinguishers or fire brigades [in rural areas], [the] best we know is to take a bucket, dip it in water and throw it on the fire.[21]
>
> – Former police commissioner RIAH PHIYEGA

> One of the hazards raised by the assessment was the possible outbreak of fire, as most of the structures have thatched roofs and are close to each other. In order to eliminate or minimise potential risks and due to water supply which was erratic, a fire pool was decided on as the most viable option for firefighting.[22]
>
> – Public Works Minister THULAS NXESI

> The fire pool should be converted into a swimming pool to be used by the children of the village.[23]
>
> – Deputy Minister of Social Development HENDRIETTA BOGOPANE-ZULU.

These comments show that, instead of seriously considering the Public Protector's report and implementing its remedial action, our elected representatives appear to have prized loyalty to Zuma over their own dignity, integrity and common sense. Their craven willingness to prostitute themselves by defending the indefensible was cringeworthy.

The EFF launched a Constitutional Court application to ensure that the Public Protector's remedial action was actually implemented. The party sought findings that Parliament had failed to fulfil its constitutional obligation to hold the President accountable. On the day of the hearing in February 2016, Zuma's senior counsel, Jeremy Gauntlett, conceded that the Public Protector's findings were binding on the President and that the police minister's exonerating report was meaningless. This concession sought to protect the President from the possibility of impeachment, which could follow from a finding that he had failed to uphold his oath of office and had broken the law. 'This is a delicate time in a dangerous year,' Gauntlett said. 'It will be wrong if this court makes a ruling which may result in a call for impeachment. The DA and EFF may try to impeach. Some have argued that the President was defiant ... [but the President argued] that it was an error in law.'[24]

In the week before the Constitutional Court hearing, Zuma had offered draft orders to settle the dispute and avoid the proceedings by agreeing to pay a percentage of the value of the security upgrades benefit, to be determined by the Auditor-General and the Treasury. These offers were rejected by the EFF and the DA.

As an aside, the concession made by Gauntlett during the Nkandla hearing was faithful to Zuma's strategy in much of his other litigation, namely to resist, oppose and delay his day in court, thereby postponing and prolonging the moment of accountability and culpability, only to collapse at the final moment with a devastating concession as to the correctness of the case against him. This mirrored his conduct in the case of the spy tapes.

But the strategy to oppose the Public Protector's Nkandla report exhibited another hallmark of the Zuma era. Madonsela was attacked by key Zuma ally, the Deputy Minister of Defence and Military Veterans, Kebby Maphatsoe, who outlandishly accused her of being a CIA agent: 'Thuli must tell us who her handler was,' said Maphatsoe,[25] adding that MK members had been trained to spot 'enemy agents':

> We know how foreign intelligence works and we are not just thumb-sucking. We've got those [sic] expertise amongst us and we are not taking chances. We have people who were in the intelligence of the African National Congress [who are] able to identify enemy agents. They [foreign intelligence] create their own person and popularise him or her. That's how they work, they create you ... they make sure you are well accepted by the people.[26]

This claim attracted other Zuma acolytes, including former ANC Youth League president Collen Maine, who said that the state was under attack from 'imperial forces' and repeated the claim that Madonsela was a CIA agent.[27] Maine added that she was also a 'stooge of white monopoly capital'.[28] For her part, Madonsela said that 'there were a lot of unfounded attacks' on her 'when there was an investigation people did not like'. The 'schizophrenia', she said, was 'designed to distract her and her team from doing their work'. She pleaded, 'For goodness sake, people, calm down!' and asked them to stop the 'childish games'.[29]

The Constitutional Court resoundingly affirmed the Public Protector's report. In doing so, it delivered a lecture to the nation about the duty of the President to uphold the Constitution, the role of the Public Protector and Parliament's oversight obligations. The court held that

> the institution of the Public Protector is pivotal to the facilitation of good governance in our constitutional dispensation. In appreciation of the high sensitivity and importance of its role, ... the Constitution guarantees the independence, impartiality, dignity and effectiveness of this institution as indispensable requirements for the proper execution of its mandate. The obligation to keep alive these essential requirements for functionality and the necessary impact is placed on organs of State. And the Public Protector is one of those deserving of this constitutionally-imposed assistance and protection.[30]

The court said that the Public Protector is 'one of the most invaluable constitutional gifts to our nation in the fight against corruption, unlawful enrichment, prejudice and impropriety in State affairs and for the betterment of good governance'. It went on to say that, because litigation is not easily available for the average citizen, especially the poor and marginalised, for this reason the Public Protector is 'the embodiment of a biblical David ... who fights the most powerful and very well resourced Goliath, that impropriety and corruption by government officials are. The Public Protector is one of the true crusaders and champions of anti-corruption and clean governance.'[31]

The court then turned to consider the nature of the rule of law in general, and the nature of the Public Protector's powers in particular:

The rule of law requires that no power be exercised unless it is sanctioned by law and no decision or step sanctioned by law may be ignored based purely on a contrary view we hold. It is not open to any of us to pick and choose which of the otherwise effectual consequences of the exercise of constitutional or statutory power will be disregarded and which given heed to. Our foundational value of the rule of law demands of us, as a law-abiding people, to obey decisions made by those clothed with the legal authority to make them or else approach courts of law to set them aside, so we may validly escape their binding force.[32]

As a result, the court found, '[n]either the President nor the National Assembly was entitled to respond to the binding remedial action taken by the Public Protector as if it is of no force or effect or has been set aside through a proper judicial process. The ineluctable conclusion is therefore that the National Assembly's resolution based on Minister Nhleko's findings exonerating the President from liability is inconsistent with the Constitution and unlawful.'[33]

The court concluded that

an order will thus be made that the President's failure to comply with the remedial action taken against him by the Public Protector is inconsistent with his obligations to uphold, defend and respect the Constitution as the supreme law of the Republic; to comply with the remedial action taken by the Public Protector; and the duty to assist and protect the office of the Public Protector to ensure its independence, impartiality, dignity and effectiveness.

Similarly, the failure by the National Assembly to hold the President accountable by ensuring that he complies with the remedial action taken against him, is inconsistent with its obligations to scrutinise and oversee executive action and to maintain oversight of the exercise of executive powers by the President. And in particular, to give urgent attention to or inter-vene by facilitating his compliance with the remedial action.[34]

285

The Nkandla case illustrates the failure of Parliament to hold the executive accountable, permitting a whitewash and allowing it to dodge its constitutional obligations. It also demonstrates the corollary: the governing party permitted baseless attacks on Madonsela and undermined the constitutional scheme with vexatious parallel processes, instead of respecting a key institution of accountability.

More fundamentally, the case also shows how adjudication is inherently political in nature, responsive to its contemporaneous context. The court's uncompromising endorsement of the binding nature of the Public Protector's powers, and recognition of the broad remedial remit of that office, was applauded and welcomed – when Madonsela was its occupant. However, once Mkhwebane took over, and found that the South African Reserve Bank's mandate should be changed and that the Constitution should be amended to permit this, she, perhaps understandably, relied on the Nkandla judgment for justification for her far-reaching remedial action. The latitude and authority defined by the Nkandla decision were then abused by the current Public Protector, and some of her reports have since been challenged in court.

This reflects the danger inherent in far-reaching court decisions on political questions in a system of precedent: what is desirable in one set of circumstances involving certain individuals can be wholly disastrous when circumstances change or other people are appointed. The question is, how to prevent this? Amending our electoral system to ensure that members of Parliament are directly elected by, and therefore accountable to, constituents may assist. And so would reform of the unilateral powers of appointment of heads of key institutions by the President. We will return to these ideas after examining another case that raises related problems.

Finally, there is another feature of the Nkandla saga that merits rueful reflection. The Public Protector's report found that

> Measures that should never have been implemented, as they are neither provided for in the regulatory instruments, particularly the Cabinet Policy of 2003, the Minimum Physical Security Standards and the SAPS Security Evaluation Reports, nor reasonable, as the most cost effective to meet incidental security needs, include the construction inside the President's residence

of a Visitors' Centre, an expensive cattle kraal with a culvert and chicken run, a swimming pool, an amphitheatre, marquee area, some of the extensive paving and the relocation of neighbours who used to form part of the original homestead, at an enormous cost to the state. The relocation was unlawful, as it did not comply with Section 237 of the Constitution. The implementation of these installations involved unlawful action and constitutes improper conduct and maladministration.

Measures that are not expressly provided for, but could have been discretionally implemented in a manner that benefits the broader community, include helipads and a private clinic, whose role could have been fulfilled by a mobile clinic and/or beefed up capacity at the local medical facilities. The measures also include the construction, within the state occupied land, of permanent, expensive but one-roomed SAPS staff quarters, which could have been located at a centralized police station. The failure to explore more economic and community-inclusive options to accommodate the discretional security-related needs, constitutes improper conduct and maladministration.[35]

In the report, the Public Protector set out steps to be taken by the president, 'with the assistance of the National Treasury and the SAPS', to determine the reasonable cost of the measures implemented at his private residence that did not relate to the President's security.[36] The key point for the reader is that the Public Protector considered other features of the construction work done at Nkandla, such as the marquee area, paving, private clinic, police quarters and helipads, to have also been the result of maladministration and irregular expenditure.

The Constitutional Court's order, in contrast, only provided that

The National Treasury must determine the reasonable costs of those measures implemented by the Department of Public Works … that do not relate to security, *namely the visitors' centre, the amphitheatre, the cattle kraal, the chicken run and the swimming pool only* (emphasis added).[37]

As a result, the list of costly features for which Zuma could have been personally liable in the Public Protector's report is more extensive than those in the court's order, and he could have been on the hook for more than the R7.8 million ultimately determined for his personal account (paid with the dubious assistance of a loan from previously unknown VBS Bank).

This raises an intriguing hypothetical consequence that could have arisen had the Constitutional Court not limited the President's liability in this manner.[38] The President is elected from among the Members of Parliament. Section 47 of the Constitution prohibits unrehabilitated insolvents from being Members of Parliament. Given that the presidential annual salary is R2.9 million, a liability of R7.8 million – or even more if the additional features for which he could have been liable had been included in his tab by the Constitutional Court – could have provided grounds to declare Zuma insolvent, potentially removing his eligibility to continue to serve as President.

The final case considered in this chapter concerns efforts to ensure that Parliament would conduct impeachment proceedings against the President given judicial findings that he had failed to uphold his oath of office, and undermined the rule of law and the Constitution.

Impeachment

Four days after the Constitutional Court had handed down its judgment in the Nkandla case on 31 March 2016, DA leader Mmusi Maimane moved a motion of no confidence in the National Assembly based on the decision. His argument was that the judgment showed that the President had failed to implement the Public Protector's remedial action and thereby had failed to fulfil his constitutional obligations and oath of office. That motion was defeated.

On 10 November 2016, Maimane moved another motion of no confidence. It was again defeated by the ANC's majority in Parliament.

In October 2017, yet another motion of no confidence was moved, but this time it was conducted by secret ballot, following the Constitutional Court's judgment in a case brought by the United Democratic Movement. The court held that a motion of no confidence was 'one of the severest political consequences imaginable – a sword that hangs over the head of the president to force him or her to always do the right thing'.[39] The court agreed that a motion of no confidence may not have 'the fatal bite' without the possibility of being conducted by secret ballot, a procedure that, in the appropriate circumstances, may 'safeguard the responsibility of Members of Parliament to vote according to their conscience when it is necessary to enforce accountability effectively and properly'.[40]

Again, one of the motivations for this motion was the President's failure to implement the Public Protector's remedial action. Tellingly, the motion was defeated by a narrow margin, with at least 30 ANC Members of Parliament likely to have voted in favour of the motion now that they could do so anonymously.

The EFF then approached the Constitutional Court for an order whereby the Speaker of Parliament would be required to put in place appropriate mechanisms to hold the President accountable for his violations of the Constitution evident in the Nkandla saga. In particular, the application directed the Speaker to convene a committee in Parliament to conduct an investigation into whether the President had violated the Constitution in a manner that was grave enough to justify his impeachment.

Section 89 of the Constitution reads:

(1) The National Assembly, by a resolution adopted with a supporting vote of at least two thirds of its members, may remove the President from office only on the grounds of –

(a) a serious violation of the Constitution or the law;

(b) serious misconduct; or

(c) inability to perform the functions of office.

(2) Anyone who has been removed from the office of President in terms of subsection (1)(a) or (b) may not receive any benefits of that office, and may not serve in any public office.[41]

Although the National Assembly had not put in place a mechanism that was specially tailored for Section 89, it had put in place a mechanism that could be used effectively for the removal of a President in terms of Section 89: an *ad hoc* committee.[42]

The Constitutional Court's decision in this case revealed a dramatic division and tensions between the judges of the court, and not just by virtue of it being a split decision. At the sitting in which the court's decision was handed down, the Chief Justice interrupted Justice Jafta, who was reading the majority decision, to insist that his minority judgment be read out as well.

The majority judgment[43] proceeded from the basis that a president can be impeached only on one of the grounds listed in Section 89. In this case, 'a serious violation of the Constitution' was the front-runner to justify removal. According to Justice Jafta, the Constitution was silent on what constitutes 'a serious violation of the Constitution' and therefore it was up to the National Assembly to make that determination before an impeachment process could begin. It followed, therefore, that the process for impeaching the President must be preceded 'by a preliminary inquiry, during which the [National] Assembly determines that a listed ground exists. The form which this preliminary inquiry may take depends entirely upon the Assembly.'[44] The problem was that no rules existed for the establishment of a mechanism to make this preliminary determination needed to proceed with an impeachment of a president. Therefore, the court found, 'without rules defining the entire process it is impossible to implement section 89'.[45]

Another fascinating feature of the decision is that the Chief Justice objected in surprisingly strong language to the order of the majority and the reasoning they had followed to reach the decision, commencing the minority decision by stating that this was 'a textbook case of judicial overreach – a constitutionally impermissible intrusion by the Judiciary into the exclusive domain of Parliament. The extraordinary nature and gravity of this assertion demands that substance be provided to undergird it, particularly because the matter is polycentric in nature and somewhat controversial.'[46]

He claimed that it was

> at odds with the dictates of separation of powers and context-sensitive realities to prescribe to the National Assembly to always hold an inquiry, and to never rely only on readily available documented or recorded evidential material, to determine the existence of a ground of impeachment. It is just as insensitive to this doctrine to hold that impeachment grounds must always be determined by the Assembly before the debate and voting on a motion of impeachment could take place.[47]

The Chief Justice concluded:

When approached for intervention, this Court's role is to help only those who are constitutionally incapable of helping themselves. And, if the solution has already been provided and it is within the applicants' remit to address their own problem effectively, this Court is duty-bound to let them do it themselves. Mindful of the dictates of separation of powers, this ought to be even more so when help-seekers are the bearers of the primary constitutional responsibility, in another arm of the State, to do what they seek to achieve through an order of this Court. The running of State affairs is a trilateral responsibility – shared by the Executive, the Legislature and the Judiciary. It would be quite concerning if a court were to grant an order that does not serve or advance any practical purpose and in circumstances where that order deals with what has been achieved already or could be improved on if only cooperation were forthcoming from applicants, in a process that is already under way.[48]

On behalf of the majority, Justice Froneman took what can only be described as strong objection to the accusations of judicial overreach made against them by the Chief Justice. He responded by saying that he concurred with the judgment of Justice Jafta, but that he would have been 'content for [this] concurrence to merely be noted in the usual manner. The Chief Justice, however, characterises the second judgment as a textbook case of judicial overreach – a constitutionally impermissible intrusion by the Judiciary into the exclusive domain of Parliament'. He recognised 'the extraordinary nature and gravity of this assertion' and said that it should not be left unanswered'. Froneman then set out his response to the Chief Justice:

It is part of constitutional adjudication that, as in this matter, there may be reasonable disagreement among judges as to the proper interpretation and application of the Constitution. The respective merits of opposing viewpoints should be assessed on the basis of the substantive reasons advanced for them. There is nothing wrong in that substantive debate being robust, but to attach a label to the opposing view does nothing to further the debate.

For the reasons lucidly set out in the second judgment, I do not agree with the reasoning of the Chief Justice and the Deputy Chief Justice in their respective judgments. I do not, however, consider the different outcome that they reach to be the product of anything other than a serious attempt to grapple with the important constitutional issue at hand. The fact that I do not agree with their reasoning or the outcome that they propose does not mean that I consider them to have abdicated their responsibility to ensure that the National Assembly acts in accordance with the Constitution.

I consider that the outcome reached in the second judgment is the product of equally serious, honest and detached reasoning on the part of Jafta J and those of my colleagues who concur in his judgment.[49]

This exchange is arguably unprecedented in South African legal history. It is commonplace for appellate judges, who do not sit and decide cases alone, to disagree with one another in cases and for the minority, whose view did not persuade the members of the court, to pen a justification for their disagreement with their colleagues.

Vituperative comments about the reasoning of colleagues is an unfortunate and routine feature of the US Supreme Court, but not (yet) of our apex court. In one such example, when the US Supreme Court decided a same-sex marriage case, Justice Antonin Scalia memorably complained about the tone of the majority decision:

The opinion is couched in a style that is as pretentious as its content is egotistic … If … I ever joined an opinion for the Court that began: 'The Constitution promises liberty to all within its reach, a liberty that includes certain specific rights that allow persons, within a lawful realm, to define and express their identity', I would hide my head in a bag. The Supreme Court of the United States has descended from the disciplined legal reasoning of John Marshall and Joseph Story to the mystical aphorisms of the fortune cookie.

The fallout between two factions of the Constitutional Court evident in the impeachment decision is, fortunately, a rare exception rather than the rule.

So, what to make of this trilogy of cases? First, they tell us something about separation of powers – the allocation of distinct and complementary roles to the executive, legislature and judiciary. They confirm that each arm of government – indeed each organ of state or institution – must do its work. The judiciary was forced to fill the void left while the legislature slumbered. And this meant that litigation, rather than politics, was the process used to resolve political challenges facing our state. This placed the judiciary in an extraordinary and undesirable position at the vanguard of politics.

The impeachment case shows how sensible lawyers can differ on where the lines are that separate the powers of the arms of government. The judiciary advanced to the very outer limits permissible under separation of powers to address state capture when it could. It stepped into the vacuum left by the hollowing out of other institutions that should ensure accountability when necessary. But the judiciary cannot be the load bearer alone. Each and every other arm or organ of state must do its part.

Secondly, the failure of Parliament to exercise effective oversight of the executive, to give effect to decisions of the judiciary and important institutions such as the Public Protector, undermined these constitutional arrangements. The governing party's political machinations turned the representatives of the people into either a chorus for the executive or an irrelevancy. The ANC's numerical majority was used to railroad outcomes – even though one would speculate that the South African electorate, including the millions of voters who support the ANC at election time but are not card-carrying members of the organisation, may have wanted something else from them, something more conscious of the national interest, in terms of accountability and sound governance.

In addition, the precedent set in these cases can have disastrous consequences when circumstances and office bearers change. This is evident in what we experienced with the Nkandla case when we compare that with the next Public Protector's incantation of those powers to amend the Constitution and the mandate of the Reserve Bank.

In sum, these cases, and all of those listed earlier in this chapter, show the extent and effectiveness of state capture. So what can be done? What structural reforms could assist in ensuring it does not and cannot happen again?

The Slabbert report by the Electoral Task Team in 2003 proposed reforms of the electoral system to introduce constituency-based accountability for Members of Parliament. This was designed to counteract party boss dominance and ensure that elected representatives owed allegiance to the electorate and the interests of the community who voted them into Parliament, rather than to caucus instructions.

Indeed, the importance of electoral reforms was raised during the secret ballot debate:

> Seemingly there is no consistent set of principles and practices which will satisfactorily resolve the tension between party demands and individual conscience. Yet what does become clear is that there is much more scope for flexibility, tolerance of dissent, and – yes – freedom of conscience in systems where MPs are directly responsible to constituents rather than, as in South Africa, they are wholly accountable to their parties.

> Is this why the ANC so forthrightly rejected the recommendations of the Van Zyl Slabbert Commission on Electoral Reform? The commission recommended a mixed electoral system, whereby MPs would be elected on party platforms but from multi-member constituencies.

> There is no escaping the necessity of party systems to get the job of government done. Voters understand the need for party discipline. Yet, as the vote of no confidence also shows, they also want MPs to have the courage to rebel.[50]

Further reforms of the presidential powers of appointment and removal to dilute the current concentration of power in that office may be appropriate. Parliamentary oversight plays a limited role in these procedures, enabling a presidential free hand to appoint beholden, incompetent or pliable leaders to key institutions. Of course, the President must appoint those who will implement government policies and decisions. But greater consultation and scrutiny of the qualification and suitability of these leaders is desirable. The President should only have unfettered choice in selecting the cabinet (subject to rationality and legality), but should not enjoy the same level of freedom to select the leaders of all of the other key organs of state.

These types of reforms, coupled with the strengthening of our politics, civil society and constitutional institutions, ensure that we do not end up living under a juristocracy. Some may have applauded a juristocracy, but that was because we did not have a functioning or functional democracy. A juristocracy cannot and should not replace our chosen constitutional democracy.

P.S.

There is one other role for judges, retired or active, frequently used in South Africa at times of crisis or following events that demand reflection and fact finding, or which present an opportunity for reform, to ensure it never happens again: the establishment of a commission of inquiry. Commissions are focused on fact finding and are generally advisory in nature. They delve into evidence to establish what happened, and provide advice and assistance to the executive on issues of policy or implementation. Recommendations often follow to amend or promulgate legislation and the like.

Commissions notionally produce accountability as well – though often incidentally. One need only compare commissions into the police killings at Marikana, the arms deal and policing in Khayelitsha to see that the spectrum of commissions runs from effective to a wholesale waste of extensive public resources.

Commissions have several undesirable features in common: huge budgets, lengthy processes, armies of lawyers – often sidelining the very people with the story to tell – and the production of voluminous reports containing recommendations for policy reforms and even criminal prosecutions. And then nothing happens. No prosecutions. No policy reforms. No consequences.

Moreover, for so long as a commission is active, law-enforcement agencies, politicians and those implicated point to the ongoing process, the daily media reports, the theatre of accountability, as the reason why they are not doing more to redress or address whatever it is that occurred.

So we need to be supportive but also sceptical of commissions, as they often seem to decommission inquiry. The displacement of events, allegations and responsibility into a process that may or may not uncover the whole truth, the facts and the role of all parties is a risk in every commission. The conduct of a commission, the priorities it sets, the topics it selects for attention mean that we may not uncover the full story.

The Nugent Commission was appointed by President Ramaphosa on 23 May 2018 to deal with the degradation of SARS as an institution. Headed by retired Justice Robert Nugent, this is a fine example of a commission that was employed to best advantage. It has laid bare the responsibility of the Zuma-appointed SARS commissioner, Moyane, for the destruction caused to this critical institution, and it did so in less than seven months. By contrast, the Zondo Commission into state capture, appointed on 9 January 2018, which admittedly has a larger brief, is likely to continue for a very long time. By the end of its first year of operation, neither Zuma nor his key supporters had given any evidence. Nonetheless, the commission's proceedings have, at the least, exposed the public to the magnitude of state capture and corruption.

Whatever the success of this commission, however, it bears emphasis that commissions of inquiry should supplement, and not be a substitute for, effective law enforcement. Hence the importance of the urgent reconstruction of the NPA.

14

CONCLUSION: PRECEDENT
AND POSSIBILITY

'It does not matter who the judge is, we do not believe that the judiciary would be able to be objective.'

– PATRICK CRAVEN, spokesperson for COSATU, reacting to news of the indictment of Jacob Zuma, cited in the *Mail & Guardian*, 12 January 2008

'South Africa cannot afford a situation whereby the courts and the judiciary become targets for unwarranted attacks whenever people in the ANC, who think they are untouchable, disagree with their decisions. It will indeed be unfortunate if their bitterness against democratic state institutions is going to be used to advance political agendas and settle scores.

The ANC and its allies must also recognise that the independence of the judiciary is not something that can be upheld only when it suits them. When ANC president Jacob Zuma was acquitted of rape, the judiciary was not criticised; when he is charged with corruption, blood in the court is threatened.'

– *THE SUNDAY TIMES*, 19 January 2008

'There is a growing observable trend by the courts to act and play a big brother role where in some, if not any [sic] cases find themselves encroaching in the terrain of other organs. We are therefore saying that courts are using their powers as if they above Parliament.'

– SIHLE ZIKALALA, ANC KwaZulu-Natal chairperson, as per the *Sowetan*, 15 May 2017

The legal doctrine of precedent reflects the duty of judges to follow rulings as set out in previous judicial decisions. The Constitutional Court has observed that the doctrine of precedent serves to 'enshrine a fundamental principle of justice: that like cases should be determined alike'.[1] The doctrine also promotes the principles of legal certainty, rationality and equality, in that a litigant can claim injustice if a previous ruling on identical facts was not applied to her. Precedent is not an inflexible constraint. It can give way to distinction between the facts on which the precedent was based and the instant case. It can be altered when an appellate court decides that the morality or social and political context that shaped the judicial thinking on which the precedent was based has changed, so as to make the precedent legally inappropriate.

Take the case of Alix Carmichele, which we discussed in Chapter 10. Here, the lower courts, being the High Court and the Supreme Court of Appeal, both followed precedent in refusing to grant Alix Carmichele any relief. It required the Constitutional Court to unshackle the restrictions of a precedent, which had given little recognition to the constitutional principle of accountability of the police and prosecution services to the public they are supposed to serve. Suddenly, the law embraced Carmichele's case, and afforded her a legal cause of action on the basis of which she was awarded damages.

Precedent also may refer to the precedent of history. The National Party government used law vigorously for its own repressive and racist purposes. It developed a pernicious form of precedent, using law as a means to subvert political opposition and to structure a society in its racist image. The *Rivonia* case represented a classic form of the political trial. On the strength of the conviction of key leading members of the ANC, the state claimed that its opponents were no more than violent criminals. That case was followed by many similar trials throughout the next two and a half decades as the Nationalist government continued to seek justification for its repression of political opposition. As the intensity of political opposition to apartheid grew during the 1980s, the template fashioned at the *Rivonia* trial was applied in two major political trials – in Pietermaritzburg in 1985 and at Delmas, which followed shortly afterwards. In both cases, the state prosecuted senior members of the United Democratic Front on grounds of treason, terrorism, murder and subversion in a desperate attempt to delegitimise the non-racial democratic opposition to its racist hegemony.

Almost 50 years of precedent shattered the lives of millions in South Africa. The pass laws dismembered black community life. In 1948 alone, 176 000 black people were turned into 'criminals' for choosing to live in a part of their country that the 'law' prohibited them from entering. By 1970, the figure had risen to 600 000 for the year – on average one person became a criminal every minute.[2] This vigorously enforced carceral system imploded after the victories in the *Komani* and *Rikhoto* cases, which we documented in Chapter 5.

This precedent of the abuse of law returned to haunt the country less than 15 years after the dawn of democracy. As we described in the previous chapter on state capture, the Zuma decade was characterised by an assault on key institutions that had been designed to uphold the rule of law and the broader aims of democracy. The NPA, the SAPS, the so-called anti-corruption unit (the Hawks), the office of the Public Protector (after Madonsela's term at the helm) and SARS all fell without political demur to Zuma and his acolytes.

There can be little doubt that Zuma reflected the precedent seen in the appointment of LC Steyn as a pliable Chief Justice rather than Oliver Schreiner in the 1960s when he overlooked Deputy Chief Justice Dikgang Moseneke and appointed instead Mogoeng Mogoeng. That Justice Mogoeng promoted the principle of judicial independence with com-mendable vigour once appointed only showed that Zuma had unwittingly committed a major blunder from the perspective of his own agenda. The precedent from the 1960s was not to be revived.

If precedent serves to connote the binding legal and political force of law through time, the word 'possibility' captures the constitutional ambition of a break with a past – a history saturated with racism, sexism, homophobia and egregious political intolerance. It was a past often accompanied by state-sanctioned violence, which – despite the obdurate refusal by the state to admit to such conduct during apartheid – was revealed in its varying shapes of horror during the TRC hearings, and the De Kock and Basson trials.

As noted, South Africa did not experience a revolution after FW de Klerk unbanned the ANC, the PAC and the South African Communist Party in 1990. Instead, the erstwhile warring parties engaged in intricate negotiations that culminated in a Constitution that promised the possibility of transformation. That term connoted that there was an imperative to take over governmental institutions and reshape political and legal concepts that had been created during apartheid in the image of non-racial and non-sexist democratic principles.

That possibility became immediately apparent after 1994, when the newly created Constitutional Court broke with apartheid precedent in key judgments it delivered, beginning with the *Makwanyane* case, in which the death penalty was declared to be unconstitutional.

Most recently, the Constitutional Court broke legal ground in its judgment in *Daniels v Scribante* when it sought to infuse property law with a fresh normative framework, which recognised the need to react decisively to a history of land dispossession. (We shall return to this decision later in this chapter.)

As we have already noted, however, law possesses a dialectical quality, in that it can operate both at the level of oppression and as a set of defensive rights. The legal 'possibility' can thus also work in a dramatically different way from its promotion of substantive democratic change, namely the possibility of law constructing a culture of authority rather than of justification, even if the authority may take on a more non-racial character in the post-apartheid era.

As an example, the employment of state violence against the Marikana miners, who were confronted by egregious employment practices of privately owned mining houses enforced by brutal police conduct, is a tragic example of the replication of the long history of South African police violence.[3] The level of violence in that incident recalled the apartheid police murder of 69 people at Sharpeville in March 1960. Meanwhile, the construction of a parallel state by the Zuma regime was effectively unfettered by the rule of law, and remained a real possibility until the election of Cyril Ramaphosa as ANC president in December 2017. At the time of writing, however, it would be naive to ignore the reality of the spectre of a parallel state, which still haunts the country and may still hamper the possibility of achieving a sustainable, viable democracy.

Although we have presented here the merits of a series of decisions of the Constitutional Court, we do not wish to be misunderstood as being advocates of constitutional fundamentalism. Courts alone cannot vindicate the vision of the Constitution. Lawfare should be the last resort, and not a default position when political solutions fail. When political impetus does fail, the Constitution itself is imperilled, whatever the court may deliver by way of progressive judgments. Section 25 of the Constitution, the property clause, is an example. For about 25 years, the government has failed to implement a coherent policy of land reform. A sensible reading of Section 25 reveals that it does not mandate a market-related awarding of compensation in the case of expropriation by the state. And it is significant that a government democratically elected more than two decades ago has never tested the scope and meaning of the section. Rather, its land policy has floundered in a morass of incoherence and non-delivery. Now, suddenly, with the executive facing opposition from populist quarters, the blame for this political ineptitude has shifted to the text of Section 25.[4] A discourse has developed to the effect that, were it not for Section 25 of the Constitution, land reform would have proceeded with coherence and have been expedited. Yet the record of the past two decades reveals that the four key elements of any meaningful land-reform programme were never implemented with all due deliberate speed: 1) broadening access to land and opening up all natural resources to everyone; 2) making insecure or weak rights stronger; 3) restoring what was lost or dispossessed on a much larger scale; 4) implementing policies to capacitate recipients of land reform, so that they could exploit the land rights that had been restored to them in a manner that would produce substantive benefits of these rights to holders and their communities.

None of these elements of a coherent land policy are compromised by the contents of Section 25 of the Constitution. However, the political ineptitude that has prevented implementation of a sensible policy would appear to be justified by blaming the Constitution. It is a luminous case of political failure compromising the possibility of the Constitution as a means to transformation.

The courts and the Constitution

We have highlighted examples of the increasing utilisation of the courts as the forum for contesting political struggles. This has placed a fierce spotlight on an invariably unelected judiciary to settle these disputes and thereby develop new precedent, which non-governmental organisations have urged courts to fashion in the image of the possibility that they seek to mine from the text of the Constitution. The danger for courts in this situation is that, as Max du Plessis has warned, 'If the court appeals only to the public and its sense of common morality in abdication of its constitutional duty it will be too easily dismissed as apologist, but if it proclaims the superiority of human rights ideals without attempting to engage with the public and its opinion, it will be criticised for being utopian.'[5]

The cases to which we have devoted entire chapters, and other important cases that we have listed here, reveal that the constitutional journey never proceeds in a single deliberate direction. The dominant trajectory will depend on the outcome of political and legal contest shaped by the prevailing political discourse, the legal traditions in the country and the available legal materials – being existing legal precedents, the facts of the particular dispute, the quality of the lawyering and the ideology of the judiciary. Hence, the role of the judicial institution has inherent limits, particularly because of the factors we have listed. This means that a judicial reading of a legal text, including the Constitution, is not an unfettered exercise of discretion.

Take the following illustration based on our reading of the South African constitutional text: the South African Constitution promotes the foundational values of dignity, equality and freedom. Manifestly, these need to be reconciled into a normative system that is not at war with itself. In our view, a libertarian conception of freedom would hardly be compatible with a commitment to a society based, in part, on a substantive conception of equality. Detailed constitutional provisions make this point clear. The Constitution contains an express commitment to substantive equality, to the constraint of private power exercised in a public fashion, which includes the power of private organisations when exercised in a manner that may affect the rights of ordinary citizens. The Constitution ensures that significant limitations are placed on all actors to safeguard the environment; workers have express rights to form trade unions, to strike and to bargain collectively.

What, for example, would happen if a South African Margaret Thatcher or Donald Trump emerged to take power in South Africa? How would courts deal with the introduction of policies of the democratically elected government that ran counter to the very foundations of the Constitution? If you wish, substitute Robert Mugabe: the game works equally well. A coherent reading requires intellectual and legal justification in order to be coherent with the text; hence a judicial reading of the Constitution does not mean that anything that calls itself an interpretation of the Constitution can pass as a justifiable legal reading.

We read the Constitution as a plan for a truly democratic and equal society. A new challenge to this plan has arisen: incorrectly claiming it as an obstacle to transformation that arose from an incoherent compromise between the ANC and the Nats. We reject this claim.[6]

We have shown that the Constitution can move beyond the constraints of this precedent to embrace a possibility for a society that has substantively broken from its past. It can provide an egalitarian framework that restores sovereignty to 55 million South Africans. That possibility is most comprehensively set out in Thabo Mbeki's 'I am an African' speech, which we referred to in Chapter 1 and which he delivered in Parliament when the Constitution was adopted into law in 1996. This result may not be inevitable – but it is possible.

In this context, the 2017 Constitutional Court decision in *Daniels v Scribante* is one in which we find sound support for our observation, and hence it merits more comprehensive discussion.

Daniels v Scribante: A riposte to the constitutional critics

Yolanda Daniels, a domestic worker, occupied a small property on the farm where she worked. The manager of the farm, Theo Scribante, behind whom were the owners of the farm, appears to have been particularly obstructive in respect of Daniels's peaceful occupation of her dwelling. Things came to a head as follows: Daniels wanted to make certain basic improvements, which included levelling the floors, paving part of the outside area and installing an indoor water supply, a washbasin, a second window and a ceiling. Even Scribante and his fellow respondents accepted that, without these improvements, the dwelling was not fit for human habitation. However, even though Ms Daniels had indicated that she was paying for these basic improvements with her own money, the respondents objected, forcing a process of litigation.

Relying on provisions of the Extension of Security of Tenure Act (ESTA), Daniels argued that the right to reside accorded to her in terms of ESTA included the right to make improvements to her dwelling. In a startling illustration that an extremely conservative legal tradition in South Africa was still alive, both the Land Claims Court and the Supreme Court of Appeal dismissed Daniels's case on the basis that, without an express provision in ESTA permitting an occupier to effect improvements, she could not encroach on the rights of the owners of the farm. At this point, the constitutional critics appeared to have been proved correct.

Daniels and her legal representatives persisted all the way to the Constitutional Court. There, Justice Mbuyiseli Madlanga, for the majority of the court, eschewed the narrow approach to interpretation adopted by the other courts and immediately consigned ESTA to the vortex of South African history: 'Dispossession of land was central to colonialism and apartheid. It first took place through the barrel of the gun and "trickery". This commenced as soon as white settlement began, with the Khoi and San people being the first victims. This was followed by "an array of laws" dating from the early days of colonisation. The most infamous is the Native Land Act.'[7]

Justice Madlanga accepted that there was no express provision in ESTA that created a right of an occupier to make improvements. However, he sought to divine the real purpose of the Act: 'It is also about affording occupiers the dignity that eluded most of them throughout the colonial and apartheid regimes. We must adopt an interpretation that best advances this noble purpose of section 25(6) and ESTA. That purpose provides context.'[8]

The context made it clear that the Act had been designed to ensure that occupiers who were protected by the legislation could live in dignity, which would not be the case if an occupier was prevented from making basic improvements. To the argument that an owner might then have to compensate the occupier for the cost of improvements if they gave up occupation, Justice Madlanga found that this hypothesis could wait determination in the appropriate case, but in the Daniels case ordered that Daniels was entitled to make the necessary improvements.

Justice Johan Froneman, supported by Justice Edwin Cameron,

penned a concurring judgment (unusual, in that it was written in both Afrikaans, Justice Froneman's home language, and English). There is a further unusual aspect to this judgment – it provides a deeply personal reflection on South Africa's horrendous past. In his judgment, Justice Froneman provides a resounding response to those who argue that the Constitution was designed to imprison South Africa within its apartheid framework. In this connection, his observations may well be a useful signpost for further legal development:

> Before we can make substantial and lasting progress in making the ideals of the Constitution a reality, at least three things must happen: (a) an honest and deep recognition of past injustice; (b) a re-appraisal of our conception of the nature of ownership and property; and (c) an acceptance, rather than avoidance or obfuscation, of the consequences of constitutional change.[9]

Conclusion

We do not claim that an entrenched Constitution and a Bill of Rights supervised by an independent judiciary alone are enough to sustain our political and economic democracy. Those rights underpin active citizenship. Active citizenship underpins the expression of a plurality of views and the dynamic discourse that follows. That discourse underpins effective politics[10]. Each of these is a requirement for our constitutional democracy to thrive and build our shared future.

Viewed in this way, the cases examined here, both before constitutional democracy dawned in South Africa and those that were litigated on the basis of the Constitution, hold significant implications for constitutional democracy in countries even beyond the borders of South Africa. The rights struggles that mark these cases are a contest against the imposition of the power of the 'one' in authority over the 'other', being the balance of society. In this sense, the possibility is not only about rights but about the existence of democratic politics.

Constitutional democracy is a robust and fragile mechanism. Today, there are lessons for us from that oldest of constitutional democracies, the USA. The rise of populism and the ideologically polarised and divided Supreme Court show that a constitutional project can be endangered.

Rights listed in a legal text alone are insufficient – constitutional essentialism (i.e. the idea that democracy is attained solely or mainly though the legal form) is not the answer. A lesson that emerges from the legal struggles described in this book is that courts cannot do the work alone; they end up isolated and ineffective. The Constitution must be recognised as the bridge away from the past, and now the plan for building our future together.

Risk to this project is heightened by the state of institutions that also have a mandate to promote accountable and transparent governance. Take, for example, the explosion of claims about the collapse of governance at Eskom, the Public Protector's report on state capture, the report by the State Capacity Research Project on the rise of a 'mafia' state or the #Guptaleaks email disclosures by amaBhungane published in the *Daily Maverick, City Press* and *The Sunday Times*.[11] In a democracy worthy of the name, these startling allegations would have immediately been investigated by the relevant police departments, the Hawks, the NPA and the Public Protector. Instead, the silence from some of these quarters is deafening, and their peripatetic lurching between paralysis and inexplicable intervention is disquieting. Clear enforcement action is needed to demonstrate that these agencies are beholden to no one.

Without these institutions and greater oversight from Parliament, and without significant public pressure and political activity to support the courts in resisting sinister and subversive political initiatives, the constitutional bridge will ultimately collapse under the weight of pressure from government and nefarious private activities that betray any promise of a democracy for some people. It is for this reason that we have made some suggestions as to how the Constitution may be amended to enhance both the principles of accountability of public institutions and public participation in our democracy.

Political activity is needed to keep alive the possibility envisaged in the Constitution. Law alone may be used or abused. Much depends on the level at and manner in which the political contest unfolds. In turn, the possibility of law can open up further space for political activity. If that possibility is not exploited by civil society, the likelihood of meaningful transformation is slim.

The politics of justification and accountability of public power, so fundamental to the construction of a constitutional bridge, might have enjoyed a relatively fruitful first decade in South Africa. But many of the pillars designed to support the bridge were weakened, if not destroyed, and that process started, it must be said, before the rise of Zuma. The precedent of the past and the possibility of a return to parts of that past began to loom on the political landscape. Although South Africa is in a far better place than it ever was under apartheid, the dream of 1994 has darkened in recent years.

The resort to crude racial populism, fuelled by a vile concoction of state capture and a PR campaign spun by Bell Pottinger, struck at the heart of a transforming society. Small wonder that the Constitution became the target as this pernicious campaign began to gain popular traction.

Our Constitution survived and was strengthened by the test, and continues to set our ambitions for the society that we are now building together. Courts cannot do it alone, nor will the text alone suffice. The possibility now is for each of us to understand our constitutional rights, to bond with others in debate and dialogue, and then to build a vibrant politics and our free, dignified and equal society.

NOTES

Foreword

1 National Treasury, 2017 Budget Review, http://www.treasury.gov.za/
   documents/national%20budget/2017/review/FullBR.pdf, accessed
   27 February 2019.
2 See https://www.concourt.org.za/images/phocadownload/justice_
   cameron/Bar-Dinner-Johannesburg-Saturday-1-November-Speech-as-
   delivered-for-website.pdf
3 Cited in Daron Acemoglu and James A Robinson, *Why Nations Fail: The
   Origins of Power, Prosperity and Poverty*, London: Profile Books, 2012.
4 Extract from Nelson Mandela's Inaugural Address as President of South
   Africa, 10 May 1994, https://www.sahistory.org.za/archive/
   mandela-quotes-and-interesting-information.

CHAPTER 1: The ascendancy of lawfare

1 Lizeka Tandwa, Nkandla judgment exemplary of ConCourt – Moseneke,
   News24, 28 January 2017, https://www.news24.com/SouthAfrica/
   News/nkandla-judgment-exemplary-of-concourt-moseneke-20170128.
2 ANC says judgement on reasons for reshuffle 'encroaches' executive
   realm, IOL, 5 May 2017, https://www.iol.co.za/dailynews/news/south-
   africa/anc-says-judgement-on-reasons-for-reshuffle-encroaches-executive-
   realm-8968594.
3 Jean and John L Comaroff (eds), *Law and Disorder in the Postcolony*.
   University of Chicago Press, 2008, 17.
4 Ibid., 27–29.

5 Ibid.

6 RW Johnson, *How Long Will South Africa Survive?* Jonathan Ball, 2015, 30. Johnson claims that Mendi Msimang, one-time treasurer of the ANC, had been sent to the then Judge President of KwaZulu-Natal, Judge Vuka Tshabalala, to suggest the appointment of Judge Squires as the presiding judge in the Shaik trial. Johnson offers no explanation as to Mbeki's preference for Squires. Significantly, the allegation has never been denied some three years after the publication of Johnson's book.

7 Amicus curiae: an impartial adviser to a court.

8 Advocates For Transformation correctly drew attention to the failure of the General Council of the Bar to appeal another Supreme Court of Appeal decision, also decided by a 3:2 split between the judges, regarding a number of advocates, including white senior counsel from the Pretoria Bar, who successfully appealed against their removal in a separate case. But this is hardly a justification not to allow the Constitutional Court to determine which side of the split court was correct. It is worth noting that Justice Leach was in the minority in both cases, consistently seeking the disbarment of those considered lacking in the required integrity to be officers of the court.

9 Duarte questions 'leaks' from populist Madonsela's office, *Mail & Guardian*, 26 August 2014, https://mg.co.za/article/2014-08-26-duarte-questions-leaks-from-populist-madonselas-office.

10 See Address by Public Protector Advocate Thuli Madonsela on the occasion of Recognition of Achiever Award function at the University of Pretoria, 14 April 2016, https://www.gov.za/speeches/address-public-protector-adv-thuli-madonsela-occasion-recognition-achiever-award-function.

11 *Southern Africa Litigation Centre v Minister of Justice and Constitutional Development* 2015 (5) SA 1 (GP) at para 37.

12 Karyn Maughn, Judiciary is last line of defence against government, *Mail & Guardian*, 12 February 2016, https://mg.co.za/article/2016-02-10-the-judiciary-last-line-of-defence-against-government.

13 Natasha Marrian, Alliance resurrects Moseneke's Zuma criticism, *Business Day*, 2 July 2015, https://www.pressreader.com/south-africa/business-day/20150702/281629598928856.

14 'I am an African', Thabo Mbeki's speech at the adoption of the Republic of South Africa Constitution Bill, 8 May 1996. For the full speech, see https://www.news24.com/SouthAfrica/Politics/I-am-an-African-by-Thabo-Mbeki-20110525.

15 Achille Mbembe, Apartheid futures and the limits of racial reconciliation, unpublished paper, Wiser Institute, 2015.

16 Joel Modiri, The crises in legal education, *Acta Academica*, 46, 3 (2014), 1–24, 11.

17 Tshepo Madlingozi, Social justice in a time of neo-apartheid constitutionalism, *Stellenbosch Law Review*, 28, 1 (2017), 123–147.

18 Theunis Roux, *The Politics of Principle: The First South African Constitutional Court, 1995–2005.* Cambridge University Press, 2011.

19 Karl Klare, Self-realization, human rights and separation of powers: A democracy-seeking approach, *Stellenbosch Law Review*, 26 (2015), 467.

CHAPTER 2: Why these cases?

1   Etienne Mureinik, A bridge to where? Introducing the Interim Bill of Rights, *SAJHR*, 10, 1 (1994), 31–48.

2   *Omar and Others v Minister of Law and Order and Others* 1986 (3) SA 306 (C). By contrast, see the judgment of Judge Goldstone in *Momoniat and Naidoo v Minister of Law and Order* 1986 (2) SA 264 (W). Omar at the time was one of the most tenacious and courageous human-rights practitioners in the country

3   *R v Abdurrahman* 1950 (3) SA 136 (A).

4   EP Thompson, *Whigs and Hunters, The Origin of the Black Act.* New York: Pantheon Books, 1975, 265–266. There was also a liberal approach to law that proved equally influential. See, for example,
E Mureinik, Dworkin and apartheid in H Corder (ed.), *Essays on Law and Social Practice in South Africa.* Cape Town: Juta, 1988.

5   Nicholas Haysom and Clive Plasket, The war against law: Judicial activism and the Appellate Division, *SAJHR*, 4, 3 (1988), 303–333.

6   Steve Mufson, *Sunday Star*, 3 May 1987.

7   Ibid.

8   When we refer to the common law, we mean that body of law that is not sourced in legislation, but which is drawn primarily from Roman-Dutch and English law, itself a reflection of South Africa's colonial past. This body of law was then adopted by the courts to meet the judicially perceived needs of the country. Thus, the rules developed by the courts, together with the legal materials of both the Roman-Dutch and English legal systems, to which courts may have recourse, constitute the structure of the legal system upon which is built a superstructure of legislation that amends, corrects, repeals and adds to the existing body of common law. Today, the common law ultimately derives its authority from the Constitution, which is also the

source for judges to effect changes to the common law. For a detailed discussion, see Francois du Bois (ed.), *Wille's Principles of South African Law.* Juta, 2007, 9th edition, Chapter 4.

9 Laurie Ackermann later left the bench to promote human rights as a law professor, heading up the first human-rights centre at Stellenbosch University.

10 Etienne Mureinik, A bridge to where? Introducing the Interim Bill of Rights, *SAJHR*, 10, 1 (1994), 31–48.

11 Alexander Bickel *The Least Dangerous Branch: The Supreme Court at the Bar of Politics.* Yale University Press, 1962.

12 Otto Kirchheimer, *Political Justice: The Use of Legal Procedure for Political Ends.* Princeton University Press, 1961.

13 Section 20(7) of the Promotion of National Unity and Reconciliation Act 34 of 1995.

14 Herman Giliomee, Hanging question over SA, *Sunday Times*, 22 August 1988.

15 Briefly, delict is that body of law that seeks to afford a right of compensation to a person who, as a result of an act of another person performed in a wrongful and culpable way, has suffered harm.

CHAPTER 3: Who can rid me of this troublesome court?
The Executive v The Judiciary

1 Dikgang Moseneke, Oliver Schreiner Memorial Lecture, University of Witwatersrand, 23 October 2008.

2 'KC' refers to King's Counsel, the most senior rank of advocate. After the death of King George VI , the title became Queen's Counsel (QC). Today, however, South African senior counsel are designated by 'SC' after their names.

3 House of Assembly Debates, 17 April 1951, col. 4584.

4 Authors' interview with Denis Cowen, November 2006.

5 David Scher, The disenfranchisement of the Coloured voters, unpublished DLitt and Phil thesis, Unisa, 1983, 96–97. This chapter owes Dr Scher a great debt, in that his superb research provided a goldmine of material.

6 Canada and Australia were the other countries recognised by Britain as dominions.

7 *Harris and Others v Minister of the Interior and Another* 1952 (2) SA 428 (A) at 471.

8 House of Assembly Debates, 20 March 1952, col. 3124–3126.

9 Ibid., 5 May 1952, col. 4922–4925.

10 Ibid., 7 May 1952, col. 5181.

11 JGN Strauss, as cited by DM Scher, The court of errors: A study of the High Court of Parliament crisis of 1952, *Kronos*, 13 (1988), 33.

12 *Minister of the Interior and Another v Harris* 1952 (4) SA 769 (A) 779/.

13 Cited by DM Scher, The court of errors: A study of the High Court of Parliament crisis of 1952, *Kronos*, 13 (1988), 25.

14 These suggestions are gleaned from the Dönges papers, as accessed by DM Scher, The court of errors: A study of the High Court of Parliament crisis of 1952, *Kronos*, 13 (1988)

15 *Die Burger*, 18 March 1953.

16 Translated from an article published in *Die Vaderland*, 25 March 1953.

17 Ibid.

18 Ibid.

19 In the Liberal Party's magazine, *Contact* (February 1955), there is a discussion of appointments to the bench and the likelihood that these would produce a servile and weak bench.

20 Edwin Cameron, Legal chauvinism, executive-mindedness and justice: L. C. Steyn's impact on South African law, *SALJ*, 99 (1982) 38–75: 40.

21 DM Scher, The disenfranchisement of the Coloured voters, unpublished Dlitt and Phil thesis, Unisa, 1983, 632.

22 House of Assembly Debates, 25 May 1955, col. 4430.

23 Ibid, 23 May 1955, cols 6003ff.

24 Ibid.

25 Ellison Kahn (ed.), *Fiat Justitia: Essays in Honour of Oliver Denys Schreiner*. Juta, 1983, 74.

26 Ibid., 40.

27 Ibid.

28 House of Assembly Debates, 19 January 1957, cols189–191.

29 *Collins v Minister of Interior and Another* 1957 (1) SA 552 (A) at 585.

30 Ellison Kahn (ed.), *Fiat Justitia: Essays in Honour of Oliver Denys Schreiner*. Juta, 1983, 44.

31 Ibid.

32 G Heaton Nicholls, *South Africa in My Time*. Allen, 1961, 243.

33 DM Scher, The disenfranchisement of the Coloured voters, unpublished Dlitt and Phil thesis, Unisa, 1983, 632.

34 Statement of the National Executive Committee on the occasion of the 93rd anniversary of the ANC, 8 January 2005, https://www.sahistory. org.za/archive/january-8th-statements-statement-national-executive-committee-occasion-93th-anniversary-anc-

35 Sabelo Ndlangisa, It's poor judgment: Mogoeng concerned about apparently baseless perceptions. *Times LIVE*, 11 July 2017, https://www.timeslive.co.za/politics/2017-07-11-its-poor-judgment-mogoeng-concerned-about-apparently-baseless-perceptions/.

36 Zuma: State capture a politically decorated expression, News24, 12 September 2018, https://www.news24.com/SouthAfrica/News/zuma-state-capture-a-politically-decorated-expression-20180912.

CHAPTER 4: The Rivonia trial: Competing visions for South Africa

1   Extract from a document found by the police at Liliesleaf Farm, 11 July 1963.

2   Authors' interview with Ahmed Kathrada, 28 December 2007.

3   Ahmed Kathrada, *Memoirs*. Penguin Random House South Africa, 2004, 156.

4   Ibid., 157.

5   Ibid., 158.

6   Anthony Sampson, *Nelson Mandela The Authorized Biography*. Harper Collins, 1999.

7   Authors' interview with Ahmed Kathrada, 28 December 2007.

8   Hansard, 1963, col. 7772.

9   Cited in an article in the *Rand Daily Mail*, 15 July 1963.

10 Authors' interview with Ahmed Kathrada, 28 December 2007.

11 Ibid.

12 Ibid.

13 *Rand Daily Mail*, 9 October 1963.

14 Hilda Bernstein, *The World that was Ours: The Story of the Rivonia Trial*. London: Persephone Books, 1984, 120.

15 Wessel le Roux, Studying legal history through courtroom architecture, *Codicillus*, 44, 1 (May 2003), 55–63.

16 Hilda Bernstein, *The World that was Ours: The Story of the Rivonia Trial*. London: Persephone Books, 1984, 120.

17 Authors' interview with Arthur Chaskalson, July 2007.

18 Ismail Mahomed, The Bram Fischer memorial lecture, *SAJHR*, 14 (1998), 209.

19 Stephen Clingman, *Bram Fischer: Afrikaner Revolutionary*. University of Massachusetts, 1998. Chaskalson recalls examining documents during the trial that had been seized earlier by the police and which should have been made available to the defence. He discovered documents that involved Fischer. When he was later asked by Fischer what he had found, he mentioned these documents. Fischer offered no comment (authors' interview with Arthur Chaskalson, July 2007).

Notes

20 Authors' interview with Ahmed Kathrada, 28 December 2007.

21 Hilda Bernstein, *The World that was Ours: The Story of the Rivonia Trial*. London: Persephone Books, 1984, 125.

22 Joel Joffe, *The Rivonia Story*. Cape Town: Mayibuye Books, 1995, 43.

23 Ibid.

24 *The Star*, 4 December 1963.

25 *Rivonia* case: Goldreich and the others planned to build an armaments factory, *Die Burger*, 5 December 1963 (translation from the Afrikaans original).

26 *The Star*, 5 December 1963.

27 *Rivonia* trial record, vol. 4, p 1.

28 Ibid., 12.

29 Bruno Mtolo, *Umkonto we Sizwe: The Road to the Left*. Durban: Drakensberg Press, 1966, 148; Hilda Bernstein, *The World that was Ours: The Story of the Rivonia Trial*. London: Persephone Books, 1984, 158.

30 Hilda Bernstein, *The World that was Ours: The Story of the Rivonia Trial*. London: Persephone Books, 1984, 158.

31 Bruno Mtolo, *Umkonto we Sizwe: The Road to the Left*. Durban: Drakensberg Press, 1966, 142.

32 *The Star*, 20 May 1964.

33 Hilda Bernstein, *The World that was Ours: The Story of the Rivonia Trial*. London: Persephone Books, 1984, 140.

34 Ibid.

35 Ibid., 188.

36 Ibid., 192.

37 The speech is to be found in the Rivonia trial record at the William Cullen Library, vol. 19.

38 Ibid.

39 Ibid.

40 Ibid.

41 Ibid.

42 Anthony Sampson, *Mandela: The Authorised Biography*. HarperCollins UK, 1999, 193.

43 *Rivonia* trial record, vol. 19.

44 RS Roberts, *No Cold Kitchen: A Biography of Nadine Gordimer*. Real African Publishers, 2005, 155–156.

45 Ibid.

46 *Rivonia* trial record, vol. 20, p 12.

47 Ahmed Kathrada, *Memoirs*. Penguin Random House South Africa, 2004, 178.

48 George Bizos, *Odyssey to Freedom*. Penguin Random House South Africa, 2009, 249–250.

49 Joel Joffe, *The Rivonia Story*. Cape Town: Mayibuye Books, 1995, 203.

50 Authors' interview with Arthur Chaskalson, July 2007.

51 Authors' interview with Ahmed Kathrada, 28 December 2007.

52 Joel Joffe, *The Rivonia Story*. Cape Town: Mayibuye Books, 1995, 208.

53 Ibid.

54 A fellow traveller is a sympathiser with the same cause who is not necessarily a member of the organisation.

55 Ibid.

56 Ibid., 211.

57 Ibid., 212.

58 *Rivonia* trial record, vol. 32.

59 Ibid.

60 Ahmed Kathrada, *Memoirs*. Penguin Random House South Africa, 2004, 191.

61 Fred Bridgland, Obituary, Percy Yutar, *The Scotsman*, 23 July 2002.

62 This interview was part of Professor Albertyn's doctoral research.

63 Lauritz Strydom, *Rivonia Unmasked!* Ostara Publications, 1965, 8.

64 HH de Villiers, *Rivonia: Operation Mayibuye*. Afrikaanse Pers-Boekhandel, 1964, 28–29.

65 Ibid.

66 Authors' interview with George Bizos, 16 June 2007. The system by which the Governor General (later the President, when South Africa became a republic in 1961) could commute a sentence of death has been documented and carefully analysed by Rob Turrell in *White Mercy: A Study of the Death Penalty in South Africa*. Greenwood, 2004.

67 Nelson Mandela, *Long Walk to Freedom*. London: Abacus, 1994, 377.

68 Authors' interview with George Bizos, 16 June 2007

69 Foreword to HH de Villiers, *Rivonia: Operation Mayibuye*. Afrikaanse Pers-Boekhandel, 1964.

70 *The Star*, 18 June 1964.

71 *Rand Daily Mail*, 17 June 1964.

72 Ibid.

73 Anthony Sampson, *Mandela: The Authorised Biography*. HarperCollins UK, 1999, 198.

74 *Sunday Times*, 7 June 1964.

75 *Cape Argus*, 18 August 1985.

76 CH Albertyn, A critical analysis of political trade in South Africa, 1948 to 1988, unpublished PhD thesis, Cambridge University, 248.

77 Ibid.

78 Cited by Albertyn in A critical analysis of political trade in South Africa, 1948 to 1988, unpublished PhD thesis, Cambridge University, 250.

79 Quoted in Business Day, 16 May 2016.

CHAPTER 5: The challenge to the pass laws: The beginning of the end

1   Influx control was governed by the Bantu (Urban Areas) Consolidation Act 25 of 1945; denationalisation by various pieces of legislation governing the homelands was incorporated into Acts such as the Status of Transkei Act 100 of 1976, the Status of Bophuthatswana Act 89 of 1977, the Status of Venda Act 107 of 1979 and the Status of Ciskei Act 110 of 1981; and the labour bureaus in terms of the Black Labour Act 67 of 1964.

2   Stephen Ellmann, Law and legitimacy in South Africa, Law and Social Inquiry, 20, 2 (1995), 407 441. The information also comes from the transcript of an interview with Rikhotso conducted by Ellmann in 1994 kindly provided by Ellmann. We have used the spelling 'Rikhoto' when referring to the case, as it is known by that name.

3   Figures provided by Michael Savage, The imposition of pass laws on the African population in South Africa 1916–1984, African Affairs (1988), 181.

4   Report of the Local Government Commission TP.7, 1922.

5   'Banality of evil' is a phrase borrowed from Hannah Arendt, who, in her work Eichmann in Jerusalem (1963), argued that the great evil in societies like Nazi Germany was not committed necessarily by fanatics or psychopaths but by ordinary people who accepted the premises of their government's policy and who therefore conducted themselves with the attitude that their actions were normal and ordinary. We want to argue that this paradigm is applicable to the conduct of the administrators who are partly the subject of this chapter.

6   General Circular No 25, 1967, para 1.

7   The applicable law was Section 10(1)(c) of the Bantu (Urban Areas) Consolidation Act 25 of 1945, which provided: 'No Black shall remain for more than 72 hours in a prescribed area unless he produces proof in the manner prescribed that ... (c) such Black is the wife ... of any Black mentioned in para (a) or (b) of this subsection and after lawful entry into such prescribed area, ordinarily resides with that Black in such area.' As

Komani qualified under para *(b)* because he had been employed for more than ten years by the same employer, his wife may have been excused for reading Section *(c)* as affording her a right to live with him.

8   That advocates, from time to time, represent clients with whom they disagree ideologically is attributable to the taxi cab rule of the Bar – if available, an advocate must take the brief offered. In this way, unpopular causes can find legal representation. Whether the rule should apply also to the state is a more controversial question.

9   In fairness, there was precedent equating ordinary residence with lawful residence, although not necessarily pertaining to the legality of the housing regulations.

10   The Black Sash was founded in 1955, initially to campaign against the removal of Coloured voters from the common roll (see Chapter 2 for more). As apartheid extended its web of control, the Black Sash began a campaign against the pass laws. White women, to cite its national director, Marcella Naidoo, speaking in 2005, used the relative safety of their white classification to don symbolic black sashes as a symbol of mourning and protest against unjust laws. The organisation played a brave and principled role as an important element of civil society, of which its advice offices were a critical component. The South African Institute of Race Relations was launched in 1929.

11   Authors' interview with Arthur Chaskalson, July 2007.

12   Authors' interview with Geoffrey Budlender, August 2007. There is a point of jurisprudential curiosity here: some 15 years later, most of the Constitutional Court, under Chief Justice Chaskalson at the time, in *Du Plessis v De Klerk* 1996 (3) SA 850 (CC), used the same approach of the limited state to decide that the new Constitution applied only to relations between the state and the individual, thus finally disposing of a controversy about the potential reach of the Constitution.

13   Authors' interviews with Budlender and Chaskalson, August 2007 and July 2007.

14   Cited by Richard Abel in *Politics by Other Means: Law in the Struggle Against Apartheid, 1980–1994.* New York: Routledge, 1995, 27. This superb book contains a comprehensive account of these cases and, accordingly, we have drawn on its material.

15   Based on an interview with Komani by Zackie Achmat in his film *Law and Freedom*, 2005.

16   The hypocrisy of people like Koornhof, who personified the cruel lack of integrity of the entire National Party enterprise (Koornhof and Pik Botha,

Minister of Foreign Affairs, were the exemplars of this approach), is seen when one compares how he opposed the *Komani* judgment with the statement he had made to an American audience a year earlier: 'I detest the dompas. I declared war on the dompas. That thing must be ousted completely and totally out of my country and I have requested my officials to work on it.' – *Time*, 4 September 1987.

17   Richard Abel, *Politics by Other Means: Law in the Struggle Against Apartheid, 1980–1994*. New York: Routledge, 1995, 31.

18   Ibid.

19   Note from Paul Kennedy to Charles Nupen, 5 March 1983, LRC papers in the William Cullen Library, University of the Witwatersrand.

20   Page 21 of the typed judgment, LRC papers.

21   Cited by Richard Abel in *Politics by Other Means: Law in the Struggle Against Apartheid, 1980–1994*. New York: Routledge, 1995, 48.

22   The comment by Rikhotso appears, as does the explanation, in Stephen Ellmann, Law and legitimacy in South Africa, *Law and Social Inquiry*, 20, 2 (1995), 407, 443.

23   Rikhotso told Ellmann of his confidence that the court in Bloemfontein would uphold his case. See Stephen Ellmann, Law and legitimacy in South Africa, *Law and Social Inquiry*, 20, 2 (1995), 443.

24   Arthur Chaskalson, The right of black persons to seek employment and be employed in the Republic of South Africa, *Acta Juridica* (1984), 33, 40.

25   Richard Abel, *Politics by Other Means: Law in the Struggle Against Apartheid, 1980–1994*. New York: Routledge, 1995, 53.

26   Ibid., 54.

27   Ibid., 53.

28   *Hansard*, 10 August 1983, col. 10994.

29   Not that it should now be assumed that all white people have shrugged off this world view.

30   *Hansard*, 10 August 1983, col. 10988.

31   Fred Ferreira, cited by Steven Friedman in Stay off Rikhoto ruling, SA government warned, *Rand Daily Mail*, 7 June 1983.

32   *Hansard*, 10 August 1983, col. 10991.

33   Quoted by Richard Abel in *Politics by Other Means: Law in the Struggle Against Apartheid, 1980–1994*. New York: Routledge, 1995, 58.

34   *Black Affairs Administration Board, Western Cape, and Another v Mthiya* 1985 (4) SA 754 (A).

35   Harold Rudolph, *Annual Survey of South African Law*, 1985, 35.

36   Richard Abel, *Politics by Other Means: Law in the Struggle Against*

Apartheid, 1980–1994. New York: Routledge, 1995, 61.

37 In some ways, this makes the achievements of this litigation even more remarkable. Unlike with the Treatment Action Campaign litigation discussed later in the book, neither litigant could rely on civil-society pressure to push his case. The combination of the political and the legal was significantly absent in these cases. It was rather the lawyers Budlender and, in particular, Nupen, who refused to withdraw from the fight and bask in the glory of court victories. Their remarkable persistence in their dealings with a recalcitrant administration ensured that the orders granted by the Appeal Court would not simply be ignored in perpetuity.

38 See Stephen Ellmann, Law and legitimacy in South Africa, *Law and Social Inquiry*, 20, 2 (1995), which reflects the litigants' feeling of satisfaction against the odds.

39 Start weeding at the roots, *Financial Mail*, 1 February 1980.

40 Commission of Inquiry into Legislation Affecting the Utilisation of Manpower, RP32/1979 (the Riekert Report).

41 See GM Budlender and DM Davis, Labour law, influx control and citizenship: The emerging policy conflict, *Acta Juridica* (1984), 141. The government was also intent on using citizenship of the so-called independent homelands as a further means of control. Making black South Africans citizens of the homelands, deportation and the use of alien status were additional tools that were used to maintain a core and a periphery of workers.

42 For a comprehensive history of the United Democratic Front, see Jeremy Seekings, *The UDF: A History of the United Democratic Front in South Africa, 1983–1991.* David Philip and James Currey, 2000.

43 Richard Abel, *Politics by Other Means: Law in the Struggle Against Apartheid, 1980–1994.* New York: Routledge, 1995, 63.

44 In an interview with the author, Geoffrey Budlender spoke in awe of the way Chaskalson confronted and then swung in his direction a hitherto hostile court.

45 Riekert Commission at paras 4.204*(h)* and 4.280*(h)*(ii).

46 PJ van der Merwe, An analysis of the Report of the Commission of Inquiry into Legislation Affecting the Utilisation of Manpower, 1979, 45.

47 *Earthlife Africa, Johannesburg v Minister of Energy* [2017] 3 All SA 187 (WCC).

CHAPTER 6: Exposing detention without trial

1 Submission to the Truth and Reconciliation Commission by FW de Klerk, 14 May 1997.

Notes

2   The first state of emergency was declared on 25 July 1985 and lifted on 7 March 1986.

3   *Weekly Mail*, 13 June 1986.

4   Truth and Reconciliation Commission Report, vol 4, p 201, paras 12–14.

5   Mac Maharaj, describing his experience in detention while tortured by 'Rooi Rus' Swanepoel; see Padraig O'Malley *Shades of Difference: Mac Maharaj and the Struggle for South Africa*. Penguin, 2008, 124.

6   Ibid., para. 14.

7   UN Security Council Resolutions 417 and 418 of October and November 1977.

8   AS Mathews and RC Albino, The permanence of the temporary, *SALJ*, 83 (1966), 16, 23.

9   *Rossouw v Sachs* 1964 (2) SA 551 (A) at 564.

10 Section 6 of the Terrorism Act 83 of 1967. The 90-day detention clause was suspended on 30 November 1964, only to be replaced in 1965 by a more widely drawn provision, which authorised detention for 180 days. That, in turn, was replaced by the indefinite clause and Section 6 of the Terrorism Act.

11 AS Mathews, *Law, Order and Liberty in South Africa*. University of California Press, 1972, 176.

12 Breyten Breytenbach, *The True Confessions of an Albino Terrorist*. Harvest Books, 1984, 19.

13 Truth and Reconciliation Commission Report, vol 6, p 618.

14 Ibid, p 619.

15 Ibid.

16 Ibid, p 621.

17 *Die Burger*, 8 November 1985.

18 *Cape Times*, 24 September 1985.

19 *Cape Times*, 8 November 1985.

20 *Eastern Province Herald*, 7 June 1990.

21 South African Institute of Race Relations, Race relations survey, 1985. Johannesburg: SAIIR, 1986, 440–441, http://psimg.jstor.org/fsi/img/pdf/t0/10.5555/al.sff.document.boo19860000.042.000_final.pdf.

22 Court papers in authors' possession.

23 Ibid.

24 Ibid.

25 Ibid.

26 Ibid.

27 Ibid.

28 *Cape Times*, 26 September 1985.

29 *Eastern Province Herald*, 7 June 1990.

30 S Browde, The treatment of detainees, paper delivered at the National Medical and Dental Association national conference, 4 April 1987.

31 M Rayner, Turning a Blind Eye? Medical Accountability and the Prevention of Torture in South Africa. Washington, DC: American Association for the Advancement of Science, 1987.

32 Nicholas Haysom and Clive Plaskett, The war against law: Judicial activism and the Appellate Division, *SAJHR*, 4 (1988), 303.

33 Richard Abel, *Politics by Other Means: Law in the Struggle against Apartheid 1980–1994.* Routledge, 1995, 257.

34 See Mahmood Mandami, Beyond Nuremberg: The historical significance of post-apartheid transition in South Africa, in Karen Engle, Zina Miller and Dennis Davis (eds), *Anti-Impunity and the Human Rights Agenda*, Cambridge University Press, 2016.

35 The reopened inquest into the death of Ahmed Essop Timol (Case No IQ01/2017), para. 47.

36 Ibid., para 67.

37 Ibid.

38 Ibid., para 148.

39 Ibid., para 242.

40 Ibid., para 243.

41 Ibid., para 253.

42 This is a formulation of the concept of *dolus eventualis* that formed the basis of the conviction of Oscar Pistorius, on appeal, after the Supreme Court of Appeal had correctly found that the trial court had made a fundamental error in respect of this basic concept of criminal law – a mistake that Judge Mothle certainly did not make in his carefully considered judgment.

43 The reopened inquest into the death of Ahmed Essop Timol (Case No IQ01/2017), para 343.

CHAPTER 7: A bridge over our troubled waters?

1   We draw heavily on the most useful information and narrative set out on the Constitutional Court's own website, http://www.constitutionalcourt. org.za. See also the comprehensive account offered by Allister Sparks, *Tomorrow is Another Country: The Inside Story of South Africa's Road to Change.* University of Chicago Press, 1996.

2   See R Spitz and M Chaskalson, *The Politics of Transition: The Hidden*

History of South Africa's Negotiated Settlement. Bloomsbury Publishing, 2000.

3   From Hansard, private members' statements of Legislative Assembly of British Columbia, Member G Brewin, p 10209, 1994, Legislative Session: 3rd Session, 35th Parliament, Friday 22 April 1994 Morning Sitting vol. 14 no. 13. The full story is to be found in Allister Sparks, *Tomorrow is Another Country: The Inside Story of South Africa's Road to Change.* University of Chicago Press, 1996.

4   Chiara Carter, Is the TRC threatening to become a cold case?, Independent Online, 8 April 2006, https://www.iol.co.za/news/politics/is-the-trc-threatening-to-become-a-cold-case-273350.

5   EA Christodoulidis, Truth and reconciliation as risks, *Social and Legal Studies*, 9 (2000), 179–201, cited in K van Marle, Law's time, particularity and slowness, *SAJHR*, 19 (2003), 245.

6   D Posel and G Simpson (eds), *Commissioning the Past: Understanding South Africa's Truth and Reconciliation Commission.* Wits University Press, 2002, 168.

7   E de Kock and J Gordin, *A Long Night's Damage: Working for the Apartheid State*, Contra, 1998, 249.

8   Ibid., 250.

9   Ibid., 251.

10 Ibid., 252.

11 Pumla Gobodo-Madikizela, *A Human Being Died That Night: A South African Woman Confronts the Legacy of Apartheid.* Mariner Books, 2004, 61.

12 Chiara Carter, Is the TRC threatening to become a cold case? Independent Online, 8 April 2006, https://www.iol.co.za/news/politics/is-the-trc-threatening-to-become-a-cold-case-273350. The remainder consisted of 556 members of the former liberation movement, and 56 AWB members also received amnesty.

13 E de Kock and J Gordin, *A Long Night's Damage: Working for the Apartheid State*, Contra, 1998, 274–275.

14 South West African People's Organisation.

15 M Burger and C Gould, *Secrets and Lies: Wouter Basson and South Africa's Chemical and Biological Warfare Programme*, Zebra Press, 2002, 191.

16 Ibid., 191.

17 Ibid., 192.

18 Ibid., 191.

19 This perception increased over the next decade, with many ordinary citizens, as is evidenced by reaction to newspapers and radio talk shows,

complaining about the law's bias some 15 years into non-racial democracy.

20 M Burger and C Gould, *Secrets and Lies: Wouter Basson and South Africa's Chemical and Biological Warfare Programme*, 2002, 218–219.

21 Ibid., 188.

22 1996 (8) BCLR 1015 (CC).

23 Ibid., para. 17.

24 Ibid., para. 9.

25 Ibid., para. 17.

26 See, in this regard, Kader Asmal, Louise Asmal and Ronald Suresh Roberts, *Reconciliation Through Justice: A Reckoning of Apartheid's Criminal Governance* (2nd ed.). St Martin's Press, 1997.

27 1996 (8) BCLR 1015 (CC), at para. 19.

28 Louis Luyt, *Walking Proud: The Louis Luyt Autobiography*. Don Nelson, 2003, 267, 299.

29 The Administration of Justice, *1999 Annual Survey of South African Law*, 779.

30 Ibid., citing RW Johnson in the *London Review of Books*, 21, 19, 30 September 1999.

31 Steven Friedman, *Business Day*, 17 May 1999.

32 The Administration of Justice, *1999 Annual Survey of South African Law*, 781, 32.

33 1999 (4) SA 147 (CC) paras 15–21.

34 Ibid., para 97.

35 Louis Luyt, *Walking Proud: The Louis Luyt Autobiography*. Don Nelson, 2003, 309.

36 Ibid.

37 James L Gibson, *Overcoming Apartheid: Can Truth Reconcile a Divided Nation?* Russell Sage Foundation, 2004, 304.

38 Defending democracy, *Sunday Tribune*, 23 September 1999.

CHAPTER 8: A break with the past, a view of the future

1 Pierre de Vos, No, the death penalty is not a deterrent and should not be re-introduced, Constitutionally Speaking, 23 November 2016, https://constitutionallyspeaking.co.za/no-the-death-penalty-is-not-a-deterrent-and-should-not-be-re-introduced/.

2 South African television coverage reproduced by Zackie Achmat, *Law and Freedom*, 2005.

3 Authors' interview with Wim Trengove and Gilbert Marcus, July 2006.

4 Makwanyane and Mchunu were released on parole after serving 22 and

23 years apiece. See The men they could not hang, *Pretoria News*, 29 June 2013, https://www.pressreader.com/south-africa/pretoria-news-weekend/20130629/282102044252554.

5 *Weekly Mail*, 17–23 February 1995.

6 Authors' interview with Sydney Kentridge, February 2008.

7 Speech by President Nelson Mandela at the inauguration of the Constitutional Court, Johannesburg, 14 February 1995, https://www.sahistory.org.za/archive/speech-president-nelson-mandela-inauguration-constitutional-court-johannesburg-14-february-1.

8 This section draws from Sadakat Kadri, *The Trial: A History, from Socrates to O.J. Simpson*. Random House, 2005.

9 https://www.amnesty.org/en/latest/news/2018/04/death-penalty-facts-and-figures-2017/

10 For a detailed discussion of the applicable studies and the evidence against the deterrent argument, see Jeffrey Fagan, Death and deterrence redux: Science, law and causal reasoning on capital punishment, *Ohio Journal of Criminal Law*, 4 (2006), 255; John Donahue and Justin Wolfers, The use and abuse of empirical evidence in the death penalty debate, *Stanford Law Review*, 5 (2005), 791. See also heads of argument in *Makwanyane* at 57 *et seq*.

11 It seems that the greatest deterrents to criminal activity are, arguably, both increasing the likelihood that a criminal will be apprehended and successfully prosecuted by the police and justice system, and addressing the socio-economic sources of crime.

12 CBS News, 12 June 2000. See also Hugo Bedau (ed.), *The Death Penalty in America: Current Controversies*. Oxford University Press, 1997.

13 Appellants' Heads of Argument at 29 n74 Kahn 'The Death Penalty in SA' (1970) 33 *THRHR* 108, 109.

14 Heads at 29 n75 and n76; Kahn 'The Death Penalty in SA' (1970) 33 *THRHR* 108, 109–111; George Devenish, The historical and jurisprudential evolution and background to the application of the death penalty in South Africa and its relationship with constitutional and political reform, *SACJ*, 1, 7 (1992).

15 Ibid., Heads at 30 n78 and n79.

16 Ibid., Heads at 30–31 n81–n85.

17 Ibid., Heads at 44; B van Niekerk, Hanged by the neck until you are dead, *SALJ*, 86 (1969), 457 and *SALJ*, 87 (1970), 60.

18 Statistics from *Journal of Criminal Justice*, 1989, 251–253.

19 Heads at 31 n74 Kahn 'The Death Penalty in SA' (1970) 33 *THRHR* 108, 109.

20 See, for example, L Angus and E Grant, Sentencing in capital cases in the Transvaal Provincial Division and Witwatersrand Local Division: 1987–1989, *SAJHR*, 50 (1991), 69.

21 Ibid.

22 Ibid., 229 and 230.

23 1988 (1) SA 868 (A).

24 CR Snyman, *Criminal Law* fourth ed. Butterworths, 2005, 260.

25 There were two Stoffel van der Merwes in the cabinet, one referred to as 'Slim' Stoffel and the other as 'Dom' Stoffel (the Minister of Home Affairs).

26 *Pretoria News*, 17 March 1988.

27 Peter Parker and Joyce Mokhesi-Parker, *In the Shadow of Sharpeville: Apartheid and Criminal Justice*. NYU Press, 1998.

28 E Mureinik, From moratorium to reprieve, *SAJHR*, 6 (1990), vii.

29 Ibid., ix.

30 To paraphrase Mureinik, From moratorium to reprieve, *SAJHR*, 6 (1990), x.

31 *S v Makwanyane and Another* 1995 (6) BCLR 665 (CC), at para 27.

32 Helen Grange, A matter of life and death, *Cape Argus*, 17 February 1995.

33 Brendan Seery, It could be the OJ trial without the blood, *Weekend Argus*, 18–19 February 1995.

34 *Annual Survey of SA Law*, 1994, 721–726.

35 Ibid.

36 1995 (6) BCLR 665 (CC), at paras 87–89.

37 Authors' interview with Zackie Achmat, 2005.

38 1995 (6) BCLR 665 (CC), at para 377.

39 Ibid., para 376.

40 Ibid., para 382.

41 *Cape Times*, 8 June 1995.

42 *Cape Argus*, 9 June 1995.

43 Ibid.

44 Roger Friedman, Their lives hang by a thread on death row, *Weekend Argus*, 18–19 February 1995.

45 Ibid.

46 Brian Stuart, Give clemency to all on death row, *The Citizen*, 17 February 1995.

CHAPTER 9: Activism, denialism, socio-economic rights (and beetroot)

Notes

In this chapter, the authors are heavily indebted to Nicoli Nattrass's comprehensive, exhaustively researched and referenced work *Mortal Combat* for the historical and empirical facts surrounding the HIV/AIDS epidemic in South Africa and the government's response to it. (See Nicoli Nattrass, *Mortal Combat: AIDS Denialism and the Struggle for Antiretrovirals in South Africa*, University of KwaZulu-Natal Press, 2007.)

1   Etienne Mureinik, Beyond a charter of luxuries: Economic rights in the Constitution, *SAJHR*, 8, 4 (1992), 464–474.

2   Ibid., 472.

3   This section draws from Letter to South Africa's President Thabo Mbeki – Expression of concern by HIV scientists, 4 September 2006, https://www. aidstruth.org/letter-to-mbeki.php.

4   Nicoli Nattrass, *Mortal Combat: AIDS Denialism and the Struggle for Antiretrovirals in South Africa*, University of KwaZulu-Natal Press, 2007, 38–39.

5   Ibid., 9.

6   Ibid., 40.

7   Ibid.

8   Xolela Mangcu *To the Brink: The State of Democracy in South Africa*, University of KwaZulu-Natal Press, 2008, 50.

9   Hein Marais, *AIDS review 2000*, Centre for the Study of AIDS, University of Pretoria, 2000.

10   Sarah Boseley, How Nelson Mandela changed the Aids agenda in South Africa, *The Guardian*, 6 December 2013, https://www.theguardian. com/world/2013/dec/06/nelson-mandela-aids-south-africa.

11   Nicoli Nattrass, *Mortal Combat: AIDS Denialism and the Struggle for Antiretrovirals in South Africa*, University of KwaZulu-Natal Press, 2007, 40–41.

12   Ibid., 41–44.

13   Ibid., 44–60.

14   The terms 'MTCTP' and 'MTCT' are used widely in the relevant literature.

15   The term 'denialist' in the context of AIDS was coined by the TAC and is used here to show the powerful way in which the organisation characterised the government's policies and the way in which this framed the MTCTP issue.

16 TAC, Mbeki shows no remorse for role in AIDS deaths, 8 March 2016, https://tac.org.za/news/mbeki-shows-no-remorse-for-role-in-aids-deaths/.

17 Xolela Mangcu *To the Brink: The State of Democracy in South Africa*, University of KwaZulu-Natal Press, 2008, 56.

18 Ibid.

19 Ibid.

20 Nicoli Nattrass, *Mortal Combat: AIDS Denialism and the Struggle for Antiretrovirals in South Africa*, University of KwaZulu-Natal Press, 2007, 75.

21 Ibid., 107, 113.

22 Ibid., 88.

23 Xolela Mangcu *To the Brink: The State of Democracy in South Africa*, University of KwaZulu-Natal Press, 2008, 57.

24 Global Policy Forum, Letter to South Africa's president Thabo Mbeki, 4 September 2006, https://www.globalpolicy.org/component/content/article/211/44977.html.

25 UN envoy Stephen Lewis decries gender inequality in closing session of the International Aids Conference, AllAfrica, 16 August 2006, https://allafrica.com/stories/200608190001.html.

26 Xolela Mangcu *To the Brink: The State of Democracy in South Africa*, University of KwaZulu-Natal Press, 2008, 62.

27 Authors' interview with Zackie Achmat, 11 December 2007.

28 See TAC, https://tac.org.za/?s=MTCT+guide.

29 Ibid.

30 M Heywood, Preventing mother-to-child HIV transmission in South Africa: Background, strategies and outcomes of the TAC case against the Minister of Health, *SAJHR*, 19, 2003, 278–315.

31 Ibid., 281.

32 Ibid., 281–285.

33 Ibid., 284.

34 Ibid., 285.

35 Ibid., 286.

36 Ibid., 286–289.

37 Ibid., 292.

38 Dr A Ntsaluba, answering affidavit 658, 665, 705, 816; M Heywood, Preventing mother-to-child HIV transmission in South Africa: Background, strategies and outcomes of the TAC case against the Minister of Health, *SAJHR*, 19, 2003, 296.

39 See South African Constitution, Chapter 2: Bill of Rights, http://www.justice.gov.za/legislation/constitution/SAConstitution-web-eng-02.pdf.

40 M Heywood, Preventing mother-to-child HIV transmission in South Africa: Background, strategies and outcomes of the TAC case against the Minister of Health, *SAJHR*, 19, 2003, 297.

41 Ibid., 299–300.

42 HRC 'has nothing new to add', *Mail & Guardian*, 23 November 2001.

43 M Heywood, Preventing mother-to-child HIV transmission in South Africa: Background, strategies and outcomes of the TAC case against the Minister of Health, *SAJHR*, 19, 2003, 300–301.

44 Thanks to our Constitution, *Sunday Times*, 16 December 2001; M Heywood, Preventing mother-to-child HIV transmission in South Africa: Background, strategies and outcomes of the TAC case against the Minister of Health, *SAJHR*, 19, 2003, 301.

45 See K Hopkins, Shattering the divide – when judges go too far, *De Rebus*, March 2002, 23–26.

46 Ibid., 23–24.

47 Address by Premier Shilowa at opening of Gauteng provincial legislature, http://www.gpg.gov.za/docs/sp/2002/sp0218.html); M Heywood, Preventing mother-to-child HIV transmission in South Africa: Background, strategies and outcomes of the TAC case against the Minister of Health, *SAJHR*, 19, 2003, 303.

48 Newshour, SABC, 10 February 2002; M Heywood, Preventing mother-to-child HIV transmission in South Africa: Background, strategies and outcomes of the TAC case against the Minister of Health, *SAJHR*, 19, 2003, 303.

49 M Heywood, Preventing mother-to-child HIV transmission in South Africa: Background, strategies and outcomes of the TAC case against the Minister of Health, *SAJHR*, 19, 2003, 304.

50 *TAC v Minister of Health* TPD Case No 21182/2001 (8 March 2002) 12–13; M Heywood, Preventing mother-to-child HIV transmission in South Africa: Background, strategies and outcomes of the TAC case against the Minister of Health, *SAJHR*, 19, 2003, 305.

51 M Heywood, Preventing mother-to-child HIV transmission in South Africa: Background, strategies and outcomes of the TAC case against the Minister of Health, *SAJHR*, 19, 2003, 306–307.

52 Ibid., 307.

53 Published in *The Star*, 5 April 2002; M Heywood, Preventing mother-to-child HIV transmission in South Africa: Background, strategies and outcomes of the TAC case against the Minister of Health, *SAJHR*, 19, 2003, 307.

54 More damage control after Manto says No, *The Star*, 25 March 2002.

55 Ministry of Health, media statement, 27 March 2002; M Heywood,

Preventing mother-to-child HIV transmission in South Africa: Background, strategies and outcomes of the TAC case against the Minister of Health, *SAJHR*, 19, 2003, 309–310.

56 1998 (12) BCLR 1696 (CC).

57 2000 (11) BCLR 1169 (CC).

58 *Minister of Health and Others v Treatment Action Campaign and Others* (No 2) 2002 (5) SA 721 at para 94.

59 Ibid., para 38.

60 Ibid., para 129.

61 M Heywood, Preventing mother-to-child HIV transmission in South Africa: Background, strategies and outcomes of the TAC case against the Minister of Health, *SAJHR*, 19, 2003, 315.

62 2002 (5) SA 721, para 118.

63 Ibid., para 99.

64 G Budlender, A paper dog with real teeth, *Mail & Guardian*, 12 July 2002; M Heywood, Preventing mother-to-child HIV transmission in South Africa: Background, strategies and outcomes of the TAC case against the Minister of Health, *SAJHR*, 19, 2003, 314.

CHAPTER 10: A special relationship

1 For this chapter, the authors are indebted to Alix Carmichele's attorney, Perino Pama, whose copious notes and file on the *Carmichele* case provided invaluable, comprehensive material, including statements and testimony excerpts. This enabled us to reconstruct events underlying the litigation. Accordingly, except where otherwise indicated, this chapter uses Pama's materials as its factual basis.

2 Darkness and light and dreams worth having, *Business Day*, 5 October 2007.

3 *Carmichele v Minister of Safety and Security and Another* 2001 (10) BCLR 995 (CC) at para 18.

4 Ibid., para 21.

5 Ibid., para 22.

6 Statement from court papers made available by attorney Perino Pama.

7 The authors have been unable to locate the actual article published in *Fair Lady* in which this quotation appears, but obtained a version of it from Perino Pama. The authors would welcome any information about the original source.

8 Similarly, the authors obtained this quotation from Pama, quoting, in turn, a *Fair Lady* article.

9   Evidence of Ms Annie Coetzee sourced in court record made available by Pama.

10   Authors' interview with Pama, 12 January 2008.

11   *Carmichele v Minister of Safety and Security and Another* 2001 (1) SA 489 (SCA) at paras 5 and 17.

12   Authors' interview with Pama, 12 January 2008.

13   From court record made available by Pama.

14   *Carmichele v Minister of Safety and Security and Another* 2001 (10) BCLR 995 (CC) at para 32.

15   Authors' interview with Wim Trengove SC, 12 December 2007.

16   MAS stands for *misdaad-administrasiestelsel* – crime administration system. Each case reported is registered in the system with a CAS (MAS) number.

17   Court record made available by Pama.

18   Cited by Carmel Rickard, *Sunday Times*, 7 November 2003.

19   Ibid.

20   Ibid.

21   Translation: 'He said over and over that she must screw him.' The correct reading was, 'He said over and over that she must turn over'.

22   Carmel Rickard, *Sunday Times*, 7 November 2003.

23   Marianne Merton, Missing stats in SAPS annual report raises questions about the functioning and capability of the criminal justice system, *Daily Maverick*, 14 August 2018.

24   2002 (132) SA 346 (SCA) at paras 1–2.

25   2005 (60) SA 419 (CC)

26   Constitutional Court, media summary issued 13 June 2005.

27   Ibid.

CHAPTER 11: Gay marriage: From possibility to reality

1   Cameron JA in *Fourie and Another v Minister of Home Affairs and Others* 2005 (SA) 429 (SCA), at para 9.

2   *Ebrahim v Essop* 1905 TS 59 at 61.

3   Pierre de Vos, The 'inevitability' of same-sex marriage in South Africa's post-apartheid state, Constitutionally Speaking, 2015, https://constitutionallyspeaking.co.za/wp-content/uploads/2015/11/The-Inevitability-of-Same-sex-marriage.pdf.

4   *National Coalition for Gay and Lesbian Equality and Others v Minister of Home Affairs and Others* (CCT10/99) [1999] ZACC 17; 2000 (2) SA 1; 2000 (1) BCLR 39 (2 December 1999), at para 54.

5   *Minister of Home Affairs and Another v Fourie and Another* (CCT 60/04)

[2005] ZACC 19; 2006 (3) BCLR 355 (CC); 2006 (1) SA 524 (CC) (1 December 2005), at paras 1–3.

6   Ibid.

7   *Fourie v Minister of Home Affairs* (SCA), at para 25.

8   *Minister of Home Affairs and Another v Fourie and Another* (CC), at para 138–139.

9   *Fourie v Minister of Home Affairs* (SCA), at para 18.

10 Ellen Ann Andersen, *Out of the Closets and Into the Courts: Legal Opportunity, Structure and Gay Rights Litigation.* University of Michigan Press, 2006.

11 135 S. Ct 2584.

12 *Obergefell v Hodges NO* 14-556 slip decision at 16–17.

13 *Obergefell v Hodges NO* slip opinion 1–2.

14 Ibid., slip at 5.

15 Cited in *The Wall Street Journal*, September 2015.

16 The acronym for lesbian, gay, bisexual, transgender, 'queer or questioning' and intersex.

CHAPTER 12: The great escape

1   *Minister of Justice v SALC* 2016 (3) SA 317 (SCA), at para 103.

2   *Foreign Affairs* 72, 1993.

3   Barbara Hogan, as cited in Danny Titus, Human rights in foreign policy and practice: The South African case considered, SAIIA Occasional Paper 52, November 2009.

4   *The Washington Post*, 11 April 2007; BBC News, 23 February 2010; see also Gwen P Barnes, The international court's ineffective enforcement mechanisms: The indictment of President Omar al-Bashir, *Fordham International Law Journal*, 34 (2011), 1580.

5   *Minister of Justice and others v Southern African Litigation Centre* 2016 (3) SA 317 (SCA), at para 7.

6   News24, 1 July 2015.

7   South Africa Investing, July 2015.

8   Legal brief, 1 August 2015.

9   *Carte Blanche*, 22 June 2015.

10 Parliament, 24 June 2015.

11 *Southern Africa Litigation Centre v Minister of Justice and Constitutional Development and Others* 2015 (5) SA 1 (TP) at para 16.

12 Diplomatic Immunities and Privileges Act 37 of 2001.

13 *Southern Africa Litigation Centre v Minister of Justice and Constitutional*

Development 2015 (5) SA 1 (GP) at para. 21.

14 Lauren Kohn, The Bashir judgment raises the red flag for the rule of law and the judiciary, *SALJ*, 133, 246 (2016): 252.

15 2015 (5) SA 1 (GP) at para 28.

16 Ibid., paras 37–38.

17 *Minister of Justice and Constitutional Development v Southern African Litigation Centre* 2016 (3) SA 317 (SCA) at paras 102–103.

18 Ibid., para 103.

19 All of these references are sourced in Stephen Grootes, When judges of the land said 'Enough!' to the ANC, *Daily Maverick*, 8 July 2015.

20 Ibid.

21 *Business Day*, 28 August 2015.

22 Natasha Marrian, *Business Day*, 28 August 2015.

23 Zak M Yacoob, cited by Lauren Kohn, The Bashir judgment raises the red flag for the rule of law and the judiciary, *SALJ*, 133, 246 (2016): 256–257.

24 1995 (4) SA 877 CC.

25 See Cora Hoexter and Morné Olivier, *The Judiciary in South Africa*. Cape Town: Juta, 2014, 361.

26 *Mail & Guardian*, 21 October 2016.

27 ENCA TV News, 21 October 2016.

28 Department of International Relations and Cooperation, South Africa's withdrawal from the Rome Statute of the International Criminal Court, http://www.dirco.gov.za/milan_italy/newsandevents/rome_statute.pdf.

29 Cited in para 4 of the judgment in *Democratic Alliance v Minister of International Relations and Cooperation* (Case No 83142/2016).

30 Ibid., para 52.

31 Ibid., para 77.

32 As cited in *Daily Maverick*, 8 March 2017.

33 Ibid., para 81.

34 ANC, International relations: ANC Discussion Document 2017, 12 March 2017, see https://www.politicsweb.co.za/documents/international-relations-anc-discussion-document-20.

35 Alexander Bickel, *The Least Dangerous Branch: The Supreme Court at the Bar of Politics*. Yale University Press, 1962.

CHAPTER 13: 'State capture' (noun)

1 Constitution of the Republic of South Africa, Section 55 (Powers of National Assembly), http://www.justice.gov.za/legislation/constitution/

SAConstitution-web-eng.pdf.

2   Ibid., Section 179.

3   Ibid., Section 182.

4   *Mail & Guardian,* 30 October 2009.

5   *Mail & Guardian,* 21 September 2006.

6   National Treasury, Republic of South Africa, Budget review 2018, Chapter 4, http://www.treasury.gov.za/documents/national%20budget/2018/review/FullBR.pdf.

7   Jacques Pauw, *The President's Keepers: Those Keeping Zuma in Power and Out of Prison.* Tafelberg, 2017.

8   Ibid.

9   Ibid.

10 Jan Gerber, Spy tapes: How the saga unfolded over the years, News24, 16 March 2018, https://www.news24.com/SouthAfrica/News/spy-tapes-how-the-saga-unfolded-over-the-years-20180316.

11 TS Eliot, *Four Quartets,* 'Little Gidding', 1942.

12 *Zuma v Democratic Alliance and Others* 2018 (1) SA 200 (SCA) 146 at paras 3–4.

13 Ibid., para 80.

14 Ibid., para 84.

15 Ibid., para 92.

16 Cited by Mogoeng C J in *Economic Freedom Fighters v Speaker of the National Assembly and Others* 2016 (3) SA 580 (CC) at para 1.

17 *Sowetan,* 28 May 2015.

18 Ibid.

19 Mail & Guardian, 31 March 2014.

20 Ibid.

21 Ibid.

22 Ibid.

23 Ibid.

24 Greg Nicolson, Nkandla, the reckoning: Zuma's skin-saving volte-face, *Daily Maverick,* 10 February 2016, https://www.dailymaverick.co.za/article/2016-02-10-nkandla-the-reckoning-zumas-skin-saving-volte-face/.

25 Mail & Guardian, 8 September 2014.

26 Daily Maverick, 9 September 2014.

27 ENCA.com 26 September 2016.

28 *Newsweek,* 28 September 2016.

29 *Business Day,* 27 September 2016.

30 2016 (3) SA 580 (CC) at para 50.

31 Ibid., para 52.

32 Ibid., para 75.

33 Ibid., para 99.

34 Ibid., paras 103–104.

35 Public Protector of South Africa, *Secure in comfort: Report on an investigation into allegations of impropriety and unethical conduct relating to the installation and implementation of security measures by the Department of Public Works at and in respect of the private residence of President Jacob Zuma at Nkandla in the KwaZulu-Natal province*, paras 10.3.2–10.3.3, https://cdn.24.co.za/files/Cms/ General/d/2718/00b91b2841d64510b9c99ef9b9faa597.pdf.

36 Ibid., para 11.1.1.

37 2016 (3) SA 580 (CC) at para 105. See part 5 of the order.

38 We are indebted for this point to retired Constitutional Court Justice Johann Kriegler.

39 *United Democratic Movement v Speaker of the National Assembly* 2017 (5) SA 300 (CC) at para 43.

40 Ibid., para 84.

41 Constitution of the Republic of South Africa, Section 89 (Removal of President), http://www.justice.gov.za/legislation/constitution/ SAConstitution-web-eng.pdf.

42 *Economic Freedom Fighters v Speaker of the National Assembly* 2018 (2) SA 571 (CC) at para 39.

43 Ibid., para 176 et seq.

44 Ibid., para 180.

45 Ibid., para 182.

46 Ibid., para 223.

47 Ibid., para 224.

48 Ibid., para 236.

49 Ibid., para 279–282.

50 Roger Southall, Lessons from South Africa: Parliamentary conscience and the courage to rebel, The Conversation, 9 August 2017, http://theconversation.com/lessons-from-south-africa-parliamentary-conscience-and-the-courage-to-rebel-82280.

CHAPTER 14: Conclusion: Precedent and possibility

1 *K v Minister of Safety and Security* 2005(6)SA 419(CC) at para 16.

2 LM Thompson and J Butler, *Change in Contemporary South Africa.* Berkeley, 1975, 184.

3   See, for example, Greg Marinovich, *Murder at the Small Koppie: The Real Story of the Marikana Massacre*. Penguin Random House, 2016.

4   See, for example, Tembeka Ngcukaitobi, Land reform needs laws and imagination, *Mail & Guardian*, 21 September 2018.

5   Max du Plessis, Between apology and utopia – the Constitutional Court and Public Opinion, *SAJHR*, 18 (2002), 39.

6   For a sustained example of constitutional denigration, see Joel Modiri, The time and space of critical legal pedagogy, *Stellenbosch Law Review*, 27, 3 (2016), 507–534.

7   *Daniels v Scribante* 2017 (4) SA 341 (CC) at para 14.

8   Ibid., para 23.

9   Ibid., para 115.

10 Peg Birmingham, *Hannah Arendt and Human Rights: The Predicament of Common Responsibility*. Indiana University Press, 2006.

11 How South Africa is being stolen, *City Press* and *The Sunday Times*, 21 May 2017.

ACKNOWLEDGEMENTS

During the period in which this book was produced, we have benefited from many people's extremely generous assistance. As indicated in a note to the text, the first part of this book draws heavily on an earlier work that we co-authored. Accordingly, for those chapters we wish to record our gratitude to the late Chief Justice Arthur Chaskalson, Justice Richard Goldstone, Justice Edwin Cameron, Sir Sydney Kentridge QC, advocates George Bizos SC, Gilbert Marcus SC, Marumo Moerane SC, Wim Trengove SC, Anton Ackermann SC and Geoff Budlender SC, as well to Zackie Achmat, Alix Carmichele, the late Professor Denis Cowen, professors Halton Cheadle, Neville Ruben and Nicholas Haysom, and to Perino Pama, Justine White, Leon Levy and the late Ahmed Kathrada. We are also grateful to Tom Rikhotso and Professor Steven Ellman for generously affording us access to an interview that Professor Ellman conducted with Mr Rikhotso, and to Veli Komani in respect of a video interview to which we had access facilitated by Zackie Achmat.

In numerous chapters we have relied on newspaper articles, op-ed pieces, journal papers and books written by a range of individuals, hopefully all credited in the endnotes, many of which would have been inaccessible to us had it not been for the kindness of Herschel Miller of the National Library in Cape Town and Michele Pickover at the William Cullen Library, Wits University Archives. Special thanks to Rowena Bihl,

Dennis's registrar, who had the unenviable job of ensuring that Dennis's contributions were typed and formatted correctly.

The entire text has been meticulously edited by Mark Ronan. We are indebted to him for his diligence and stoicism in ensuring that the text was written in the most accessible and coherent manner possible. A huge thank you goes to Jeremy Boraine of Jonathan Ball Publishers for the tolerance and patience that he exhibited over a number of years, during which we failed to comply with his extremely reasonable deadlines. His encouragement and the further efforts of the team at Jonathan Ball Publishers have ensured the publication of this work.

We are privileged and indebted to Minister Pravin Gordhan, one of the true custodians of the constitutional vision, for penning the foreword.

To our respective partners, Timothy and Claudette, our families and friends, and the armies of waiters, baristas and barmen who ensured endless hours of productive discussion and debate during the decade taken to draft this book. Simply put, we could not have done it without you.

Michelle Le Roux
Dennis Davis

INDEX

A

Abel, Rick 106, 110, 115, 141
Abrahams, Shaun 10, 94–95, 270, 274, 278
absolution from the instance 225, 229–230
accountability 2, 7–8, 19, 36, 41, 295,
  306–307
Achmat, Zackie 201–202
Ackermann, Anton 159–160, 162
Ackermann, Laurie 29, 185, 228, 241, 263
adjudication, models of 31–32
adoption 241
Advocates for Transformation 10
African National Congress (ANC)
  Al-Bashir case 12, 258
  elective conferences 5, 277, 278
  ICC 265–266
  judiciary 7, 13, 63–64, 293, 297
  Nkandla case 281
  Rivonia trial 35, 66–69, 76, 78–85, 93
  SARFU case 169
  Scorpions 8, 272
  transformation 16
  transition from apartheid to democracy
    148–150, 152–154
  Treason Trial 80
African regional court 264
African Union (AU) 254, 255
African vernacular (customary) law 17–18,
  191–192

Afrikaner Weerstandsbeweging (AWB)
  152, 153
Aggett, Neil 129
AIDS Law Project 202
Al-Bashir, Omar 12–13, 250–253, 274
Al-Bashir case
  Al-Bashir's visit to South Africa
    250–251
  foreign policy and 248–250
  in High Court 251–253, 255–257
  ICC and 250, 255, 258, 260–266
  reactions to 253–255, 258–261
  significance of 12–13, 40–41, 264–266
  in Supreme Court of Appeal 257–258
Albertyn, CH 89–90, 93
Albertyn, PK 54
Albino, RCL 124
amaBhungane 306
amnesty 38, 156, 159–160, 164–166
ANC *see* African National Congress
Angus, L 180
answering affidavits 136–137
antiretroviral (ARV) drugs *see* TAC case
apartheid 16, 18–19, 22–26, 30–32,
  179–183, 299–300
Apleni, Mkuseli 252–253
Appeal Court 34, 50–51, 105
Appellate Division 31–32, 34, 55–57, 61,
  141, 182

339

Appellate Division Quorum Act 55–57
arms deal scandal 273, 275, 277–280
arms of government 2
ARVs *see* TAC case
assessors 161
Athlone Advice Office 100
atrocities *see* torture
AU *see* African Union
Auditor-General 2–3, 155
AWB *see* Afrikaner Weerstandsbeweging
AZAPO (*Azanian People's Organisation*)
  case 38, 148, 163–166

B
Baartman, Elizabeth 118
Bantu (Urban Areas) Consolidation Act
  100–101, 104–107, 112
Baqwa, Selby 271
Bashir, Omar al- *see* Al-Bashir, Omar
Basson, Adriaan 6
Basson, Wouter (*Basson* case) 156–158,
  160–163, 299
Batohi, Shamila 9
BBC 198
Bell Pottinger 16, 307
Bernstein, Hilda 70–71, 78–79, 80
Bernstein, Lionel 'Rusty' 67, 70, 74, 85
Beyers, Andrew 44, 49–50, 53–54
bias 37, 162, 168–172, 179
Bickel, Alexander 33, 266
Biko, Steve, death in detention 123,
  131–132
Biko family 38, 148, 163–166
Bill of Rights 3, 17, 27, 40, 186, 205,
  228–229
Bisho massacre 151
Bizos, George 70, 90–91, 185, 187–189,
  193
Black Lawyers' Association 186
Black Sash 100, 114
Bloomberg, Abe 48, 50
Bogopane-Zulu, Hendrietta 282
Boipatong massacre 150
Bonthuys, Cecilia Johanna 242
Booysen, Johan 270
Bophuthatswana 149, 153
Boswell, James 176
Botha, Chris 206–207, 214

Botha, DH 54
Botha, PW 27, 93, 148
bowls 58–59
Bozalek, Lee 118
Breitenbach, Andrew 226–228
Breytenbach, Breyten 125–126
bridge metaphor 30–33, 37, 149, 155, 164,
  166, 195, 306–307
Brink, Judge 57, 60
Britain 36, 176
Broome, Francis 91
Budlender, Geoffrey 35–36, 100–103, 105,
  204, 215
Burger, Die 76–77, 127
Burger, M 162
Burgers, Carol 216, 221
Bush, George W 245
Buthelezi, Mangosuthu 152–153
Butler, Rab 92

C
cabinet reshuffle, March 2017 1, 274
CALS *see* Centre for Applied Legal Studies
Cameron, Edwin 8–9, 39, 56, 198, 239,
  240, 242–243, 304
Canada 150–151
Cape Nguni 191–192
Cape Times 48, 127, 128, 138–139
capital punishment *see* death penalty
Carmichele, Alix 40, 216, 220–228,
  234–235
Carmichele case
  attack on Alix Carmichele 216, 220–222
  background of Francois Coetzee
    216–220, 222
  compensation claim 234–235
  in Constitutional Court 228–229
  in High Court 222–226, 229–232
  impact of 235–238, 298
  in Supreme Court of Appeal 226–228,
    232–234
Carte Blanche 254
CASAC *see* Council for the Advancement of
  the South African Constitution
Centlivres, Albert 49–51, 53–54, 56–57, 59,
  60, 61–62
Centre for Applied Legal Studies (CALS)
  28–29, 228

Chapter 9 institutions 2–3, 7–8, 293
Chaskalson, Arthur
    death penalty 174–175, 186, 190
    Komani case 36, 100–105, 115, 116
    Legal Resource Centre 35–36
    Mthiya case 113
    Rikhoto case 36, 107, 109–110, 116
    Rivonia trial 70, 72, 86, 88
    SARFU case 168, 170
    TAC case 208
Cheadle, Halton 122–123, 129–134, 137, 140
Chetty, Dayalin 223, 225, 226, 231–232
Chief Justice, position of 13, 64–65
Chikane, Frank 157, 160
China 118, 249
Christodoulidis, EA 157
Cilliers, Jaap 160
civil society 5, 33
Civil Union Act 246
Claassen, Beverley 217–218, 219
Cleaver, Roger 234
Clingman, Stephen 73–74
CODESA *see* Convention for a Democratic South Africa
Coertze, Ignatius 48
Coetsee, Kobie 179, 240
Coetzee, Annie 217, 219, 224, 230–231
Coetzee, Francois 216–227, 230–232, 234
    see *also Carmichele* case
Collins, William David 47, 53, 59
Collins case 34, 55–62
Coloured vote cases
    background to 46–48
    Collins case 34, 55–62
    Harris cases 32–33, 43–45, 47, 48–56, 58, 59–60, 61, 111
    lessons from 63–65
Columbia University 178
Comaroff, Jean and John 1, 4–5
Commission for Gender Equality 2–3
Commission for the Promotion and Protection of the Rights of Cultural, Religious and Linguistic Communities 2–3
Commissioning the Past 157–158
commissions of inquiry 6, 37, 166–172, 295–296

common law 28, 29, 31, 34, 102–103, 105, 228
common purpose, legal doctrine of 38, 181
communism 36, 92–93
Communist Party *see* South African Communist Party
comparative law 190
Conference for a Democratic Future 148
Congress of South African Trade Unions (COSATU) 150, 154
Conservative Party 111, 154
Constitutional Assembly 37, 152, 153–155
Constitutional Committee 154
Constitutional Court 37–39, 147–149, 154–155, 166–172, 183–191, 194–195, 229, 298, 300
constitutional essentialism 305–306
constitutional fundamentalism 301
Constitution of the Republic of South Africa
    Al-Bashir case 251, 256, 258
    as bridge 22, 30–33
    Carmichele case 40, 227
    Chapter 9 institutions 2–3, 7–8
    Coloured vote cases 53–54, 64
    courts and 301–303
    criticisms of 14–19, 305, 307
    gay marriage 40, 239–240
    human rights 184, 196–197
    Nkandla case 11, 280–281, 288–289
    SARFU case 166–172
    state capture 268
    transformation and 17, 303
    transition from apartheid to democracy 2, 37–38, 148–149, 152–155
    withdrawal from ICC 261–262
    see *also* Interim Constitution
Convention against Torture and Other Cruel, Inhuman or Degrading Treatment or Punishment 163
Convention for a Democratic South Africa (CODESA) 149–150, 183–184, 239
conviction rates 173, 236
Corbett, Michael 101–102
corruption 8–9
COSATU *see* Congress of South African Trade Unions

Council for the Advancement of the South
African Constitution (CASAC) 261, 263
Cowen, Denis 48
Crause, Herman 127
Craven, Patrick 297
crime 236
criminal censure 34–35
Criminal Procedure and Evidence Act
178–179
Curlewis, David 180–181

D

DA *see* Democratic Alliance
Dalai Lama 41, 249
Daniels, Enver 255
Daniels, Yolanda (*Daniels v Scribante*)
300, 303–305
Deane, Edgar Arthur 47, 53
death penalty
history of 38, 176–177, 178–183
Interim Constitution 183–184
justifications for 173, 177–178, 190, 192
Makwanyane case 39, 173–176,
184–195, 300
Rivonia trial 89–92
Sharpeville Six case 38–39, 181–182
De Beer, Eddy 57, 59
debtors 176
De Klerk, FW 39, 120, 142, 148, 150, 153,
182, 193
De Kock, Eugene (*De Kock* case)
156–160, 299
delays due to pending litigation 3–4 see
also Stalingrad litigation strategy
delict 40, 229
De Lille, Patricia 277
Democratic Alliance (DA) 261, 268, 270,
271, 277–278, 283, 288
Democratic Party 154, 155
Deputy Chief Justice, appointment of 13
Derby-Lewis, Clive 152, 193
Desai, Siraj 271
detention without trial
deaths in detention 128–129, 143–146
history of 36–37, 120–122
legal context of 123–126
public knowledge of 126–129
Rivonia trial 70

torture 36–37, 121–122, 126–129,
134–136, 138–146
Wendy Orr case 36–37, 122–123,
129–143
De Villiers, Dawid 45, 53, 56, 57, 59
De Villiers, HH 90–91
De Villiers, William 167–168
De Vos, Pierre 173, 240–241
De Wet, Quartus 71–72, 75, 77–78, 81–91
Didcott, John 29, 165, 175, 187–188, 191
Diplomatic Immunities and Privileges Act
254–257
diplomatic immunity 254–257, 260, 264
Directorate for Priority Crime Investigation
see Hawks
Directorate of Special Operations *see*
Scorpions
Dlamini, Enoch 'Knox' 161
Dlamini-Zuma, Nkosazana 197–198
doctrine of common purpose 38, 181
Dönges, Eben 52, 54–55, 57–58
Duarte, Jessie 11, 253–254
Dugard, John 28–29
Duncan, Graeme 44, 48, 59
Duncan, Sheena 105
Du Plessis, Max 302

E

Earthlife Africa 118
Eastern Province Herald 138
Economic Freedom Fighters (EFF) 11,
268, 274, 275, 276, 282–283, 289
efficacy, of courts 33
Eksteen, Judge 138–139
elections 46, 152–153
electoral system 46, 269, 294
Eliot, TS 278
Ellmann, Stephen 108
English case law 226
equality *see* inequality
Equality Foundation 240
Erasmus, Deon 223
Erasmus, Paul 144
ESTA *see* Extension of Security of Tenure
Act
Eurocentric attack on Constitution 14–19
executive 2, 33, 41, 124, 207, 211–213,
261–263, 293

Index

Executive Council, Western Cape Legislature v President of the Republic of South Africa 260

Extension of Security of Tenure Act (ESTA) 303–304

F

Fagan, Henry 56
faith in the law 24, 35
family life 101–102
Farlam, Ian 232, 242
Ferreira, Fred 111
Fischer, Abraham 72–73
Fischer, Bram 35, 70–75, 81, 85–86
Fischer, Percy 72
Foreign Affairs 248
foreign policy 40–41, 248–250
Forum for Black Journalists 171
Foster, Don 127–128
Fourie, Adriaana 242
Fourie case 240–246
Franklin, Edgar 47, 53
freedom 32, 34, 302–303
Freedom Charter 80
Freedom Front 153
Friedman, Gerald 24–25, 29
Friedman, Steven 169
Frolick, Cedric 282
Froneman, Johan 291–292, 304–305

G

Gauntlett, Jeremy 11, 99, 103, 113, 257, 283
gay marriage 40, 239–247
Gazi, Costa 206
Gender Research Project 228
General Convention on the Privileges and Immunities of the Organisation of African Unity 255–256, 261
General Council of the Bar 10
General Law Amendment Act 123
Genocide Convention of 1948 163
Gibson, James 171–172
Giliomee, Hermann 38
Ginwala Inquiry 270
Glauber, Ian 186–187
Glenister, Hugh (*Glenister* cases) 8–9, 262, 272, 273

Goddard, Robert 174
Goldberg, Denis 70, 76, 85, 89
Goldreich, Arthur 67–70
Goldstone, Richard 29, 228, 263
Goodman, Isabel 252
Goon Show, The 96–97, 101
Gordhan, Pravin 21, 94–95, 272, 274, 275, 276
Gordimer, Nadine 83–84
Gosling, Julie 216–217, 219, 220–221, 224, 226
Gould, C 162
Government of National Unity 152–153, 197
Gqobona, Sicelo 135
Graaff, De Villiers 125
Grant, E 180
Grootboom case 212
Gupta family 14, 94, 272, 275–276, 280, 306
Guterres, António 263
Gwala, Harry 78

H

Hani, Chris, assassination of 152
Hanson, Harold 86, 88
Harare Declaration 148
Harms, Louis 6, 232–234
Harris, Ganief 47, 53
Harris cases 32–33, 43–45, 47, 48–56, 58, 59–60, 61, 111
Hartzenberg, Willie 161–162
Havenga, Cornelius 174
Hawks 8–9, 10, 259, 271–272, 273, 299, 306
Haysom, Fink 123, 133–134
healthcare *see* TAC case
Helen Suzman Foundation 8–9
Heywood, Mark 203, 204, 208
High Court of Parliament 52–54, 61
high courts 13, 185, 236
HIV/AIDS
    Constitutional Court 207–213, 214–215
    Constitution and 196–197
    High Court 206–209
    policies in South Africa 196–201, 203
    public opinion 213–214
    TAC case 39–40, 201–215

Hoek Street Law Clinic 107
Hoexter, Oscar 56–57, 61–62
Hoffman, David 192–193
Hogan, Barbara 249
homelands 153
housing 112, 303–305
Human, Wessel 181
human rights
  under apartheid 25, 27–29
  Bill of Rights 3, 17, 27, 40, 186, 205,
    228–229
  death penalty 175, 183–184, 186, 188,
    191–192
  foreign policy 41, 248–250, 264
  Komani case 102
  'minimum core' conception of 212
  TAC case 196–197, 205, 212
  TRC 156, 163–166
Human Rights Commission *see* South
  African Human Rights Commission

I
'I am an African' speech, by Thabo Mbeki
  18, 303
ICC *see* International Criminal Court
identity 15, 18–19
IFP *see* Inkatha Freedom Party
immigration laws 241
impeachment of Jacob Zuma 12, 283,
  288–293
Implementation Act 257–258, 261–262
Independent Electoral Commission 2–3
inequality 16, 19, 302–303
influx control *see* pass laws
Inkatha Freedom Party (IFP) 149,
  152–155
Interim Constitution 147, 153–154,
  163–164, 183–184, 224, 240 see *also*
  Constitution of the Republic of South
  Africa
Internal Security Act 129
International Convention on the
  Suppression and Punishment of the
  Crime of Apartheid 163
International Criminal Court (ICC) 12, 250,
  255, 258, 260–266
Inxeba (film) 247

J
Jafta, Chris 290
Jaga, Ranjan 223
Jansen, Erns 113
Jeffery, John 254–255
Jiba, Nomgcobo 10, 270, 274
Joffe, Joel 70, 76, 87–88
Johnson, RW 7, 169
John Vorster Square Police Station 128,
  143
Jones, Judge 139–140
Jordan, Pallo 161
Joubert, CP 103
judges
  Al-Bashir case 259
  in apartheid era 27–28, 31–32, 55–57,
    59–60, 64, 115–117
  AZAPO case 164–165
  Constitutional Court 185
  death penalty 175, 189, 194–195
  impeachment 290–293
  Omar case 24–26
  SARFU case 169–170
  TAC case 210–211
Judicial Service Commission 13, 273
judiciary
  adjudication 31–32
  appointments 55
  attacks on 14, 63–65, 168–169, 297
  bias 37, 162, 168–172, 179
  detention without trial 127
  effectiveness of 32–33
  overreach 13, 207, 211–213, 254, 258,
    259–260, 290–293
  role of 2, 243–246, 254, 263, 266, 268
  state capture 273–276
  trauma of victims 232–234
juristocracy 5, 295

K
Kalangula, Peter 161
Kannemeyer Commission 133–134
Kantor, James 70, 75
Kasrils, Ronnie 161
Kathrada, Ahmed 67, 68–70, 84, 85, 89–90
Kennedy, Anthony 245
Kennedy, Paul 107
Kennedy, Robert 244

Kentridge, Felicia 36, 105
Kentridge, Janet 228
Kentridge, Sydney 175
Kidson, David 73
Kirchheimer, Otto 34
Klare, Karl 18
Klein, Inspector 230–231
Kodwa, Zizi 1
Koloane, Bruce 272
Komani, Nonceba 98–106
Komani, Veli 35–36, 98–106
Komani case 35–36, 98–106, 108–119, 299
Koornhof, Piet 105–106, 108, 111–112, 114
Kriegler, Johann 29, 168, 169–170, 188, 263
Kruger, Renier 109
Krynauw, Dr 132–133

L
Land Claims Court 304
land reform 16, 301
Lang, Ivor 131–132, 141
Langa, Pius 168, 169, 172
lawfare
    concept of 4–5
    duality of 5, 19–20, 300
    increase in 4–14, 265, 301
law of delict 40, 229
Lawyers for Human Rights 179
Legal Aid Board 99–100
Legal Resources Centre (LRC) 35–36, 107, 114
legitimacy of courts 33, 112, 126, 171–172
Le Grange, Louis 140
Le Roux, 'Fef' 223
Le Roux, Frank 111
Lewis, Stephen 201
LGBTQI community *see* gay marriage
liberal legalism 33–34, 55, 93
Liliesleaf Farm 67, 69–70, 74
litigation strategies 27–28
Louw, Charles 99
Louw, Dian 219–221, 224, 230
Louw, Eric 55
Lowen, George 75
LRC *see* Legal Resources Centre
Luthuli, Albert 93–94
Luyt, Louis 37, 148, 167–172

M
Mabelane, Matthews Mojo 129
Madlanga, Mbuyiseli 304
Madlingozi, Tshepo 17
Madonsela, Thuli 10–11, 271, 281, 283–284, 286–287
Maduna, Penuell 209
Magashula, Oupa 94
Maharaj, Mac 121–122, 143
Mahomed, Ismail 73, 164–166, 175, 187
Mail & Guardian 277
Maimane, Mmusi 288
Maine, Collen 284
Majola, Bongani 204
Makwanyane, Themba 174
Makwanyane case 39, 173–176, 184–195, 300
Malan, DF 47, 50, 51–52, 96–97
Malan, Sailor 62–63
Malele, Elmon 128–129
Malema, Julius 94, 276
Malmesbury Prison 222
Mandela, Nelson
    arrest and imprisonment 68
    Constitutional Court 175–176
    foreign policy 248
    HIV/AIDS 197–198
    on legitimacy of courts 260
    Rivonia trial 35, 70, 75, 79–85, 90, 92–93
    SARFU case 37, 148, 166–168, 170
    transition from apartheid to democracy 16, 148, 152–153, 155
Mandela, Winnie 71
Mangcu, Xolela 198
Mangope, Lucas 153
Mantashe, Gwede 11, 13, 254, 258
Maphatsoe, Kebby 283–284
Marais, Hein 198
Marcus, Gilbert 122, 130, 174, 204
Marikana massacre 276, 300
marriage *see* gay marriage
Marriage Act 242
Marshall, Margaret 244
Mashitane, Thomas 67
Mass Democratic Movement 148
Masutha, Michael 260–261
Mathews, Tony 124, 125

Mbeki, Govan 68, 70, 85
Mbeki, Thabo
  on Constitution 14–15
  foreign policy 248–249
  HIV/AIDS 198–200, 203, 207–208
  'I am an African' speech 18, 303
  judiciary 7
  NDPP 270
  Jacob Zuma and 6, 277
Mbembe, Achille 15–16
Mbete, Baleka 12, 64
McCarthy, Leonard 277
Mchunu, Mavusa 174
Mdluli, Richard 10, 275
media tribunal 5
Medicines Control Council *see* South
  African Medicines Control Council
Meyer, Roelf 150–151, 154
Mhlaba, Raymond 70, 85
Miller, Solly 101–102, 104
Mini, Vuyisile 183
'minimum core' conception of human
  rights 212
MK *see* Umkhonto we Sizwe
Mkhwebane, Busisiwe 271, 286
Mlambo, Dunstan 251, 252
Mlangeni, Andrew 70, 85
Modiri, Joel 16–17
Moerane, Marumo 208, 210
Mogoeng, Mogoeng 13, 65, 259, 271, 299
Mohamed, André Gregory 236–237
Mokaba, Peter 200
Mokgoro, Yvonne 263
Mokhari, William 251–252
Molteno, Donald 44, 46, 48
Mondlane, Gibson 161
Moreno Ocampo, Luis 250
Moseneke, Dikgang 1, 8–9, 13, 43, 64–65,
  167, 258–259
mother-to-child transmission prevention
  (MTCTP) 198, 202–215 see *also* HIV/
  AIDS
Mothle, Billy 143–146
motions of no confidence 268, 274, 275,
  288–289
Motlanthe, Kgalema 270, 271
Motshekga, Mathole 258
Motsoaledi, Elias 70, 85

Moyane, Tom 272–273, 276, 296
Mpshe, Mokotedi 269–270, 274, 277–280
Mrwebi, Lawrence 10, 274
MTCTP *see* mother-to-child transmission
  prevention
Mthiya, Mr 113
Mtolo, Bruno 67, 78–79
Mufson, Steve 27–28
Multiparty Negotiating Forum 152, 153
Mureinik, Etienne 22, 30, 182–183, 196,
  197
Mushwana, Lawrence 271
Mxenge family 38, 163–166
Mzobe, Magasela 282

N
Namibian amnesty of 1989 161
Natal Mercury 110
National AIDS Convention of South Africa
  197
National Assembly 12, 153, 285–286,
  289–290
National Association of People Living with
  HIV/AIDS 201
National Director of Public Prosecutions
  (NDPP) 9–10, 94–95, 269–270, 273, 274,
  277–280
National Energy Regulator of South Africa
  (NERSA) 118–119
National Medical and Dental Association
  141
National Party
  Appellate Division 34
  Coloured vote cases 32–33, 45, 47–48,
    52, 54–55
  Constitution 154, 240
  De Kock case 158
  detention without trial 126, 143
  elections 46
  judiciary 63, 298–299
  pass laws 98
  Rivonia trial 90
  Suppression of Communism Act 46
  transition from apartheid to democracy
    148–150, 152–154
  TRC 142–143
National Prosecuting Authority (NPA) 4,
  10, 269–270, 271, 274, 277–280, 299, 306

National Union of South African Students (NUSAS) 100, 107, 109, 244
Ndlwana case 50–51
NDPP *see* National Director of Public Prosecutions
negative liberty 32
neoliberal attack on Constitution 14–19
NERSA *see* National Energy Regulator of South Africa
nevirapine 202–208
New Yorker, The 151
Ngcuka, Bulelani 269, 277
Nhleko, Nkosinathi 281
Nicholson, Chris 6, 21, 270, 277
Nkandla case 1, 10–12, 14, 41, 274, 280–289, 294
Nkoana-Mashabane, Maite 260–261
N K v Minister of Safety and Security 237–238
notice of motion 134
NPA *see* National Prosecuting Authority
Ntlemeza, Berning 10, 273
nuclear power scheme 26, 117–119, 274
Nugent Commission 276, 296
Nupen, Charles 107
NUSAS *see* National Union of South African Students
Nxasana, Mxolisi 10, 270, 274
Nxesi, Thulas 282
Nzimande, Blade 259

O
OAU *see* Organisation of African Unity
Obergefell et al v Hodges 245
Odendaal, Brigadier 128
O'Donovan, Bryan 107–108
Omar, Dullah 24–25, 160, 193
Operation Mayibuye 66, 68, 81, 85
O'Regan, Kate 174, 208, 237–238, 242–243, 263
Organisation of African Unity (OAU) 148, 256
Orr, Wendy 122–123, 126, 129–138, 140–142 see *also Wendy Orr* case

P
PAC *see* Pan Africanist Congress
Palace of Justice, Pretoria 71

Pama, Perino 222, 224–225, 227, 229
Pan Africanist Congress (PAC) 69, 149
Parliament
    under apartheid 49, 50–51, 124
    Nkandla case 12, 41, 283, 286, 293
    role of 2
    state capture 268–269
    withdrawal from ICC 262–263
parliamentary committees 268–269
pass laws
    Goon Show logic 96–97, 99, 101
    history of 35–36, 97–101
    Komani case 35–36, 98–106, 108–119, 299
    Rikhoto case 35–36, 97, 106–119, 299
    significance of 117–119
Paton, Alan 86–88, 92
Phiyega, Riah 282
Pikoli, Vusi 269–270
Pilkington-Jordan, RD 53
Pillay, Ivan 94, 275
Pityana, Barney 206
political issues
    Carmichele case 227
    death penalty 191, 195
    judiciary 14, 43
    lawfare 1, 3–7
    Nkandla case 11–12, 286
    pass law cases 115–116
    Rivonia trial 34–35, 72
    Sharpeville Six case 39
    state capture 293
    TAC case 206–207, 210–211, 214
    withdrawal from ICC 265
populism 305, 307
'possibility' 299–300
poverty 16, 19, 179
power 26
precedent 298–299
Precedent & Possibility 3
Presidential AIDS Advisory Panel 199
presidential powers of appointment 13, 295
Pretorius, Petrus 174
Price, Terry 223, 226
private law 227, 229
Progressive Party 44
Project Coast 160, 162

Promotion of National Unity and
Reconciliation Act 38, 156
property clause of Constitution 16, 301
property law 300, 303–305
provinces, ARV roll-outs in 204, 207–208
public opinion 77–78, 187–190, 195
Public Protector
Constitution and 2–3, 268
Nkandla case 10–11, 281, 283–287
Reserve Bank 286, 294
role of 270–271
state capture 299, 306
Public Safety Act 24, 129

Q
Quorum Act *see* Appellate Division
Quorum Act

R
Rabie, Pierre 27–29
race 10, 55, 103, 111, 123, 157–158, 179
railway coaches, segregation in 25
Ramaphosa, Cyril 9, 10, 150–151, 154,
278, 296, 300
Rand Daily Mail 69, 70, 91–92
rape *see* sexual assault
'reasonableness' approach to human rights
212–213
Reserve Bank *see* South African Reserve
Bank
retributive justice 177–178
Ribeiro family 163–166
Rickard, Carmel 233
Riekert Commission 114–115, 116
rights *see* human rights
Rikhoto case 35–36, 97, 106–119, 299
Rikhotso, Mehlolo Tom 35–36, 97–98,
107–109, 114
Rivonia trial
background to 66–70
defence's case 79–85
judgment 85–89
Liliesleaf Farm 67, 69–70, 74
opening of 70–78
significance of 20–21, 34–35, 89–95,
175–176, 298–299
state's case 78–79
Robb, Noel 100

robes 185
'rogue unit' reports 273, 274, 275
Rome Statute 12, 250, 254–255, 256,
257–258, 260–261, 263–266
Romney, Mitt 244–245
Rose Innes, James 239
Roux, Theunis 17
Rubicon speech 93
Rumpff, Frans 102–104, 115
Russia 26, 118, 177

S
SABC *see* South African Broadcasting
Corporation
Sabotage Act 72, 90
Sachs, Albie 17, 124–125, 168–170,
187–188, 191–192, 242–243, 246
same-sex marriages *see* gay marriage
Sampson, Anthony 68, 83, 92
sanctions against South Africa 123
SAP *see* South African Police
SAPS *see* South African Police Service
*SARFU (South African Rugby Football
Union)* case 37, 148, 166–172
SARS *see* South African Revenue Service
Satchwell, Kathy 241
Sauer, Paul 55
Save Our Babies 203
Scalia, Antonin 245–246, 292–293
Scher, David 50, 62–63
Schnetler, Brigadier 137–138
Schock, Philip 99
Schreiner, Edna 61
Schreiner, Oliver 56–57, 58–59, 61–62, 65,
108
Schulman, André 128
Scorpions 8, 271–272, 273, 277
Scribante, Theo 303
secret ballot, for motion of no confidence
vote 275, 289, 294
Secure in Comfort report 281
security police *see* South African Police
Selebi, Jackie 270
Senate Act 57–62
Separate Representation of Voters Act 47,
51
separation of powers
ANC 13

Coloured vote cases 45
concept of 2, 20
Fourie case 243
impeachment 291–293
Dikgang Moseneke on 43
TAC case 215
withdrawal from ICC 266
Separation of Voters Act 53
sexual assault 179, 228, 232–235
Sexwale, Tokyo 193
Shaik, Schabir (Shaik trial) 6–8, 211, 269, 277
Sharpeville Six case 38–39, 181–182
Simelane, Menzi 9, 270, 273
Sisulu, Albertina 71
Sisulu, Walter 35, 68–70, 79, 84–85, 92
Slovo, Joe 67, 68
Smuts, Jan 47–48, 96–97
Snitcher, Harry 44, 48
social change 19, 35, 242
Society for the Abolition of the Death Penalty 179
'sodomy case' 240–241
Soga, John Henderson 191–192
Sogoti, Mbulelo Joseph 135–136
Soobramoney case 212
South Africa Act 46, 48–49, 58
South African Broadcasting Corporation (SABC) 26, 77, 209, 274
South African Communist Party 46, 67, 69, 73, 76–77, 79, 81, 150
South African Human Rights Commission 2–3, 154, 206
South African Institute of Race Relations 100, 154
South African Medical and Dental Council 131–132
South African Medicines Control Council 198, 204, 205
South African Police (SAP) 33, 36–37, 46, 69–71, 120–126, 133, 162
South African Police Service (SAPS) 33, 186, 236, 271, 287, 299, 300
South African Reserve Bank 286, 294
South African Revenue Service (SARS) 4, 94, 268, 272–273, 275, 276, 296, 299
South African Rugby Football Union (SARFU) case 37, 148, 166–172

Southern Africa Litigation Centre 12, 250–251, 252, 255
Southern African Faith Communities' Environment Institute 118
Sowetan 108, 110
Sparks, Allister 151
Speaker of the National Assembly 289
Special Investigating Unit 272
'special relationship', between state and persons 226–227
'spy tapes' case 41, 274, 277–280
Squires, Hilary 277
Sri Lanka 249
St Albans Prison 132, 135, 138
Stalingrad litigation strategy 7, 279–280, 283
Stallard Commission 97
Star, The 77, 91, 208
State Capacity Research Project 306
state capture
    commissions of inquiry 295–296
    Hawks 271–272
    impact of 41
    impeachment 288–294
    judiciary 65, 273–276
    National Prosecuting Authority 94, 269–270
    Nkandla case 280–288, 293–294
    parallel state 23, 300
    Parliament 268–269
    Public Protector 270–271
    reforms against 294–295
    Scorpions 271–272
    South African Revenue Service 272–273
    'spy tapes' case 277–280, 293–294
    state institutions 7–8, 267–268, 306
state institutions 2–3, 4, 7–8, 267–268, 293, 306
states of emergency 27, 28–30, 36–37, 120, 140–141
State v Makwanyane see Makwanyane case
State v Nelson Mandela and Others see Rivonia trial
State v Safatsa and Others see Sharpeville Six case
Statute of Westminster 49, 50–51, 58
Stephenson, Hugh 92

Steyn, Lucas 56, 60–61, 65, 100, 125, 299
strategy *see* litigation strategies
Strauss, JGN 48, 53
Strijdom, JG 56, 58, 97
sub judice rule 7
Sudan 250
Sunday Star 27–28
Sunday Times 92–93, 207, 233, 273, 297
Superior Courts Bill 64
Suppression of Communism Act 46, 72, 124
Supreme Court (USA) 305
SWAPO 161
Swart, CR 57, 60

T

TAC (Treatment Action Campaign) case
background to 39–40, 201–205
in Constitutional Court 207–213, 214–215
Constitution and 196–197
in High Court 206–209
issues in 205–206
public opinion 213–214
significance of 39–40
Terblanche, Doreen 219, 223–224
Terblanche, Eurena 218–219, 222, 223, 230–231
Terre'Blanche, Eugène 152, 153
terrorism 36, 125
Thompson, EP 25–26, 28
Thompson, Matthys 174
Thompson, Ogilvie 124–125
Time 199
Timol, Ahmed, death of 128, 143–146
Tipp, Karel 109
Torch Commando 62–63
torture 36–37, 121–122, 126–129, 134–136, 138–146 see *also Wendy Orr* case
transformation 14–17, 19, 30–31, 191, 303
transition from apartheid to democracy
AZAPO case 163–166
Basson case 160–163
CODESA 149–150
Constitution 2, 148–149, 152–155
Constitutional Court 147–149
De Kock case 158–160
Government of National Unity 152–153

Interim Constitution 147, 153–154, 163–164
SARFU case 166–172
talks between Ramaphosa and Meyer 150–152
transformation 147–148, 300
TRC 155–158
violence 151–153
World Trade Centre 152
TRC *see* Truth and Reconciliation Commission
Treason Trial 71, 80–81, 90, 102
Treatment Action Campaign (TAC) *see* TAC case
Trengove, Wim 133–134, 138–140, 174, 184–185, 228, 230–231, 234, 237
Truth and Reconciliation Commission (TRC) 37–38, 122, 126–127, 142–143, 147–148, 155–158, 159–160, 163–166
Tshabalala-Msimang, Manto 197, 199–200, 203–204, 208–210, 213, 214
Tshwete, Steve 167
Tucker, Benjamin 132

U

ubuntu 189, 191–192
Umkhonto we Sizwe (MK) 67–68, 72, 73, 76, 81
UN *see* United Nations
UNHRC *see* United Nations Human Rights Council
United Democratic Front 115, 148, 299
United Democratic Movement 289
United Nations (UN) 148, 201
United Nations Human Rights Council (UNHRC) 249
United Nations Security Council (UNSC) 123, 249, 250
United Party 47, 53, 63, 92
United States of America (USA) 27, 36, 177, 244–246, 292–293, 305
UNSC *see* United Nations Security Council
Unterhalter, Jack 39
Urban Areas Act 110
USA *see* United States of America

V

Valkenberg Hospital 220

Van den Berg, HJ 52
Van den Bergh, Hendrik 69
Van der Merwe, AJ 49–50
Van der Merwe, PJ 116
Van der Merwe, 'Slim' Stoffel 181
Van der Merwe, Willem 159
Van der Westhuizen, Jacob 127
Van Eeden, Ghia (*Van Eeden v Minister of Safety and Security*) 236–237
Van Heerden, Hennie 109–110, 115
Van Niekerk, Johannes 145
Van Riebeeck Festival 49–50
Van Schalkwyk, Gerrit 103–104
Van Wyk, Theo 44–45, 49, 53–54
Van Zyl, Diko 127
Van Zyl, Francois 7
Van Zyl, Helm 127
VBS Bank 288
Verwoerd, Hendrik 92, 96–97
victims, re-victimised by law 232–235
Viljoen, Constand 153
violence 82–84, 92–93, 151–153, 299–300
Virodene 198
Vlakplaas farm (unit C10 headquarters) 158–159
Vlok, Adriaan 157
Von Bratt, Kevin 224, 226
Von Lieres und Wilkau, Klaus 186, 188
Vorster, John 69, 100

W
Wallis, Malcolm 248, 253, 257
Walus, Janusz 152, 193
Waterkloof Air Force Base 251–253, 272, 275
Weekly Mail 120
Wendy Orr case 36–37, 122–123, 129–143
Whigs and Hunters 25–26
'white monopoly capital' 16, 284

Williams, Cecil 68
'will of the people' 52, 63–64
Wolpe, Harold 69–70
World Trade Centre 152
Wynne, George 45

Y
Yacoob, Zak 168, 169, 259–260, 263–264
Yutar, Percy 74–75, 77–82, 84, 87–90

Z
Zapiro 199
Zondo Commission into state capture 296
Zuma, Jacob
  Al-Bashir case 259–260
  cabinet reshuffle, March 2017 1, 274
  charges of corruption 6–7, 21
  foreign policy 249–250
  Forum for Black Journalists 171
  impeachment of 12, 283, 288–293
  judiciary 64–65, 259–260, 273–275
  lawfare 5, 26
  motions of no confidence 274, 275, 288–289
  National Prosecuting Authority 9–10, 269–270
  Nkandla case 1, 10–12, 14, 41, 274, 280–289, 294
  nuclear power scheme 26, 117–119
  as president 8
  Public Protector 271
  Scorpions 8, 272
  South African Revenue Service 272–273
  'spy tapes' case 277–280
  on state capture 65, 267
  state institutions 299
Zwane, Mosebenzi 5, 275